TEACHER
ACTION
RESEARCH

This book is dedicated to my family.
To my wife Mary: Without her caring and loving support there would be no book.
To our sons and their wives: David and Jane, Sean and Gail.
To our daughter: Maureen.
To our grandchildren: Katelyn, Molly, Kevin, and Jack.

TEACHER ACTION RESEARCH

BUILDING KNOWLEDGE DEMOCRACIES

GERALD J. PINE
Boston College

Los Angeles • London • New Delhi • Singapore • Washington DC

For information:

SAGE Publications, Inc.
2455 Teller Road
Thousand Oaks,
  California 91320
E-mail: order@sagepub.com

SAGE Publications Ltd.
1 Oliver's Yard
55 City Road
London EC1Y 1SP
United Kingdom

SAGE Publications India Pvt. Ltd.
B 1/I 1 Mohan Cooperative
  Industrial Area
Mathura Road, New Delhi 110 044
India

SAGE Publications Asia-Pacific
  Pte. Ltd.
33 Pekin Street #02-01
Far East Square
Singapore 048763

Printed in the United States of America

Library of Congress Cataloging-in-Publication Data

Pine, Gerald J.
Teacher action research : building knowledge democracies/Gerald J. Pine.
    p. cm.
Includes bibliographical references and index.
ISBN 978-1-4129-6475-3 (cloth)
ISBN 978-1-4129-6476-0 (pbk.)
  1. Action research in education. 2. Teaching. I. Title.

LB1028.24.P56 2009
370.72—dc22   2008022447

This book is printed on acid-free paper.

08   09   10   11   12   10   9   8   7   6   5   4   3   2   1

Acquisitions Editor:	Steve Wainwright
Editorial Assistant:	Julie McNall
Production Editor:	Catherine M. Chilton
Copy Editor:	Jacqueline Tasch
Typesetter:	C&M Digitals (P) Ltd.
Proofreader:	Liann Lech
Indexer:	Sylvia Coates
Cover Designer:	Gail Buschman
Marketing Manager:	Nichole M. Angress

Contents

Preface

Teacher Action Research: Building Knowledge Democracies is a text written for graduate students, experienced teachers, and administrators. It has been developed for use in such action research courses as teacher research, teacher action research, educational action research, inquiry seminar, and classroom research. It also could serve as a supplemental text for courses in research methodology, qualitative research, staff development, school change, and educational administration and policy. Finally, it would be a useful resource for in-service and staff development programs in school districts interested in implementing a unique research approach to improve teaching and student learning.

The book is set apart from others by its emphasis on helping schools to build knowledge democracies through the process of teacher action research. The text argues that through teacher action research, schools can become knowledge democracies where teachers provide the intellectual leadership for nonhierarchical, egalitarian, participatory, collaborative, and democratic construction of knowledge. In such democracies, inquiry permeates every aspect of the school's organization, programs, activities, and culture. This means that any function of the school is open to inquiry, including teaching, learning, curriculum, leadership, professional development, university-school partnerships, and parental involvement. Teachers, students, and parents work together in conducting caring inquiry in the classroom, school, and community to construct knowledge for meaningful change. They become committed to collaborative enlightenment and consciousness raising to increase potentials for self-affirmation and renewal; to support the principles of democracy in education; to construct authentic practical knowledge that makes a difference in the lives of students, parents, and teachers; and to advance the principles of social justice within the school and the community. The book is cutting edge in developing the concept of schools as knowledge democracies, in its comprehensive treatment of action research as a distinct generative paradigm, and in its reconceptualization of research validity.

❖ PURPOSES OF THE BOOK

The purposes of the book are to engage and help the reader to

1. Develop an appreciation and understanding of teacher action research as a critical and unique intellectual practice and mode of thinking

2. Learn how teacher action research can empower the active and ongoing inclusion of nontraditional voices in the research process—students and parents

3. Focus on understanding the historical, philosophical, and theoretical foundations of action research—to internalize action research as more than a technical "cookbook" approach to conducting inquiry

4. Develop an appreciation and understanding of action research as a paradigm as opposed to a method

5. Develop a different and unique view of validity, a view that encompasses a variety of processes to demonstrate and differentiate the trustworthiness of action research

6. Understand how teachers, parents, and students, through collaborative action research, can create a knowledge base for the improvement of teaching and learning and the construction of a knowledge democracy

7. Learn how the practices of action research are intersecting processes and mental dispositions rather than discrete techniques for conducting a research study

8. Learn how to build a school research culture through collaborative inquiry

9. Understand the role of the professional development school as a generative venue for constructing a knowledge democracy

10. Develop insightful perspectives on the complexities, challenges, and possibilities of action research to change educational practice

❖ PERSONAL INFLUENCES IN THE WRITING OF THIS BOOK

I believe that we teach and write who we are. We bring to our work, our actions, and our daily living our worldviews, identity, values, memories, prior experiences, expectations, and attitudes. My ideas and approaches to teaching, doing, and writing action research have been shaped throughout my professional life by many profound experiences participating with school and university colleagues in a variety of collaborative action research studies over a span of 40 years. These experiences have informed my perspectives and thinking about action research and nurtured the ideas and concepts I have brought together in this book, *Teacher Action Research: Building Knowledge Democracies.*

Included among the more powerful educational action research experiences I have lived are: a 3-year study at the University of New Hampshire funded by the U.S. Teacher Corps project on using collaborative action research to adapt research findings for the improvement of K–12 teaching and learning; a National Institute for Education study on collaborative action research conducted through the University of New Hampshire and Oakland University; the establishment of the Institute for Action Research and Professional Development funded by the Kellogg Foundation and Oakland University; and the convening of a national invitational conference on collaborative action research supported by Oakland University. Finally, for the past 10 years, I have been involved in facilitating and guiding more than 1,000 teacher research studies among master's degree students in the teacher education program at Boston College.

Through these experiences, I have learned firsthand the reality of action research. I have seen how it empowers teachers and addresses authentic problems in the classroom. An influential and unique form of professional development, action research improves student learning situations and illuminates teaching practice; it creates change through a process of recursion and generates deeper understandings and insights of teacher and student life in the classroom. I have come to know and experience how teacher knowing is related to adult development, how inseparable are feeling states and thinking states, and how vital are the interconnections between intellectual, affective, and social processes in conducting inquiry and constructing knowledge.

Then, too, I have learned about the difficulties, complexities, and messiness of doing action research in the turbulent environment of the school. School schedules can change abruptly depending on the weather, a special program, or an unexpected crisis, and events in the community intrude on the rhythms of the school. Unplanned and unexpected events in the school disrupt the best of planning, while personal issues of illness, distress, and conflict affect focus and commitment. New demands on teachers deflect their time and energy, but the fragility of collaborative relationships requires sustained attention, communication, and support. Staff assignments and reassignments alter the energy, timing, and pacing of the inquiry process, and projects and initiatives launched by district administration can put action research studies on the back burner. In addition, high-stakes testing programs can sap teacher attention, energy, and time. Informal and formal power relationships affect the process of collaboration.

I have also learned of the difficulties inherent in university and school structures and reward systems; these can get in the way of establishing authentic partnerships between schools and universities. As a university faculty member working in a number of different schools, I experienced the cultural clashes between university values and the daily practice in schools. University norms include autonomy and individuality, allocation of time for reflection and research, traditional views and valuation of research, tolerance for ambiguity, faculty control of time and workplace pacing, and rewards for research. In contrast stand the school's norms of efficiency, structured time, daily routines, and "busyness." Teachers lack control over the pacing, timing, and outcomes in a variety of situations, as they face the constant imperative to ensure that all students are receiving appropriate instruction and are learning and the hovering cloud of high-stakes testing. Despite all its espoused virtues, coordination of university and school resources, I learned, demands an extraordinary investment of time. All of these situations and issues have constituted the ever-changing and challenging terrain in which my experiences in conducting or participating in action research studies have been located.

Despite the complexities and challenges embedded in doing collaborative action research, my commitment to the process of teacher action research has been deeply affirmed by the impact I have witnessed among more than 1,000 teachers and graduate teacher interns who have participated in conducting classroom action research. Over many years, written commentaries collected from teacher-researchers have indicated that they made instructional and curricular changes in their classrooms. They perceived themselves as changed professionals in terms of their knowledge, skills, and attitudes about classroom inquiry and problem solving and of their knowledge and understanding of education. They shared their work at regional, state, and national conferences. They noted that they were practicing new ways of communicating, sharing, and developing collegiality and that they had significantly increased their ability to identify, analyze, and solve problems in their classrooms and schools. They perceived themselves as empowered, reflective professionals whose opinions were valued and respected and who felt less intimidated and more comfortable in conducting research. Most important, they saw themselves improving student learning in critical ways.

❖ VOICES

It is important to note that in addition to the voices of scholars, teacher and student voices are cited and quoted throughout this book. The use of their voices brings the real world of teaching, learning, and education to bear on the practices and ideas discussed here. I also include my own voice to acknowledge who I am as a teacher, writer, and action researcher and to acknowledge that, in all research, subjectivity is invariably present. I encourage my students to own their research by using the personal pronoun *I* or the collective personal pronoun *we* to assert their ownership of their research questions and their personal agency in addressing their research problems. I hope using my own voice will model for my students and for the reader that I am not disembodied from the ideas in this book and that I have been attentive to my own subjectivity.

❖ USE OF THE RESEARCH LITERATURE

The literature on action research in all its forms is massive and deep. I have drawn from the contemporary literature of action research, with more than 200 references dating from the year 2000, as well as the long, rich, vibrant, and eloquent history of action research. I choose not to be ahistorical but to draw deeply from the historical roots of action research. I hope the reader will resonate to this blend of the contemporary and the historical.

And finally, throughout this book, I share my personal beliefs and values, which have emanated from 40 years of experience in action research and reflections on that experience. I share these beliefs and values in the hope of stimulating a silent dialogue between me and you, the reader. You may agree or disagree with the ideas developed in this book. Whatever your response, I hope that the book engages your attention, intellect, and thought and that the engagement will advance your professional and personal goals.

❖ ORGANIZATION OF THE BOOK

This book is divided into three major parts and 11 chapters:

Part I: Understanding Action Research focuses on the nature and character of action research, its history and development, and different forms of action research. It addresses questions of validity by reconceptualizing validity and generalizability, and it establishes the uniqueness of action research as a generative paradigm for creating knowledge and changing practice. This section of the book is historical, philosophical, and theoretical and lays the groundwork for developing a deep understanding and fundamental grasp of the nature and character of action research. Without such a fundamental understanding, the implementation of action research in education can become merely a mechanical, instrumental process open to exploitation of students and teachers.

Chapter 1, "The Disconnection Between Educational Research and Practice: The Case for Teacher Action Research," discusses the gap between educational research and practice and the need for a different research approach to close the gap. This chapter discusses the complexities of schools and argues for research approaches that recognize the power of context in teaching and learning. It argues that, through action research, contextual variables can be accommodated and the historical gap between educational research and practice can be closed. The chapter concludes that we can build knowledge democracies in which the construction of knowledge is not for a privileged few but engages the expertise of teachers, administrators, parents, and students in the service of democratic problem solving.

Chapter 2, "Teacher Action Research: Collaborative, Participatory, and Democratic Inquiry," tells what action research is and how it came about; it describes the intellectual and philosophical influences of postmodernism and feminism, which have shaped its development, as well as different approaches to doing action research in education. Specific instances of how action research has been employed by teachers and administrators are included, along with direct quotes from teachers about the value of doing action research.

Chapter 3, "A Paradigm of Teacher Action Research," argues that action research is not a method but rather a different paradigm that embraces many methodologies. I examine how it differs from other

major research paradigms. As an evolving paradigm, it reflects epistemological, ontological, and axiological assumptions about knowledge
creation, human experience, and human values. To understand
action research and its ramifications for the improvement of human
well-being, one must thoughtfully consider and reflect on the
nature of action research as a paradigm. This chapter is written to
help the reader do just that.

Chapter 4, "The Validity of Action Research," addresses the critical question of research validity. How truthful is action research?
What claims can be made to support its validity as a rigorous
research approach? To what extent can the findings of action
research be generalized? The chapter addresses these important
questions and describes different ways of confirming validity, which
represent a significant departure from the more traditional validation procedures of the social sciences. Twelve categories of action
research validity are discussed, with 9 or 10 questions in each category; participants in collaborative action research can respond to
these questions and use them at any point in the action research
process to promote dialogue and to improve and strengthen the
research while it is in progress and being implemented on a day-to-
day basis.

Chapter 5, "Teacher Action Research as Professional Development,"
makes the point that action research is more than a process of research.
It involves knowledge construction and learning and consequently is a
powerful form of professional development. This chapter delineates a
continuum of approaches to professional development, ranging from
traditional strategies on one end of the continuum to action research
on the other end. Using six criteria, the differences in the continuum
are explored, and the implications for conceptualizing action research
as professional development are discussed. The teacher outcomes of a
major study on action research as professional development are
shared, and the meaning and consequences of these outcomes for the
future of action research as a process of professional development are
elaborated.

*Part II: Collaborative Action Research: Foundation for Knowledge
Democracies* consists of three chapters that establish the philosophical
and practical foundations for building a knowledge democracy. This
section of the book broadens the concept of collaborative action
research to include new partners in the inquiry process—students and
parents—and deals with a number of critical issues, such as time,
resources, and culture, which need to be confronted if schools are to
evolve into knowledge democracies.

Chapter 6, "Collaborative Action Research," provides an overview and discussion of the history, development, processes, and characteristics of collaborative action research and its power to liberate teachers to function as constructors of knowledge and agents of change. A critical focus in this chapter is on the school becoming a center for collaborative inquiry. This chapter lays the groundwork for Chapters 7 and 8, which are central to the theme of the book and important in developing the school as a knowledge democracy.

Chapter 7, "Conditions for Building a Knowledge Democracy," delineates in detail the necessary conditions for creating a knowledge democracy. It contends that parents and K–12 students must be active participants in conducting research and gives examples of parents and students who have conducted research on a variety of educational issues. The chapter focuses on significant questions dealing with real and practical concerns of finding time to do research, developing relational and systemic trust, learning how to collaborate, and addressing the challenges of collaboration. Examples of K–12 student action research studies and of parents conducting action research are included, along with practical suggestions for helping teachers to find time to do action research in schools and for supporting teacher research as an enduring practice. The chapter also discusses (a) concrete ideas for developing a research culture in schools; (b) working principles of collaboration developed and used by a team of teacher education graduate students; and (c) operational ideas for building personal and systemic trust and for advancing the collaborative action research process.

Chapter 8, "Creating Knowledge Democracies: Professional Development Schools," argues that the professional development school (PDS) is an ideal organizational venue where collaborative action research and the democratic construction of knowledge can flourish through an egalitarian research partnership of teachers, parents, students, administrators, university faculty, and teacher interns. The defining characteristics of a PDS, the development of an embedded research culture, the facilitation of collaborative inquiry, and the outcomes of a PDS as a knowledge-creating school are examined.

Part III: Practicing Action Research deals with the practical aspects of conducting individual or collaborative action research. The goal of Chapters 9, 10, and 11 is to illuminate the practice of the action research process; they should be considered within the context of the preceding chapters on the power of action research to build knowledge democracies. Although practice is the focal point of these chapters, the philosophical and theoretical bases of practice are examined.

Chapter 9, "Fundamental Practices for Teacher Action Research," makes the point that reflection, observation, journaling, narrative writing, and critical dialogue are dynamic and interacting processes and should not be considered as technical, isolated, or mechanical tools for carrying out an action research study. Within their theoretical and philosophical contexts, each of these processes is described in detail with concrete suggestions for implementation. The chapter includes concrete steps for becoming more deeply reflective; a four-phase observational/reflective cycle of practice; specific guidelines for journaling and documentation; practical ideas for stimulating writing; and questions that teachers may address to facilitate observation, journal writing, and reflection about teaching and learning in the classroom.

Chapter 10, "Case Study and Teacher Action Research," describes case study as an inherent methodology of action research. It explores the theoretical and philosophical assumptions of the case study approach. Different types of case studies are delineated, including three major approaches: appreciative inquiry, cultural inquiry process, and the descriptive review.

Chapter 11, "Conducting Teacher Action Research," written with my pedagogical voice, enjoins the reader to consider each step in implementing an action research study as part of the recursive spiraling process that characterizes action research. Each step of the process—framing the research question, conducting the literature review, identifying data sources, collecting and analyzing the data, drawing conclusions, and finding meaning—is described in detail with extensive discussion of all the practical issues affecting the implementation of action research. The chapter is dedicated to providing a practical blueprint for doing collaborative action research; it includes several tables that list teacher, student, classroom, and school variables that classroom teachers and students have identified as affecting the design and outcomes of their action research studies. It also offers exemplary research questions generated by graduate students who have conducted action research studies and a list of data sources that students and classroom teachers have identified as being helpful to them in conducting action research.

The appendixes consist of (a) a list of annotated teacher action research Web sites and a list of curriculum and instruction Web sites that teachers and students have found to be useful sources for information about ideas and ways for doing action research and (b) examples of complete teacher research studies written by graduate students and experienced classroom teachers.

❖ ACKNOWLEDGMENTS

I wish to thank Camille Fitzpatrick, my graduate assistant in 2006, and Janice Jackson, faculty colleague, who read the first drafts of this book and provided invaluable feedback regarding the book's organization and content. I am forever indebted to my faculty colleagues at the University of New Hampshire, Oakland University, and Boston College whose ideas and questions over the years have intellectually nourished and challenged my thinking about action research, educational change, and professional development. I also want to thank all the graduate students and teachers with whom I have been privileged to collaborate in conducting teacher action research studies over the past 40 years; their impact on my own growth and learning in teacher action research has been immeasurable. I am grateful for the sustained and thoughtful support I received throughout the publication process from the Sage editorial team. Jacqueline Tasch's copy editing was splendid in her attention to the smallest details and in her caring editorial suggestions. The assistance of Julie McNall, editorial assistant, and Catherine Chilton, production editor, has been very helpful. Finally, I wish to extend my deepest thanks to Steve Wainwright, acquisitions editor, whose enthusiasm, encouragement, and initiative made possible the publication of *Teacher Action Research: Building Knowledge Democracies*.

I would also like to thank the following reviewers:

Jennifer Borek
University of Memphis

Miguel A. Guajardo
Texas State University-San Marcos

Cathy Mogharreban
Southern Illinois University at Carbondale

Sharon L. Gilbert
Southern Illinois University at Carbondale

Deborah M. Hill
Southern Utah University

Sara S. Garcia
Santa Clara University

Helen L. Harrington
University of Michigan

Ronald G. Helms
Wright State University

George R. Meadows
University of Mary Washington

Amy Suzanne Johnson
University of South Carolina

Michael L. Slavkin
University of Southern Indiana

Ronald S. Beebe
Cleveland State University

Penny L. Burge
Virginia Tech

Carrie Dale
Eastern Illinois University

Lynne Masel Walters
Texas A&M University

Ray M. Gen
Chapman University

Sylvia Peregrino
University of Texas–El Paso

Amanda Haertling Thein
University of Pittsburgh

Richard A. Couto
Antioch University

Part I

Understanding
Action Research

The first five chapters of this book focus on the context for conducting action research: its history, different approaches to doing action research, the validity of action research, action research as a paradigm, and action research as professional development. This section of the book is historical, philosophical, and theoretical and lays the groundwork for developing a deep understanding and fundamental grasp of the nature and character of action research. Without such a fundamental understanding, the implementation of action research in education can become merely a mechanical and instrumental process open to exploitation of students and teachers.

1

The Disconnection Between Educational Research and Practice

The Case for Teacher Action Research

Whatever impact does educational research have on individual classroom teachers and their students? To what degree does educational research make a positive difference in the lives of teachers and their students? To what extent does educational research affect teaching and learning? In this chapter, I attempt to address these questions by examining and distilling nearly 40 years of professional literature dealing with the relationship between educational research and practice. In examining that relationship, I conclude this chapter by arguing that teacher action research must play a prominent role in making research work to affect teaching and learning and to transform the school into a knowledge democracy. As you read through this chapter, I believe it would be helpful to reflect on your own experience in using or not using educational research. To what degree have you used educational research to inform your teaching practice? If you have tried to use educational research, what were its benefits and shortcomings? What are the difficulties of translating educational research into practice? What resources do you use in the search for and implementation of educational research? How has educational research affected your practice?

❖ HISTORICAL CONTEXT

Historically, educational research consistently has been caught in a fundamental dilemma between the practical or "doing" aspects and the scientific or "knowing" aspects of a problem. On one side are the real, practical demands of teaching, which are multidimensional, multilayered, context dependent, site specific, and continually evolving and changing. On the other side are the demands of the scientific: that knowledge must be generated with rigor and recognized principles of scientific inquiry and that such knowledge is generalizable so that it can be shared and used by a larger community than those with direct experience of a specific event.

Although it has always been assumed that educational research and practice should be intimately tied together, research and practice seem to be more disconnected and alienated from each other than ever before, a situation starkly portrayed by Miller (1999) in his article, "The Black Hole of Educational Research." Asked why academic studies play such a minimal role in efforts to improve the schools, he asserts that educational research on classroom change and school reform has been inconclusive and weak and that, even in areas of good scholarship, research has little influence on what happens in classrooms. Despite a membership of more than 20,000 in the American Educational Research Association (AERA), despite countless numbers of researchers presenting their findings to more than 12,000 participants at annual AERA meetings, and despite more than 100,000 educational publications and reports produced annually, educational research has had little impact on changing schools or improving student learning because of its disconnection from practice. In the face of the imperative questions, demands, and problems challenging education, education cannot afford a separation between research and practice. It never could. The integration of educational research and practice is essential if any genuine progress is to be achieved in addressing compelling, complex, and significant issues in education. Such integration requires an analysis of the reasons for the divide between research and practice and a reconceptualization of what constitutes beneficial educational research.

More than 20 years ago, Eisner (1985), in describing the chasm between educational research and practice, portrayed a discomforting reality:

Practitioners seldom read the research literature. Even when they do, this literature contains little that is not so qualified or so compromised by competing findings, rival hypotheses, or faulty design that the framework could scarcely be said to be supported in some reasonable way by research. . . . If educational research is to inform educational practice, researchers will have to go back to schools for a fresh look at what is going on there. We will have to develop a language that is relevant to educational practice, one that does justice to teaching and learning in educational settings, and we will need to develop methods of inquiry that do not squeeze the educational life out of what we study in such settings. (pp. 450–451)

And Bok (1987), a few years later, said of the gap between research and practice:

The prevailing view is that scholars have contributed little to improve practice in schools. Not that the field has lacked for effort: over 100,000 articles are published every year. Nevertheless, education journals are repeatedly described as filled with projects that are imperfectly designed, shoddily researched, and poorly reasoned. Topics are often chosen on the basis of the social significance of the subject with little heed as to what questions are truly researchable. Methods of inquiry are frequently questionable and conclusions politically biased or only loosely related to the evidence. . . . Few undertakings are more baffling than the effort to isolate the influence of formal education from the myriad of factors that shape the development of a human being.

Both Bok's and Eisner's comments establish past understanding of the disconnection between research and practice. Today, the current situation shows little evidence of any progress in bridging the gap between research and practice. Commenting on their work over many years as National Science Foundation senior program officers, Sabelli and Dede (2001) say:

Decades of funded studies that have resulted in many exciting programs and advances have not resulted in pervasive, accepted, sustainable, large scale improvements in actual classroom practice, in a critical mass of effective models for educational improvement, or in supportive interplay among researchers, schools, families, employers, and communities. (p. 2)

Today, even with programs specifically designed to bring research into the classroom, teachers seldom use research findings to improve their practice and inform their teaching. There is continuing concern that educational research has had minimal impact on improving teaching and learning and that translating research into practice remains a persistent, almost intractable, problem (Heibert, Gallimore, & Stigler, 2002)—a situation which the national publication *Education Week* (Viadero, 2003) deemed serious enough to warrant a series of articles on finding ways to develop "useable knowledge" that could be implemented in the classroom. Four years later, *Phi Delta Kappan,* believing the gap between research and practice was still wide, opened its April 2007 issue with four articles focusing on the Research/Practice Divide. And in June 2007, the entire issue of the international journal *Educational Research and Evaluation* was devoted to addressing the gap between educational research and practice.

Recognizing the gravity of the problem, the most ambitious and long-term approach to bridging the gap between research and practice has been launched by the National Academy of Sciences and the National Research Council through the formation of the Strategic Education Research Partnership (SERP). SERP is a 15-year program of research and implementation designed to find a way to make significant research findings part of the working vocabulary of teachers, school administrators, and education policymakers (National Academy of Sciences, 2003; National Research Council, 2004). SERP "would foster enduring relationships between the research community, educators, and policy makers so that research is influenced by the needs and insights of those who work most closely with students" (National Academy of Sciences, 2003, p. 3). As an organization, SERP would be an accessible place for teachers and policymakers to go for carefully screened, reliable knowledge with the goal of building and supporting effective demand for research among practitioners.

I am guardedly optimistic about this effort and hope that SERP will not be plagued by the history of similar efforts, which assumed that teachers were simply clients—consumers of research and technicians in research application—with no role as active researchers. Past efforts to transmit research have reflected the traditional research and development (R&D) approach of knowledge transmission. While hopeful, I am troubled that in trying to bring teachers and researchers together, the very language of SERP's documents reflects a deep commitment to an R&D approach and reveals a continuing conceptual separation of the research community from teachers. As I will discuss further in this chapter, the R&D model is problematic and has not had a history of great success in bridging the gap between research and practice.

Finally, it should be noted that dismay and disenchantment with the impact of educational research on teaching and learning practice is not limited to concerns in the United States. Frost, Durrant, Head, and Holden (2000), commenting on the status of educational research in England, note:

> Educational research is under scrutiny. Those professing to engage in research activities are challenged with questions about the quality and the validity of their work, its subject and context, its application and dissemination. There are questions over who conducts the research, who funds it, and who has the power over what is researched and how the results are subsequently used. Despite the vigor of the debate in academic circles, it has been suggested that the impact of current research on the consciousness and practice of individual teachers is minimal. (p. 109)

And from the Netherlands, Korthagen (2007) offers his viewpoint on the gap between research and practice:

> All attempts at enhancing the dissemination of research results have not led to a clear, successful, and generally accepted approach to bridging the research-practice divide and despite all these attempts, the gap between research and practice seems to have increased rather than diminished during the second part of the twentieth century. (p. 303)

❖ WHY THE DISCONNECTION BETWEEN RESEARCH AND PRACTICE?

What accounts for the gap between educational research and practice? Many explanations have been identified by a number of writers over the past 38 years (Atkin, 1989; Bangs, 1998; Barlow, Hayes, & Nelson, 1984; Barnard, 1999; Biesta, 2007; Broekkamp & van Hout-Wolters, 2007; Clifford & Guthrie, 1988; Davis, 2007; Fenstermacher, 1987; Frost et al., 2000; Goodlad, Klein, & Associates, 1970; Goodson, 1993; Graham, 1978; Henson, 1996; Kennedy, 1997; Korthagen, 2007; Lagemann, 2000; McIntyre, 2005; McKenna, 1978; Nuthall, 2004). I summarize them here:

1. Teachers judge much of the research to be lacking in practicality and to be inconsistent with classroom realities. They have been put off by the deadening jargon and the esoteric language of educational research, its concepts of experimentation, and its narrowly conceived

search for illusory proofs that one treatment or approach is superior to another. Research has not been sufficiently persuasive to motivate teachers to change their practices, and research findings are not communicated in ways that engage and motivate teachers. Explaining the problem of jargon and language, which distances teachers from research, Back (2001) notes:

> Scholarly writing has become self-referential and full of convoluted argot. It seems that we are writing too much to impress our peers. This produces a kind of surfeit of meta-language that passes largely unread from the desktop to the university library. But in order to be published in the right places, work has to conform to conventions that value academic technique over accessible prose.

2. Over the years, the continuing efforts of trying to link educational research with practice has constituted a history of intellectual compromise. Faculties in schools of education located in prestigious universities became ensnared in the academic and political cultures of their universities and neglected their professional allegiances. They became "marginal men, aliens in their own worlds" (Clifford & Guthrie, 1988, p. 3). As a ticket of admission to the university, they bought into a positivistic epistemology inherent in the university culture and construed professional knowledge as the application of research producing an institutional separation between research and practice.

> In short, schools of education entered into a devil's bargain when they entered the academic milieu. The result was their mission changed from being primarily concerned with matters central to the importance of schooling towards issues of status passage through more conventional university scholarship. (Goodson, 1993, p. 2)

In this embrace of conventional disciplinary methodologies, the relevance of educational research to practice was seriously compromised.

3. Many university researchers have lost touch with the reality of schools and the multiple demands, forces, and issues that affect the daily lives of teachers and students. Teaching is besieged with multilayered complexities that are not discernible or well understood by researchers who are removed from the ever-changing contexts of schools.

Only a modest number of faculty members have actually taught in public schools, and, for those who have, many years have passed since their public school teaching days. . . . For many of my colleagues, their understanding about life in schools is based on their exposure to the literature, their own particular strand of research, episodic campus visits, or the anecdotal reports of those who work in schools. (Davis, 2007, pp. 570–571)

Davis advises practitioners not to trust everything he and his colleagues have to say about schools.

4. Emanating from the institutional separation of knowledge from practice, the R&D model of knowledge dissemination became dominant in educational research. The R&D model assumes that teachers, as consumers of knowledge, will adapt and use knowledge developed by researchers in universities, research institutes, and educational foundations, outside and far removed from the specific situational contexts and circumstances that affect the work of teachers. This view contrasts sharply with Paulo Freire's (1973)—"The person who has the problem has the solution." The importation and imposition of solutions from experts in academe to apply within specific school contexts has been fiercely resisted by classroom teachers.

5. Teachers have not been actively involved in identifying research questions and in designing and implementing research studies. Too often, teachers have been the subjects of studies, treated as variables to be controlled and manipulated in experimental studies, regarded at best as peripheral to the conduct of educational research, and not respected for their craft knowledge. "Even in cases . . . where teachers and researchers have worked together, teachers report that their concerns and those of researchers usually do not overlap. Hence, the teacher's curiosity and needs remain unresolved" (Stevenson, 1987, p. 234).

6. In the quest to imitate the physical sciences, researchers often tailor educational questions and problems to fit the research design rather than asking the right questions and then deciding on methodologies appropriate to the questions. Because so often the research designs have driven the questions, the research outcomes have been too narrow and limited in application.

7. Until recently, teacher education programs did not prepare teachers to function as inquirers about their own classrooms. Although preservice teachers had been exposed to some study of research, it was

often in isolated courses focusing on teachers as consumers of research. No matter how much knowledge is generated by researchers, the practices and expectations of teacher educators largely determine the degree to which prospective teachers come to value and apply research. What teachers learn or don't learn about research is far more a product of the subliminal scholarly ethos and culture in their preparation program than the result of formal instruction. Even in teacher education programs, which now offer such courses as teacher action research, inquiry seminar, collaborative action research, or educational action research, unless inquiry permeates the entire teacher education curriculum, it becomes an isolated "one shot" experience not fully integrated into teachers' attitudes and behaviors.

8. Positivistic/empirical research approaches, particularly experimental, quasi-experimental, and process-product approaches, have failed to capture the critical elements of effective teaching and learning and ignored profound cultural and contextual factors affecting teaching and learning. Behaviors that foster success in one year or one classroom do not necessarily have the same effect the following year or in another classroom. "Ensuring that the same treatment is really the same is really difficult, and even if one could do that, the supposedly same treatment could have different effects in different places" (Lagemann, 2000, p. 221).

9. Traditional positivistic educational research has been viewed by teachers as exploitative, with researchers collecting "data from schools to publish in esoteric academic journals without giving anything back to teachers or their schools" (Frost et al., 2000, p. 155). In a nutshell, teachers feel they have been used by academe to serve the selfish interests of university faculty.

10. Traditional positivistic research has excluded school and community stakeholders and has been conducted within Eurocentric paradigms of logic and ethnocentric norms of reference, producing a racist and sexist knowledge base in which multiple ways of knowing and being are cast as deficiencies, further marginalizing already marginalized groups (Harris, 1992; hooks, 1994; Seidl & Friend, 2002; Stanfield, 1993). Positivistic research is described as a colonizing construct (Mutua & Swadener, 2004, p. 1), and there are calls for a decolonization of research methodologies (Smith, 1999). A new research paradigm is needed to address issues of racism, diversity, equity, and social justice—issues that deeply affect teaching and learning.

❖ RESPONDING TO THE GAP: RENEWING AN OLD DEBATE

Notwithstanding the numerous critiques of positivistic research and especially experimental and quasi-experimental designs, these approaches have received new life, renewing vigorous debate between proponents of quantitative and qualitative methodologies. In an attempt to make accountability the centerpiece of the educational agenda, to base school improvement efforts more on research-based evidence, and to improve the quality and usefulness of educational research, Congress and the administration of President George W. Bush, through the No Child Left Behind Act of 2001, mandated a scientific basis for educational research, modeled after medical research. Emphasizing **experimental** and **quasi-experimental research**, the Act defines scientifically based research as

(a) research that involves the application of rigorous, systematic, and objective procedures to obtain reliable and valid knowledge relevant to education activities and programs and (b) includes research that:

- employs systematic, empirical methods that draw upon observation or experiment;
- involves rigorous data analyses that are adequate to test the stated hypotheses and justify the general conclusions drawn;
- relies on measurements or observational methods that provide reliable and valid data across evaluators and observers, across multiple measurements and observations, and across studies by the same or different investigators;
- is evaluated using experimental or quasi-experimental designs in which individuals, entities, programs, or activities are assigned to different conditions and with appropriate controls to evaluate the effects of the condition of interest, with a preference for random-assignment experiments, or other designs to the extent that those designs contain within-condition or across-condition controls;
- ensures that experimental studies are presented in sufficient detail and clarity to allow for replication or, at a minimum, offer the opportunity to build systematically on their findings; and
- has been accepted by a peer-reviewed journal or approved by a panel of independent experts through a comparably rigorous, objective, and scientific review. (Section 7891, p. 35)

Reaction to this mandated definition has ranged from concerns that the legislative language is ideological, pressing for a mechanistic application of a particular set of research methods, to a measured response from the National Research Council (2004), which in its report *Advancing Scientific Research in Education* concluded that although good research adheres to core scientific principles, a wide variety of legitimate designs are available for education research and that research methodology may vary widely, depending on the research question. The report explicates the complexity and contextual nature of education, which affect educational research:

> Education is multilayered, constantly shifting, and occurs within an interaction among institutions (e.g., schools and universities), communities, and families. It is highly value laden and involves a diverse array of people and political forces that significantly shape its character. These features require attention to the physical, social, cultural, economic, and historical environment in the research process because these contextual factors often influence results in significant ways. Because the U.S. education system is so complex, attention to context is especially critical for understanding the extent to which theories and findings may generalize to other times, places, and populations. (Committee on Research in Education and National Research Council, 2005, p. 37)

Some writers suggest that the National Research Council's report does not go far enough in presenting an inclusive view of science and in capturing the complexity of scientific work in education, that its emphasis on methodology diverts attention from fundamental issues of epistemology, and that it marginalizes certain epistemologies and methodologies (Berliner, 2002; Ericson & Gutierrez, 2002; St. Pierre, 2002). The issue of **epistemology** in educational research is crucial if we accept the idea that there are different ways of knowing the world and thereby investigating it. Consequently, there can be no single epistemology governing all science. These are issues that I will discuss in subsequent chapters.

Despite the critiques of the National Research Council's response to the No Child Left Behind Act, I believe the Council's report offers a trenchant reminder of the essential role of context in educational research. In several sections, the report brings a balanced perspective to the debate regarding the renewed emphasis on experimental and quasi-experimental research designs. However, the report restrictively concludes that the way to go in educational research is the quantitative road. It is patently clear that although particular quantitative research designs are appropriate for some research questions, they have several significant limitations in investigating questions dealing with educational innovation, intervention, and change and with the complexities of classroom teaching and learning.

❖ LIMITATIONS OF EXPERIMENTAL AND QUASI-EXPERIMENTAL DESIGN

A major problem in integrating educational research and practice has been research methodology and design. Because the quantitative methods of the physical sciences, rooted in **positivism,** enjoyed and still enjoy the highest academic status, over the years, educational researchers "went empirical with a vengeance." Quantitative methodology, as it percolated down through physical sciences, became exceedingly popular in educational research, often resulting in forced fits between research methodologies and educational problems. The emphasis on quantitative methodologies, particularly experimental and quasi-experimental design, limited the selection of research topics to problems that could be addressed by such methods or, worse, led us to believe that these methods were sufficient to address any issue that was at hand (Graham, 1978). Carpenter's (2000) perspective as a classroom teacher reflects a common view held by many of his colleagues:

> Among the many issues, one that stands out in my reading of 10 years worth of articles is that much educational research involves single-variable studies in schools so complex that, to change anything, one must change many things. In fact, the argument can be made that the public schools have so many variables and inherent contradictions that reform attempts, however well intentioned, are ultimately useless. Although studying one element of schooling in isolation may give valid, reliable, and sometimes even generalizable results such studies seldom account adequately for the richness and contradictions of the school environment, much less for out of school factors. (p. 385)

Many educators have argued that quantitative and experimental research models borrowed from the physical sciences cannot fully address the major issues and questions of education. Gardner (2002) notes,

Minds are not the same as bodies; schools are not the same as home or workplace; children cannot legitimately be assigned to or shuttled from one condition to another the way agricultural seeds are planted or transplanted in different soils. (p. 72)

Traditional experimental research places confining conceptual boxes on the complexities of human experience in the school and classroom.

Rigorously controlled experimentation, statistical analysis of observed correlations of variables, or disinterested theoretical speculation finds little place to stand in the turbulent world of practice, which is notoriously uncontrolled, where problems are usually ill formed, and where actors in the practice situation are undeniably interested. (Schön, 1995, p. 29)

Thus, positivistic **empirical research** is problematic when the subjects of study are self-reflecting, choosing human beings who have the capacity to change themselves, their organizations, and their situations and to create and shape their own futures. Human behavior cannot be understood without reference to the meaning and the purpose that human beings assign to their activities and experiences.

The disparity between research and the real-life problems suggested by the frontline work of teachers in the classroom, along with the awareness that experimental and quantitative research designs no longer work in all cases, has raised a number of questions about the appropriateness of traditional experimental research approaches. Human phenomena present problems of access and measurement different from those presented by physical objects. Not only are access and meaningful interpretation mediated by perception and inference, but in the conduct of human affairs, there is contextual instability. When human phenomena are reduced to isolated and linearly related factors, the resulting studies tend to lose meaning by oversimplification and the omission of context (Habermas, 1971). The fundamental question is posed and answered by Longstreet (1985):

Can one ever validly generalize from the non-existing case of an isolated variable studied under "controlled" and thus necessarily unrealistic circumstances to situations of complex human interactions imbued with consciousness, independence of will and cultural diversity? Given our present state of knowledge, the response must be in the negative; the leap from isolated variables to complex human relations is too great, and there is too much evidence in between that is missed. (p. 9)

The context of educational innovation and change illustrates the problem of fit between experimental design and the improvement of educational practice. Measuring and evaluating student learning and academic achievement is a paramount concern of any educational innovation or reform, but particularly of initiatives that focus on the adaptation of the latest research and on what is commonly referred to as "best practices." The ultimate goal of many contemporary research adaptation initiatives is to introduce and demonstrate innovative research-based instruction and curricula or "best practices" to increase the effectiveness of education for low-income, special needs children, children of color, and bilingual learners. What happens to student learning when research—validated best practices, products, and processes—are systematically implemented and adapted to bring about organizational, instructional, curricular, and behavioral change? Will students demonstrate significant gains in learning? Will they be more motivated to learn? Will students change their perceptions of self and others? What kinds of attitudes and behaviors will change in students and their teachers? To what extent will preservice and in-service programs for teachers focusing on best practices affect student cognitive and affective growth?

In the past, the experimental method often has been used to attend to these kinds of questions, along with myriad other issues. But using the experimental method for evaluating student growth and achievement as outcomes of an educational innovation or intervention has three major limitations. First, the application of the **experimental design** requires that experimental and control conditions be held constant throughout the length of the experiment. This means that all students and teachers assigned to one treatment must receive it consistently to avoid contamination of the data and design. If data about differences between students and teachers participating and not participating in the program are to have meaning, treatments cannot be modified while the experiment is in progress.

In accepting the rigorous conditions of the experimental method, researchers are asked to fit the program to the design rather than vice versa. The use of the experimental method would, then, conflict with the fundamental principle that inquiry should lead to the continual improvement and modification of a reform effort. Teachers cannot be expected to limit their demonstration efforts and activities to accommodate the constraints of a research design, just to guarantee internally valid data. As teachers learn about the strengths and weaknesses of their project activities, they may have to change and sometimes radically alter the project to meet the needs of the project's constituents and clients: students, teachers, and parents.

A second limitation of the experimental method is that it yields data about the effectiveness of an instructional or curricular innovation after the fact. Therefore, although it may be useful as a summative device, it has little value as a formative decision-making tool. Post hoc data are not provided at appropriate times to enable teachers to determine what their project should be accomplishing or what should be changed. Often, by the time experimental data have come in, it is too late to make decisions about plans and procedures that could make the difference between success and failure.

Finally, the experimental method is typically used to study discrete elements of an educational problem and, therefore, often yields isolated factors associated with specified outcomes that have doubtful application to the complexities, convolutions, and changing contexts of varied school and classroom situations. Random sampling and experimental controls require the neglect of all other variables that may affect findings. It is unrealistic to assume that any experiment can actually control all pertinent factors in multidimensional, multilayered, evolving classrooms, save the independent variable. The salient factors in children, parents, teachers, classrooms, curricula, communities, homes, and in the simultaneous interaction of all these variables with each other and with other causal factors are not understood. The fact is, in real life, people do not get assigned to each other, to problems, and to time and place with rigorous experimental randomness and neat designs with all contextual factors parsed out or controlled. To illuminate and understand the real "messy" life of the classroom, of the school, of teaching and learning, researchers must study real life in the changing contexts of classrooms and schools. Ignoring the contextual nature of education seriously compromises the findings of educational research.

Context Stripping

Mishler (1979) made one of the most incisive criticisms regarding the weakness of experimental methodology and other quantitative methods in accommodating the changing and multidimensional contextual nature of education. In a seminal article, "Meaning in Context: Is There Any Other Kind?", he argues that traditional research approaches, which have dominated the social sciences and education, have largely ignored the importance of context and, in the search for universal context-free laws, have primarily used context-stripping methods. He begins his argument by noting a fundamental paradox:

> [On the one hand] we all know that human action and experience are context dependent and can only be understood within their contexts. . . . We rely on context to understand the behavior and speech of others and to ensure that our own behavior is understood, implicitly grounding our interpretations of motives and intentions in context. . . .
>
> [and on the other hand] this ordinary and commonsense understanding of meaning as context dependent has been excluded from the main tradition of theory and research in the social and psychological sciences and in the application of this tradition to educational research. . . . we tend to behave as if context were the enemy of understanding rather than the resource for understanding which it is in our everyday lives. (Mishler, 1979, p. 2)

It is virtually impossible to imagine any human behavior that is not mediated by the context in which it occurs. Mishler then critiques the standard methods of experimental design, measurement, and statistical analysis, noting that subjects of such studies are removed from their natural settings; their normal roles and social networks are left behind; and variables are isolated from the personal and social contexts in which they operate. "Subjects are randomly assigned to different experimental treatments, as if they were as interchangeable as the seeds of different strains of corn or alfalfa," he says. As a result of the historical dominance of traditional quantitative and experimental research methodologies, researchers have been tempted "to restrict the focus of their interest to short-run events and a limited range of meanings, and, thus, methods tend to determine the problem investigated rather than the other way around" (Mishler, 1979, p. 3).

Sigmond Koch's (1959) famous analysis of psychology's "mistake" could be applied to education today in that educational research, like psychology, adopted the logical positivistic construals of scientific practice before properly thinking through whether these methods would be appropriate to understanding the subject matter of educational inquiry—namely human beings. Thus, as Howard (1988) notes:

We were left with methodologies that possessed a lopsided preference for (a) certainty over authenticity (Gibbs, 1979), (b) manipulation over understanding (MacKenzie, 1977), (c) method over meaning (Koch, 1959), (d) rigor over sensitivity to human subtlety (Sanford, 1965) and (e) narrow quantification over broad qualitative inquiry (MacLeod, 1964). (p. 94)

Mishler's and Howard's critiques suggest that the ecology of teaching, the ecology of implementing educational innovations, and the ecology of initiating change require an emphasis on hypothesis-generating and qualitative methodologies that capture the complexity of being human in an interacting social world of teaching and learning. Teaching and learning are complex relational phenomena that defy "control of variables." An awareness of the multidimensionality and complexity of teaching and learning, curriculum development, and educational change provides a compelling argument that we should search for methodologies that facilitate the study of the many dimensions, variables, and meanings that appear and interact simultaneously in the classroom (Tickunoff, Ward, & Griffin, 1979).

Classroom Complexities

Classroom teaching and learning are embedded in a complex network of interdependent variables, all of them situation-specific, constituting a complex array of human/environmental behavior and variables that influence classroom events, phenomena, and processes. This complex array is captured by Doyle (1986), who has identified several definitive attributes of the classroom that affect teachers and learners: (1) multidimensionality: the large number of events and tasks, multiple consequences of a single event, and many people with a broad range of personal and social objectives that must be taken into account in classroom decision making; (2) simultaneity: the reality that many things happen at once in the classroom and that the teacher and the students must attend to many things at the same time; (3) immediacy: the rapid pace of classroom events, providing teachers with little time to reflect before acting; (4) unpredictability: because classroom events are socially constructed, it is often difficult to anticipate how any particular activity will unfold; (5) publicness: events, especially those involving the teacher, are often witnessed by a large proportion of students; and (6) history: the accumulated set of shared experiences, routines, norms, and understandings that provides a context for classroom events. Finally, it should be noted that classrooms exist within educational systems that themselves are composed of numerous multiple interactive and dynamic variables. Interaction between these variables is nonlinear, and the boundaries of the system are open or fuzzy; consequently, the system often generates new interactive variables challenging the best research practices. (See Radford, 2007, for a discussion on action research and the challenge of complexity.)

To grasp this complex array of variables and to gain understanding of the meaning and significance of individual and classroom differences in teaching and learning, one must develop information and understanding about the contexts of teaching and learning, including the subject matter taught, the physical and social settings of the classroom, the persona of the teacher, the culture of the school, parental and community expectations and values, peer values and student culture, the emotional exchanges between students and teacher, and student opinions and interpretations of behavior. More than 30 years ago, Goodlad (1977) made a similar point relative to the school curriculum, and Carini (1975) argued that to understand the phenomena of education, it is essential to include perceived reality, particularly participants' views of educational situations. Today, the situation remains unchanged. Gallagher (2002) sums up the challenge inherent in educational research: "Educational research is different. It does not deal with the physical or biological world but with the social and behavioral world, a research environment where contextual variations matter greatly but are elusive to gauge" (p. 52). And Berliner (2002, pp. 18–20) calls educational research "the hardest science of all" because of "the power of contexts," "the ubiquity of interactions," and the "short half-life of our findings."

❖ SCHOOL CONTEXT AND EDUCATIONAL RESEARCH

There can be no doubt that contextual factors significantly affect the conduct of education research and our understanding of the meaning and implications of research findings. When thinking about conducting research in schools, it is essential to remember that classrooms do not exist in a vacuum. The events and life in a school cannot be fully apprehended and understood without an understanding of the school's context. The power of context is captured by Cazden and Mehan (1989):

> The relationship of an event to its context is like the relationship of a word to the sentence in which it appears. While it is possible to

consider the meaning of a word separate from any sentence—as in
a dictionary definition—the meaning of the word, in any instance
of use, will both determine and be determined by its context. (p. 47)

In addition to understanding how the complexities of classroom
teaching and learning impinge on the conduct and design of educational research, it is essential to attend to and grasp the contextual variables of the school and their impact on educational practice. "Existing
school contextual conditions inevitably mingle with the change process
to yield substantially different results from school to school" (Corbett,
Dawson, & Firestone, 1984, p. xii). What mode of research can best
accommodate the nuances, subtleties, and convolutions of the changing situations of the school? School contexts and environments are
dynamic. They shift and change and are affected by unpredictable
events and forces. Sarason (1982, 1996) reminds us that one of the most
difficult obstacles to addressing the major problems in our schools lies
in the fact that one cannot see culture or systems the way one sees
individuals.

Educational change and improvement efforts must respond to the
way things are in the school and the classroom but, at the same time,
work to change those traditions and practices that are dysfunctional
and block necessary school and classroom change. This means that
studying the impact of any change effort must include a consideration
of the contextual variables of the school, such as role definitions of the
school, the normative relations among and within groups, the social
climate of distance that permeates the school, the issues of power and
control that dominate, the issue of collegiality versus isolationism, the
ambiguity of goals and processes, parental and teacher expectations,
student culture, the subliminal values and organizational culture of the
school, the invisible curriculum, and the variety of arenas for interaction within and between groups.

❖ THE SEARCH FOR SCHOOL CONTEXT

However, the search for school context as a holistic entity has troubled
researchers, who cannot agree on either the possibility or desirability of
identifying and encapsulating the buzzing confusion of simultaneously existing, multilevel, mutually interacting variables. Anderson
(1982, pp. 371–372) uses three metaphors to illuminate perspectives of
school context. He indicates that some researchers view school context
as a possible but not desirable focus of research; like the albatross, it is

only a burden to policymakers who need information on mechanisms that can be easily manipulated to affect student outputs. For other researchers, school context is seen as a desirable focus of study but one that is unattainable; it takes on the qualities of the unicorn, a mythological beast that people hoped to and dreamed of seeing but never found. Then, there are more optimistic researchers, who view school context as both possible and desirable—a phoenix born of the ashes of past school research. This last metaphor reflects the viewpoint of this book. To begin to grasp and understand the subtle and elusive quality of the gestalt of school context, it is helpful to look at schools from a sociological point of view as represented in the following frameworks: schools as turbulent environments, schools as workplaces, and schools as cultures.

Schools as Turbulent Environments

Schools can be characterized as turbulent environments. The environment of any change effort in a school reflects its complexity and unpredictability. The numbers of different variables that act on a change create their own complexity. The roles of students and teachers disappear in a welter of different needs, motivations, values, interests, and characteristics the more an educational innovation becomes involved in the local system, providing evidence of a "turbulent" environment. Unlike more placid and stable environments, turbulent environments affect all phenomena in any system under investigation.

> These are environments in which there are dynamic processes arising from the field itself which create significant variances for the component systems . . . dynamic properties that arise not simply from the interactions of the system . . . where the dynamic field emerges as an unplanned consequence of the actions of the constituent systems. (Emery & Trist, 1973, p. 35)

Each school has its own history, programmatic and behavioral regularities, role definitions, time perspective, culture, and modal process of change. An understanding of these elements is a necessary precondition for studying educational change, the impact of an educational innovation, and classroom teaching and learning. The school is a social system—a complex and interdependent set of activities, interactions, and sentiments. The school can be understood as a turbulent social system in terms of five elements:

- Relations in schools are based on position within the organization.
- Authority and power are derived from legality.
- Roles and tasks in schools are prescribed and clearly differentiated; division of labor is stressed.
- The social climate of schools is marked by social distance.
- Schools must respond to the larger social system of the external environment.

Schools as Workplaces

The school can also be considered as a workplace. The school as a workplace is extraordinarily powerful in influencing teacher behavior and student learning. The prevailing patterns of interactions and interpretations in each school demonstrably create certain possibilities and set certain limits. How the school is governed and organized, whether the school is resource adequate in providing minimum tools and conditions necessary for teaching, how the school provides levels of opportunity for teachers to develop professionally, the extent to which the organizational environment encourages problem solving rather than "problem hiding," and whether the reward structure of the school supports growth, risk taking, and change are organizational attributes that significantly affect teacher behavior, development, and aspiration (McLaughlin & Yee, 1988).

The organizational attributes that appear most consequential are those that are least often studied, least visible in any clear or systematic way to teachers, and least often addressed in programs of educational improvement and reform. Most at issue are the norms of collegiality and experimentation in accounting for receptivity toward new ideas (Little, 1982, 1999). In many schools, teacher collegiality is a departure from existing norms of teacher isolation, privacy, and autonomy. Contained in classrooms or constrained by departmental walls, teachers often work alone as they struggle, without the help of their colleagues, to deal with teaching, curriculum, and management issues. In these circumstances, it is difficult to alter teaching practice, to change curriculum, to find support for trying out new approaches, and to participate in collaborative inquiry. It should be noted, however, that some school workplaces do foster norms of collegiality and experimentation, and I will discuss how these schools develop such norms in supporting collaborative action research.

Schools as Cultures

Every school has its own history and culture. Any organization, such as a school, has social norms, values, expectations, rituals, beliefs, power relationships, shared meanings, and patterned ways of perceiving, believing, acting, and evaluating held by groups of people in the organization. Schools are social institutions embracing teachers, administrators, students, support personnel, and parents, who through their daily interactions and conversations construct social conventions, meaning, expectations, and norms that can affect teaching and learning. Moreover, these attributes of culture often are not formally reflected in organizational charts, mission statements, and other school documents but exist at an informal level not immediately discernible to the uninitiated members of the school or to outsiders. For members of the school culture, many of these attributes lie at the unconscious level not easily accessible to deliberate examination.

In every school, then, there is an underground stream of norms, values, beliefs, traditions, and rituals that develop as people work together, solve problems, and confront challenges (Deal & Peterson, 1998). These attributes of culture are developed over time, are subject to modification by members of the group, and comprise a continually evolving culture. Within the larger culture of the school are subcultures (Firestone & Louis, 1999) created by different groups of students, teachers, and other school personnel. Culture influences the actions and spirit of school life; shapes a school's motivation, commitment, effort, and focus (Peterson, 1999); and plays a major role in school restructuring (Newmann & Associates, 1996) and school improvement efforts (Fullan, 1998). Indeed, the power of culture in schools is acknowledged whenever we speak of "reculturing schools," that is, changing schools by changing and developing new beliefs, values, and norms. The impact of a school's culture and subcultures on teacher behavior and ultimately student learning cannot be underestimated, yet all too frequently, it is not considered or represented as a significant variable in research designs.

Patterson, Purkey, and Parker (1986) highlight the significant features of school culture, which, in my judgment, must be given appropriate attention when we study teaching and learning in schools:

- School culture affects the behavior and achievement of elementary and secondary school students (though the effect of classroom and student variables remains greater).
- School culture does not fall from the sky; it is created and thus can be manipulated by people within the school.
- School cultures are unique; whatever their commonalities, no two schools will be exactly alike—nor should they be.

- To the extent that it provides a focus and clear purpose for the school, culture becomes the cohesion that bonds the school together as it goes about its mission.
- Culture can be counterproductive and an obstacle to educational success; culture can also be oppressive and discriminatory for various subgroups within the school.
- Lasting fundamental change (e.g., changes in teaching practices or the decision-making structure) requires understanding and, often, altering the school's culture; cultural change is a slow process. (p. 98)

In summary, the social context of research (schools as turbulent environments, workplaces, and cultures) has too often been neglected as a critical factor in educational research, with deleterious impacts on the design and conduct of inquiry and the application of findings. Lagemann (2000), in writing on the history of educational research, observes:

> To look at the history of education research is to discover a field that was really quite shapeless circa 1890 and quite well shaped by roughly 1920. By that date, research in education had become more technical than liberal. It was more narrowly instrumental than genuinely investigatory in an open-ended playful way. The field's applied emphasis had resulted in the marginalization of most subject matter that did not appear to be immediately "relevant" to the professional concerns of school administrators and, to a lesser extent, teachers. . . . the psychology that had come to stand at the core of educational scholarship was not only excessively and narrowly behaviorist, but also distinctly more individualistic than social. *It simply ignored the degree to which multiple factors, including subtle interactions between and among individuals, groups, cultural traditions, and social structures, all combine to influence teaching and learning.* (p. 236) (emphasis added)

❖ TRANSCENDING THE R&D MODEL OF KNOWLEDGE TRANSFER

Integrating research and practice without the full involvement of and collaboration with the person responsible for classroom life—namely the teacher—is impossible. Teacher and student interpretations of the meanings of experiences and events are the sine qua non of research that can improve student learning. Natural classroom settings must be maintained, even though a vast array of variables may be studied. More than 37 years ago, Goodlad et al. (1970), in their book *Behind the Classroom Door*, suggested that innovations in schools come about not from the usual kind of dissemination of research findings but only when teachers and administrators seek to find solutions to their own problems. This perspective is in contrast to the R&D model of research dissemination, as exemplified in current attempts to have schools adopt "best practices."

The R&D model has an inherent flaw: It assumes that knowledge is separate from practice and that teachers will adopt, internalize, and use knowledge that has been developed by someone else—outside experts and researchers in other contexts. It focuses on "fixing the parts and the people" in education by transferring, adopting, and implementing specific educational innovations—"best practices" in schools. This remedial strategy is based on the rational-scientific R&D perspective, which assumes that teachers are passive knowledge users and that people accept and use decontextualized and disembodied information that has been developed by researchers in other educational settings. The focus is on the transfer and implementation of specific educational innovations, assuming the role of the teacher as a willing recipient of "outside" knowledge and ignoring what teachers know, think, and do.

In the R&D model, then, teachers function more as technicians rather than reflective educators (Cochran-Smith & Lytle, 1993; Fullan & Hargreaves, 1996). Research dissemination programs may center on specific curricular content or on teaching practices. The idea is to "fix" the ineffective or inadequately performing parts (people, programs, and curriculum) of education by implementing one or another new approach through "fix the people" professional development programs—programs that are typically organized to disseminate a knowledge base constructed almost exclusively by "experts." As a result of the R&D approach, teachers

> too often implement the initiatives of others; we pass on someone else's idea of what is valuable to know or experience, and we cultivate a sense of "objectivity" as the greatest good. We become passionless, non-thinking, uninvolved, and we hand over important considerations to "the experts," evading our deepest responsibility and marooning ourselves with merely the technical. (Ayers, 2001, p. 20)

❖ EMBRACING AN EPISTEMOLOGY OF PRACTICE

The interacting variables, unsynchronized intentionality, shifting circumstances, and unintended turbulence of school context require dynamic, responsive, recursive inquiry and multiple data collection procedures. As educators, we need to emancipate ourselves from the intellectual straitjacket of decontextualized experimental and process/product designs and recognize that meaningful research can be conducted in many different ways. In addition to understanding and grasping the complexities of context, we need to recognize that there are different ways of knowing schools, classrooms, and teaching and learning. University faculty, classroom teachers, parents, students, school board members, and administrators know and experience schools and classrooms in different ways. Different ways of knowing suggest that we need different ways of studying the phenomena of education. What is required is an epistemology of practice that acknowledges our different ways of knowing and that takes fuller account of school context and the circumstances of teacher practice: uncertainty, uniqueness, complexity, conflict, and change. We need an epistemology of practice that "avoids the three dichotomies of scientific positivistic research: the separation of means from ends, the separation of research from practice, and the separation of knowing from doing" (Schön, 1983, p. 165).

Beneficial research that advances student learning and teacher development recognizes the powerful impact of school context on teaching and learning. It recognizes that school contexts are natural and not contrived and that there are no predefined boundaries for inquiry. Beneficial research requires grounded reality, moral purpose, critical consciousness, personal commitment, patience, focus, and a sustained stance of inquiry. With preparation in processes of documentation and reflection, participatory/observation, case study approaches, the use of audio/videotaping systems, the Internet, personal journals, narrative writing, and thoughtful record keeping, teachers can bring about a renaissance of school-based inquiry that characterized the latter years of the Progressive era in education and contributed valuable ideas and practices for the education of children.

❖ MOVING TOWARD A KNOWLEDGE DEMOCRACY

Alternative approaches to educational research must reflect more than a passive role for the classroom teacher as a consumer of knowledge waiting to be "fixed" by the expertise of external authorities. We need to move from the outsider approach to creating knowledge toward an insider view of schools and classrooms, which helps to uncover inside perspectives and theories. We need "to conceptualize teacher development across the lifespan as a learning problem rather than a training problem" (Cochran-Smith, 2002, p. 373). Viewed in this way, teacher development requires "more opportunities for teachers to work with others in learning communities; raise new questions about students, subject matter, assessments, equity, and access; and generate local knowledge through collaborative analysis and interpretation" (Cochran-Smith, 2002, p. 373).

If we are to close the artificial separation of knowledge from practice and achieve an authentic and deep integration of research and practice, then alternative approaches to research and knowledge construction are needed to understand educational reality in its own phenomenological terms. Alternative approaches must include the role of the teacher as an active agent in creating knowledge for the improvement of teaching and learning. We need to develop knowledge democracies characterized by collaborative, participatory, and democratic relationships between and among teachers, university faculty, students, and parents, who together build communities of inquiry that promote the democratization of the knowledge-building process. These democratic relationships are essential to integrating research and practice and to fundamentally improving education for all children. Such democratic working relationships are epitomized in teacher action research, a paradigm of research with the potential to bring about democratic educational change from the bottom up and the inside out.

❖ TEACHER ACTION RESEARCH AND KNOWLEDGE DEMOCRACIES

Through teacher action research schools can become **knowledge democracies** where teachers provide the intellectual leadership for nonhierarchical, egalitarian, participatory, collaborative, and democratic construction of knowledge. In such democracies, inquiry permeates every aspect of the school's organization, programs, activities, and culture. This means that any function of the school is open to inquiry, including teaching, learning, curriculum, leadership, professional development, university-school partnerships, and parental involvement. Teachers, students, and parents work together in conducting caring inquiry in the classroom, school, and community to construct knowledge for meaningful change. They become committed to collaborative enlightenment and consciousness raising to increase potentials for self-affirmation and renewal, support the principles of democracy in education, construct authentic practical knowledge, interact around knowledge, transform knowledge, and apply knowledge that makes a difference in the lives of students, parents, and teachers and advances the principles of social justice within the school and the community.

Knowledge for democratic change emanates from democratic deliberation marked by an open and inclusive process of public sharing, debate, reflection, and sustained study—a process of public problem solving through which everyone in the school becomes privileged to construct knowledge and to create a dynamic, recursive knowledge base for improving education. Knowledge becomes a resource that affects decisions and actions that can be widely shared, jointly generated, and used to help all participants to gain voice, reframe issues and debates, and expand their visibility and influence. Teachers, students, parents, and others join in the social construction of knowledge, awareness, and action.

❖ SUMMARY

For nearly 40 years, consistent documentation of the gap between educational research and classroom practice reveals that school context, complexity, and culture have a profound impact on the implementation of research findings. To address the gap, it is argued that teacher action research, which encompasses school culture, complexity, and context, is a powerful research approach for improving teaching and learning and for building a knowledge democracy.

In a knowledge democracy, a transformational knowledge infrastructure characterized by systemic and relational trust evolves over time to support and facilitate the engagement of teachers, parents, and students in all aspects of the inquiry process. A culture of collaborative inquiry emerges and becomes embedded in the school. In the school's democratic climate of knowledge development, the voices of those who have been silent or silenced are raised and heard—knowledge construction is not for a privileged few but invokes the unique expertise of everyone in the service of democratic problem solving. As a paradigm of collaborative, participatory, and democratic inquiry, teacher action research is the intellectual and affective heart and soul of a knowledge democracy. Within educational contexts, it addresses critical epistemological questions such as: What is knowledge? What knowledge is of value? Who constructs knowledge? In whose interests? For what purposes? As Cochran-Smith and Lytle (1998) observe:

> Teacher research can help to question and reinvent the whole idea of a knowledge base, disrupting the existing relationships of power among knowers and known—who decides what "knowledge" and "practice" mean? Who decides how knowledge ought to be interpreted and used to improve practice? Who decides what kinds of "change" and "improvement" are possible/desirable in schools and universities? (p. 33)

In the following chapter, I try to convey how action research is the intellectual heart and soul of a knowledge democracy by discussing in considerable detail what action research is, its history and origins, the intellectual and philosophical ideas that have influenced its development, and major approaches to conducting educational action research.

2

Teacher Action Research

*Collaborative, Participatory,
and Democratic Inquiry*

The literature on action research is immense and deep. In this
chapter, I draw from that literature to discuss the early history, origins, theory, and development of action research. The integration of
action research into school settings and the benefits of action research
for teachers are delineated. The influence of postmodernism and
feminism on the nature and character of action research is reviewed.
Different approaches to action research are described. I hope that as
you read this chapter you will develop a fundamental grasp of the
historical, theoretical, and epistemological underpinnings of action
research as well as an appreciation for action research as intellectual
practice and a way of thinking.

❖ WHAT IS TEACHER ACTION RESEARCH?

Action research is a paradigm and not a method. As a paradigm, action
research is a conceptual, social, philosophical, and cultural framework for
doing research, which embraces a wide variety of research methodologies

and forms of inquiry. Unlike positivism, with its emphasis on prediction, control, and generalization through quantitative methodologies, action research is a paradigm that reflects the principle that reality is constructed through individual or collective conceptualizations and definitions of a particular situation requiring a wide spectrum of research methodologies. Characteristically, action research studies a problematic situation in an ongoing systematic and recursive way to take action to change that situation.

Action research is a process of concurrently inquiring about problems and taking action to solve them. It is a sustained, intentional, recursive, and dynamic process of inquiry in which the teacher takes an action—purposefully and ethically in a specific classroom context—to improve teaching/learning. Action research is change research, a nonlinear, recursive, cyclical process of study designed to achieve concrete change in a specific situation, context, or work setting to improve teaching/learning. It seeks to improve practice, the understanding of practice by its practitioners, and the situations in which practice is located (Carr & Kemmis, 1986, p. 165). Although it is focused on actions leading to change, action research is also a mental disposition—a way of being in the classroom and the school—a lifelong habit of inquiry. It is recursive in that teacher-researchers frequently work simultaneously within several research steps and circle back to readdress issues and modify research questions based on reflection for, reflection in, and reflection on action. The reflection-action-reflection-action process can be considered a spiraling cyclical process in which research issues change and actions are improved or discarded or become more focused. In education, action research generates actionable hypotheses about teaching, learning, and curriculum from reflection on and study of teaching, learning, and curriculum to improve teaching, learning, and curriculum.

Action research assumes that teachers are the agents and source of educational reform and not the objects of reform. Action research empowers teachers to own professional knowledge because teachers—through the process of action inquiry—conceptualize and create knowledge, interact around knowledge, transform knowledge, and apply knowledge. Action research enables teachers to reflect on their practice to improve it, become more autonomous in professional judgment, develop a more energetic and dynamic environment for teaching and learning, articulate and build their craft knowledge, and recognize and appreciate their own expertise. It assumes practice is embedded in the science of the unique, recognizing that human events are idiosyncratic; they vary with time, place, cultural circumstances, the ecology of the moment, serendipity, obliquities, and unforeseen circumstances.

Action research assumes caring knowledge is contextual knowledge, with the understanding that human actions always take place in context and must be understood in context. It assumes knowledge is tentative and probabilistic, continually subject to modification. It views "not knowing" and ambiguity as resources for learning. Action research assumes teacher development involves lifelong learning in changing and multidimensional contexts. Action research is grounded in the reality of the school, classroom, teachers, and students. It is a process in which study and inquiry lead to actions that make a difference in teaching and learning, that bridge doing (practice), learning (study), and reflection (inquiry). Action research reflects deliberate attention to the ways that what we know is caught up in what we do and who we are. Through action research, we intellectually and affectively nurture ourselves, our classrooms, and our students. Classrooms and schools become sites where new meanings and understanding are created and shared.

Action research challenges certain assumptions about the research process and educational change (Grundy, 1994, pp. 28–29). It challenges the separation of research from action, the separation of the researcher from the researched, assumptions about control of knowledge, and assumptions about the nature of educational reform. Action research is *by, with, of,* and *for* people, rather than *on* people (Reason & Bradbury, 2001, p. 2).

In educational action research, teachers, who traditionally have been the subjects of research, conduct research on their own situations and circumstances in their classrooms and schools. They conduct their research according to Lewin's basic dictum, "No research without action—no action without research" (as cited in Marrow, 1977, p. 10). Teachers are privileged through the action research process to produce knowledge and consequently experience that "knowledge is power." As knowledge and action are joined in changing practice, there is growing recognition of the power of teachers to change and reform education from the inside rather than having change and reform imposed top down from the outside. Through action research, "teachers transcend the truth of power through the power of truth" (Whitehead, 1989).

❖ ACTION RESEARCH: CHANGING PRACTICE

During the 1970s and early 1980s, the writing process movement contributed to the vitalization of action research in schools throughout the country. The major focus of these action research studies, which involved collaboration between university and teacher-researchers, was on the teaching of writing. These projects were initiated through the work of the Bay Area Writing Project, which later emerged as the National Writing Project, the Philadelphia Writing Project, and the Breadloaf School of English; it also found expression in the naturalistic and contextualized studies of writing by such people as Nancy Atwell, Lucy Calkins, Janet Emig, and Donald Graves.

In recent years, action research has been employed to study a variety of classroom and schoolwide issues (see Table 2.1). Based on an analysis of 73 published reports of action research studies conducted by classroom teachers, Kochendorfer (1997) identified seven types of classroom action research studies and the kinds of questions they addressed:

1. Changes in classroom practice (e.g., What effect will daily writing have on my students?)

2. Effects of program restructuring (e.g., How will a Foxfire approach affect student work habits?)

3. New understandings of students (e.g., What happens when at-risk students perceive they can be successful?)

4. Understanding of self as teacher (e.g., What skills do I need to refine to be more effective in teaching students to work together?)

5. New professional relationships with colleagues and students (e.g., How can regular and special education teachers effectively co-teach?)

6. Teaching a new process to the students (e.g., How can I teach third graders to use reflection?)

7. Seeking a quantifiable answer (e.g., To what extent are portfolios an appropriate assessment tool for kindergartners?)

❖ ACTION RESEARCH: TEACHERS' VOICES

All of these studies suggest that action research has been and continues to be a process of practical and grounded inquiry that reflects in its origins the empowerment of teachers to identify and solve their own problems. A good example is found in the remarks of Sharon Jeffrey (1996), who writes about the impact action research has had on her as a classroom teacher:

Table 2.1   Topics of Action Research Studies

- At-risk students (Leonard, 1997)
- Becoming a teacher (Phillips & Carr, 2006)
- Block scheduling (Marshak, 1997)
- Bully prevention (Bailey & Rios, 2005)
- Conflict management in schools (Kenway, 1997)
- Classroom behavior management (Daniels, 1998)
- Creating equitable classrooms (Caro-Bruce, Flessner, Klehr, & Zeichner, 2007)
- Development of basic literacy skills among urban minority students (Wilson, 2007)
- Inclusive education (Armstrong & Moore, 2004; Oyler, 2006)
- Online learning (McPherson & Nunes, 2004)
- Parental involvement (Brough & Irvin, 2001; Reynolds-Johnson, 1997)
- Professional development of teachers (Goodwin, 1999; Marion, 1998; Senese, 2002; Zeichner, 2003)
- Role of instructional coordinator (Clay, 1998)
- Science and mathematics teaching (Goldstone & Shroyer, 2000; Capobianco & Feldman, 2006)
- School improvement (Durrant & Holden, 2006; Gross, 2002; Halsall, 1998; Hendricks, 2006; MacDonald, 1997; Raymond, 2001; Rudduck & Flutter, 2004)
- School's mentoring program (Sharp, 1996)
- Silent reading among middle-grade students (Gibbons, 1997)
- Staff collaboration in the school restructuring process (Suarez, 1997)
- Social justice (Lynn & Smith-Maddox, 2007)
- Special education (Boardman, Arguelles, Vaughn, Hughes, & Klinger, 2005)
- Teachers' beliefs (Moore, 1996; Prejean, 1996)
- Teaching geography (Bednarz, 2002)

Action research transformed my relationship with students because I could no longer conceive of researching without seeking their insights, reflections, and questions about teaching and learning. In the process, my students became more reflective and aware of their own learning. . . . Action research became the most transformative experience of my teaching career. Suddenly, my classroom was fascinating and exciting in ways I had never considered. I always enjoyed students, but after ten years of teaching, the anti-intellectual routine and stifling structures of the school system took their toll. I seriously explored other careers. . . . Action research integrated with my teaching and formed the core of my new career. Each year now, I systematically pursue research and gain a deeper understanding of teaching and learning, and the implications for student learning, teacher education, and school reform. (p. 96)

Sandy Crepps (1999), a fifth-grade teacher in the Anderson Elementary School in Dixon, New Mexico, describes teacher research as a kaleidoscope:

I can never resist picking up a kaleidoscope and being surprised and delighted by mirrored patterns. Teacher research is like that to me. It focuses me on my classroom and by sharing my experiences with other teachers I am able to see new images of not only what I am doing, but what I could be doing. These images come from other teachers' perspectives and also as I hear myself explaining or when I am writing about what I am doing. I begin to see patterns that I didn't realize existed. These new perspectives open up new possibilities and new insights, allowing me to see my students, my teaching, the curriculum, differently than I had before. . . . That is why I do teacher research. The journaling, the networking with other teacher researchers, and the questions I pose all lead me to reflect on my teaching: the good, the bad, and the complexities of life in a classroom of thirty-two students. (p. 10)

Jennifer Moore (2002), a teacher at Coronado High School, Coronado, California, tells how her teacher research taught her to listen:

One of the most exciting aspects of teacher research is that it helped me focus on the vital questions related to my instructional prac-tices. Through the intense introspection involved in teacher research, I had, in effect, invited myself to be videotaped running students off the road. While my initial goal in allowing for that close examination of my practice may have been to critique student stride or speed, I wound up recognizing how my own actions and pedagogical methods affected their results and feelings about the run itself. Writing about the experience has deepened my under-standing of my role in my students' learning and how to apply what I have learned to this year's team of "runners." A teacher researcher is a listener—someone actively engaged in making new discoveries about her students, her teaching and herself. In my first year of this process, I learned that listening is, indeed, the most important part. (p. 10)

And Maria Mercado, a bilingual teacher with the Albuquerque Public Schools, in discussing the effects of teacher research on her classroom, says:

Teacher research enhanced my classroom teaching, strengthened my oral and written articulation of what was occurring in the classroom, and in this way improved my practice. The daily journal writing along with my conversations about teaching and learning processes in the classroom served to transform my teaching on a daily basis. What has become evident to me in the examination of this process is my growth as a researcher, a student of bilingual education, and a classroom teacher. (quoted in Fischer et al., 2000, p. 9)

The voices of these teachers document the transformative power of action research in changing teaching approaches, in developing deeper understanding of their students and of who they are as teachers, in enhancing their confidence and self-esteem, in gaining new perspectives, and in revitalizing their careers. Finally, they affirm that teacher action research is a valid and energizing process for constructing knowledge about teaching and learning and for empowering teachers to take leadership in bringing about educational change.

❖ ACTION RESEARCH: OUTCOMES FOR TEACHERS

Practicing the strategies and skills of teacher action research can help aspiring teachers in designing their own meaningful pedagogy, shift the identity of teacher as expert to one of inquirer, and make it more difficult to take the dynamics of the classroom for granted (Britzman, 2003, p. 239). For example, a study of beginning teachers, with 1 to 5 years of experience (Campbell, 2004), documented that teachers who learned to do teacher research as part of their preservice program carried their learning about teacher research into their own classrooms, using data collection procedures to construct knowledge about teaching, specifically in five categories of knowledge: knowledge of classroom structure, knowledge of self, knowledge of students, knowledge of curriculum and instruction, and knowledge of theory.

Mohr (1985, pp. 127–128) found that teachers who engaged in teacher research wrote more honestly about classroom problems, became more self-assured, began to see teaching more as a learning process, found their research plans became their lesson plans in response to discoveries they were making in their classrooms, and changed their focus from teaching to finding out what their students knew and then helping their students to learn.

In addition, teachers were able and encouraged to try new ways of teaching as they became sensitive to classroom variables and examined the classroom context simultaneously with their teaching, moved from evaluating issues and events to documenting issues and events, asked more questions and listened more to their students and colleagues, and grew more tolerant of creative chaos in their thinking, which led them to become more understanding of creative chaos in their students' thinking and writing.

In a study of the CRESS Teacher Research Program, Brookmyer (2007, pp. 123–133) found that among a sample of 114 teachers who had conducted action research studies from 1985 to 2005,

- 89% indicated that teacher research is an important information base for reflective practice
- 85% indicated that teacher research is an important foundation on which to develop greater professionalism
- 84% responded that teacher research provides valuable knowledge for classroom practice
- 75% believed that teacher research provides a context for the transformation of practice.

And finally, Onwuegbuzie and Dickinson (2006), after conducting an extensive review of the literature on action research, identified 27 positive outcomes associated with the conduct of action research (see Table 2.2).

What, then, is it that makes action research a productive venue for classroom teachers? What is the nature and character of action research, and how did it all start? What makes action research different from other forms of research? To address these questions, one has to understand the history of action research and how it evolved into a unique way for constructing knowledge to inform action.

❖ THE ORIGINS OF ACTION RESEARCH

Action Research and Social Justice

Action research is rooted in a concern for social justice, which was and is the foundation for action research. Action research's participatory

Table 2.2   Advantages of Action Research for Teachers

- Develops an increased awareness of the discrepancies between goals and practices
- Improves teachers' ability to be analytical about their practices
- Increases receptiveness to educational change
- Improves instructional effectiveness
- Improves decision-making skills/awareness
- Helps teachers view teaching as a type of inquiry or experimentation
- Increases reflection about teaching
- Increases understanding about the dynamics of a classroom
- Heightens the curiosity of teachers
- Empowers teachers by giving them greater confidence in their ability to promote change
- Can expand career opportunities and roles for teachers
- Can revitalize teaching and reduce burnout
- Increases appreciation for theory, provides an avenue for informing theory, and demystifies research
- Encourages positive change and enables teachers to become agents of change
- Identifies or verifies which methods work
- Increases awareness, evaluation, and accountability of decisions made
- Promotes ownership of effective practices
- Promotes the selection of research questions that are personally meaningful
- Encourages teacher-researchers to be active learners
- Increases willingness to accept research findings for use in teaching
- Encourages more critical and responsive consumers of research
- Increases teachers' knowledge about situations and contexts
- Facilitates defense of pedagogic actions
- Strengthens connection between pure and applied research
- Increases commitment to goals they have formulated themselves rather than those imposed on them
- Increases opportunity to gain knowledge and skill in research methodology and applications
- Makes distinction between researcher and teacher irrelevant

SOURCE: Onwuegbuzie and Dickinson (2006).

action-oriented form of inquiry originated outside the field of education in the work of John Collier, social worker, anthropologist, and author. After holding several positions in community organizations, serving as the executive secretary of the American Indian Defense Association, and editing the magazine, *American Indian Life*, Collier was appointed in 1933 by Franklin D. Roosevelt as the U.S. Commissioner for Indian Affairs, a position he held for 12 years, making him the longest-serving person in this position. Reversing federal Indian policies, his "Indian New Deal" approach officially rescinded the repression of American Indian language and promoted tribal self-government, cultural preservation, and religious freedom for Native Americans. Specifically, Collier promoted the passage of the Indian Reorganization Act, which encouraged tribes to develop their own constitutions and establish themselves as membership corporations to conduct tribal business. He founded the Emergency Conservation Work program, which employed 22,000 Indians in "the building of secondary roads, trails, telephone lines, fire lookouts, nursery work, and seed collection," which led to the development of "Indian-built, Indian-maintained, and Indian-used projects" around soil conservation, forestry, and the general recovery and regeneration of Indian lands (Collier, 1963, p. 187).

Collier was appalled by the egregious record of the U.S. government's inhumane treatment of the American Indian, and he developed a collaborative action research approach designed to reverse deeply discriminatory, racist, and destructive practices and to restore the integrity and dignity of Indian society and culture. In his efforts to establish a living democracy in Indian societies and to implement more democratic policies and approaches in the Bureau of Indian Affairs, he saw action research as an imperative:

> We had in mind a particular kind of research, or, if you will, particular conditions. We had in mind research impelled from central areas of needed action. And since action is by nature not only specialized but also integrative of specialties, and nearly always integrative of more than specialties, our needed research must be of the integrative sort. Again, since the findings of the research must be carried into effect by the administrators and layman, and must be criticized by them through their experience, the administrator and the layman must themselves participate creatively in the research, impelled as it is from their own area of need . . . such research has invariably operated to deepen our realization of the potentialities of the democratic way, as well as our realization of our own extreme, pathetic shortcomings. (Collier, 1945, pp. 275–276)

After completing his 12 years of service as Commissioner of Indian Affairs, Collier (1945) published an article describing the Bureau of Indian Affairs as a laboratory of ethnic relations and outlined his participatory research methodology, which he called action-serving research. He concluded his article by citing the distinctive strengths of action research:

> We have learned that the action-evoked, action serving, integrative and layman participating way of research is incomparably more productive of social results than the specialized and isolated way; we think we have proved that it makes discovery more central, more universal, more functional, and more true for the nascent social sciences. (pp. 300–301)

The participative collaborative model of inquiry championed by Collier was a congenial match with the work of the social psychologist Kurt Lewin, who studied the dynamics of group interaction seeking to counteract racism and to improve intergroup relations. Lewin (1946) was familiar with Collier's work in action research, referring to it approvingly in an article he wrote on action research and minority problems. Both Collier and Lewin shared deep interest in and commitment to democracy as a way of life and the conviction that action research could strengthen democratic relationships. During the 1930s and 1940s, Lewin and his colleagues developed the concept of action research as a way to study and improve group and intergroup relations and to address conflict, crises, and change. They viewed action research as a collaborative process in which participants sharing power in conducting studies of their own situations and circumstances could work together to understand and solve social and organizational problems.

Lewin was invited to establish a Research Center for Group Dynamics at MIT in 1944, where he and his staff launched action research projects to combat racial discrimination and to improve intergroup relationships (Lewin, 1945). These studies focused on such issues as anti-Semitic gang behavior, resistance to hiring black sales personnel, the effects of integrated versus segregated public housing, the socialization of street gangs, the cause and cure of prejudice in children, and ways of dealing with public remarks made by bigots.

> Lewin was particularly concerned to raise the self-esteem of minority groups, to help them seek "independence, equality, and cooperation" through action research and other means. He wanted

minority groups to overcome the forces of "exploitation" and colonization that had been prominent in their modern histories. (Adelman, 1993, pp. 7–8)

Lewin (1946) introduced and coined the term *action research* in his article on action research and minority problems; he described action research as "a comparative research on the conditions and effects of various forms of social action and research leading to social action" using a process of "a spiral of steps, each of which is composed of a circle of planning, action, and fact finding about the result of the action." The spiral of steps or cycles consisted of a basic cycle of activities: identifying a general idea, engaging in reconnaissance, making a general plan, developing the first action step, implementing the first action step, evaluating, and revising the general plan. From this basic cycle, the researchers then spiral into a second cycle of activities: developing the second action step, implementing, evaluating, revising the general plan, developing the third action step, implementing, evaluating, and so on continuing into a third, fourth, fifth cycle of activities. Lewin's work affirmed the idea that a practitioner's reflection on knowing and reflection in action can lead to actionable theory that can be generalized to other situations.

Educational Action Research

Building on the work of Collier and Lewin, the great promise inherent in practical inquiry involving the collaboration and mutual support of university professors and classroom teachers soon came to fruition. Collaborative action research was initiated, pioneered, and demonstrated in the 1940s and 1950s by Stephen Corey and others at Teachers College, Columbia University, in cooperative action research projects that brought together teachers and professors primarily to improve curriculum, supervision, and instruction. Working in the Horace Mann Institute of School Experimentation, Corey (1953) advocated and advanced action research as an alternative to traditional research in schools, based on the belief that "research methodology will not begin to have the influence it might have on American education until thousands of teachers, administrators, and supervisors make more frequent use of the method of science in solving their own practical problems" (p. 18). In *Action Research to Improve Schools,* he set forth his ideas on action research, how it differed from traditional research approaches, and how it could be implemented within complex contextual school environments, primarily through collaborative inquiry involving teachers, administrators, parents, and university faculty. Recognizing teachers' reluctance to implement someone else's ideas in their classrooms, Corey vigorously argued that teachers should be equal partners in "cooperative action research" and play a major role in the design of classroom research and in the collection and interpretation of data.

Corey (1953, pp. 40–41) viewed action research as a recursive process proceeding through spiraling cycles of planning, actions, reflections, and change reflected in five stages:

- Identifying a problem area about which an individual or a group would be sufficiently concerned to want to take action
- Selecting a specific problem, formulating a hypothesis, and specifying a goal and a procedure for reaching it
- Carefully recording the actions taken and gathering and analyzing data to determine the degree to which the goal has been achieved
- Inferring, from the evidence collected, generalizations regarding the relationship between the actions and the desired goal
- Continually retesting these generalizations in action situations

Within these stages, problems, hypotheses, questions, and actions could be changed, reflecting the recursive nature of the research, with each cycle of research affecting previous and subsequent cycles. Like Lewin's conception of spiraling cycles, the stages are not linear but rather are considered as interacting loops of research activities.

In his book *The School as a Center of Inquiry*, Schaefer (1967) extended the concept of action research to make it an integral part of the school culture, suggesting that teachers use action research to make schools collegial centers of inquiry rather than distribution centers for information developed outside the schools. He argued:

> We can no longer afford to conceive of the schools simply as distribution centers for dispensing cultural orientation, information, and knowledge developed by other units. The complexities of teaching and learning in formal classrooms have become so formidable and the intellectual demands upon the system so enormous that the school must be much more than a place of instruction. It must be a center of inquiry—a producer as well as a transmitter of knowledge. (p. 1)

Schaefer urged that students as well as teachers become involved in academic inquiry and that experimentation with teaching and learning become the school norm. Through inquiry, collaborating teachers would design new instructional approaches and curriculum materials and try them out to see what worked and what didn't work. Their work would then inform further inquiry and trials, and their schools would become "knowledge creating schools" in which the intellectual assets of teachers would be deeply valued and supported (Hargreaves, 2001).

Embedded in action research, as conceived by Collier, Lewin, Corey, and Schaefer, is Dewey's idea of inquiry—thought intertwined with action, reflection in and on action—which proceeds from doubt to the resolution of doubt to the generation of new doubt. For Dewey, doubt lies not in the mind but in the situation. Inquiry begins with situations that are problematic; that are confusing, uncertain, and conflicted; and that block the free flow of action. Schon (1995) elaborates Dewey's concept of inquiry:

> The inquirer is in, and in transaction with, the problematic situation. He or she must construct the meaning and frame the problem of the situation, thereby setting the stage for problem solving, which in combination with changes in the external context, brings a new problematic situation into being. Hence, the proper test of a round of inquiry is not only "Have I solved this problem?" but "Do I like the new problems I've created?" (p. 31)

Hence, he introduces the notion of action research as a habit of continuing inquiry—a Deweyan attitude of questioning one's practice that teacher-researcher Carol Battaglia (1995) embraces:

> I now believe that action research is as much a process of asking questions about one's practice as it is deciding what to do about solutions. Action research enables you to live your questions; in a way they become the focal point of your thinking. My questions took on an almost mantra-like quality; they seemed to seep into my thinking and conversation, creep into my reading and writing when I'd least expect it. They also kept me focused. I appreciate how professionally healthy it might be to adopt an "action research mentality" whereby one is always thinking about or attempting to polish another facet of the work one does. Perhaps then action research is an attitude or becomes an attitude that is brought to one's practice. (p. 107)

The Growth and Development of Action Research

In the late 1950s and during the 1960s, action research went into somewhat of a decline, partly because of its association with radical positive activism (Stringer, 2007, p. 10), but mostly because it was not viewed as genuine research. Critics of action research, representing behavioristic and positivistic views, argued that action research was not real research because it did not use quantitative methods in controlled experiments to generate generalizations, was statistically unsophisticated, was conducted by teachers who were amateur researchers not well prepared in their teacher education programs to conduct rigorous research, and was just a form of commonsense problem solving (Hodgkinson, 1957). In other words, action research was viewed as too much of a departure from experimental science and therefore less rigorous. Furthermore, critics argued that action research couldn't be conducted by classroom teachers, who were inundated with too many tasks and had little time or preparation for doing real research. These critiques came under fire with the emergence of postmodernism, feminism, and a vast literature that raised fundamental questions about social science paradigms and the basic epistemology and methodologies of positivism on which the critiques of action research rested. Perhaps the most scathing attack on the social sciences can be found in the words of Sanford (1970), who, in addressing the question Whatever happened to action research? wrote:

> Like other industries, social science has been polluting its environment. Not only has it been spoiling its research subjects by treating them as means rather than ends; not only has it been disseminating a monstrous image of researchable man; it has been creating a large amount of waste in the form of useless information. (p. 18)

Since the early 1970s, there has been a significant and dramatic surge in the practice of action research in a variety of venues all over the world. Several factors fueled the growing momentum of recognition, legitimization, and practice of action research (Carr & Kemmis, 1986, pp. 166–167): the professionalization of teaching, reflecting the idea of teachers investigating their own practice; the perceived irrelevance of much contemporary educational research for practice; the revival of interest in the "practical" in the curriculum (Schwab, 1969); the emergence of "new wave methods" in educational research with their acknowledgement of participants' knowledge, perspectives, and categories in shaping educational practices and situations; the adoption of a self-monitoring role in teaching to address issues of accountability by highlighting good practice and sensitively critiquing working conditions; the organization of teacher support networks committed to the continuing development of education; and the increased recognition that action research provides an understandable and workable approach to the improvement of practice through critical self-reflection.

Postmodernism and Action Research

To this list of reasons, I would add that **postmodernism** (Brown & Jones, 2001) has been a pivotal influence in advancing the legitimation and widespread practice of action research throughout the world. The foundational principles of contemporary action research reflect the generative ideas of postmodernism (Tarnas, 1991, pp. 395–410):

- Reality and knowledge are plastic and subject to constant change.
- Reality is a fluid, unfolding process, constructed in the mind.
- Reality is at once multiple, local, and temporal without demonstrable foundation.
- Concrete experience takes priority over fixed abstract principles.
- No single a priori thought system should govern belief or investigation.
- Meaning systems coexist and interpenetrate.
- Imagination plays a mediating role in human experience, and philosophical and scientific statements are inherently metaphorical.
- Human knowledge is subjectively determined by a multitude of factors, and all truths and assumptions must be continually subjected to direct testing.
- Knowledge is created through open discourse.
- The search for knowledge is endlessly self-revising, and respect for contingency and discontinuity limits knowledge to the local and the specific.

Feminist Scholarship, Critique, and Action Research

Within postmodern thought, perhaps the most powerful intellectual influence, and one that has affected the conceptual evolution of action research, is **feminism**. Tarnas (1991) makes a strong case for this assertion:

Considered as a whole, the feminist perspective and impulse has brought forth perhaps the most vigorous, subtle, and radically critical analysis of conventional intellectual and cultural assumptions in all of contemporary scholarship. No academic discipline or human experience has been left untouched by the feminist reexamination of how meanings are created and preserved, how evidence is selectively interpreted and theory molded with mutually reinforcing circularity, how particular rhetorical struggles and behavioral styles have sustained male hegemony, how women's voices remained unheard through centuries of social and intellectual male dominance, how deeply problematic consequences have ensued from masculine assumptions about reality, knowledge, nature, society, the divine. Such analyses in turn have helped illuminate parallel patterns and structures of domination that have marked the experience of other oppressed peoples and forms of life . . . long established categories that had sustained traditional oppositions and dualities—between male and female, body and spirit, self and other—have been deconstructed and reconceived, permitting the contemporary mind to consider less dichotomized alternative perspectives. (p. 408)

Feminist scholarship and critique continue to inform and affect the development of action research (Belenky, Clinchy, Goldberger, & Tarule, 1986; Britzman, 2003; Grumet, 1988; Hicks, 1999; Hollingsworth & Cody, 1994; Kohli, 2000; Lather, 1991; Lykes, 1997; Maguire, 1987, 2001, 2002; McIntyre, 2007; Miller, Maguire, & McIntyre, 2004; Naples, 2003; Skelton & Francis, 2005). They focus attention on the relationship between the knower and the known; power relationships in the construction of knowledge; understanding of subjugated knowledge; the connections between feelings and knowledge—emotion and inquiry; the connection between gender and ways of knowing; and indigenous people's epistemology. The fundamental operating principles for these scholars are that human knowledge is created in relationship, that everyday experience is gendered, and that the everyday is experienced through multiple identities and the web of oppression.

Maguire makes the case that

it remains impossible for action research to be a transformative approach to knowledge creation until action researchers learn more about feminism with all its diversity, critically examine their own multiple identities and implications for their work, and open up to feminist voices and visions. (Bryden-Miller, Maguire, & McIntyre, 2004, p. 132)

Maguire (2001) elaborates five current emergent themes that demonstrate how feminists inform the work of action research—gender, multiple identities and interlocking oppressions, voice and silence, everyday experiences, and power. Within the theme of gender, it is recognized that gender is a central category of human experience and is the structure in which all individual lives are framed. Action researchers need to examine how their gendered identities affect their personal and professional lives. The theme of multiple identities and interlocking oppressions captures the sensitivity to the ways in which gender oppression is experienced within other oppressions, such as those based on race and class, and suggest that those who conduct action research need to raise their consciousness about the ways in which gender, race, and class are interconnected and to become more attentive to systems of domination that oppress marginalized groups. Voice and silence are themes that need to be explored in the action research process, for far too many people have been silenced because of their gender, race, class, or power status. A primary goal of action research is to break these silences and free up the voices of people who have been marginalized or who feel powerless.

Maguire argues that researchers must recognize that everyday experience is a source of legitimate knowledge and a place to begin inquiry and the construction of knowledge. To have meaning, these everyday experiences should be examined within context and connected with the social and institutional structures that affect our lives. The final theme of power is reflected in the challenges that action research makes to the power structure of knowledge construction. Who constructs knowledge? Which knowledge is considered privileged?

There are other themes, like Maguire's, that suggest feminist research is foundational to current action research practices: not viewing the researcher/researched relationship as a hierarchical relationship; seeing emotions as valuable aspects of the research process; abandoning conceptualizations of "objectivity" and "subjectivity" as binaries or dichotomies; taking into account the researchers' intellectual autobiography in considering their conclusions; recognizing the existence and management of the different "realities" or versions held by the researchers and the researched; acknowledging the issues surrounding authority and power in research; and finally recognizing that there is authority and power in the written representation of research (Stanley & Wise, 1993, p. 189).

Power relationships, transparency in the research process, and plurality of viewpoints are key issues for feminist researchers, as noted by Kirsch (1999):

> Feminist grounded action research opens knowledge creation conditions to scrutiny, attempts to unsettle and equalize power relations between researchers and participants, facilitates conditions for empowerment and reciprocity, wrestles with dilemmas

of representation and interpretation, and experiments with polyvocal research accounts. (quoted in Maguire, 2001, p. 66)

Extrapolating from the stance of feminist research on power relationships, one can say that educational action research empowers teachers and participants in the research process to "unsettle" and balance the power relationships between the researchers in the "academy" and K–12 classroom teachers. As a process of empowerment, action research takes many forms and shapes.

❖ APPROACHES TO ACTION RESEARCH

Carson and Sumara (1997, p. xxi) offer three criteria for determining how any particular form of inquiry would be identified as action research. When any form of inquiry meets all three criteria, it can be considered a form of action research. The three criteria include any form of inquiry that seeks to learn about the complexly formed, ecologically organized relations of lived experience; is specifically organized around questions of learning, understanding, and/or interpretation; and self-consciously attempts to alter perception and action, that is, it is transformational in nature.

Using these criteria, a number of different approaches to action research can be identified. It should be borne in mind, however, that although each of these approaches has some distinct features, in my judgment, they all share common action research elements: the recursive, spiraling nature of the research; the emphasis on collaboration and critical dialogue; the empowerment of practitioners in generating knowledge, self-reflection, and reflection for-in-on practice. They also share common values and commitments, including

a rejection of a means-end conception of rationality and of a technical-rationalist view of human worth; a commitment to personal autonomy and its rational components of honesty and sincerity; emancipatory concerns; liberal and democratic politics; an idea of genuine knowledge as essentially purposeful rather than inert; a transcendental justification. (Parker, 1997, p. 32)

The differences, then, seem to be more in degree of emphasis rather than in the fundamental nature and character of the particular action research approach. Reason and colleagues (Reason & McArdle, 2004, p. 1; Reason & Torbert, 2001, pp. 11–17) differentiate action research by considering three strategies of inquiry that are highly interdependent:

1. **First-person research**/practices address the ability of individual researchers to foster an inquiring approach, to act awarely and choicefully, and to assess effects in the outside world while acting. First-person inquiry skills are essential for those who would provide leadership in any social enterprise. (Reason & McArdle, 2004, p. 1).

In first-person research, the teacher-researcher attends to such questions as: Who am I? What is important and meaningful to me? What values, ideologies, worldviews, assumptions, and perspectives do I bring to the process of inquiry? First-person methodologies include autobiographical writing, journal writing, narratives, and reflection on audio- and videotapes of one's behavior.

2. **Second-person research**/practices such as cooperative inquiry address our ability to inquire face-to-face with others into issues of mutual concern, usually in small groups. In cooperative inquiry, a small group of peers work together in cycles of action and reflection to develop both understanding and practice in a matter of mutual concern (Reason & McArdle, 2004, p. 1). In a typical cooperative inquiry group, six to twenty people work together as co-researchers and co-subjects (Reason & Torbert, 2001, p. 11).

3. **Third-person research** and practice includes a range of practices which draw together the views of large groups of people and create a wider community of inquiry involving persons who cannot always be known to each other face-to-face. Under this heading we include, for example, practices which "network" small inquiry groups, the range of large-scale dialogue and "whole system" conference designs, and the "learning history" approach (Reason & McArdle, 2004, p. 1).

Third-person research/practice attempts to create conditions that awaken and support the inquiring qualities of first- and second-person research/practice in a wider community, thus empowering participants to create their own knowing-in-action in collaboration with others.

In their documentation and analysis of first, second, and third person-centered research activities that occurred over time in a consulting intervention with 10 different organizations, Chandler and Torbert (2003) constructed a $3 \times 3 \times 3$ model of a new vision of action research. Using three dimensions of time (past, present, future), three dimensions of research practices (first person, second person, and third person), and three research voices (first-person research on first-person practice, second-person research on second-person practice, and third-person research on third-person practice), they generated 27 flavors of action research. They suggest that the 27 flavors of action research model can be used

> as a heuristic for engaging with a wider universe of potential action research interventions as well as for designing particular actual interventions to increase joint inquiry in the present, to increase mutuality and joint ownership over time, and to increase eventually measurable transformational impact. (Chandler & Torbert, 2003)

For our purposes in exploring and understanding the process of action research as it affects teaching and learning and educational change, I have identified four major approaches that reflect first-person, second-person, and third-person research/practices. These approaches are not mutually exclusive of each other—there is a great deal of overlap between and among them—and yet their histories, purposes, and approaches differ sufficiently to mark them with their own identities.

Collaborative Action Research

Action research becomes collaborative when it is done in partnership with colleagues, or with students, or with university faculty, or with parents, or a combination of partners. It engages both first- and second-person research/practice and, in large collaborative action research networks, third-person research/practice. The process emphasizes growth through group dialogue, reflection, and action. Participants may pursue individual studies bound together by a common theme, concern, or problem and then come together to share their work and develop a common set of recommendations for educational improvement. Or participants may form research teams to study one particular issue over time. Collaborative action research often involves school-university partnerships. Historically, this approach has been integral to the action research process from the very beginning; it will be elaborated in much detail in Chapter 5.

Teacher as Researcher

Perhaps the earliest effort to engage teachers as researchers can be found in the work of Lucy Sprague Mitchell. The first dean of women at the University of California–Berkeley, she was friendly with John Dewey and greatly influenced by his writings. Committing her life to improving schools for children, she established the Bureau of Educational Experiments in New York City in 1916. She gathered a team of psychologists, a social worker, a doctor, and a number of classroom teachers around her to study jointly, in as free an atmosphere as possible, children, children's language development, teaching, and a variety of new experimental approaches to education. Eventually over time, while continuing to conduct research, the bureau expanded its mission to include developing a model teacher education program, which ultimately became the foundation for the Bank Street College of Education.

The contemporary teacher-as-researcher movement (involving first-, second-, and third-person research/practice) began in England with the work of Stenhouse (1975, 1983) and the Humanities Curriculum Project. Stenhouse, who coined the term "teacher-as-researcher," believed that teaching should be based on research, that the classroom was a natural laboratory for the study of teaching and learning, and that research and curriculum development were the privileged preserve of teachers. Building on the work of Stenhouse, the Ford Teaching Project focused on the self-monitoring role of teachers who examine their practices in collaborative action research study groups (Elliott, 1977, 2006; Elliott & Adelman, 1975). The ideas of Stenhouse, Elliott, Whitehead, and McNiff migrated to the United States, where they stimulated the further development and refinement of the concept of the teacher-as-researcher. In the meantime, the momentum for teacher action research in England continues to accelerate as reflected in the work of Whitehead and McNiff (2006).

As a burgeoning movement in the United States, teacher research has been defined by Cochran-Smith and Lytle (1993) as "systematic intentional inquiry by teachers about their own school and classroom work" (pp. 23–24). It is systematic in that it involves ordered ways of gathering data, documenting experiences, and producing a written record. It is intentional in that the research is planned and deliberate rather than spontaneous. It is inquiry in that the research emanates from or generates questions and "reflects teachers' desires to make sense of their experiences—to adapt a learning stance of openness toward classroom life" (p. 24).

Cochran-Smith and Lytle (1993) offer a working typology of teacher research that groups four types of teacher research into two broad categories: conceptual and empirical research. **Conceptual research** refers to theoretical/philosophical work or the analysis of ideas. The focus of conceptual research is essays that deal with teachers' interpretations of the assumptions and characteristics of classroom and school life and/or the research itself. Empirical research refers to the collection, analysis, and interpretation of data gathered from teachers' own schools and classrooms. Under empirical research are listed three types of research: journals, oral inquiries, and classroom/school studies. **Journals** are teachers' written accounts of classroom life over time, including records of observations, analyses of experiences, and reflections and interpretations of practices. **Oral inquiries** are teachers' oral examinations of classroom/social issues, contexts, texts, and experiences including collaborative analyses and interpretations and explorations between cases and theories. **Classroom/school studies** are teachers' explorations of practice-based issues using data based on observation, interview, and document collection involving individual or collaborative work.

Cochran-Smith and Lytle (1993) place great emphasis on teachers' ways of knowing, teacher knowing through systematic subjectivity, and teacher emic or "insider's perspective that makes visible the ways students and teachers together construct knowledge and curriculum" (p. 43). They distinguish among three conceptions of teacher learning. The first of these is knowledge for practice, in which university researchers generate formal knowledge and theory for teachers to use to improve practice. Within this conception of teacher learning, teachers are viewed primarily as consumers of research. The second conception is knowledge in practice, in which the emphasis is on knowledge in action, knowledge that is embedded in the exemplary practice of experienced teachers. The knowledge in action conception suggests that good teaching can be coached and learned through reflective supervision or through a process of coaching reflective teaching. Learning is viewed as assisted performance. Both of these conceptions of teacher learning are hierarchical, distinguishing between expert and novice teachers as well as formal and practical knowledge.

The third conception of teacher learning is knowledge of practice, which assumes "that the knowledge teachers need to teach well emanates from systematic inquiries about teaching, learners and learning, subject matter and curriculum, and schools and schooling. This knowledge is constructed collectively within local and broader communities" (Cochran-Smith & Lytle, 1999, p. 279). Within this conception of teacher learning, there are no distinctions between formal and practical knowledge. Teachers are viewed as constructors and generators of knowledge and curriculum. Knowledges of practice and teacher research are viewed as mutually interchangeable. Cochran-Smith and Lytle (1999) argue that teacher inquiry is a powerful way of articulating local knowledge and for redefining and creating a new knowledge base for teaching and learning. They also advocate that teachers study "what is taken for granted," challenge "school and classroom structures and deliberate about what it means to know and what is regarded as expert knowledge . . . and attempt to uncover the values and interests served and not served by the arrangements of schooling" (Cochran-Smith & Lytle, 1999, p. 279).

One of the most distinctive and significant contributions Cochran-Smith and Lytle (1999) make to the teacher-as-researcher movement is their construct of **inquiry as stance,** which Cochran-Smith (2002) distinguished from "inquiry as a time-bounded project or activity within a teacher education course or professional development workshop" (p. 15). Inquiry as stance suggests an orientation to the construction of knowledge and its relationship to practice. With this stance, the work of teachers in generating local knowledge through inquiry communities is considered social and political, "making problematic the current arrangements of schooling, the ways knowledge is constructed, evaluated, and used, and teachers' individual and collective roles in bringing about change" (Cochran-Smith, 2002, p. 15). Inquiry as stance positions teachers to link their inquiry to larger questions about the ends of teacher learning in school reform and to larger social, political, and intellectual movements emphasizing that teacher learning for the next century needs to be understood as a long-term collective project with a democratic agenda.

The outcomes emerging from an inquiry stance are transformative (Cochran-Smith, 2002, pp. 12–34). One outcome is that teachers learn to raise questions and try to change routine practices challenging common expectations and reconceptualizing what teaching and learning are all about. A second outcome is that teachers question and challenge the external assumptions, values, and beliefs held by others regarding practice and the internal assumptions, values, and beliefs held by teachers themselves. Finally, an inquiry stance raises teachers' consciousness and develops awareness that decisions regarding all dimensions of teaching and learning need to weigh complex and sometimes conflicting values, information, and viewpoints. The inquiry stance characterizing teacher-as-researcher is more than an attitude and posture regarding inquiry; it is a transformative worldview of knowledge construction, teaching practice, and the nature of learning.

Participatory Action Research

One form of action research that emphasizes a recursive collaborative approach with the goal of taking political and social action is **participatory action research (PAR)**, sometimes referred to as emancipatory action research (Atweh, Kemmis, & Weeks, 1998; Carr & Kemmis, 1986; Kemmis & McTaggart, 1988; McIntyre, 2007). PAR originated in Latin America and in other third world countries and can be considered a prime example of engaging first-, second-, and third-person research (Fals Borda, 2001). PAR is a social participatory process that engages participants in the study of reality in order to change it. It assumes that ideology, epistemology, knowledge, and power are bound up together. It is emancipatory, helping people to "recover, and unshackle themselves from, the constraints of irrational, unproductive, unjust, and unsatisfying social structures which limit their self development and self determination" (Atweh et al., 1998, p. 24). It is also a collective critical process in which participants deliberately contest and reconstitute unproductive, unjust, and alienating ways of interpreting and describing their ways of working and ways of relating to others. Through spirals of critical and self-critical action and reflection, participants learn how they can change the ways they interact in their social world, democratize education and the research process, change power relations in the educational and social world through the production of "people's" knowledge, and empower oppressed groups to change their lives and circumstances.

PAR, translated into community-based action research (Stringer, 2007, p. 11), is enacted through an explicit set of social values:

- It is democratic, enabling the participation of all people.
- It is equitable, acknowledging people's equality of worth.
- It is liberating, providing freedom from oppressive, debilitating conditions.
- It is life enhancing, enabling the expression of people's full human potential.

A fundamental tenet of PAR is that knowledge and the research that produces knowledge are an exercise in politics as much as understanding. To understand research, one must not only explore methodology but also inquire about the ways knowledge is produced and the benefits, resources, advantages, and power that accrue to people who control the processes of knowledge production. The writing on PAR has an evangelical quality—its advocates often are quite critical not only of traditional research models but of any kind of research, including other kinds of action research that are nonparticipatory and that do not have transformative goals for creating a more just and humane society. For example, Kemmis (1988) critiques educational action research as being too individualistic, saying that it has been "captured and domesticated in individualistic classroom research, which has failed to establish links with political forces for democratic educational reform." He then goes on to argue that it is only through exploration of more collective processes that the "genuine possibility of changing education from within" can be achieved.

Such collective processes are found in the participatory action research process practiced in Latin America, which reflects the work of Paulo Freire and embraces collective thinking, dialogue, and action and several other features that distinguish this form of action research:

- The point of departure in the research is a vision of social reality as a totality.
- The community is fully involved and actively participates in the research process.
- Social processes and structures are understood within a historical perspective.
- Theory and practice are integrated.
- The subject-object relationship is transformed into a subject-subject relationship through dialogue.
- Research and action (including education itself) become a single process.
- The synchronic and quantitative nature of traditional research is replaced by a diachronic orientation and an integration of quantitative and qualitative elements.
- The community researchers collaborate to produce critical knowledge aimed at social transformation.
- The results of research are immediately applied to a concrete situation with the goal of radically transforming social reality and improving the lives of people.

Participatory action research "is a process that is biased in favor of the least powerful." It seeks "to bring all the parties together in a way which gives those with less historic, cultural, or economic voice a more prominent place at the table" (Hall, 2001, p. 175). This perspective, reflecting the signifying feature of PAR as a politically liberating process, has been brought to educational inquiry by Carr, Kemmis, and McTaggart, among others. Their argument for a fundamental transformation of education through collaborative emancipatory research embraces the liberating concept of teachers, students, and community constructing knowledge to change themselves, their educational institutions, and their communities.

Schoolwide Action Research

Schoolwide action research (Anderson, Herr, & Nihlen, 2007; Calhoun, 1993, 1994, 2002; Clauset, Lick, & Murphy, 2008) is different from individual teacher research or from collaborative action research, in which a group of teachers conducts research or everyone in the school is involved in the research. It's a way of saying, "Let's study what's happening at our school, decide if we can make it a better place by changing what and how we teach and how we relate to students and the community; study the effects; and then begin again" (Calhoun, 1994, p. 4). Schoolwide action research reflects Schaefer's concept of the school as a center of inquiry. It engages first-, second-, and third-person research/practices.

To facilitate collective inquiry and action of the magnitude involved in this kind of action research, Calhoun (2002) has developed the Schoolwide Action Research Matrix, which includes a place to identify the student learning goal that a faculty selects for its collective focus as well as six domains, or cells, of inquiry and action. The structure of the matrix is designed to help groups study and use on-site and external information about student learning and the learning environment to establish benchmarks and desired levels of performance for students and to identify interventions and actions to study and implement in their classrooms and schools. The sequence of the matrix is designed to help staff explore the research base and move beyond what is currently known or done in their school or setting. However, it is only a guide to domains of inquiry and action, not a rigid set of steps.

Schoolwide action research seeks to improve the school as a problem-solving entity, to improve equity for students, and to involve the entire school community in the process of inquiry, thereby creating a knowledge democracy. It is a process of conducting inquiry about the school to improve teaching and learning and to make the school a self-renewing organization permeated by inquiry. The challenge inherent in schoolwide action research is that it calls for full participation on the part of all members in the school to identify issues for inquiry, to agree on improvement goals, to collect and analyze data, to draw implications and develop plans and recommendations for action, to try out actions and collect data on the schoolwide impact of these improvement efforts, and then repeat the research cycle again, investigating new questions that emanate from the inquiry.

This is a tall order when we think of facilitating the group processes that are involved in dealing with resistance to change and in building schoolwide trust, consensus, collaboration, reflection, commitment, problem solving, and a culture of sustained inquiry. It is one thing for five or six members of a collaborative action research team to work on these issues, which require empathic listening skills, critical dialogue, mutual support, and the freedom to confront and disagree with each other in facilitative ways. These processes are complex and take an enormous amount of time and energy to nurture and develop in a small group, let alone an entire school. Schoolwide action research also requires administrative support at the school and the district level. Schoolwide action research may be the most complex kind of action research to conduct:

> Schoolwide action research may feel messy and uneven, and conflict may arise during the first few cycles—all of which is to be expected when a diverse community is learning to apply a complex process. However, the very complexity generates important side effects: chiefly that all participants have to learn a lot about building colleagueship, about managing the group process, and about aspects of curriculum and instruction that they may not have reflected on had they worked alone. (Calhoun, 1994, p. 12)

As an approach for change, schoolwide action research is strongly affected by the culture of the school. Four cultural markers predict whether action research will be a force for change in a school (Sagor & Curley, 1991):

1. A common focus. In schools where action research took hold, there was clarity about school goals, priorities were protected, and there were high expectations.

2. A collective locus of control (efficacy). In schools that embraced action research, a significant cultural factor was the faculty's collective sense of efficacy. In these schools, faculty felt they had the collective power to change teaching and learning in meaningful ways.

3. Common cultural perceptions. In schools where action research made a difference, faculty members perceived their school culture in strikingly similar ways. In schools struggling with

action research, teachers had widely varying perceptions of school norms.

4. An appreciation of leadership. In schools that persevered with action research, teachers saw that their work was supported by the school's leadership, that the leadership was committed to high expectations, and that there was an appreciation of leadership, whether it came from administrators or teachers.

One form of schoolwide research is found in "whole-faculty study groups" (Clauset et al., 2008; Dana & Yendol-Hoppey, 2008; Lick, 2000; Lick & Murphy, 2006; Murphy & Lick, 2005). In whole-faculty study groups, the entire faculty of a school participates in study groups, with each group responsible for conducting inquiry focusing on a specific aspect of school improvement and change. The driving question for faculty study groups is: What is happening differently in the classroom as a result of what you are doing and learning in study groups? The fundamental goal of the whole-faculty study group process is to facilitate schoolwide change and enhance student learning. "Whole-faculty study groups are teacher centered, inspire reflection, provide authentic learning experiences, and motivate teachers to go beyond traditional boundaries and construct new learnings and meaning" (Lick, 2000, p. 44).

Schoolwide action research as a strategy to reform schools has been promoted through the Coalition for Essential Schools, League of Professional Schools in Georgia, the Northeast and Islands Regional Educational Laboratory at Brown University, and the Center for Leadership in School Reform in Kentucky. It is being used by the Broward County Schools of South Florida as a framework for long-term whole school renewal. I believe the greatest promise for schoolwide action research is found in the concept of the professional development school (PDS). A PDS is a long-term partnership between a university, a local school district, and the community dedicated to improving education for children through the improvement of preservice and in-service teacher education, instructional and curriculum development, educational change, and inquiry. University faculty collaborate with classroom teachers, parents, and school administrators, working on site in a local school or schools to turn the school into a site for teacher education and research. Within the context of the PDS, schoolwide research has been employed to implement a new mathematics curriculum and instructional approach in an elementary school, to restructure a middle school, to integrate instructional technology throughout the entire curriculum of a high school, and to integrate student action research in every content area in a middle school. The school change agenda of PDSs seems to be a congenial home for the implementation of schoolwide action research and, subsequently, the creation of knowledge democracies.

Self-Study Research

There is a growing interest in the **self-study** of teacher education practice in the United States, the United Kingdom, Canada, and Australia (Cole & Knowles, 1996a, 1996b; Hamilton, 1998; Knowles & Cole, 1996; Loughran, Hamilton, LaBoskey, & Russell, 2004; Loughran & Russell, 2002; Mitchell, O'Reilly-Scanlon, & Weber, 2006; Russell & Korthagen, 1995; Zeichner, 2007). Self-study is a form of action research or teacher research that focuses inwardly on teacher education and, in some instances, professional development (Dantonio, 2001) in a "no holds barred" way, leaving no area of teacher education sacrosanct from inquiry. The growth of self-study is represented in the establishment of the Self Study of Teacher Education Practices, a special interest group (SIG) of the American Educational Research Association, which was established in 1994 and grew rapidly into one of the largest SIGs in AERA.

Self-study in teacher education has two broad purposes: facilitating personal-professional development of teacher educators, in which studies focus primarily on the improvement of an individual's own teaching; and developing deeper understanding of teacher education practices, processes, programs, and contexts, in which studies focus on broader programmatic and institutional issues. Although these purposes are not necessarily mutually exclusive, they are concerned with refining, reforming, and rearticulating teacher education (Cole & Knowles, 1996b, p. 1). In reforming the work of educating teachers, self-study examines teacher education practice in a critical and probing way, primarily through reflective, qualitative, personal, subjective, and practically oriented inquiry, which is typically communicated in narrative form. Like other forms of action research, self-study can be conducted individually, for example via an autobiographical self-study of one's evolution as a teacher educator (Samaras, 2002), or collaboratively, using a wide range of research methodologies (Loughran & Russell, 2002).

Just as teachers conduct inquiry about teaching and learning practices and issues, in self-study, teacher-educators conduct research about their own practices. They examine their own teaching; program issues; contradictions between espoused values and program practices; the tensions, dilemmas, and concerns embedded in practice; issues of social justice, race, and gender; questions of control and power; the social and political contexts of practice; the cultural modalities of practice; the "telling and showing" model of teaching; unexamined program assumptions; and new ways of knowing.

In examining the scholarship in teacher education, Zeichner (1996) asserts that self-study is "probably the most significant development ever in the field of teacher education research" (p. 8). Although self-study appears to be a burgeoning movement in teacher education, it struggles to move from a marginalized activity to a respected and legitimate form of inquiry. Critics of self-study charge that it is narcissistic, solipsistic, self-indulgent, low-quality inquiry. There is considerable concern about the validity and trustworthiness of self-study research. Feldman (2003, pp. 27–28), responding to these critiques, argues that it is a moral obligation for self-study researchers to attend to the question of validity and suggests four ways to increase the validity of self-study:

1. Self-study research needs to clearly and carefully describe in detail how data are collected and make explicit what counts as data in the research.

2. Self-study research needs to clearly and carefully describe in detail how representation was constructed from the data. For example, if readers had some knowledge or insight into the way the researcher transformed data into artistic representation, it would increase the validity of the representation.

3. Self-study research needs to "extend triangulations beyond multiple ways to represent the same case study. Because one data set can lead to a variety of representations, it is important to show why one has been chosen over the others" (Feldman, 2003, p. 28).

4. Self-study research needs to "provide evidence of the value of the changes in our ways of being teacher educators" (Feldman, 2003, p. 28). There should be some evidence of the values of any changes in one's ways of being a teacher-educator. Such evidence can make a convincing case for the validity of the self-study.

Dinkelman (2003) offers a five-part theoretical rationale for promoting the use of self-study in teacher education programs, arguing that self-study has the potential to animate the idea of teaching as reflection, generate knowledge about promoting reflective practice, model an inquiry-based approach to pedagogy, provide opportunities for beginning teachers to reflect on learning to teach, and generate rich understanding that can be used to facilitate program change. (p. 16)

Self-study is viewed by its practitioners as a means to liberate teacher education from the conservative and confining epistemology and traditions of higher education. The ultimate goal of self-study is reform—the systemic and substantive transformation of teacher education through sustained inquiry. Unfortunately, most universities have not "elevated the status of action research in their institutions enough for it to count as a powerful tool for transforming their own teacher education programs" (Catelli, Padovano, & Costello, 2000, p. 237).

❖ SUMMARY

In this chapter, the history, origins, and development of action research are traced, and different approaches to action research are described. Varieties of action research have arisen as alternatives to traditional positivistic scientific research approaches that cannot reasonably be adapted to the turbulent changing school contexts in which the research is applied. The traditional positivistic scientific approach to research requires the temporary suspension of attention to surrounding conditions, changing contexts, and evolving circumstances. An action research approach to the study of change in teaching and learning would have to reflect in its criteria the applied dynamic and recursive nature of teaching and the ongoing need for teachers to act, a need that cannot be deferred until research results have achieved a preestablished level of certainty. The approach would recognize, for example, that regardless of the state of the research dealing with how young children learn to read, teachers would go on teaching reading and literacy.

The importance of shifting contextual circumstances and of circumstances only secondarily related to the focus of the study would need to be given attention at the very least by not assuming that all else would remain constant while the teachers and the school are under study. In addition, any action researcher would need to acknowledge the continuous cultural shifts in human behavior that are likely to render any conclusions obsolete within a relatively short period of time. What are the criteria, then, that would distinguish action research as a paradigm for studying educational action and change in classrooms and schools? This is the question I address in Chapter 3.

3

A Paradigm of Teacher Action Research

C hapter 3 makes the argument that action research is more than a method—it is a **paradigm**. Four major research paradigms are described: the empirical-positivistic-quantitative paradigm; the constructivist-interpretive-qualitative paradigm; the critical theory-postmodern-praxis paradigm; and the eclectic-mixed methods-pragmatic paradigm. Evolving from these paradigms, the action research paradigm is distinguished by 12 defining features: reflexive critique and intersubjectivity, axiology, context, ongoing tentativeness, recursion, dialectical critique, collaboration, risk, plurality, connotation, moral/political ethos and purpose, and embrace of emotion. The integration of these characteristics in the teacher action research paradigm and the implications of these features for practice are discussed.

❖ WHAT IS A PARADIGM?

The term paradigm became popular as a result of the work of Thomas Kuhn (1962), represented in his book *The Structure of Scientific Revolutions*. He is commonly acknowledged as the progenitor of the concept of paradigm as it applies to the history and philosophy of science. Paradigm comes from the Greek, *paradeigma*, meaning a pattern, model, or plan. More than 40 years after the publication of Kuhn's book, the use of the concept and the term paradigm is widespread in the social sciences and education. According to Kuhn (1962),

> a paradigm is what the members of a scientific community share and conversely a scientific community consists of members who share a paradigm—a tacit commitment by a community of scholars to a "taken for granted" conceptual framework which offers a way of seeing, framing, and making sense of the world. Scientific theories are constructed around basic paradigms. (p. 10)

Paradigms provide an overarching conceptual view as well as a social and cultural framework for doing research, shape how we understand ourselves, determine what counts as valuable and legitimate scientific knowledge, and define the experiences that can legitimately lead to knowledge and the kinds of knowledge that are produced. "A paradigm is like a new pair of glasses; it affects the way you see everything in life" (Covey, 1989, p. 125).

Guba and Lincoln (as cited in Heron & Reason, 1997) argue that

> paradigms may be viewed as sets of basic beliefs about the nature of reality and how it may be known; and these beliefs are thrown into relief by three fundamental and interrelated questions: the ontological question, "What is the form and nature of reality and, therefore, what is there that can be known about it?"; the epistemological question, "What is the relationship between the knower or would-be knower and what can be known?"; and the methodological question, "How can the inquirer find out whatever he or she believes can be known about?" (p. 277)

Heron and Reason (1997) believe that a fourth question is the axiological question:

> which we think is an essential defining characteristic of an inquiry paradigm along with ontology, epistemology, and methodology. The axiological question asks what is intrinsically valuable in human life, in particular what sort of knowledge, if any, is intrinsically valuable. (p. 277)

As we consider the evolving action research paradigm that I present in this chapter, these four fundamental questions are pivotal issues embedded in the paradigm.

❖ FOUR RESEARCH PARADIGMS

Four major paradigms have significantly influenced educational research. The **empirical-positivist-quantitative paradigm** is the most established of the paradigms, reflecting a belief in a mechanistic, determinist reality whereby parts can be separated from wholes, and cause and effect relationships among parts can be determined. Physical and social reality is independent of those who observe it. Observations of this reality, if unbiased, constitute scientific knowledge. The goals of inquiry are the definition, prediction, control, and explanation of physical phenomena as revealed through experience (induction) and experiments (deduction). There is a reliance on measuring variables and analyzing relationships among them with descriptive and inferential statistics. Adherents of this paradigm believe that if something exists, it can be measured. They seek to explain changes in aspects of reality through controlled experimentation. Detachment from the object under study is preferred to maintain objectivity. Mathematical analysis and statistical significance are held in the highest regard. Some consider this paradigm to be the antithesis of principles of action research (Susman & Evered, 1978; Winter, 1989).

The **constructivist-interpretivist-qualitative paradigm** (Denzin, 1984, 1989; Denzin & Lincoln, 1994; Geertz, 1973, 1983; Lincoln & Guba, 1985; Schwandt, 1994; van Manen, 1997, 2002) reflects the belief that humans individually and collectively construct reality. Social reality is constructed by the individuals who participate in it. Aspects of the social environment do not have an existence apart from the meanings that individuals construct for them. Analysis of curriculum and instructional programs attempts to expose the values underlying these phenomena. There is emphasis on the need to put analyses in context, presenting the interpretations of many, sometimes competing groups interested in the outcomes of education.

Human beings are seen as the primary research instruments, rejecting the mathematical modeling of phenomena on which the quantitative paradigm depends so heavily. For advocates of this paradigm, "Truth is a matter of consensus among informed and sophisticated constructors, not correspondence with an objective reality" (Lincoln & Guba, 1985, p. 44). The focus is understanding the nature of this constructed reality from multiple perspectives, emphasizing the roles of culture, gender, context, and other factors in the construction of reality. Immersion in the context of a research study is highly preferred over the detachment of the classical laboratory scientist. Within this paradigm, many different anthropological and sociological methodologies, especially human observation, have been adopted.

The **critical theory-postmodern-praxis paradigm** (Carr & Kemmis, 1986; Freire, 1970, 1973; Giroux, 1989, 1997; hooks, 1994; Lather, 1991; McLaren, 1997, 1998; McLaren & Lankshear, 1994; Shor, 1992) relates to a concern with questions of power, control, and epistemology as social constructions that have benefits for some and not for others. The real world—while still there—cannot be seen by anyone because of the biases and values that they possess. The values system that is used in scientific inquiry reflects the political power of some groups over others; inquiry is a political act.

Proponents of this paradigm view themselves as forces of emancipation engaged in conflict with powers of oppression. The goal of inquiry is to empower those who are not in political power to see their oppression so that they can transform the world. Praxis is the art of acting on the conditions one faces in order to change them. Proponents seek to deconstruct the texts inherent in educational products, programs, and processes and reveal the contradictions and the exclusion of minority interests. Deconstruction is the process of revealing hidden meanings of texts. A dialogical approach to methodology is emphasized to eliminate false consciousness and facilitate transformation. There is a desire to abandon the search for truth as sought by empiricists or understanding as desired by interpretivists in favor of seeking what I call "little truths which are situationally appropriate." Skepticism and questioning are basic tenets of this paradigm.

The **eclectic-mixed methods-pragmatic paradigm** (Brewer & Hunter, 2005; Caracelli & Greene, 1997; Chatterji, 2004; Creswell, 2003; Creswell & Plano-Clark, 2007; Johnson & Onwuegbuzie, 2004; Onwuegbuzie, 2002; Plano-Clark & Creswell, 2007; Reeves, 1996; Sechrest & Sidana, 1995; Tashakkori & Teddlie, 2003; Teddlie & Tashakkori, 2008) is the most recent paradigm to emerge in the postmodernist era. The name refers to its openness in borrowing the methods of the other three paradigms to collect information and to solve complex problems. Within this paradigm, "mixed methods research is formally defined as the class of research where the researcher mixes or combines quantitative and qualitative research techniques, methods, approaches, concepts, or language into a single study" (Johnson & Onwuegbuzie, 2004, p. 17). In an age of methodological pluralism, the mixed methods approach is viewed as softening the competition between methodological paradigms. The mixed methods paradigm is deemed to be the paradigm of epistemological and methodological pragmatism most capable of handling the complexity of postmodern society. As a paradigm, the mixed methods approach to research supports (Greene, Caracelli, & Graham, 1989):

- *Triangulation* of the study by its use of more than one research methodology
- *Complementarity,* allowing the researcher to seek a fuller understanding of the research problem by approaching it from a variety of viewpoints
- *Development* of the study, which is generated because one method in the study develops and informs the other method
- *Initiation* in discovering paradox, contradiction, and the recasting of questions or results from one method to questions and results from another method
- *Expansion* because it increases the scope of the research study to extend its breadth and range

Multiple perspectives are necessary to "triangulate" or "bracket" information and conclusions regarding complex phenomena. "The pragmatic aspect of this paradigm reflects the practical orientation that, although ultimate prediction and control may never be achieved in education through any one approach, things can get better" (Reeves, 1996, p. 4). The mixed methods "logic of inquiry includes the use of induction (or discovery of patterns), deduction (testing of theories and hypotheses), and abduction (uncovering and relying on the best of a set of explanations for understanding one's results)" (Johnson & Onwuegbuzie, 2004, p. 17).

Although critics argue that a combination of research methods can result in a "garbage can approach" (Shulman, 1986), other observers (Howe, 1988) assert that such an epistemological thesis does not exist and that epistemological paradigms need not dictate the exclusive use of quantitative or qualitative methods.

> Research is a creative act . . . don't reconfigure your thinking about it to specific approaches. Researchers creatively combine the elements of methods in any way that makes sense for the study they want to do. . . . The research question to be answered really determines the method. (Krathwohl, 1998, p. 27)

Proponents of the mixed methods paradigm rarely concern themselves with ultimate conceptions of reality, preferring to deal with the practical problems that confront them as educators. The bottom line is the results yielded to solve problems.

> They view modes of inquiry as tools to better understanding and more effective problem solving, and do not value one tool over another any more than a carpenter would value a hammer over a saw. A tool is only meaningful within the context in which it is to be used. . . . They also recognize the weaknesses of their tools, and struggle against the odds that either science or creativity will affect problem solving more than politics, ignorance, intuition, habit, and prejudice. (Reeves, 1996, p. 4)

Where is teacher action research located among these paradigms? As I have indicated at the beginning of this chapter, action research is not a method but rather a paradigm that embraces a variety of research methodologies including case studies, descriptive studies, survey studies, interview studies, observational studies, phenomenological studies, quantitative studies including quasi-experimental designs, and historical research. Indeed, almost every methodology has been employed at one time or another in the conduct of action research.

Some of the leading writers in the educational action research or teacher-as-researcher movement would identify their work as falling under the critical theory-praxis paradigm, whereas others would see themselves aligned with the constructivist-interpretivist paradigm and still others with the eclectic-mixed methods-practical paradigm. For Heikkinen, Kakkori, and Huttunen (2001, p. 22), this is a productive situation. They argue that the strength of action research is that it is multiparadigmatic, enabling a variety of perspectives to be maintained preventing "any given hegemonic paradigm from forming the only criterion of truth."

❖ DISTINGUISHING CHARACTERISTICS OF AN ACTION RESEARCH PARADIGM

Does this mean, then, that action research is located in a particular paradigm depending on the unique circumstances and contexts of inquiry, or is action research a new paradigm itself? To put it another way, is there a unique action research paradigm, or is action research a miniversion of traditional research, writ small enough for practitioners? If action research is a unique paradigm, what makes it different from other paradigms? If we view action research as an open, expansive, and evolving paradigm and not a final product, what can we say about the present characteristics of action research, which collectively distinguish it from other forms of research? In response to this question, the work and ideas of Atweh et al. (1998); Biel, Eek, Garling, and Gustafson (2008); Carr and Kemmis (1986); Collier (1945); Corey (1953); Elliott (1991); Frost et al. (2000); Gary (2007); Guba (1990); Heron and Reason (1997); Kemmis and McTaggart (1988); Kemmis and Wilkinson (1998); Law (2004); Lewin (1946); Longstreet (1982, 1985); McTaggart (1991); Oja and Smulyan (1989); Reason (2001, 2003); Sherman and Torbert (2000); Stringer (2007); and Winter (1989, 1996); among others, suggest the following as distinctive salient features that characterize and distinguish action research as an evolving and unique paradigm:

Reflexive Critique and Intersubjectivity

What is reflexivity? What does it mean to be reflexive?

There are two types of reflexivity: personal reflexivity and epistemological reflexivity. "Personal reflexivity" involves reflecting upon the ways in which our own values, experiences, interests, beliefs, political commitments, wider aims in life and social identities have shaped the research. It also involves thinking about how the research may have affected and possibly changed us, as people and as researchers. "Epistemological reflexivity" requires us to engage with questions such as: How has the research question defined and limited what can be "found?" How has the design of the study and the method of analysis "constructed" the data and the findings? How could the research question have been investigated differently? To what extent would this have given rise to a different understanding of the phenomenon under investigation? Thus, epistemological reflexivity encourages us to reflect upon the assumptions (about the world, about knowledge) that we have made in the course of the research, and it helps us to think about the implications of such assumptions for the research and its findings. (Willig, 2001, p. 10)

To be reflexive is to be self-aware. An account of a situation, such as notes, transcripts, or official documents, will make implicit claims to be authoritative, that is, it implies that it is factual and true. Truth in a social setting, however, is relative to the teller. As data are being interpreted, they are filtering through the existing knowledge, beliefs, values, and experiences of the researchers. The principle of reflexive critique (Winter, 1987, 1996) ensures that people reflect on issues and processes and make explicit the interpretations, biases, assumptions, and concerns on which judgments are based. In this way, practical and subjective accounts can give rise to theoretical considerations. In action research, there is a move away from the "objective" position on inquiry; instead, it tries to move researchers to an intersubjective perspective that includes their social location, personal experiences, and self-awareness. In action research, teacher-researchers are continually being transformed through writing reflective journals, processing data, and participating in continuing discussions regarding changing cycles of research questions and actions; thereby, they become more aware of themselves and the processes they are using. In achieving reflexivity, action researchers acknowledge that their understanding of their educational world cannot be developed apart from their own knowledge of themselves and their location in the educational world.

Longstreet (1982, p. 149) notes that avoiding the subjective involvement of the researcher in whatever is being researched has tended to exclude, in most studies on teaching and learning, the most direct and relevant source of observation: the classroom teacher. Teachers have the most in-depth information about their changing human situations and contexts. However, the subjective involvement of teachers in their classrooms is undeniable, and following the scientific paradigm, subjectivity is usually avoided in favor of detachment. Such research might rely on guest observers sitting in the back of the classroom or the administration of a survey by an outside researcher. This strategy loses a major and direct source of data, the classroom teacher, and the presence of an outside observer or even the use of a survey instrument tends to influence the phenomenon under study.

"It is not that objectively gathered empirical evidence is undesirable, but rather that too much evidence vital to the understanding of the complexities of change is being lost or ignored for the sake of achieving this scientific criterion of research" (Longstreet, 1982, p. 149). In the context of research on educational change, the question is how to deal with data that can be obtained only from subjectively involved teachers teaching in a context of frequently changing and emotionally charged situations. Action research incorporates the teacher-researcher's subjective involvement in collecting and sorting the data while still acknowledging that such data contribute to a greater understanding of teachers, classrooms, and schools and how they change. Longstreet (1982) argues:

Dealing with subjectivity means finding ways of achieving inter-subjectively derived evidence that would serve as the basis for tentative generalizations. On the surface, this would not appear to be too different from the requirements of the scientific paradigm and may be only one of degree. Unlike objectivity, intersubjectivity is achieved whenever two individuals share a similar (not the same, but similar) experience. There is no need for widespread agreement and/or reproducibility of experience necessary to the scientific method. As the number of individuals and the diversity of perspectives brought to data collection increase, intersubjectivity increases if agreement about observations is achieved, and the distinction between intersubjectivity and objectivity diminishes. It is not eliminated. (p. 150)

Intersubjectivity, based on a continuing analysis of subjective inputs, allows for the subjective involvement of the teacher-researcher in whatever is being researched. It allows for several teachers to discuss what they have experienced subjectively and to determine what in their experience is shared in a similar way.

If intersubjective agreement about tentative generalizations is to be achieved, there needs to be some established format for recording observations, which would insure that the observations made by one action researcher could be compared and collected with those of other action researchers. Intersubjectivity implies the utilization of some common, rationally established categories for filing and storing data. Recursion adds an additional requirement: that categories of data be sufficiently general so that the delineation and subsequent revision of problems may occur without requiring continual modification of the categories. (Longstreet, 1982, p. 150)

Axiology

Another defining characteristic of action research is axiology, which deals with the nature of value and captures the value question of what is intrinsically worthwhile? Axiology is derived from two Greek roots, *axios* (worth or value) and *logos* (logic or theory); it means the theory of value. Heron and Reason (1997) argue that axiology addresses the issue of "values of being, about what human states are to be valued simply because of what they are" (p. 287). The axiological question is addressed by the action research paradigm in terms of human flourishing—"a process of social participation in which there is a mutually enabling balance, within and between people, of autonomy, co-operation, and hierarchy . . . seen as a means to an end which enables people to be involved in the making of decisions, in every social context, which affect their flourishing in any way" (Heron, 1996, p. 11). Inherent in action research is the goal of producing practical knowledge that will enhance the well-being of people economically, politically, psychologically, educationally, and spiritually and thereby contribute to the flourishing of people and communities (Reason & Bradbury, 2001). Action research values emancipatory learning, which enables people to come together to achieve more autonomy, independence, and control over their own lives; to significantly advance greater equality and social justice; and to sustain progressive social change (Thompson, 2000). Human flourishing and emancipatory learning are reciprocally related processes that characterize the values of action research.

Context

Action research is contextually bound (Mishler, 1979). It focuses on real-life issues and problems and on actions to address problems. Traditional research approaches have ignored the pivotal role of context in human experience. The action research process reflects the principle that human action and experience are context dependent and can be understood only within their contexts. Rather than strip away context, action research recognizes that context deepens our understanding of human actions, experience, and behaviors and enriches the process of inquiry.

Ongoing Tentativeness

In action research, continuous cultural change in the school as well as the unsynchronized intentionality of individual teachers is reflected in the elimination of results or conclusions typically presented as the culmination of scientific study. The conclusions reached are never more than tentative generalizations subject to continuous revision. Tentative generalizations are based on the accumulation of observations and reflection, offering a basis for hypothesizing about the dynamics of individual, classroom, or school change. Action research is ongoing in conception rather than periodic and composed of discrete entities. Instead of verification or replication, ongoing revision is the standard followed.

In addition, ongoing tentativeness is applied not only to the generalizations emanating from the gathering of data and evidence but also to the statement of the problem. In the study of individual and school contextual variables, the statement of the problem is in constant flux. Rather than clearly delineated, stable parameters, problems shift in their nature and meaning as the context and environments shift. Ongoing revision of the parameters of the research questions as well as the outcomes is one of the defining characteristics of action research (Longstreet, 1982, p. 147).

Recursion

Action research is a recursive process. The data, the generalizations, and even the research questions are reviewed, reconsidered, and revised along with other new and emerging data to develop tentative findings and conclusions. Unlike positivistic research, in which the questions are stated and fixed at the start and do not change, in action research, the questions change and shift from the very beginning in a cyclical process of data discussion and analysis. Recursion as a fundamental action research process assumes that there are no fixed conclusions but rather continuing, infinite revision. Action research constantly draws on its own results for generating new results and direction. Tentative generalizations lead to inquiries and questions about classroom and teaching changes, which in turn lead to new data; these are accumulated with the existing data so that tentative generalizations may be revised, which leads to the revision of the problem and questions, which leads to new data, and a continuing process of revision (Longstreet, 1982, p. 148).

Recursion is fundamental in the process of ongoing tentativeness inherent in action research studies. Recursion is captured by the concept of the action research spiral, one of the legacies left to us by Kurt Lewin. The action research spiral in Figure 3.1 is Hingley's (2008) modification of the action research cycle depicted by Carr and Kemmis (1986, p. 186). Theirs is a cycle of action and reflection, broken into phases of planning, acting, observing, and reflecting. The cycle can begin at any stage, and it does not stop after one cycle is completed but begins another cycle and becomes more of a spiral.

Most significant, through the recursive process, theory and practice are continually transformed (Winter, 1987, 1996). For action researchers, theory informs practice, and practice refines theory, in a continuous transformation. In any setting, people's actions are based on implicitly held assumptions, theories, and hypotheses; with every observed result, theoretical knowledge is enhanced. The two are intertwined aspects of a single change process. It is up to the researchers to make explicit the theoretical justifications for the actions and to question the bases of those justifications. The ensuing practical applications are subjected to further analysis, in a recursive transformative cycle that continuously alternates

Figure 3.1   The Action Research Recursive Spiral

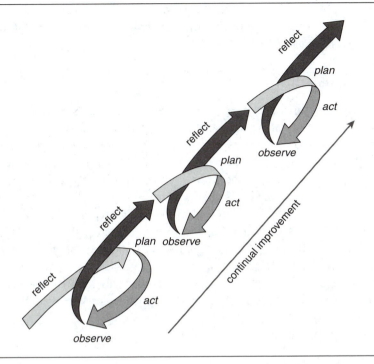

between theory and practice. This transformative cycle between theory and practice is captured by teacher-researcher Avery (1990), who writes:

> Now theory informs my practice in the classroom and classroom practice informs my theory making. I continue to research, rethink, and revise. I develop patterns of learning for myself that influence my teaching. I know there will be no pat answers, no universal strategies or techniques. I know that many factors influence the implementation and outcome of specific teaching strategies. I have learned to be a learner. (p. 44)

Dialectical Critique

Closely related to the idea of recursion is dialectical critique, which is a way of understanding the relationship between various aspects of our own work contexts. Reality, particularly social reality, is consensually validated, which is to say it is shared through language. Phenomena are conceptualized in dialogue; therefore, a dialectical critique is required to understand the set of relationships between the phenomenon and its context and between elements constituting the phenomenon. The key elements are those constituent elements that are unstable or in opposition to one another. These are the ones most likely to create changes (Winter, 1987, 1996).

Collaboration

Participants in action research projects are coresearchers. The principle of collaborative research assumes that each person's ideas are equally significant as potential resources for creating interpretive categories of analysis, negotiated among participants. It strives to avoid the skewing of credibility stemming from the prior status of an idea holder. It especially makes possible the insights gleaned from noting the contradictions between many viewpoints and within a single viewpoint. Intersubjective dialogue becomes critical in opening and refining different ways of knowing. Collaboration has always been a concept basic to the educational action research process as demonstrated in the work of Corey (1953) and Schaefer (1967). It is indispensable in identifying research problems and potential solutions to those problems (Winter, 1987, 1996).

Risk

The change process potentially threatens all previously established ways of doing things, thus creating psychic fears among practitioners. In action research, risking disturbance means developing an understanding of our own taken-for-granted processes and assumptions and being willing to subject them to critique. One of the more prominent fears comes from the risk to ego stemming from open discussion of one's interpretations, ideas, and judgments. Initiators of action research use this principle to allay others' fears and invite participation by pointing out that they, too, will be subject to the same process and that whatever the outcome, learning will take place (Winter, 1987, 1996).

Plurality

The nature of the research embodies a multiplicity of views, commentaries, and critiques, leading to multiple possible actions and interpretations. This plural structure of inquiry requires a plural text for reporting. This means that many accounts are made explicit, with commentaries on their contradictions, and a range of options for action are presented. A report, therefore, acts as a support for ongoing discussion among collaborators, rather than a final conclusion of fact (Winter, 1987, 1996).

Connotation

Longstreet suggests that in studying research questions dealing with topics such as teacher, student, classroom, and school change, it would be important to avoid assigning a denotative definition to the concept of change, which is a word that in ordinary usage shifts its nuances and even its meaning in ways that are often unclear. The development of connotations in an action research study means that vaguely used key terms such as change are the object of analysis to determine the range of connotations or changing meanings attributable to them and the relationship of varying contexts to the differing interpretations. The need is to understand the actual usage of the concept of change, not to establish a standard to which the usage must conform. Mapping the extensions and variations of the meanings of change and how such meanings impact teachers is a critical dimension of the action research process. Parallel to the effort to achieve greater connotational understanding in the ordinary daily usage of key terms regarding change is the de-emphasis on the precise delimitation of the research questions. A connotational and organismic approach to data collection is more appropriate in action research dealing with the phenomena of classroom and school change (Longstreet, 1982, p. 151).

Moral/Political Ethos and Purpose

I would add the element of moral/political ethos and purpose as a distinguishing characteristic of action research. Embedded in action research is a moral/political ethos that evokes congruence between inquiry and service to improve the human condition. The origins, history, and implementation of action research throughout the world reflect a deep and abiding concern for social justice and for bringing about educational, social, and political change. The language of action research (e.g., emancipation, participation, collaboration, action, change, dialogue) reflects moral and political values. "The practice of action research is not a value free process; it raises questions of values, morals, ethics, and is intended to contribute to the flourishing of human persons, communities, and the eco-systems of which we are a part" (Reason, 2006, p. 201). In action research, "reality" is investigated in order to transform it. Actions are taken to advance human learning and human existence. Action is informed by research, and research is informed by action—all for the purpose of introducing and studying a change to improve a given situation. Knowledge in combination with action becomes transformational. Researching and implementing curriculum, pedagogical, and organizational changes in the classroom and/or school, when motivated by a desire to improve student learning and student personal development, are moral and political actions that distinguish action research as a paradigm.

Embrace of Emotion

In action research, emotions are recognized, acknowledged, and accepted as integral to the research process. Emotions, feelings, and actions count as much as cognition and rationality. There is no conscious dichotomy between emotions and thinking. Emotions and thinking are inextricably interconnected in the action research process (McLaughlin, 2003). Dadds (cited in McLaughlin, 2003, p. 67) contends that "passionate and committed teacher research is driven by affective as well as cognitive epistemologies" and that emotion acts as a motivational force as well as a spur to action.

One of the strongest cases for the role of emotion in the reasoning process is made by Antonio Damasio (1994) in his book *Descartes' Error.* Damasio stakes his position early in the book when he writes in the introduction:

> I began writing this book to propose that reason may not be as pure as most of us think it is or wish it were, that emotion and feelings may not be intruders in the bastion of reasoning at all; they may be enmeshed in its networks, for worse and for better. (p. 1)

He argues that emotion and reason are not completely separate, and in fact, they are quite dependent on one another in the normally functioning human being. Through historical examples as well as his own cases, Damasio provides convincing evidence that impairments to portions of the brain responsible for emotion also impair the ability to use reason or behave rationally. For Damasio, emotions are integral to thinking and serve as evaluative filtering.

de Sousa (2003, pp. 17–18), in the *Stanford Encyclopedia of Philosophy,* claims that emotions are conscious phenomena that involve more pervasive bodily manifestations than other conscious states; vary along a number of dimensions in terms of intensity, type, and range; are indispensable in determining the quality of life; contribute crucially to defining our ends and priorities; play a significant role in the regulation of social life; protect us from an excessively slavish devotion to narrow conceptions of rationality; and have a central place in moral education and the moral life. In her study of information-seeking behavior, Kuhlthau (1993) found that as people moved through various stages of searching for information, investigating a topic, finding a focus, completing collection of data, and making a presentation, they initially experienced uncertainty, apprehension, and then optimism, followed by feelings of confusion, frustration, and doubt, in turn, followed by feelings of confidence and a sense of direction, concluding with feelings of satisfaction or accomplishment.

Making judgments, problem solving, drawing conclusions, testing out ideas, taking risks, taking action, working in collaboration with others, recognizing and accepting the emotional character of teaching, searching for meaning in one's work and inquiry, participating in dialectical discussion, listening with empathy, and developing relational and systemic trust are inter- and intrapersonal processes deeply rooted in emotions about the self, about others, and about the world. In action research, we need

> to take absolutely seriously the role of emotions in research. To ignore them and to attend only to reason will distort the balance necessary to engage in the loss of control, risk taking, and confusion that is the research process. Emotional blindness will not enhance the research process; it will only drive underground the examination of assumptions and processes in individuals and groups that hinder fruitful exploration. (McLaughlin, 2003, p. 76)

❖ CHALLENGES FOR ACTION RESEARCH

1. Action research has great appeal as a paradigm for classroom-based research. The democratic language of action research, with its emphasis on empowerment, emancipation, and teacher leadership, is engaging, attractive, and seductive, and yet, we have to be careful that the same language and appeal do not become another means of subtle external control. In their critique of action research, Clandinin and Connelly (1992) argue that action research could become another externally imposed curriculum reform reflecting a deficit view of teachers and characterized by predetermined objectives and the assumption that teachers must change in pre-established ways to address deficits. They are concerned that in externally initiated action research projects, the intentions of external agencies such as foundations, universities, and government agencies are to direct how teachers are "required to develop

knowledge, undertake research, change, grow, reflect, revolutionize their practice, become emancipated, emancipate their students, engage in group collaboration, assume power, and become politically active" (p. 377). We need to recognize the tensions and the problems that can come with well-meaning but subliminal and undermining actions of control that often accompany externally funded action research efforts. It is only through authentic collaboration and critical dialogue among participants in an action research study that the integrity of the action research process can be maintained.

2. As a process for change, action research is vulnerable in another way. Gibson (1985) states the case well:

> To the educational equivalent of the poor and powerless, the action research movement has evidently brought balm, comfort, some easing of local ills, and a sustaining faith in its own shared vision. But it possesses the same Achilles heel as the Salvation Army: its powerlessness, even irrelevance in the face of structural inequality and injustice. (p. 59)

Through the process of authentic collaborative action research, these two cautionary issues can be addressed. Educational, personal, social, and political change can come only through a process of collective inquiry and action in which power resides with participants engaging in critical reflection and dialogue to conceptualize and solve their own problems.

❖ SUMMARY

In summary, then, action research is an evolving paradigm reflecting epistemological, ontological, and axiological assumptions about knowledge creation, human experience, and human values. It is a "living theory" (Whitehead, 1989; Whitehead & McNiff, 2006) of practice, reflection, inquiry, action, change, and ongoing revision—practice informs theory, theory informs practice. As an evolving paradigm, action research is open to continuous scrutiny, dialogue, and debate about its assumptions, processes, and goals. As situations, institutions, organizations, societies, and the world change, so do paradigms. Although the action research paradigm is open to continuous revision, it provides a fundamental framework for research that can make a significant difference in the enhancement and advancement of "human flourishing."

In closing this chapter, I note that the collaborative nature of the action research paradigm empowers participants to take charge of their classrooms, to improve teaching, and to advance student learning. What is meant by collaboration? Why is collaboration important in the action research process? What are the distinguishing characteristics of collaborative action research? How is a collaborative research culture created and nurtured in schools? What is the intellectual and political power in collaboration? These and other questions are addressed in subsequent chapters.

4

The Validity of Action Research

G iven the widespread practice of different forms of action research in a variety of venues throughout the world, it is inevitable that the question of the **validity** of action research would emerge. How real, how authentic, how truthful is action research? What level of confidence can be placed in the research? What criteria ought to determine the validity—the truthfulness and accuracy, the appropriateness, the logic and the technical adequacy of the action research process or any action research study? In this chapter, I address these questions and propose a reconceptualization of the term; I also describe different approaches to determining the validity of action research studies.

❖ WHAT IS VALIDITY?

The validity of traditional positivistic research methodologies has been guided by the gold standards of internal and external validity, which were created by Campbell and Stanley (1963). The concepts of internal and external validity have been widely used to determine the value and trustworthiness of experimental and quasi-experimental research studies. According to Campbell and Stanley, **internal validity** is the basic minimum requirement without which any experiment is uninterpretable: Did the experimental treatments, in fact, make a difference in the specific circumstances of the study? **External validity** asks the question of generalizability: To what degree can the effects observed under experimental conditions be generalized to other populations and contexts? To address these questions, positivistic educational research has confined its view of validity to sophisticated measurement and statistical techniques for prediction and generalizability. Judgments on the trustworthiness of educational research studies were dominated by these measurement concepts until the widespread emergence of alternative research approaches, which have yielded different conceptions of validity.

For instance, an interesting and provocative perspective on the issue of validity has been offered by Winter (1989), who argues that action research needs to have some sound basis for validity. If action research cannot "claim improved validity for its outcomes, why should anyone do action research, and why should anyone take it seriously?" (pp. 35–36), he asks. Action research should go beyond just being pragmatic in a local situation. If it is worth the investment of our time and energy, then it must help us: to grow in understanding, insight, and knowledge; to check and question our opinions, beliefs, and assumptions; and to lay out a more solid foundation for our practice. Winter suggests that the issue of validity in action research is represented by the question not of how we can ensure that our findings are valid but rather of how we can ensure that our procedures are specific and rigorous. In making his case for establishing a clear difference of procedure between action research's form of data gathering and analysis and positivist procedures, he notes that the failure to do so will result in the outcomes of action research being met with such taunts as:

> "We knew that already," "We're doing that already," or, more precisely: "Is that all action research is? Gathering and analyzing data?" "We do that every day of our lives." In a word: Action research procedures need to be specific. We have already seen post-positivist procedures characterize everyday decision making as well as the methods of large-scale social science surveys. Unless action research can be differentiated from both these activities, it will risk being confused with one or the other and attacked as either too minimal to be valid as a form of investigation, or too elaborate to be feasible as a form of practice. (Winter, 1989, p. 35)

Winter (1989) concludes that to achieve more rigor for inquiry into action that goes beyond the everyday practices of professional life and that is differentiated from the concept of rigor defined by positivist research, we need to ask four crucial questions:

1. How can action research procedures be economical?

2. How can action research procedures be specific?

3. How can action research procedures be accessible?

4. How can action research procedures be rigorous?

❖ TRIANGULATION

A common procedure used to ensure the rigor of action research is triangulation, a process in which multiple forms of diverse and redundant types of evidence and perspectives are used to check the validity and reliability of action research outcomes. There are four types of triangulation, according to Denzin (1984): *data source triangulation*, when several different sources of data are used involving time, space, and people, as the researcher looks for the data to remain the same in different contexts; *investigator triangulation*, when several researchers investigate the same phenomenon; *theory triangulation*, when investigators with different viewpoints interpret the same results or when more than one theoretical scheme is used in the interpretation of the phenomenon; and *methodological triangulation*, when one approach is followed by another, to increase confidence in the interpretation or when the study uses more than one method and may consist of within-method or between-method strategies.

In addition to these four types of triangulation, Freeman (1998, p. 97) suggests a fifth approach: *triangulation in time and/or location*, when the same form of data is collected and/or the same methods are used over a given time period or with the same sources in several different locations. When the researcher combines in one study multiple observers, theoretical perspectives, sources of data, and methodologies, then multiple triangulation occurs. By bringing different kinds of evidence and approaches into relationship with each other, they can be compared and contrasted. This means that a problem or issue is researched using a number of different methods, each of which can partly transcend its own limitations by functioning as a point of comparison with another.

Minimally, in triangulation, three methods or points of view are required for comparisons and contrasts to be illuminating and to allow conclusions. When multiple data sources, methodologies, and evidence are brought together so that points of difference, agreement, and disagreement can be identified and noted, then there are more cross-checks on the validity and reliability of the findings. For example, a teacher conducting inquiry on designing and implementing learning centers to improve reading skills can gather data from her students, her colleagues, and other external observers, as well as her own reflections and observations using a variety of approaches such as surveys, video-taping, journaling, and interviews. The likelihood of concurrence regarding the findings on the study's outcomes then increases. Where significant disagreement about the findings does occur, a critical and analytical discussion of the point(s) of disagreement can lead to new insights and questions or a reconceptualization of the research.

❖ VALIDITY AS INQUIRY

The emergence of nonexperimental qualitative methodologies has raised new questions about the concept of validity and how it should be defined, particularly questions about the appropriateness of applying conventional ideas of validity to nonexperimental designs. For example, Mishler (1990) distinguishes between validity and validation, indicating that a search for validity yields an increasingly static abstract construct, whereas a search for validation produces the following living processes:

- Focusing on activities rather than static properties of tests, instruments, and scores
- Focusing on functional criteria rather than abstract rules
- Focusing on validation rather than truth finding
- Reformulating validation as a social discourse between and among teachers, students, and researchers
- Articulating contradictions through social discourse

Mishler's work suggests that validation is not a statistical property but rather a social, mutual, and cumulative process of formulating and implementing practice, collecting data on the results of implementing practice, sharing and discussing the results, refining the questions, and trying out recalibrated practices, always striving for better and more valid practice based on an analysis of data. Rather than seeing validity criteria as a form of intellectually "policing" research, we need to move toward "validity as incitement to discourse" (Lather, 1986). In response to the questions and critiques of positivistic concepts of validity, alternative validity standards for qualitative and action research have evolved over time and are conceptualized in different ways (Altrichter, 1993; Corey, 1953; Dadds, 1995; Eisenhart & Howe, 1992; Elliott, 1991; Feldman, 2007; Lather, 1986, 1991; Lincoln, 1995; Lincoln & Guba, 1985; Mishler, 1990; Roman, 1989; Stenhouse, 1975, 1983; Stevenson, 1996; Winter, 2000).

I resonate to Winter's (2000) argument that "validity is not a single, fixed, or universal concept, but rather a contingent construct, inescapably grounded in the processes and intentions of particular research methodologies and projects" (p. 1). Assuming that validity is complex, dynamic, context sensitive, and not a unitary concept, I would argue that validity can be located at different and concomitantly multiple stages in the action research process. Furthermore, if we also view validity as a mutual collaborative process of discourse and inquiry, involving the participants in an action research study in critically examining the truthfulness of the public and hidden aspects of action research, then everything is open to scrutiny for the truth, for example, power relationships governing who produces knowledge, the openness of dialogue, the embedded values in the study, and the positionality of the researchers. Through validation meetings involving researchers and participants, validity can be examined as if it were a crystal: "Crystals are prisms that reflect externalities and refract within themselves. . . . What we see depends on our angle of repose" (Richardson, 1994, p. 522).

The following is a synthesis and integration of proposed criteria for judging the validity of an action research study. What I have done here is to identify 12 different validity criteria based on a review of the literature previously cited above. For each validity criterion, a series of questions is posed to stimulate critical discussion, examination, and inquiry regarding the validity of an action research study in terms of its goals, intentions, contexts, assumptions, relationships, processes, methodologies, questions, changes, and outcomes. For example, one might question the validity of an action research study in terms of its validity as a dialogical study. Is this a valid dialogical study of differentiated instruction? Has the research encouraged debate about the theory and practice of differentiated instruction in the school? To what degree has the research encouraged and generated a reflective and critical dialogue among the participants in the research? And so on. By changing the verb tenses in each question, validity inquiry can be conducted at the beginning, the middle, and the end of the research cycle or at any other time in the cycle. Validity then becomes formative rather than summative. These criteria may overlap in some cases, but I believe each of the criteria captures the more dynamic, nuanced, and subtle elements of action research. Because teachers conduct research for different purposes and in different contexts, they will use different aspects of these validity criteria, depending on the motivation and circumstances of their research.

1. *Catalytic validity* (Lather, 1991; Stevenson, 1996). To what extent has the research energized participants to know and understand reality so they can transform it? Has the research been transformative, leading to changes in the researchers' understandings, actions, and situations? Has the research been emancipatory, freeing participants from institutional constraints and social structures that limit their self-development and self-determination? To what extent is there a willingness on the part of participants to take risks, to try something different? Has the research led to self-transformation for participants as well as programmatic and institutional transformation?

2. *Consequential validity* (Messick, 1993). What are the value implications of the research? What are the potential social consequences of the research? What can be speculated as the unintended consequences of the research? Will the research lead to useful, meaningful, and fair decisions regarding student learning and teacher development? What are foreseen as the value, social, and emotional consequences for all the participants in the study? What plans have been made to identify the consequences of the research? To what extent will the consequences of the research be just and sound for all participants and the people affected by the research? What are the implications of the research for equity and social justice?

3. *Democratic validity* (Anderson et al., 2007; Dadds, 1995; Stevenson, 1996). To what degree has the research been done in collaboration with all stakeholders who have a vested interest in the problem under study? How does the research involve those whose actions constitute practice and those affected by the practice? Have multiple perspectives and interests been taken into account? Has the research been genuinely collaborative in including all stakeholders who are affected by the research and respecting their perspectives? Have decisions about what to study and how to study it been made, and have the relationships between researchers and other participants been established with deep

respect for the voices and interests of all participants? Who determines the quality and the importance of the research? In whose interests has the research been conducted? Who owns and benefits from this research? How have democratic values been actualized in the conduct of the research?

4. *Dialogical validity* (Anderson et al., 2007). To what degree has the research encouraged and generated a reflective and critical dialogue among all the participants in the research? Has the research encouraged debate about theory and practice in the school? Has there been a critical dialogue about the outcomes of the research? Has the research engaged participants in examining their knowledge and assumptions and in seeking to understand one another's viewpoints? Has there been an openness and trust to speak one's mind and to listen to others? Have the participants inquired into their own and one another's beliefs, values, and perspectives to better understand how they construct meaning in their teaching and in the school? To what extent have participants been able to develop their own "voice"? Has the research created space for student voices? Parental voices? Other voices? Has the research silenced any voices?

5. *Ethical validity* (Campbell & Groundwater-Smith, 2007; Eisenhart & Howe, 1992; Zeni, 2001). Have the elements of human subjects protection such as permissions, confidentiality, privacy, and truth telling been present throughout the research process? If children have been involved, have their educational and developmental needs been addressed in the process of the research? Has the technical quality of the research been balanced against risk to participants? Have the risks as well as the possible benefits of the study been described to students, teachers, and other participants? In the design and conduct of the research, have all relevant people, committees, and authorities been consulted? Have the principles guiding the research been accepted in advance by all participants? Have the wishes of those who do not want to participate in the research been respected? To what extent has the research reflected an ethic of caring for all participants? Has the development of the research remained visible and open to suggestion from others? Has there been equal access to information generated by the process for all participants? Have researchers been explicit about the nature of the research process from the beginning, including all personal biases and interests? Have all participants been allowed to influence the conduct of the research? Have the contributions of participants to the research been acknowledged? Who will own the success or failure of the research?

6. *Interpersonal Validity.* Was the research characterized by interpersonal openness and trust? To what extent were each person's views and ideas accepted? How were interpersonal differences addressed? Was time taken to build effective working relationships and communication among participants? To what degree did research participants listen attentively to each other? How were interpersonal confrontations handled? What did participants learn from interpersonal differences and confrontations? Were the voices of the silent and the silenced heard? Did researchers communicate trustworthiness and respect in themselves as knowers, inquirers, and engagers of others?

7. *Outcome validity* (Anderson et al., 2007; Dadds, 1995). To what extent are the findings of the study worth paying attention to? To what extent are the outcomes authentic and life affirming? To what degree has the completion of the research cycle generated an action or actions for change? To what degree do the actions, which have evolved from the study, lead to a resolution of the problem under investigation? Are the proposed actions of the study clearly stated? Can they be carried out within the classroom or school by the teacher-researchers? By other participants in the study? Has the research been aborted before any action has been taken to address the research problem? What is the quality of the knowledge and the actions generated by the research? Do the outcomes enhance teacher development? Are the conclusions drawn from the data applicable to practice? Do they lead to actions that are critically responsive? How does the research inform and improve educational practice? Do the outcomes enhance student learning? Are the outcomes life affirming and enhancing?

8. *Process validity* (Anderson et al., 2007; Eisenhart & Howe, 1992). To what degree has triangulation been used to guard against biased views of events? Have multiple data sources, methodologies, theoretical schemes, and evidence been brought together so they can be compared and contrasted? Have the processes of problem identification, data collection, and analysis been adequate and thorough? How carefully has the study been designed, conducted, and presented? What is the fit between research questions, data collection procedures, and methods of analysis? Does the research reflect clarity, coherence, and competence? Are the data thorough and based on a variety of sources? Are the conclusions consistent with the nature of the data? Have the researchers considered various explanations for what is discovered in the study? Have the researchers been alert to and able to use knowledge outside the particular perspective or

tradition in which they have been working? Is the research naturalistically generalizable, in that other teacher-researchers have sufficient information about the context of the research to draw analogies to their own situations?

9. *Public validity* (Eisenhart & Howe, 1992; Stevenson, 1996). To what extent have the researchers made the results of their research public and engaged in a dialogue about it? What texts have been produced to represent the research? Written reports? Film? Paintings? Poetry? Dramatic productions? What is the quality of the text that is produced to represent and share the research? Has the research been communicated in ways that are accessible and understandable to and debatable by many and various audiences? Have the richness and the complexity of the research been clearly articulated? Has the action research process been made sufficiently transparent so that outsiders have adequate information to determine whether the research is relevant to their situations?

10. *Recursive validity* (Stevenson, 1996). Has research been systematically conducted but in a way that is responsive to evolving understandings and circumstances in the research? Have questions, problem statements, methodologies, and outcomes been revised, reflecting changes in conceptions, contexts, circumstances, and the action research process itself? How has the research helped participants study reality in order to change it and to change reality in order to study it? To what extent have descriptions, emerging interpretations, and conclusions been fed back to research participants and refined in light of participant perspectives and researcher reactions?

11. *Social justice validity.* To what extent has the research addressed issues of social justice, diversity, equity, civic discourse, and caring? Has the research generated changes in teaching and curriculum more responsive to the wide range of differences among students? Has the research promoted more understanding and respect for cultural, racial, ethnic, class, and gender differences? To what extent has the research promoted access for students with disabilities? Has the research addressed issues of inclusivity? Has the research led to greater consciousness of more democratic and just forms of education? Have the participants become more aware of the power that accrues to people who control the production of knowledge? What is the research silent about? Has the research created spaces for the voices of those who are normally silent and/or silenced? Has the research empowered participants to take more control over their situations?

12. *Values validity.* Have the researchers articulated and justified their own intentions and beliefs for the research? Have the researchers declared their positionality in conducting the study? To what extent have the researchers articulated the rationale for and the educational significance of the study in a way that connects it to their own value commitments and experiential and theoretical knowledge? What has been the interplay between the researchers' values and actions, where values inform actions and actions inform values? Have the researchers disclosed their own preconceptions and how they might affect the research? How have the values of democracy and social justice been actualized through the research process? Has the research uncovered the ideological self of the researchers? What values have been actualized in the research?

❖ GENERALIZABILITY IN ACTION RESEARCH

Are the findings of action research studies generalizable? That is a significant question of external validity that often arises among practitioners and critics of action research. Action research projects many times have been viewed as less generalizable than empirical positivistic studies, which are quantitative and use random sampling to select a population that is representative of a larger population to which generalizations can be extended. In contrast, action research studies are localized and conducted with an existing group of people, who may or may not represent a random selection from a larger population. But Lomax (1994) dismisses this concern regarding generalizability:

> The question of generalization is also "old hat." . . . Generalization in the sense that an experiment replicated in exactly the same controlled conditions will have the same results a second time around seems a nonsensical construct in the hurly burly of social interaction. However, I do believe it important that action research projects have an application elsewhere, and that action researchers are able to communicate their insights to others with a useful result. The way in which this can be done seems common sense to me. The action research process needs to be made transparent so that a knowledgeable outsider has sufficient information to judge whether the research is relevant to their situation. (pp. 118–119)

A number of deficiencies with the concept of generalizability have been identified by Lincoln and Guba (2000), who indicate that generalizations are limited by:

1. Dependence on the assumption of determinism

2. Dependence on inductive logic, thereby closing out the rules of deduction

3. Dependence on the assumption of freedom from time and context

4. Entrapment in the nomothetic-idiographic dilemma ("The trouble with generalizations is that they don't apply to particulars," Lincoln & Guba, 2000)

5. Entrapment in a reductionist fallacy

Early in the history of action research, questions were raised about the generalizability of action research studies. In response to these questions, Corey (1953) suggested that "action research studies are undertaken not to make possible lateral extensions of generalizations but to make possible vertical extensions, with the vertical line going into the future" (p. 14). In other words, if a fifth-grade teacher conducts action research to assess the effectiveness of implementing learning centers to improve reading in her classroom, then the conclusions of her study would have their greatest validity and general applicability to groups of fifth-grade children she might teach in the future. This kind of vertical generalizability was viewed by Corey as reflecting the spirit and intent of action research.

However, Kember (2000) and Elliott (1991), among others, argue that evidence and conclusions from action research studies are generalizable in the traditional sense, even for single case studies. They argue that if an action research study finds that a particular instructional or curriculum change works well, then it makes sense to recommend that other teachers try implementing the innovation if they are faced with similar situations of instruction and curriculum. Adapting the innovation from one situation to another with similar contexts and circumstances could be considered a form of provisional testing rather than an unqualified recommendation (Stenhouse, 1975, p. 142).

Following Stake's (1995) concept of naturalistic generalizability, teachers who wish to use the results of an action research study would make judgments about the similarities between their own contexts and situations and that of the research. "The argument is essentially that lessons learned from one action research project may be utilized by others facing similar issues in related contexts" (Kember, 2000, p. 42). If hundreds of action research studies were regularly and systematically collected over time and housed in university and school libraries, then studying similar action research projects (for example, studies dealing with classroom management) through the lenses of intersubjectivity and triangulation would yield a generalizable body of practical knowledge that could significantly affect teacher practice. What would be required in these action research reports is a sufficiently rich description of their contextual details so that other teacher-researchers would be able to draw analogies to their own situations (Stevenson, 1996).

❖ SUMMARY

By using the validity criteria described in this chapter and by aggregating, comparing, and contrasting existing action research studies, cross-study conclusions can be drawn and generalized. Over time, a new knowledge base will emerge as communities of university researchers and teacher-researchers converge in one collaborative knowledge infrastructure to share and build trustworthy knowledge for teaching and learning (Heibert et al., 2002). One of the ways in which the convergence of research communities in such a knowledge infrastructure can be accomplished is through a reconceptualization of action research as a form of professional development, which I discuss in the following chapter.

5

Teacher Action Research as Professional Development

As I have argued in the previous chapters of this book, teachers as researchers can advance and enhance the professional status of teaching, generate theory and knowledge, improve student learning, increase the effectiveness of reform efforts, and promote teacher development. Unfortunately, teachers' potential and role as agents of inquiry and change have too often been neglected. Rather, teachers frequently have been disenfranchised by many educational practices and innovations, especially those involving "teacher proof" curricula and "best practices." They have been socialized to receive knowledge generated by others rather than trust in their own capacities to assign meaning through action and reflection. Thirty years ago, Chittendon, Charney, and Kanevsky (1978) captured the situation well in language that could apply to many professional development approaches today:

SOURCE: All material in this section adapted from D. Miller & G. Pine (1990), "Adapting Professional Inquiry for Educational Improvement Through Action Research," *Journal of Staff Development, 11*(3), 56–60. Reprinted with permission of the National Staff Development Council, www.nsdc.org, 2008. All rights reserved.

Historically teachers have been told that the source of knowledge about learning resides somewhere outside their classrooms, perhaps in curriculum or research labs. Given such conditions, it is not surprising to find some teachers so lacking confidence in their own views that they doubt the legitimacy of their experience with children when confronted with "expert" evidence that goes against it. Insofar as teachers are unable to look critically at their classrooms, their teaching suffers. It becomes uninteresting and takes on qualities of routine and mindless practice that characterize too many elementary schools. (p. 58)

Knowledge in context is an essential component of efforts to improve practice. Too often the examination of teaching and learning has been stripped of the many real-life variables that affect children. Because many educational studies have examined discrete elements of a problem at the expense of the ever-changing context of the classroom, teachers often find research meaningless and irrelevant. Without a regard for context, action is uninformed. With a respect for the realities of the classroom, action becomes relevant and meaningful.

When teachers engage in their own classroom-based inquiry, they use their own expertise, experience, initiative, and leadership. This offers teachers active participation in the development of meaning and knowledge. What does it take for teachers to value and honor their own experience and skill as a source of expertise, to initiate and direct their own inquiry, to analyze their experience with students, to engage in the construction of knowledge, and to make their inquiry public?

❖ ACTION RESEARCH/PROFESSIONAL DEVELOPMENT

Action research can be conceived as a form of professional development characterized as an ongoing process of systematic study in which teachers examine their own teaching and students' learning through descriptive reporting, purposeful conversation, collegial sharing, and critical reflection for the purpose of improving classroom practice. Teacher action research as professional development is characterized by (a) a collegial environment and community of inquiry in which teachers reflect, question, hypothesize, document, and evaluate; and by (b) a safe and supportive environment in which teachers commit to, risk, and implement experimental actions. Under these conditions, the process can produce change, generate informed action, and produce knowledge through reflection on practice (Kyle & Hovda, 1987a,

1987b). As a process of professional development, action research empowers teachers to study their own circumstances, transform their experiences, develop and articulate craft knowledge, take purposeful responsibility for improving practice, and secure ownership of professional knowledge.

Action research is not the exclusive territory of those with technical and methodological expertise. Rather, this mode of research is suited to teachers who cultivate thoughtful, analytic habits of mind. Barritt, Beekman, Bleeker, and Mulderij (1985) propose that action research can engage everyone who teaches:

> We believe that everyone who teaches, and we mean teachers in the broadest sense, including parents as well as professional teachers, should be engaged in research. Informally they already are. Everyone who watches, thinks about what they have seen, and acts on that information is engaged in research. Research isn't separate from life; it is a special way of regarding life. It is a habit of mind which all of us have more or less and which can profitably be cultivated in everyone. (p. 69)

The facilitating effect of action research on educational improvement efforts may be better understood by considering a continuum of approaches to professional development. The continuum ranges from traditional programs to action research projects and strategies. This range of approaches to professional development can be described using six factors, or dimensions, which are examined later. Let us consider the following examples on this continuum.

In School System A, 4 days in the school calendar are dedicated to staff development. Nationally known speakers offer one-day workshops for all the teachers. The workshops address a theme identified by the school administration as a generic concern for K–12 teachers. Each teacher has the freedom to implement the workshop ideas in ways that fit his or her classroom situation.

School System B, as part of a statewide and grant-supported staff development thrust on instructional effectiveness, conducts a series of training workshops on a particular technique or model. The goal is to train all the teachers in the school system in the designated model.

In School System C, school-based study teams have been established to conduct projects on a curriculum or instructional topic of their own choosing. They meet regularly (often weekly) to reflect on their experiences, to discuss classroom observations, and to examine their data. They collaborate with and support each other in systematically

Table 5.1   Continuum of Approaches to Professional Development for Teachers

Factors	Traditional Approaches	Action Research
1. Source of expertise	External authority	Participating practitioners
2. Locus of knowledge	Formalized outside the context	Located in context and problem situations
3. Experience	Draws from a formalized body of knowledge	Draws from teacher interactions with each other, with learners, and with situational realities
4. Initiative	Arises from system and administrative problems and priorities	Emerges from teaching and learning situations and needs
5. Leadership	Program and school administration	Group-centered leadership
6. Mode of organization	Individual and passive	Collaboration for engagement

SOURCE: Miller, D., & Pine, G. (1990), "Advancing Professional Inquiry for Educational Improvement Through Action Research," *Journal of Staff Development*, 11(3), p. 58. Reprinted with permission of the National Staff Development Council, 2008. All rights reserved.

studying and modifying their practice (Livingston, Castle, & Nations, 1989; Miller, Snell, & Snell, 1987).

Table 5.1 presents a conceptual framework for comparing the relationship of these and other approaches along a continuum of professional development. At the left end of the continuum is the traditional program, characterized by maintenance functions and by teachers' responsibilities for implementation only. At the other end of the continuum is action research, with leadership status for teachers defined in terms of their initiative, experience, judgment, and insights as professionals. The continuum is elaborated by the various ways in which assumptions, provisions, and outcomes are combined in six areas: expertise, knowledge, experience, initiatives, leadership, and mode of organization.

On the left side of the continuum, teachers have limited opportunities for developing their potential as professionals or for making creative contributions. This characterizes traditional approaches to educational innovation and staff development for teachers. As a result of this approach teachers are often concerned with following prescribed procedures and goals and do not have any delegated responsibility for adaptations in their own classroom, in their own school, or most important, to the particular learning needs of their own students. In contrast, the right side of the continuum challenges teachers and offers significant participation in educational improvement.

In making this comparison, I do not suggest that traditional staff development programs are dysfunctional or serve no appropriate purpose. Rather, it is argued that educational improvement should involve teachers in ways that respect and engage their observations, ideas, craft knowledge, analytic strategies, interpretations, and formulations.

In this continuum, each approach serves a different purpose and has different effects on the professional status and efficacy of teachers. The continuum is not a continuous scale of positive and negative elements. Rather it is a nominal scale, indicating relative distinctions among professional development approaches. Each of the six factors is now examined more thoroughly.

Source of Expertise

Traditional staff development programs have assumed that valid expertise about teaching and learning comes from those not involved in the day-to-day world of teaching and that expertise lies with those who have administrative authority or who have published scientific theory and knowledge with claims of universal generalizability and invariance (Schön, 1983). Traditional programs have reflected the view that authoritative knowledge is to be imparted to and then applied by practitioners. This approach has several consequences: (a) tightly prescribed training has been developed, as is found in teacher-proof curriculum packages; (b) teacher accountability systems have been designed; (c) contextual aspects of teaching and learning have been disregarded; (d) passive teaching and learning methods have been valued; and (e) a hierarchical separation of research and practice has been reinforced.

In contrast to traditional approaches, action research posits a dynamic and context-based view requiring the exercise of professional judgment. Expertise can emanate from teacher-initiated action, teacher reflection, discussion, and dialogue. In brief, meaning can be constructed through an action-reflection-action cycle. Rather than being the subjects of research, teachers become articulate experts whose expertise reflects a dynamic blend of experience and reflective knowledge.

Locus of Knowledge

Knowledge is power. Whoever generates and disseminates knowledge can affect the goals, agenda, expectations, and values of a profession. Recognition and acceptance of where knowledge is located determines the rights and privileges of access to knowledge and the power of influence. What is knowledge? Who creates knowledge? How and to whom is it disseminated? For what purposes? Responses to these questions affect the nature, character, and direction of teacher development and educational improvement.

In traditional programs, the locus of knowledge has often been determined by a high regard for distant authority and by a corresponding suspicion of teachers. This view has given priority to knowledge from external sources: experts, textbooks, technical journals. Hence, the efficacy of practice has rested in the hands of researchers, textbook publishers, the testing industry, curriculum developers, administrators, and scholars—all of whom are external to the teaching-learning situation. In contrast, action research assumes that significance and meaning lie in the actual situations of teaching and learning. It also assumes that knowledge of, about, and for teaching and learning should be determined by what teachers and learners actually do. This suggests that if effective teaching and learning are to occur, teachers must have a central role in the development of knowledge that affects the care, education, and development of children.

In chronicling her journey as a young teacher candidate, Marilyn Kroeker Motlong (2000), a fourth-grade teacher in Pawtik, Ontario, speaks to teacher centrality in the development of local knowledge and personal and professional confidence:

> The focus of my action research has been to develop into a more confident teacher, better able to understand my students' needs. In part I have done this by better understanding myself. My research questions related to this focus emerged and changed as the year progressed, and my concerns about my practice diminished. One key question was, How can I ensure that I am modeling appropriate values and morals, and not imposing them? Another was, How can I teach, effectively, the content of the curriculum, particularly in mathematics? . . . I believe that the most amazing transformations in my thinking are occurring because of my action research and the reflective practice it engenders. I have confidence in myself even in the occurrence of failure.

I believe this is a strong characteristic to have—strength when you have been defeated. My growth in confidence is giving me an improved ability to explore and "test" my own beliefs and practices.

Role of Experience

To understand the role of teachers in generating knowledge, the reciprocal relationship between knowledge and experience must be recognized. As teachers go about the business of teaching, their skillful action shows them to be knowledgeable in a special way. They have "know-how." To understand the reciprocity between knowledge and experience, it is useful to distinguish at least three kinds of knowledge (Reason & Heron, 1986): (a) *experiential* knowledge (gained through direct encounter with people, places, or things); (b) *practical* knowledge (knowing how to do something—demonstrated by a skill or competence); (c) *propositional* knowledge (knowing about something—expressed in statements and theories).

Traditional staff development programs have disregarded teachers' experience and practical knowledge because they are deemed subjective, particular, and place-bound. The underlying assumption of the typical staff development program is that teachers should be the recipients of knowledge (Reason & Heron, 1986). This has meant that authoritative external knowledge has been used to make judgments about practice.

The way teacher experience has been traditionally evaluated and studied has been captured by Ross and Cronbach's (1976) metaphor of watching a train versus being on board a train. From the traditional perspective, to gain knowledge about a train and its passengers, observations are made at the station, during the journey, and on arrival at the final destination. The observations are made from points outside the train. Action research emphasizes the knowledge consequences of boarding the train; riding for the entire journey; talking with the passengers, the conductor, and the engineer; and looking out the windows.

Action research seeks to capture the pulse and vitality of life "on board the train" (i.e., the classroom). It provides the conditions for manifesting teacher know-how through reflection-on-experience. It enables teachers to describe and interpret their intentionality and explore the boundaries of their meanings. It is an iterative process in which knowledge arises from an examination of practice. It values personal knowledge (Polanyi, 1962).

Opportunities for Initiatives

Teacher growth initiatives arise when teachers define goals, weigh possible alternative actions, and make decisions. Such initiatives involve risk and commitments that step beyond the existing state of affairs. In traditional programs, initiatives usually arise from needs, problems, and priorities identified by the district and administrators, rather than by teachers and learners. Typically, these initiatives have been based on needs assessments that reflect a deficit ideology. Such assessments often are disconnected from context and look at symptoms, not underlying capacities. Consequently, traditional programs may be characterized by imposition and prescription. In action research, initiatives for improvement are responses to the dynamics of ongoing teaching-learning activities in terms of goal-oriented efforts. Initiatives emerge when participants define the problems. Teaching is viewed as an experimental, improvisational, and recursive process always subject to improvement through action, reflection, and documentation.

Leadership Responsibility

A major function of leadership is to formulate goals and develop agendas for action. Leadership involves obtaining and allocating resources to support the achievement of valued goals. Leadership is essential for integrating staff interests, energy, interrelationships, and talents for a shared purpose, promising benefits for the common good. In traditional programs, leadership responsibility has been treated as a prerogative of administrators. Often, leadership has been marked by unilateral judgment and decision making. Too often, these administrators have made decisions but never experienced the consequences of their own decisions.

On the other hand, in action research, leadership arises in response to needs and goal seeking. It is flexible and responsive to the functional needs of a group. Action research enables teachers to undertake leadership to become more autonomous in judgments and to exercise initiative.

Mode of Organization

The way in which professional development activities are organized affects program outcomes. Consideration of organizational forms and structures is important because they significantly affect the allocation of resources, time, and energy. In one school district, staff development may be a subunit of the personnel office organized to respond to the district's collective bargaining agreement. In another district, staff development may be organized as a semiautonomous unit to support curriculum and instructional programs. In a third district, staff development may be a function located in the superintendent's office, organized to support a districtwide strategic plan.

In traditional programs, organizational matters center around the system, not students and teachers. Modes of organization have typically been the domain of administrators. These modes have usually been static and centrally controlled. System efficiency has been a major criterion for selecting the modes of staff development organization. Information is gathered for management purposes, for defining teacher roles, and for assigning tasks (Oja & Pine, 1987). In action research, the organization of the activities centers around problem solving. Information is generated as a resource for all participants. The organization of the activities is viewed as fluid and adaptable, roles are overlapping and flexible, and inquiry is participatory and collaborative, creating a context of action research that starkly differs from the traditional school context (see Table 5.2).

❖ ACTION RESEARCH AS PROFESSIONAL DEVELOPMENT: TEACHER OUTCOMES

In a collaborative action research study that Sharon Oja and I facilitated (Oja & Pine, 1983, 1987), teams of middle school teachers conducted research on schoolwide problems of teacher leadership, student learning, and scheduling over a period of 2 years. Teachers on the action research teams identified several outcomes with respect to their role as researchers: (a) an increased understanding of the relationship between scheduling, curriculum, and school philosophy; (b) the creation of new patterns of communication, sharing, and collegiality; (c) the building of a common body of knowledge; and (d) an increased ability to identify, analyze, and solve classroom problems.

Teachers valued their group process and perceived growth in themselves as a result of the process. Although their concerns focused on how the action research results would contribute to improved school practice, student learning, and educational theory, it was their experiences on the team that all teachers said they would transfer into

SOURCE: This section adapted from S. Oja & G. Pine (1987). Collaborative Action Research: Teachers' Stages of Development. *Peabody Journal of Education, 64*(2), 96–115. Reprinted with permission from Taylor & Francis. 2008. All rights reserved.

Table 5.2   A Continuum of Contexts

Traditional School Context	*Collaborative Action Research Context*
1. Change is initiated and managed from the top	1. Change is initiated and managed from the bottom, middle, and top
2. Hierarchical, principal-managed	2. Nonhierarchical, self-managed
3. Information is generated for management—management information system	3. Information is generated for everyone
4. Norm of mutual tolerance	4. Norm of collegiality
5. Norm of convention	5. Norm of experimentation
6. Power is concentrated in the principal's office	6. Power is diffused in the team
7. Teachers handle limited specific roles and functions	7. Teachers handle different roles and functions, roles exchanged
8. Tasks are assigned to teachers	8. Teachers develop their own tasks
9. Teachers' roles are defined and structured	9. Teachers' roles are overlapping and flexible
10. Individual "private cycle" of problem solving is limited to the classroom	10. Group "public cycle" of collaborative problem solving involves inside and outside the classroom
11. "Behaviorally" busy setting–reactive thinking–cognitive constriction	11. A setting of pause-reflective thinking-cognitive expansion
12. Directed and reactive inquiry	12. Participatory and collaborative inquiry
13. Detached "out of classroom" perspective of classrooms and school	13. Immediate, concrete, "in classroom" perspective of classrooms and school
14. Short-term and quick "on demand" problem solving	14. Sustained deliberate inquiry
15. Recipe knowledge	15. Deep recursive knowledge

their own classrooms, schools, and districts. For them, the process of action research as a professional development experience was one of the most personally significant outcomes—an outcome holding the greatest potential for effecting change in their schools.

Through their participation in collaborative action research, all teachers became more familiar with research language, methodology, and design. Their involvement also made them better consumers of educational research and stimulated them to become more skilled researchers. Teachers shared their research methodologies and findings at national, regional, and local conferences in addition to their own school districts' professional development committees, school boards, and university facilities.

Teachers on the teams expressed a variety of different perceptions regarding the school context, collegiality with other teachers, themselves as researchers, and action research approaches to school problems. Among the variety of teacher-perceived outcomes were the following.

School Context

- Gaining a better understanding of the dynamics and inner workings of the school
- Gaining a clearer and more nuanced understanding of the problems and decisions faced by school administration
- Acquiring greater knowledge of the complexity of decision-making processes in the school among faculty as well as administration
- Developing better understanding and more fundamental grasp of contextual and organizational issues affecting teaching and student learning
- Gaining a more fundamental grasp of the interrelationships between scheduling, curriculum, and school philosophy
- Developing a greater appreciation of the impact of school history on current problems and issues of curriculum and change

Collegiality

- Creating new patterns of communication, collegiality, and sharing on the team
- Developing knowledge of the dynamics of collegiality and its influence on school problem solving; applying knowledge of the dynamics of collegiality and sharing within the team
- Demonstrating greater willingness to communicate concerns and to experiment with solutions
- Gaining support and emotional strength from team members in confronting day-to-day problems and issues
- Sharing and building a common body of knowledge
- Feeling more comfortable in the school and able to cope with pressures of the school day
- Working to develop greater schoolwide collegiality

Teacher Skills and Attitudes as Action Researchers

- Choosing a schoolwide review of the state of practice to develop a conceptual basis for their work
- Using internal resources in the school to examine a problem (school history, statements of philosophy, demographic data, curriculum guides)
- Collecting information from the thinking of other teachers (through survey data and interviews) to define and address problems
- Seeing research design as recursive rather than static
- Viewing research as less intimidating and feeling more comfortable and knowledgeable in conducting research
- Perceiving themselves as professionals whose opinions were valued and respected

The Collaborative Action Research Process

- Seeing action research as an effective problem-solving model that could be applied in a variety of school situations
- Valuing collaborative action research as a model of professional development
- Viewing collaborative action research as a process for refining and using teacher capabilities
- Developing a more comprehensive understanding of educational problems and their possible solutions
- Experiencing collaborative action research as a source of personal and professional renewal and intellectual stimulation

Temporary Systems and the Collaborative Action Research Process

Formed together out of a desire for personal, professional, and classroom change, the teacher research teams evolved into *temporary systems* (Benne, Bradford, Gibb, & Lippitt, 1975; Goodman & Goodman, 1976; Miles, 1964; Morley & Silver, 1977). A temporary system consists of a group of individuals who engage in a joint task for a limited period of time (Miles, 1964). People come together, interact, create something, and then disband. Examples include conferences, workshops, institutes, retreats, study groups, and projects.

Such systems are brought into being to develop an idea, a plan, a product, a service, or to make something happen. When the task is completed, or the time set has expired the system is dissolved. Permanent systems, in contrast, exist to carry out relatively repetitive operations, or to provide services for which there is a continuing need. (Gant, South, & Hansen, 1977, p. 7)

The research teams functioned as temporary systems in the permanent systems of their middle schools. Within temporary systems, individuals and groups may behave differently than those in the permanent system. New structures and norms can be substituted for existing ones and can be tested to determine their value. Power and status differentials may be minimized to facilitate new patterns of communication and to locate areas of needed change. For instance, where teachers can freely interact as peers, new patterns of problem solving and new approaches to decision making can be tried.

The teacher research teams (temporary systems) operated in ways that were very different from the ways in which the schools (permanent systems) operated. Instead of relying on students for most of their human contact in the harried atmosphere of the classroom, teachers were able to sit in relatively uninterrupted settings to discuss professional matters; instead of making decisions about a single classroom individually, they became involved in joint planning for the entire school; and instead of having few, if any, adult sources of feedback and encouragement about their teaching performance, they worked in a supportive environment in which commendations for action were frequent from peers and outside experts. Pursuing what would be considered "non-discussable" questions in the larger context of the school became an ongoing process within the context established by the teacher research teams.

Peer support, the sharing of ideas, and the experience of collegiality and group decision making were especially prized by these teacher-researchers. As temporary systems, the teacher research teams involved professional development, providing teachers with opportunities to experience and practice different roles and functions; and group development, providing teachers with the opportunity to experiment with interdependent behavior and to use different methods of problem solving and decision making to achieve the objectives of their inquiry.

The downside of action research teams morphing into temporary systems is that they can create a sense of artificiality. McTaggart (1991, p. 45) warns that action research groups can become "special" in a way that establishes an insulated sense of privacy and status and enhances their own work but makes extension of that work to others extremely difficult. The greater the difference between life in the temporary system of an action research team and life in the permanent system of the school, the greater the problem of entry or reentry when members of the temporary system go back to their usual tasks with the notion of affecting change in the permanent system. Action research groups need to commit themselves to extending their influence as well as their understanding. Failing to help other teachers join them may result in action research being dismissed as the domain of the "enlightened few."

Creating New Contexts

The research teams created their own operational contexts, which contrasted markedly with the operational context of their schools (see Table 7.2). They organized, operated, and developed new norms and structures in a fashion that highlighted different assumptions about what makes for effectiveness in running schools—their schools, in particular. That is, by varying the principles used to organize and to operate themselves, the teams made more visible corresponding and contrasting principles in use in their schools. Consequently, within the contours of the research projects, the process of action research emerged as more significant than the product.

At the end of the project, teacher-researchers were impressed not only with the prospect, probabilities, or specifics of school change but also with the process of collaborative inquiry, which led to personal and professional growth. In the teachers' view, the process of collaborative teacher research is what has enduring value. This perspective of effecting change through the action research process is expressed clearly in the final reports of the teacher research teams, which recommended that

- Collaborative action research be applied in all future professional development and school change efforts
- Collaborative action research be used to give teaching staff a significant role in formulating the questions and developing the agenda for school, classroom, instructional, and curriculum change
- The collaborative action research process be used to study, develop, and implement school instructional schedules
- Teachers' knowledge and skills in the collaborative action research process be used to promote the process with other school staffs at other sites
- The context created through the collaborative action research process become the school's context for decision making and initiating change

❖ ACTION RESEARCH AS PROFESSIONAL DEVELOPMENT: TEACHER VOICES

Sustained educational improvement is accomplished most successfully through action research that engages teachers in advancing professional inquiry. Engaging teachers in action research will lead to sustained educational improvement, and it also has the potential to enhance the teaching profession. If classroom teaching in elementary and secondary schools is to come of age as a profession—if the role of teacher is not to continue to be institutionally infanticidal—then teachers need to take the responsibility for investigating their own practice systematically and critically, by methods that are appropriate to their practice (Ericson, 1986).

Cary Avery (1990), a classroom teacher-researcher, illustrates the transformational power of teachers investigating their practice when she says:

> As a practitioner, my traditional role was to be concerned with what my students were doing and how I enabled them to do it. As a teacher researcher, I became a learner in the classroom concerned with what my students were learning and how they were learning. I experienced my classroom as a collaborative venture and examined not only how I functioned, but also how we worked together and why strategies did or did not work. (p. 44)

Michelle Pasko (2004), a third-grade teacher in Anne Arundel County Public Schools in Maryland, describes how she grew as a teacher through action research:

> In spite of this, though, the most important result was within my soul as a result of this project. This is a time when many of us feel that the job of teaching is overwhelming and even impossible. Sometimes it feels that we spend so much time assessing and so little time teaching. We feel that we just aren't good enough and don't "teach to the tests" enough. We feel that if we aren't teaching "by the book" and sticking to the scheduled minutes, we aren't doing a good job. Well, I took a risk by teaching outside of the curriculum and interrupting the precious "language arts block" to complete an action research project. At the end of it all, I learned something so valuable: sometimes it is OK to take risks and to follow our hearts. Our students will learn amazing things, and

teachers will be reminded of what teaching is all about: the magic and excitement of seeing students learn.

Even though Barbara Bell Angus (2003), a special needs teacher, didn't accomplish everything she wanted to do through her action research project, she tells her own story of professional transformation:

So although I haven't addressed my original question, which I continue to think is important and deserving of investigation, I have improved my effectiveness in dramatic and noticeable ways. In fact, the power of having students review videotapes of their classroom interactions was so powerful that it was noticed by my teaching neighbor, who asked me to come into her classroom to videotape. Everything that I have found as a result of my attempt at action research seems so obvious. But it was only through scrutiny of videotaped recordings and subsequent reflection that I was able to make these observations and, consequently, to change my approach to teaching my high needs students. So, although I have experienced incredible frustration and confusion and I still don't have a neatly packaged research article, I have experienced incredible unpredicted growth as a teacher and consequently, my students have benefited as well. (p. 6)

Comparing her professional development experiences with her experiences as an action researcher, Christine Jamieson (2000), an English teacher at Ernestown Secondary School in Ontario, Canada, writes:

Often my experience with professional development opportunities has been predetermined by the school I was employed in. This is typically delivered by an outside expert who parachutes in and I am often left wondering at the end of it, if that time was well spent, as it frequently does not change, inform or improve my teaching practice. I always feel that a "one size fits all" approach can never meet the needs of a diverse group of teachers. Action research has allowed me to identify an area that I had questions about and to pursue this question vigorously using reflective practice. This research framework allowed for a distillation of the recurring themes and patterns that promoted constructivist teaching and learning and initiated new teaching practices. It has led to a deeper understanding of constructivist theory and the transformative power of action research to increase my knowledge about my own teaching and learning. (p. 6)

❖ SUMMARY

The experiences of these teachers affirm that to achieve educational improvement and enhance the teaching profession, professional development programs must be created that (a) enable teachers to be leaders, (b) value teachers as experts, (c) facilitate teacher initiative, and (d) promote teacher inquiry. Action research as professional development liberates teachers from the maintenance mentality of traditional in-service education and offers significant participation in activities that advance sustained educational improvement (Goswami & Stillman, 1987; Hustler, Cassidy, & Cuff, 1986; Kyle & Hovda, 1987a, 1987b; Olson, 1988; Stevenson, 1991). The implementation of action research as a form of professional development enables schools to become centers of inquiry where administrators, teachers, interns, and university faculty can share ideas and grow together to improve educational practice, improve student learning, and facilitate student development. Sustained action research is our best hope to integrate research and professional development in order to significantly advance the quality of teaching and student learning and development.

Part II

Collaborative Action Research

*Foundation for
Knowledge Democracies*

This section consists of Chapters 6, 7, and 8, which establish the philosophical and practical foundations for building a knowledge democracy. This section of the book broadens the concept of collaborative action research to include new partners in the inquiry process—students and parents—and deals with a number of critical issues such as time, resources, and culture, which need to be confronted for schools to evolve into knowledge democracies.

6

Collaborative
Action Research

C hapter 6 begins with a historical review of collaborative action research, discusses its characteristics, and then offers concrete examples of a variety of collaborative action research programs located across the country. I argue throughout this chapter that collaborative action research liberates teachers to assume leadership roles as constructors of knowledge and agents of change in helping schools to become centers of inquiry. The chapter concludes with specific but brief examples of a number of middle school teachers collaborating to support each others' research studies.

Collaborative action research represents a renaissance within educational research. The idea of such collaborative efforts was initiated, articulated, and demonstrated by Corey (1953) and Schaefer (1967), then renewed and reinvigorated by the National Institute for Education, which sponsored three major studies that gave impetus and national visibility to the rebirth and renewal of collaborative action research: the Interactive Research and Development on Teaching Study (Tickunoff et al., 1979), the Interactive Research and Development on Schooling Study (Griffin, Lieberman, & Jacullo-Noto, 1983), and the Action Research on Change in Schools Study (Oja & Pine, 1983). In addition to these studies, a major replication of the Tickunoff study conducted by Huling (1982) gave further support to the importance of collaborative inquiry. All of these studies involving university faculty and classroom teachers focused on collaborative action research as a process characterized by several elements:

- Research problems are mutually defined by teachers and university faculty. "Knowledge is not produced for a scientific community, but rather for an interpretive community, consisting primarily—though, not exclusively—of school practitioners" (Oja & Pine, 1987, p. 96).
- University faculty and classroom teachers collaborate in seeking solutions to identified problems. They participate in a process of collaborative reflection and critical dialogue.
- Research findings are used and modified in solving problems. The tensions inherent in integrating action and research are captured in the term traditionally used to describe this type of inquiry: action research.
- Teachers develop research competencies, skills, and knowledge, and university faculty engage in field-based qualitative and naturalistic research methodologies.
- Teachers, as a result of participating in the action research process, are better able to solve their own problems and renew themselves professionally. They find their "voice" and develop a sense of agency. Action research is professional development.
- Teachers, or teachers together with university faculty, produce research reports for publication.

Collaborative action research values teachers' knowledge; accentuates their capacity to conduct their own research in the interests of their students' learning and in the interests of improving their own teaching; emphasizes problems that are explored from teacher/student perspectives; and liberates the mental dispositions of teachers for critical reflection, questioning, and the continuous pursuit of inquiry, contributing to the development of inquiry as a lifelong stance.

❖ THE COLLABORATIVE NATURE OF ACTION RESEARCH

Historically, action research was, from the very beginning, collaborative in nature (Collier, 1945; Lewin, 1946). Lewin emphasized the importance of collaboration in gathering data, in discussing findings, and in making decisions and commitments to action. In the major and significant application of the action research paradigm in education,

Corey (1953) embraced the collaborative ethos, which conceives action research as a cooperative activity involving teachers, students, supervisors, and administrators. While acknowledging that action research does not necessarily have to be a collaborative activity, he argued that, in most instances, cooperation among participants is highly desirable; as many people as possible who would be affected by the research should participate in doing it. For Corey (1953), making action research a cooperative effort would "result in better problem definition, more realistic consideration of action hypotheses, easier translation of these hypotheses into action, and better interpretation of the evidence accumulated" (p. 144). Nearly 30 years later, Brown, Henry, Henry, and McTaggart (1982) affirmed Corey's views:

> Action research is distinguished by its adherence to a collaborative ethic. Action research is a collaborative endeavour in which groups of practitioners work together to understand better their own practice, to increase their own awareness of the effects of their practice, and of their control over the situation in which they work. (p. 4)

Elliott (1991) makes the case that collaborative action research provides a creative outlet for responding to the imposition of a paradigm of school management based on an accountability and control surveillance model:

> I would argue that the widespread emergence of collaborative action research as a teacher-based form of curriculum evaluation and development is a creative response to the growth of technical rational systems of hierarchical surveillance and control over teachers' professional practices. Out of the still smoldering embers of the traditional craft culture the phoenix of a collaborative practice arises to offer creative resistance to the hegemony of the technocrat. (p. 56)

Kemmis and Wilkinson (1998) argue that action research is best conceptualized as a collaborative process because action research is a social process "directed towards studying, reframing, and reconstructing practices which by their very nature are social. If practices are constituted in social interaction between people, then changing practices is a social process" (p. 22). It has also been argued that individual action research is a limited form of action research and that action research is not individualistic (Kemmis & DiChiro, 1987, p. 103).

The theme of the collaborative nature of action research continues to be supported in the work of Frost et al. (2000, p. 67), who maintain that collaboration is a source of moral support for beginning and sustaining action research, a process for transcending competing agendas and conflicting priorities to sustain the momentum of inquiry, a vehicle for managing change through dialogue based on shared experience and data analysis, and a means for generating a critical perspective through the power of critical discussion and reflexive study.

Examples of Collaborative Action Research

Collaborative action research is inquiry-based service, a process of teams or groups of researchers concurrently inquiring about problems in education and acting on them. It assumes that effective educational practice that will make a difference in teaching and learning is the first business of education, that there is a generic need to improve educational practice, and that the improvement of educational practice requires the confrontation of real problems in the school by conceiving alternatives and testing them out. Through action research, teachers form communities of reflective practitioners who together engage in cycles of research and action that lead to professional growth and improved practice. Practice through collaborative inquiry then becomes the crucible for innovation, a distinctive measure of assumptions, speculations, and theories.

Collaborative action research teams can be structured in different ways for different purposes. Dana and Yendol-Hoppey (2008) suggest four different structures for teachers and prospective teachers to collaborate in conducting inquiry. *Shared inquiry* is a form of collaboration in which teachers define and conduct a single research study together. *Parallel inquiry* occurs when members of a team of teachers simultaneously conduct parallel but different individual research studies, working together to support each other's individual projects. *Intersecting inquiry* is a collaborative structure in which teachers conduct individual research studies that focus on the same topic but examine different questions and dimensions of that topic. Collaboration occurs at the point of intersection. *Inquiry support* is a configuration of teachers who assume full ownership of their research project but invite the participation of other colleagues who are not conducting any inquiry to serve as "critical friends" to raise questions and provide feedback on research design, data collection, and interpretation of data.

Several examples illustrate different patterns of collaborative action research and varied configurations of collaborative action research teams. Here I have chosen to select exemplars of collaborative action research, including several examples that do not involve university faculty, with the intention of documenting that collaborative action research does not always require a partnership with a university. Indeed, a substantial and steadily increasing amount of collaborative action research has been and continues to be conducted across the country by teams of teachers, teachers and students or parents, or community workers and youth working together in a school, school district, or local community.

For example, in Hartford, Connecticut, the Institute for Community Research, a nonprofit community organization, sponsors the Youth Action Research Institute (YARI). YARI promoted the use of action research for personal, group, and community development and employs a prevention research educator to work with teachers, youth workers, and youth action researchers in schools and afterschool programs throughout Connecticut. Youth/adult teams are trained in ethnography-based action research approaches and facilitation skills; they are helped to conduct in-depth analysis of their data, to present and use their research findings for social problem solving, advocacy in a peer leadership program, and community change. They also work as part of youth/adult training teams to disseminate action research approaches, methods, and strategies to other adults and young people who wish to do similar work in their schools and communities.

The Youth Action Research Group (YARG) operates in the Washington, D.C. neighborhoods of Mount Pleasant and Columbia Heights, where high school students and community activists, with the help and financial support of the Georgetown University Volunteer and Public Service Center, founded YARG after a series of monthly after-school meetings and community forums that focused on neighborhood issues. YARG was established with the goal of developing new leaders and engaging more people in community organizing and local citizenship. The high school students initially were trained in collaborative participatory action research and ethnography and participated in a 3-month community-based research project in the neighborhood where the students lived and went to school. Today, YARG is concerned about gentrification, displacement, loss, abandonment, and greed in their neighborhoods; it strives to investigate, document, and include the untold stories of the people who live in, work in, and build communities in neighborhoods undergoing massive transformation.

In Concord, New Hampshire, teams of teachers meet every Tuesday using the collaborative action research process to improve the district's mathematics program. Teams work together to ask questions, examine assumptions, analyze data, and develop action strategies to improve instruction and student learning. The process is based on an inquiry approach developed by Love (2001) that calls for looking at an instructional/learning problem through many lenses and for disaggregating test data to highlight results for individual subsets such as grade level and gender, ethnic, or economic group. Teachers use a variety of data sources, including standardized tests, performance assessments, student work, enrollment figures, classroom observations, and interviews. Solutions are revised to reflect changing contexts and goals. "In (these) inquiry-based schools, teachers and administrators continually ask questions about how to improve student learning, experiment with new ideas, and rigorously use data to uncover problems and monitor results" (Love, 2001, p. 111).

At the Action Research Laboratory in Highland Park High School in Highland Park, Illinois, teachers conduct inquiry in their classes to improve student learning. Interdisciplinary teams of three teachers collaborate in research, using both qualitative and quantitative methodologies, to study new ideas in instruction, curriculum development, and assessment that will increase student learning. Several teachers who have participated in the research promoted by the Action Research Laboratory now function as facilitators for other research teams.

In the Crewe Primary School, Virginia (Reynolds-Johnson, 1997), a team of parents, teachers, and the school administrator conducted an action research study focusing on issues of parental involvement. The team's study generated a number of strategies that were used to enhance the involvement of parents in their children's education. In applying the action research process to the problem of parent involvement, the team also learned how to use action research to address other areas in the school requiring improvement.

Throughout the nation in 10 different locations, 150 teachers participate in the Teachers Network Policy Institute, which connects the data from their action research studies to the development of policy recommendations to improve student achievement (Meyers, 2003). Classroom teachers conduct action research studies on a variety of issues in their classrooms and schools and document their work in papers and publications, which are then disseminated locally and nationally. The teachers, who are fellows of the network, participate in major conferences, join influential task forces, and present their work to local districts and school boards—all for the purpose of using their research to influence policy in their schools, districts, and unions, as well as at the state and national levels.

In the Seattle-Puget Sound, Washington, area, 40 teachers from 10 high schools conduct collaborative action research on block scheduling and effective teaching and learning (Marshak, 1997). Seeking to build a knowledge base about the relationship between block scheduling and effective teaching and learning, four teachers from each of the participating high schools form research teams facilitated by a university professor from Seattle University. Each team formulates its own questions, develops data collection procedures, collects and analyzes data, writes its own conclusions about the meaning of the studies and their implications for practice, and then shares the studies for critique by two teams of Puget Sound-area high school teachers.

The faculty at Aire Libre Elementary School in Phoenix, Arizona, was concerned about student differences in achievement and attitudes toward mathematics design. Teachers conducted a quasi-experimental study comparing mastery learning in mathematics with traditional mathematics instruction (Schaefer, 1989). Data sources include scores on district-developed criterion-referenced tests, along with lesson plans and information about instructional methods and materials, variations in group size, grouping procedures, student evaluation procedures, and criteria. Their data analysis generates research-based instructional and curriculum decisions for the improvement of student achievement.

The Supporting Teachers as Researchers Project (STAR) provides teams of two to four teachers in the Elkhart Community School system in northern Indiana with opportunities to conduct classroom action research studies on topics of mutual interest (Mettetal & Cowen, 2000). More than 100 teachers have participated in the STAR program, investigating a variety of instructional and curriculum issues: the use of a multiple intelligence approach to teaching mathematics, the use of the Internet to enhance learning in the classroom, and the effect of multiage classrooms on student learning. Research proposals are submitted early in the school year, and final research reports are presented in May at a research fair and dinner. Abstracts and reports are made available to all schools in the Elkhart system. Follow-up studies indicate that the STAR program has had a positive impact on student learning, increased active learning in the classroom, and increased reflective practice and collegiality among teachers.

Ways of Knowing: Teachers as Constructors of Knowledge

These examples demonstrate that collaborative action research places great emphasis on the involvement of those who have traditionally been "researched" to identify problems, collect data, interpret information, and apply findings to solve problems. Knowledge is power. Collaborative action research answers the question of who has the right to create knowledge by arguing that the expected beneficiaries of research (teachers, students, parents) should design and carry out their own research. Three assumptions underlie this approach: (1) parity in decision making among the participants conducting the study, (2) respect for the unique perspective of each constituency, and (3) equal assumption of responsibility among each participant in the collaborative research and theory development process (Mergendoller, 1979).

Seven critical practices that facilitate collaborative work and cut across the traditional boundaries and cultures of universities and schools include talking about teaching, sharing planning and teaching, making classroom observations, developing pedagogical skills, engaging in systematic and collegial study, conducting team research, and communicating with a wide audience (Rosaen, 1995). The interaction and the cumulative effect of these practices foster a collegial learning environment, a process of professional development, and knowledge construction in which teachers' learning is grounded in the practical work they do and research is viewed as integral to the realities of classroom life.

Teacher construction of knowledge involves an awareness of different ways of knowing, how these ways of knowing interact, and how relations between these ways of knowing can be changed so that thoughtful action is grounded in them (Heron & Reason, 1997). *Experiential knowing* is tacit knowing involving direct face-to-face encounters with a person, place, or thing. It arises through participation with others; it is knowing through empathy and resonance, and it is very difficult to put into words. *Presentational knowing* emerges from experiential knowing and provides its first expression through forms of imagery such as poetry and story, drawing, sculpture, movement, and dance. It bridges experiential knowing and propositional knowing. *Propositional knowing* "about" something is knowing through ideas and theories, is expressed in abstract language or mathematics, and ultimately is grounded in our experiential articulation of a world. *Practical knowing* is knowing how to do something, demonstrated in a skill or competence.

In an important sense, practical knowledge is primary (Heron, 1996).

It presupposes a conceptual grasp of principles and standards of practice, presentational elegance, and experiential grounding in the situation within which the action occurs. It fulfills the three prior forms of knowing, brings them into fruition with purposive deeds, and consummates them with an autonomous celebration of excellent accomplishment. (Heron & Reason, 1997, p. 281)

In collaborative action research, then, teacher knowing becomes more valid, richer, deeper, more true to life, and more useful—if these four ways of knowing are congruent with each other; if teachers' knowing is grounded in their experiences, expressed through their stories and images, understood as their personal theories that make sense to them, and expressed in worthwhile action in their classrooms and schools.

Awareness of these ways of knowing is essential to developing a "reframing mind," which "continually overcomes itself, divesting itself of its own presuppositions" (Torbert, 2004, p. 211). Constructing knowledge requires critical consciousness about our ways of knowing, which necessarily includes the processes of collaborative action research: sharing experiences, participating in critical dialogue, providing feedback, formulating new ideas and questions, and exchanging knowledge and insights with others. In collaborative action research, then, participants work together reflecting on their experiences and problematic situations to define the educational questions they wish to explore and develop the methodology for their exploration (propositional knowing); they apply their methodology in their world of educational practice (practical knowing); doing so generates new forms of encounter with their classroom or school world (experiential knowing); they identify approaches to represent this experience in meaningful patterns (presentational knowledge); this leads to revised propositional knowledge of the originating questions, thus completing one cycle through these four forms of knowing—a cycle that may be repeated several times (Heron, 1996; Heron & Reason, 1997; Reason & Heron, 1995). Moreover, as teachers cycle through these forms of knowing, they not only identify practical theories that apply to their own idiosyncratic settings but also formulate these practical theories as general hypotheses that have the potential for generalizability in contexts similar to their unique settings.

Finally, in collaborative action research, knowledge is developed through relationships with others, acknowledging that there is a ceiling to how much we learn and grow if we keep to ourselves (Fishman & McCarthy, 2000; Fullan & Hargreaves, 1996). Knowing and learning are communal acts. They require a continual cycle of discussion, disagreement, and consensus over what has been said and what it all means. The process of constructing knowledge in relationship with others suggests that the dominance of the metaphor of knowing as power can be transcended by a new metaphor—knowing as loving (Palmer, 1983). Instead of viewing reality as something to be mastered, analyzed, formed, and shaped to our ends or learning as "mastering" ideas, "grasping" concepts, "wrestling" with problems and "cracking" them, this *relational knowing* sees another kind of knowledge is available to us, one that begins in a different passion and is drawn toward other ends. . . . This is a knowledge that originates not in curiosity or control but in compassion or love—a source not celebrated in our intellectual tradition but in our spiritual heritage . . . the act of knowing is an act of love, the act of entering and embracing the reality of the other, of allowing the other to enter and embrace our own. (Palmer, 1983, p. 8)

Magolda (1995) contrasts this kind of relational knowing with patterns of impersonal knowing, which are characterized by separation, abstraction, autonomy, objectivity, and rationality. Relational knowing is at the heart of collaborative action research, where knowing starts from a relationship between self and other; where knowing involves acting in relationships and creating meaning in our lives with others; where relationships with others inform inquiry and practice to construct knowledge out of caring and love for students.

Teachers as Agents of Change

In addition to generating new knowledge, the collaborative research process can be of immediate and direct benefit to a school and its constituents in advancing change. Through collaborative action research, schools become centers for change as opposed to targets for change. "One would have to look long and hard to find a single school endeavor that incorporates more of the essential findings of the change literature than collaborative action research" (Sagor, 1997, p. 193). Although it is important that the school and the community gain from the results of the ongoing research, it is just as important that they gain from the action research process itself. This means that teachers, students, and members of the community—as they participate in the research process—are able to articulate emerging problems and to initiate processes to find solutions. Teachers who identify real problems of concern to themselves give considerable thought to creating interventions to change their situations and to assessing whether these interventions work.

For example, Mohr (1987) found that teachers participating in a collaborative teacher research project on writing transformed their teaching. As they studied their own classroom issues, they became more confident and open to change. They became more willing to confront and engage difficult questions about their teaching and to interrogate their beliefs and attitudes about themselves and their students. As their research and teaching melded, they began to see teaching more as a learning process rather than a daily routine or performance. Teaching and research became integrated. Teachers moved from evaluating their classroom experiences, positive or negative, to documenting what was happening in the classroom. They refined and revised their teaching as they refined and revised their research. As they became more sensitive to the complexities of classroom context, they risked trying new ways of teaching. The nature of classroom discourse changed, and teachers and students moved toward a more collaborative relationship in advancing the quality of learning and teaching.

In changing their teaching, these teachers illustrated that the fundamental principle of collaborative participatory research and its point of most radical departure from orthodox research is that the research process is based on a system of discussion, investigation, and analysis in which teachers, students, and parents, who in traditional research were the "researched," are now the researchers. Theories are neither developed beforehand to be tested, nor drawn by the researcher from his or her involvement with reality. Reality is described by the process through which a school, community, and its teachers, parents, and children develop their own theories and solutions about themselves and their situations.

Teachers want to make a difference in the lives of their students, and they bring a sense of moral purpose to their work. Their moral purpose is embedded in their commitment to making improvements in teaching and student learning—the raison d'être of collaborative action research. The process of collaborative action research facilitates the development of personal vision building, inquiry, mastery in the form of growing indigenous expertise, and of course, collaboration— four essential ingredients for teachers to become effective change agents (Fullan, 1993).

Because action research is essentially a process of change, teachers participating in collaborative action research become more aware of the change process. Indeed, they become agents of their own change, using action research to grow personally and professionally, developing understandings, insights, skills, and dispositions that empower them to solve problems and improve educational practice. Their approach to change is not naïve. They understand and experience the complexities and difficulties of change, both small incremental changes in their instruction and more substantial changes in the school curriculum or organization. In addressing these complexities of change, they develop understandings and skills in coping with the stress, uncertainty, and contextual boundaries that affect any change effort.

Collaborative Action Research and Scholarship

Collaborative action research yields its own findings regarding the effectiveness of different research-based strategies in different situations with different pools of available resources and for different kinds of content. As Massanari (1978) suggests,

> Such findings should be collected, synthesized, and disseminated to the education community. They would be valuable and needed contributions to the knowledge base that supports professional development. Publications such as "What's Working Where" and "What Didn't Work Here" would be welcomed by the education profession. (p. 53)

Collaborative action research involving university and school partnerships requires the coordination of the publication and research interests of university faculty, the thesis research of graduate students, and the term paper requirements of graduate and undergraduate students with the problem-solving and professional development needs of teachers. It offers the opportunity for intensive involvement between university and school faculty and consequently the implementation of cross-contextualized research, which integrates academic and school contexts. It offers mutual sharing and stimulation of curriculum development, teaching, and measurement problems and the sense of participating in intellectually coordinated research on "large" educational problems (at least as contrasted to the more typical thesis and term paper topic).

Most important, collaborative action research is substantial professional inquiry and scholarship in its scope, its epistemology, and its outcome. A teacher with this orientation and skill in action research is no longer static or dependent on others for professional progress. The teacher's own professional growth and competence are enhanced. Teachers feel professionally alive, and they feel effective—in that they can do something about their profession. If action research meets these goals, then we are really describing a generic process of inquiry and growth that has the potential to reform education.

University faculty, graduate students, and teachers learn and grow together in the collaborative process to develop communities of inquiry that produce knowledge from practice. The intellectual and professional process of producing new knowledge about problems in teaching, curriculum, and school change is the raison d'être of action research. Producing knowledge from practice results from an alternating cycle of reflection and action, critical thinking, careful practice, and evaluation designed to generate a more comprehensive understanding of educational problems and their possible solutions.

Teacher-oriented inquiry and the view of the school and the class-room as the proper focus of research action will come about when pro-fessors and teachers change their attitudes and perceptions about inquiry and research. Some time ago, McKenna (1978) spoke clearly to this point:

> Many researchers will have to revise their posture that scholars mustn't get their hands dirty with the clay; that the potting must be done by others, once the scholars have prescribed the clay mix and kiln temperature. More specifically, the attitude that you can't learn much in the "messy" situation of the ordinary class-room will need to be replaced with one that accepts real schools as the most appropriate places for conducting research and development. And researchers will need to come to recognize teachers as peers, as colleagues, who have much to contribute to improving the R&D process, from identifying researchable issues, determining research design, data gathering and analysis, to planning programs based on findings. Once these are accom-plished, new strategies for conducting research may need to be devised and tested in order to inquire into the multidimensional problems that are identified for study. Teachers on their part will need to reconceptualize their roles to include involvement in inquiry and problem-solving on instructional issues. And they will need to gain confidence on their ability to contribute on a parity basis to the research and development process. (p. 3)

Schools as Centers of Inquiry

The integration of research and service through collaborative action research can help our schools become centers of inquiry (Schaefer, 1967), where university faculty and teachers inquire sys-tematically on such fundamental issues as what is to be taught, how, by whom, where, and with what outcomes for students and teachers. The process of systematic inquiry constitutes effective and meaningful professional development. Significant learning and growth occur when teachers and university researchers work together in carrying out research to solve problems that concern themselves and the schools. Collaboration of this kind generates opportunities for teachers and university faculty to develop a common language and multiple conceptual frameworks for exploring and reflecting on what happens in classrooms.

The school is a fertile and abundant field for research. In any one school, there are innumerable authentic researchable problems for teachers to investigate, research that warrants the support and attention of foundations, universities, and governmental agencies. Jackson (1968) notes that the classroom teacher typically engages in as many as 1,000 interpersonal exchanges during the course of a 6-hour day in the classroom, frequently averaging 200 to 300 interpersonal transactions per hour, an observation that testifies to the complexity and immediacy of the daily situation in which every teacher is forced to make decisions. A single school is a "research goldmine" in terms of important questions, variety and richness of data, and numbers of potential researchers. I believe very deeply that educational research must be fashioned from the fabric of the questions and problems of the school. The practical orientation of the school provides a research perspective that fits the unique and rich character of educational problems and questions. The dominant chord of school- and classroom-oriented research supplants the ethos of knowledge for the sake of knowledge, with inquiry that generates useable knowledge that spawns decision, action, and change.

Paradoxically, it is the knowledge generated from practice that will enrich our conceptual understandings and educational theory. The action-reflection-teaching-evaluation cycle feeds on itself epistemologically. Collaborative action research adds to both conceptualizing and practice by validating one against the other.

> To suggest that theoretical and practical research can be conceived as thesis and antithesis enables the possibility of synthesis. It runs the risk, admittedly, of oversimplification; but surely there must be hope for productive combinations of practical and theoretical orientations. (Schubert, 1980, p. 23)

❖ THE INTERACTION OF INDIVIDUAL AND COLLABORATIVE ACTION RESEARCH

The effectiveness of teacher action research as a way to improve education and as a professional development process has been demonstrated by a number of middle school teachers who, in collaboration with university faculty, conducted studies to address curriculum, instructional, and learning problems (Pine, 1979). The teacher-researchers engaged in parallel studies and met weekly in groups to share their work, to provide feedback to each other on research design and implementation and data analysis, to identify common themes emanating from their studies, and to build a culture of collaboration and support for each teacher's work.

What is competency testing? Who determines what competencies students must master? How are they measured? Who designs competency tests? How are they used to help children? John Stokel and Marian Fritz, middle-school mathematics teachers, were concerned about these questions and translated their concerns into a comprehensive, ongoing research study involving the use of computers and a humanistic approach to working with students. Both of these teachers, while taking a graduate course on tests and measurements, decided to study the application of the principles underlying competency testing to individualize instruction in mathematics. Their study generated data that promoted individual student learning in the mathematics program by constructing tests to provide specific individualized feedback to advance each student's understanding of mathematical concepts.

Inappropriate student behavior is a concern for many classroom teachers; among them is Lorna Healey, who was responsible for providing instruction for special needs students with behavioral problems. Lorna was interested in studying ways to help students develop more positive classroom behavior. With her colleagues, she developed an approach using a combination of learning reinforcements and individualized instruction to change the inappropriate behavior of one of her students. She wrote a case study that provides rich detail identifying the significant variables that influence behavior and indicates how these factors can be dealt with in changing behavior. Her case study yields useful observations for all those interested in helping special needs youngsters realize their potential.

Bob Blomquist, an eighth-grade mathematics teacher, studied the question of how teaching and learning styles can be appropriately matched to improve instruction. Through computerized library searches and extensive reading, he conducted a comprehensive review of the literature dealing with teaching and learning styles. He then generated a process that enables teachers to analyze teaching and learning styles and to match the teaching styles most appropriate for each individual student's learning style. His review of the literature proved to be of great practical value and demonstrates that synthesizing and adapting previous research can be very useful for the classroom teacher who wants to reach each student.

Teaching writing is a national educational concern and an area that has been addressed by many action research studies. Sandra Woodworth, an English teacher who was interested in improving instruction in writing, studied the professional literature of action research and assessment to determine the most valid approach for assessing a student's writing and the most effective ways of teaching writing. She conducted a study on students' perceptions of what constitutes good writing. Her study focused on student interests and perceptions and how these could be best assessed and used in generating high-quality writing that reflected the individual voices of her students.

Lois Cynewski had long been interested in an individualized and independent learning approach to home economics. She developed a large number of independent learning packages, which she used and revised in the home economics curriculum. Her study focused on what she learned in developing her unique approach and how her findings could be used by other home economics teachers. She conducted a study on reading levels of home economics instructional materials, developed a collection of recipes that appeal to junior high school-age students, and designed a thorough, systematic, and carefully thought out approach for promoting independent learning in home economics. Her work is of great value to middle-school home economics teachers and contains many concrete ideas, which she has carefully evaluated.

How do you evaluate the teaching performance of an instructor who has implemented an individualized and open approach to education? Concerned about this question, Peter Frechette designed an evaluation system that incorporated student evaluation, self-evaluation, and supervisor evaluation of the teacher, using an individualized approach to instruction. He tested this approach and evaluated and continually modified it, collecting data from students, colleagues, and the principal. His study included a number of instruments that can be used by other teachers who are individualizing instruction and who wish to have their performance evaluated within the context of a philosophy of individualization. Among the instruments included in this study were Student Assessment of Instruction, Instructor Self-Evaluation, and an Observation Form for Assessing Individualized Instruction. How these instruments were used and the process of evaluation are described in Peter's study, which should be of great interest to principals and teachers concerned about alternative approaches to teacher evaluation.

Jean Woodworth, an English teacher, introduced a number of changes in her classroom, then studied how effective these changes were in improving the classroom learning climate and the effectiveness of instruction. She introduced a system of peer observation and feedback to improve classroom climate, small-group and individualized learning approaches, the use of student journals to record personal reactions about learning, and the use of moral dilemmas to generate moral sensitivity and ideas for group discussion and student writing. Jean also redesigned her classroom to facilitate structured and nonstructured approaches to teaching. Her retrospective study documents the implementation of these approaches and their impact on student learning and growth.

Jean Arsenault, a home economics teacher, tried out individualized learning packets and was concerned about whether they were effectively addressing the individual learning needs of students in her heterogeneously grouped classes. She documented the introduction and implementation of the units and described how they have been revised and what their impact was on student learning. Included in her research is a diagnostic procedure that helps her and her students in identifying the appropriate learning units to be used with each student. Her study evaluates the effectiveness of this individualized approach and offers a guide with a number of recommendations for teachers who wish to implement a similar approach in home economics.

Peer teaching has generated many research findings that appear in the professional literature. Bernie Smith, a mathematics teacher, implemented a peer tutoring program, which required identification and training of student instructors and the development of an effective management system for using student instructors. He compared the effectiveness of this approach with other approaches to teaching mathematics and collected data to determine the impact of peer tutoring, not only on learning but also on the attitude of middle-school students toward themselves and their peers. He gathered these data primarily through a questionnaire that included objective and open-ended items for collecting information about the results of peer tutoring on the affective and cognitive aspects of learning.

An intriguing question for some teachers is how an individualized approach to instruction can be introduced and phased into their classrooms while other, more traditional approaches are maintained. Sue Parr, a social studies teacher, investigated the problems and the effects of partial individualization of her social studies curriculum. For 2 or 3 days a week, she individualized her classroom, and the other days, she used more traditional group-centered approaches. She developed a number of curriculum units to facilitate individualization and addressed the question of how to engage students to use learning stations in the social studies curriculum. She designed several learning stations, which, in combination with her curriculum units, constituted the main thrust of her individualization program. Her research documented this approach and its effects on student learning.

Walter Barrett and Louise Novak used a multilevel individualized approach to teaching mathematics. Their approach is characterized by a great deal of flexibility, which enables students to move in and out of different levels of mathematics according to their interests and abilities. They designed their program to meet the individual needs of all middle-school students in their math classes. They collected data from 150 students to determine how students feel about multilevel individualized instruction. The results of their study proved to be of value to other middle-school mathematics teachers concerned about maximizing learning for all students in mathematics.

Ronald Fortier, a social studies teacher, was interested in simulation theory and how it could be translated into practical approaches to facilitate moral development. He designed several simulations and tested them in his classroom. The design of the simulations required an extensive review of the professional literature and a careful consideration of how simulation theory can be best translated in authentic ways within the context of a middle-school social studies curriculum. His research described the implementation of the simulations, their revisions, and the ultimate impact of the simulations on student learning.

❖ SUMMARY

In summary, these authentic examples make evident the value of action research in addressing instructional and learning problems. The process of conducting classroom and school problem-centered research with systematic peer support and collaboration constitutes one of the most promising ways to improve learning for students. The middle-school teachers who conducted the studies described here give evidence of the commitment and collaborative involvement of inquiring professionals, who are continually learning, innovating, and evaluating to enhance the learning of their students. Finally, they demonstrate the potential of collaborative action research as a supportive and an energizing strategy for school improvement and as a powerful form of professional development.

7

Conditions
for Building a
Knowledge Democracy

In this chapter, I discuss in some detail the critical elements of collaborative action research that are essential to building a knowledge democracy. These elements include developing a "work with" posture, establishing systemic and relational trust, finding enough time to build relationships and conduct research, confronting issues inherent in building collaboration between university faculty and classroom teachers, including students and parents as research partners in collaborative action research studies, and learning how to collaborate and dealing with the challenges of collaboration.

❖ DEVELOPING A "WORK WITH" POSTURE

Collaborative action research liberates teachers' creative potential, stimulates their abilities to investigate their own situations, and mobilizes human resources to solve educational problems. Collaborative research begins when university researchers, teachers, and other combinations of partners assist each other in developing the skills to identify and conceptualize problems.

Collaborative action research is a process in which teachers and researchers work with parity and assume equal responsibility to identify, inquire into, and resolve the problems of classroom teachers. Such collaboration recognizes and utilizes the unique insights and skills provided by each participant while, at the same time, demanding that no set of capabilities is assigned a superior status. It assumes a *work with* rather than a *work on* posture—the latter being more frequently the modus operandi when teachers are asked to join researchers in a linear R&D endeavor. (Tickunoff, Ward, & Griffin, 1979, p. 15)

The *work on* posture has been typical of traditional research approaches characterized by technical processes in which educational researchers keep the key decisions outside the school and away from teachers. This approach prevents teachers and the school from becoming the subject of their own transformation. Freire (1973) insists that methodological failings can always be traced to ideological errors. An implicit ideology of paternalism, social control, and nonreciprocity between experts and "helpees" underlies traditional positivistic research. (In the traditional research study, one finds the word *subjects*—interesting language, which suggests that someone must be the *ruler* or the manipulator.) To adopt the collaborative action research model, which fosters dialogue and reciprocity, one must first be ideologically committed to equality, to the abolition of privilege, and to nonelitist forms of research leadership wherein special qualifications may be exercised but are not perpetuated.

The tradition and culture of the academic research establishment are difficult to change and could be problematic in collaborative action research. More than 60 years ago, teachers were encouraged to conduct research on educational problems (Buckingham, 1926, 1939; Dewey, 1929; Good, Barr, & Scates, 1936; Waples & Tyler, 1930), but they served primarily as assistants to university researchers and not as genuine partners. Even today, it would be easy for teachers to become consultants to, rather than full participants in the research process, a situation in which teachers' voices might be "selectively appropriated" in service of university values and ideologies (Hargreaves, 1996). Thus, action research would become colonized in promoting the agenda and research interests of teacher-educators; university academics would become the sole directors of the research while the practitioners become simply the "cooperative" objects of study. Indeed, Elliott (1991) warns that action research could be "hijacked" by university academics:

Action research and the teacher as researchers' movement are enthusiastically promoted in academia. But the question is: are the academics transforming the methodology of teacher-based inquiry into a form which enables them to manipulate and control teachers' thinking in order to reproduce the central assumptions which have underpinned a contemplative academic culture detached from the practices of everyday life? (p. 14)

And Cochran-Smith and Lytle (1998) sound another warning about the potential consequences inherent in the emerging paradox of teacher research:

As it [teacher research] is used in the service of more and more agendas and even institutionalized in certain contexts, it is in danger of becoming anything and everything. As we know however, anything and everything lead in the end to nothing of consequence. It would be unfortunate indeed if the generative nature of teacher research contributed either to its marginalization and trivialization on the one hand or its subtle cooptation or colonization on the other. (p. 21)

If teachers are to be full partners in research, they must be co-researchers who share with university partners the responsibility for identifying the questions and the problems to be studied, establishing the design and execution of the research, and participating in the interpretation and dissemination of the results (Gajewski, 1978). If genuine, authentic, and sustained collaboration between university researchers and teacher-researchers in building communities of inquiry is to be achieved, then a number of principles need to be taken into account (Gore & Zeichner, 1995, p. 19, as cited in Grundy, 1994):

- Democracy is required in partnerships and hierarchical relationships; situations in which expertise is seen to belong more clearly to one set of participants than another are to be avoided.
- In planning the partnership, the distinctive interests of all parties need to be taken into account.
- Trust, communication, and understanding of each partner's perspectives should be developed.
- Participants must acknowledge and address problems associated with a lack of, or limits on, rewards and recognition of individuals in universities and schools for collaborative activities.

- All involved in the partnership should be jointly responsible for and involved in the planning of the partnership from the very beginning.

The principles listed here suggest a new way of thinking about collaboration involving university faculty and K–12 classroom teachers. Soltis (1994) voices the emerging nature of authentic collaboration between teachers and university faculty: "Genuine collaboration will not only require new teachers in new school cultures and structures, but also new teacher educators, new cultures in schools of education, and altered university structures" (p. 255).

So the obvious question is, How do we in education build genuine collaboration, a new kind of collaboration that can fundamentally change our knowledge base for significantly improving teaching and learning? The challenge is great, but we can create the conditions required for building a knowledge democracy through collaboration by developing systemic and relational trust; finding time to do what needs to be done; dealing with the issues confronting classroom teachers and university faculty; actively engaging students, parents, and community members as equal partners in our collaboration; and deliberately and explicitly focusing on what it takes to achieve full collaboration.

❖ ESTABLISHING TRUST

Trust is an essential condition for conducting collaborative action research (Tschannen-Moran & Hoy, 2000, 2001). Systemic trust is invisible but a necessary condition for collaborative inquiry. In contrast, systemic mistrust defeats the goals and the process of collaborative research. Indeed, collaborative action research provides one of the best mechanisms for exploring the dynamic tensions between trust and mistrust. Most of us regard trust as a personal characteristic, but Niklas Luhmann (1980), in his work *Trust and Power*, has shown that it has a systemic character as well. For example, money is a medium of trust because it communicates fixed expectations at a general level. Even though we may occasionally worry about banks, we go about our daily lives with reasonable confidence that money can be exchanged for goods. Another example of system trust is generated by specialized authority or expertise. We assume the car mechanic will fix the automobile and that newspaper accounts have some degree of reliability.

When we call for a taxi, we assume that we will be safely delivered to our destination. Legitimate political power also builds trust because it is based on expectations about what will be done when the officeholder is elected; it assumes a style of decision making that will be acceptable enough for the individual to live in a given society.

Familiarity is closely related to trust because both are complementary ways of absorbing complexity. Trust is an attitude that one learns from experience and then expands to other phenomena. In contrast, mistrust increases complexity: One can never be sure of others, so one must check to confirm information, operate independently, and be on guard.

Trust, however, contains an element of risk because it can be misplaced. According to Luhmann (1980, p. 24):

> One who hopes has confidence despite uncertainty.
>
> Trust reflects contingency. Hope ignores contingency.

According to Luhmann, the greatest value of trust is that it is a way of dealing with complexity. Because all systems in turbulent environments are threatened with instability, information overload, and uncertainty, this function of trust is important. Any researcher trying to understand phenomena that exist under such conditions must learn how to deal with complexity. In sum, because complexity is characteristic of turbulent environments, trust becomes a tool of inquiry.

How does trust deal with complexity? First, it orders information processing into the system. Because reality is too complex to control, trust substitutes for complexity. It is no longer necessary to absorb all information: Only some is relevant. Trust enables the selection to be made with ease. By trusting another person or a medium that communicates trust, one has the opportunity to act spontaneously and quickly. Through trust, individuals and systems gain time to react: System risks are kept under control. Moreover, complexity is reduced because it is possible to go beyond available information to generalize expectations of behavior. Trust "replaces missing information with an internally guaranteed security" (Luhmann, 1980, p. 93). In other words, collaboration requires trust as an input condition in order to stimulate facilitative and supportive processes to minimize uncertainty and system risk. Thus, trust depends on risk reduction mechanisms such as language and organization, but it cannot be reduced to these.

Trust involves relationships and interactions with other people. Systemic trust is bound up in *relational trust* (Bryk & Schneider, 2002), which is an organizational property defined through the reciprocal exchanges among participants in an organization such as a school. Bryk and Schneider (2002, pp. 22–26) indicate that these exchanges reflect a dynamic interplay among four ways of viewing each other: with respect, with competence, with personal regard for others, and with integrity. As a fundamental element of relational trust, respect is reflected in the ways in which we acknowledge one another's dignity and ideas, the extent to which we interact in courteous ways with each other, and our ability to talk genuinely and to listen empathically to each other. Competence is expressed through our belief in each other's ability and willingness to fulfill our responsibilities effectively. Do we have faith and confidence in each other's ability to perform our duties and responsibilities completely? Personal regard is demonstrated in genuine caring about each other both personally and professionally. It manifests itself to the degree we are willing to go beyond what is expected—to transcend our roles and responsibilities—to go the extra mile to help each other. The fourth element of integrity requires that a moral and ethical perspective guide our work in putting the interests of children first, especially when the most difficult decisions have to be made, and that we keep our word.

Trust involves vulnerability and risk. Trust is based on trust in ourselves, repetitive interactions, predictability of human behavior, reliability, dependability, meaningful communication, reciprocity, honesty, concern for others, and a reasonable degree of certainty in an often uncertain world. Trust is nurtured in a school environment characterized by good communication, shared decision making, opportunities for collegial learning, networking with outside environments, a norm of experimentation, and a commitment to continuous inquiry (Fullan & Hargreaves, 1996).

The paradox of systemic/relational trust is that as it reduces one level of risk, at another level, it creates opportunities for risk taking. Systemic and relational trust provide freedom to engage in projects that one would not or could not undertake on one's own; it is an essential requirement for collaborative inquiry (Solomon & Flores, 2001):

> Trust opens new and unimagined possibilities. Trust is not bound up in knowledge as much as it is with freedom, the openness to the unknown. This means moving beyond the realm of Knowing What We Know to the richer realm of Knowing What We Do Not Know, and the even richer realm of learning What We Do Not Even Know That We Do Not Know. This is not a realm that most of us can enter alone. We can arrive there only with and through other people. And for that, we have to trust them. (p. 50)

Trust is more than an attribute or product—it is

an empathic procedure to guide action and interaction . . . trust connects knowledge and knower in a meaningful way; it honors relationships and experience. Trust, in friendship and in research, directs what we can know and how we can know, and confirms intelligence as a social relation. (Donawa, 1998, p. 4)

As a relational and social ethic, trust involves five key elements:

- *Benevolence.* Having confidence that another party has your best interest at heart and will protect your interests is a key ingredient of trust.
- *Reliability.* Reliability refers to the extent to which you can depend upon another party to come through for you, to act consistently, and to follow through.
- *Competence.* Similar to reliability, competence has to do with belief in another party's ability to perform the tasks required by his or her position.
- *Honesty.* A person's integrity, character, and authenticity are all dimensions of trust. The degree to which a person can be counted on to represent positions fairly makes a huge difference in whether or not she or he is trusted by others.
- *Openness.* Judgments about openness have to do with how freely another party shares information with others. Guarded communication provokes distrust because people wonder what is being withheld and why. (Tschannen-Moran & Hoy, 1998)

In recognizing how essential trust is for risk taking, we face certain inevitable conclusions about collaborative research activities. Building collaboration involves building trust. First of all, to generate trust in processes adds significant costs of time and energy. Everyone involved in the collaborative inquiry must find time, allocate resources, and give serious importance to building relationships and systemic trust. Trust is learned as well as earned. Trust requires a personal investment of attention and commitment to developing and maintaining relationships over time. We trust first in people, then in social relationships, in processes, and in structures. Second, trust requires that all who participate in action research assume serious ethical commitments in the process of conducting inquiry to protect the rights and privileges of teachers, students, and parents; to ensure that no party is exploited for the purposes of research; and to protect the school site from exploitation.

Finally, trust becomes the main criterion in reporting research findings. It is more than protecting those involved in the generation of data: It demands that reports are documents of integrity that provide understanding, insight, and wisdom as well as information.

❖ FINDING ENOUGH TIME

In *New Rules,* a prescient book, Yankelovich (1981) observed that a significant number of people now have aspirations that are less family bound than people's goals just several decades ago. Their time commitments are dictated primarily by their own aspirations for self-fulfillment. They maintain complex personal time schedules, often involving major commitments to education, travel, personal health and exercise programs, and experiments in interpersonal living and child care arrangements. They are involved in a variety of what used to be called "leisure pursuits," as well as in their work as a source of both income and personal satisfaction.

The dynamics of these people's lives are a countervailing force to the time demands imposed by the older family-bound industrial order. As a result, many employers and employees have been experimenting with a variety of new personal time styles for individual workers. Implementing flexible work schedules and job sharing, reallocating work time, making released time provisions, shifting work online to home offices, compressing work schedules, and using other work time schemes increase the flexibility of institutional time systems to respect a variety of personal time schedules and styles and to accommodate easy movements of individuals into and out of work environments.

Where do teachers fit into this kind of time experimentation? Briod (1982), in his study of the American school time system, hypothesized that teachers are viewed as a base of traditional middle-class reliability in American communities, teaching under a relatively unbending school time system at the very period in our history when experimentation with work, personal, and social time is increasing in society at large.

Although those outside the school community may point with envy to those vaunted summer vacations, and with anger to what seems like short daily time schedules, they require the regularity and reliability of school time in order to plan their own flexible schedules. Teachers, on the other hand, feel dissonance about a school time system that seems excessively bureaucratic, vaguely sensing that the American "time revolution" is passing them by.

The lonesomeness and isolation of teaching have been well documented by Lortie (1975) and Sarason (1982). The boundaries of the classroom and the cellular forms of school organization minimize teacher-teacher interaction, the rewards of teaching are experienced in isolation from peers, contacts with a variety of adults are limited, almost all of a teacher's time is spent with children, and consequently, teachers are psychologically alone even though they are in a densely populated setting. The isolation, autonomy, and loneliness of teaching mitigate a sense of common purpose and responsibility, a sense of belonging, give-and-take discussion, reflection, collaboration, and a norm of innovation and experimentation. Satisfaction in the classroom is no palliative for loneliness and isolation. The need to plan and prepare instruction and materials jointly, to share concerns, and to build relationships is not completely fulfilled in the classroom. Collegiality and collaboration require time arrangements that build continuity and opportunity for developing relationships—a significant element for supporting teacher action research.

Time and the allocation of time in schools, then, is more than a measurable resource. As we shall see,

> time imposes a social order, and how things are handled in time conveys status and intention. The pacing of events, the rhythms of life, the sequence in which things are done, and the durations of events all become subject to symbolic interpretation. (Schein, 1992, pp. 114–115)

Private Time Versus Public Time

As a principle of differentiation, time serves to keep apart the private and public spheres of life (Zerubavel, 1981). Time is a major organizational principle that facilitates the institutionalization of privacy as well as segmentation of individuals along the lines of their various social and occupational involvements. By providing some rigid boundaries that segregate the private and public spheres of life from one another, time has become indispensable to the regulation and maintenance of individuals' social and occupational involvements. We can view the relative degree of the individual's social and occupational involvement at any given time as a proportion between *private time* and *public time*. For teachers, the boundaries of private and public time are blurred. Their occupational role claims their allegiance at home, on weekends, and into the night as they grade and evaluate papers and projects, write reports, fill out report cards, plan lessons, develop and write curriculum, attend afterschool and evening meetings, and assess student performance. Teaching can seem to be never ending, reaching into the private time of teachers, sapping them of energy, and creating feelings of guilt, resentment, and frustration.

Inert Time Versus Productive Time

Time conflicts and problems are continually frustrating to teachers, administrators, and all those who work within the school time system. Time is a precious resource and is "the single most important general resource teachers possess in their quest for productivity and psychic award; ineffective time allocations are costly" (Lortie, 1975, p. 177). Teachers have fought to get control over the use of their time; many collective bargaining agreements have detailed specifications on the extent to which management can make extra time demands on teachers. Contracts are likely to concentrate on "extra" time outside the regular working day. Teachers have bargained to reduce the proportion of *inert* to potentially *productive* time in the working day (Lortie, 1975, p. 176). Inert time refers to occasions when the potential for learning is absent or very low because the teacher's activities are not instructional. Clerical duties, frequent interruptions, time pressures, and extra duties all involve inert time. Potentially productive time refers to the occasions when the teacher is engaged in direct instruction of students or in activities closely related to instruction, such as the construction of lessons or curriculum units.

Sacred Time Versus Profane Time

Temporal segregation of time to distinguish between the sacred and profane spheres of life historically has been a way for societies to assign days or periods of time when religious life is separated from work life. The Sabbath, Sundays, and other periods of time traditionally have been set aside by various religious groups as time for reflection, rest, renewal, worship, and sanctification. Durkheim (1965) noted this fundamental bipartite division of time into two distinct parts that are mutually distinctive—the one being devoted to everyday "profane" activity and the other being assigned to religion:

> It is necessary to assign determined days or periods to the (religious life), from which all profane occupations are excluded. . . . There is no religion, and, consequently, no society which has not known and practiced this division of time into two distinctive parts, alternating with one another. (p. 347)

There is no question that in our contemporary world, the lines separating sacred and profane time have become blurred. Weekends, Sundays, and Sabbath no longer are viewed as special times reserved for religious observance or for rest and renewal of body and spirit. For some, these periods of time have become part of the normal working week; for others, they are a time to attend to work brought home from the office and to squeeze in shopping, household chores, and various sundry other activities. For most people, the distinction between time for the spirit, for renewal, and for refreshing the self and time for the everyday profane spheres of living has vanished. Nowhere is this more evident than in the world of teaching. As the voices of these middle school teachers, with whom I collaborated on a teacher action research study (Oja & Pine, 1983), attest, the interminability of workload reaches into precious "sacred" time:

> I just am spending most of my weekends checking papers and I begin to resent that already and it's just October. And like you said, this past weekend, I just felt like telling the kids no, I didn't get to it this weekend sorry, it was a nice sunny day and we wanted to enjoy the day too, and, you know, you get caught in guilt. I see that it's a real problem, too.

> This weekend I was exhausted. It seems so unfair to me there are so many things I want to do as a woman, and a wife, and home-maker, that I want to do as a teacher professionally, and I can't find the time to do it all. I can't do it all!

> You know what, I find the guilt trip wears you out. It wears me out. If anybody would say that you suffer, you put the guilt on yourself, I'd say I do not, but I do. I make it worse for myself. I come in on Monday after the weekend and I think, I told them I'd have the papers done today, a hundred and twenty papers, and I want to say I need a life too!! Before I know it I'm in there shaking, I'm not really shaking but the guilt inside of me is eating me so badly, I think, oh, God, please don't let one ask me because I'll just crumble. It's horrible.

Monochronic Versus Polychronic Time

Teachers see administration allocating the resource of time, which matters so much to them. Within a framework established by a school system's administration, time schedules are worked out under the principal's supervision, and the principal's decisions about schedules profoundly affect the teacher's work life. Control over the allocation of time is one of the principal's sources of power, influence, and authority. The principal's decisions in this area vitally affect teachers' working conditions and their attitudes. The principal is also the person in the school who has the most discretionary time, a characteristic of professional autonomy and status not unlike that of the lawyer, doctor, or dentist and a source of envy among teachers. The busy teacher juggling relationships with different children, trying to individualize instruction, asking and answering questions, attending to the needs of inclusion students, responding to parents, assessing student work, and making the countless decisions teachers make in a day experiences time in a polychronic time frame as opposed to a monochronic time frame (Bluedorn, Kaufman, & Lane, 1992; Hall, 1959; Hall & Hall, 1987).

Polychronic time is characterized by doing several things at once, completing transactions, being highly sensitive to context, and having an orientation toward people and relationships. Busy school administrators organize their time in a *monochronic* time frame doing one thing at a time, tending toward linear arrangements of activities, having a low sensitivity toward context, and putting an emphasis on the completion of tasks, schedules, and procedures. Polychronic time frames are common in smaller organizations, Latin and Native American cultures, and among women. Monochronic time frames are characteristic of Western culture, larger organizations, and males.

The juxtaposition of these two time frames can create tensions and conflict in any educational change effort. Restructuring a school's time frame to support a stance of inquiry and the regular conduct of teacher research is a daunting challenge. There is no question that one of the most formidable difficulties teachers encounter in doing action research is finding the time to collaborate, plan, dialogue, schedule and conduct team meetings, analyze data, and write. Teachers, by and large, view the primary allocation of teacher time as time spent in the classroom in direct contact with students. The time framework of schools has been constructed around this tradition of direct and sustained contact with students; and teacher understandings of their power, status, and efficacy are intimately related to that time framework. When teachers are asked to devote time to activities that have not been part of that tradition, as they are in restructuring time to make action research integral to their work, it can create substantial disequilibrium (Cambone, 1995).

In summary, then, teachers and administrators assign different meanings to time, and this affects how they view and allocate time. To change a school's time framework means that teachers and administrators need to reflect on the meanings they attach to time and then find ways of real-locating time in accordance with their new understandings and commitments. Because time is most precious for teachers, who are inundated with a variety of demands and expectations, it is not surprising that in one major collaborative action research study (Oja & Pine, 1983), a team of middle school teacher-researchers identified school scheduling as the primary focus of their research:

> We see scheduling affecting all dimensions of the middle school. Time is one of the most valuable resources in the educational system and decisions about its allocation affect the curriculum, student learning, student/teacher relationships and opportunities for innovation. The schedule reflects priorities and values about the educational process in the school. It can provide significant flexibility or severely limit flexibility. It can promote collegiality or fragmentation. The schedule can serve the school and its students or it can make the school and students its servants. The ramifications of scheduling are pervasive and touch upon almost every aspect of the school. In our judgement it is an area worthy of action research. (p. 3)

One member of the team writes in his unpublished journal about his frustration in seeking to research and to change the schedule:

> Schedules pose a problem every year in this school. I would like to research: 1.) state laws on allocation of class time, classes necessary, school time; 2.) ideal class time length for middle school students; 3.) staggered schedules and different ways of finding time to do a better job of teaching. Whenever an idea comes up about changing the schedule you always get the same answers from administrators. Money, staffing, bus schedules, lunch programs, prevent changes. I hate the way the schedule changes we make are made because of money, convenience, and all these other factors—seldom for the good of student learning.

A Challenge for Classroom Teachers

How can the time be found in the teacher's regular teaching load for collaborative discussion, reflection, investigation, and speculation? The answer to this question is essential in making action research foundational in building a knowledge democracy. The challenges of making action research integral to teaching and school life have been identified by Cochran-Smith and Lytle (1993):

Maintaining teacher-research communities over relatively long periods of time also presents a number of challenges. How can a group meet the needs of both new and experienced members? Can a group become too large or too small? What happens to a group when members come and go? How can a group avoid being locked into procedures and continue to be receptive to critique and change even when many members feel satisfied with the status quo? How can teacher-researcher groups be increasingly responsive to special interests without fragmenting the organization? If teacher-researcher groups are to be more than the latest educational fad or the newest theme of staff development programs, they must be analyzed and reconceptualized as enduring structures subject to many of the same problems as other voluntary organizations that exist over time. (p. 91)

If teacher research is to become an enduring practice in education, then time must be built into school schedules for inquiry and dialogue. Michael Kirst (1982) has suggested that public schools can improve in hard times by attending to four alterable variables that do not add to costs. The first such variable is time; present practices in the use of time, he says, "undoubtedly need reform" (p. 7). How then can time be obtained to support teacher research? Here are some suggestions for gaining time to do action research in schools and to support teacher research as an enduring practice:

- Release teachers from nonteaching duties (such as lunch and hall duty) and replace these assignments with a common meeting time.
- Pair teachers; in addition to having many instructional advantages, paired teachers may sometimes combine classes for selected whole-class activities, which allows one teacher to participate in research team meetings or to observe, collect data, and so on.
- Form a school-university partnership, perhaps with a professional development school, and increase the number of teacher-interns in the school and the amount of fieldwork in all teacher preparation courses and practica. In this way, prospective teachers can teach more classes, and teachers can build in common time to plan and do action research studies.
- Seek out school restructuring grants and use funds to pay stipends to staff for research team meetings after contracted hours.
- Schedule time in blocks so that classroom teachers can meet as research teams at a common time.

- Create an electives block that is primarily staffed by community volunteers (or community people who receive stipends) while staff meet to plan and conduct research.
- Create a weekly community service learning block, staffed by a coordinator, in which all students participate in a structured community service learning experience while teachers meet in a common planning time for action research.
- Hire long-term substitutes to come in one day weekly to teach classes while teachers meet in research teams.
- Organize the majority of professional development time around school-based collaborative action research.

School systems throughout the country have found a variety of ways to use these ideas to gain time to support teacher development and action research. Imaginative restructuring designs for securing time for these purposes have been implemented in the Iowa City Schools; the Hefferan Elementary School in Chicago; Rufus King High School in Milwaukee, Wisconsin; Central Park East Secondary School in New York City; Freemont High School in Sunnyvale, California; Wells Junior High School in Wells, Maine; Holt High School in Holt, Michigan; and Jackson Road Elementary School in Montgomery County, Maryland (Pardini, 1999). When there is sufficient time and space for doing action research, then all participants can commit themselves to developing a school research culture.

❖ CONFRONTING UNIVERSITY VERSUS CLASSROOM ISSUES

Issues for Classroom Teachers

Teachers need to be willing and open to having other adults in the classroom and to see this as a positive factor not interfering with teaching and learning. It is helpful if participating teachers draw on their abilities to describe and analyze aspects of their own behavior, not just their students' behavior. Teachers who have not thought about classroom teaching and learning in such critical and reflective ways may need time to explore these aspects of their classrooms with others as they enter the collaborative action research process. Teachers need to consider how to restructure their time because action research may require time away from the classroom. Depending on their prior experiences in conducting research, teachers may need documentation and observation skills; they also may need to become familiar with data collection strategies and to feel comfortable with analyzing and interpreting data, drawing conclusions, and writing reports of their studies. This requires a supportive school atmosphere, as well as a climate and opportunities for teachers to practice action research over time. Finally, teachers need to have their research sanctioned and respected by school leadership and by universities. "Even after their involvement in educational action research teachers are reluctant to say they really did research; even if they admit to having done research they maintain that it was unscholarly or of low quality" (Kincheloe, 1991, p. 18). This perception about their own work can change if university faculty throw off their expert mantles and act like ordinary curious people with practically oriented questions that are pursued in schools through collaboration with teachers.

Issues for University Faculty

University faculty members of the action research team may need to take some time in learning to recognize and explore the naturalistic dimensions of school- and classroom-based action research. Gaining access to what teachers know about the classroom requires that university faculty have excellent listening and facilitative skills, patience, and the ability to ask the right questions in the right manner. University faculty members gain such access through professional relationships that are based on trust and long-term commitments to the school and its teachers and students. Teachers' willingness to share ideas, open up their classrooms, critique and try out research strategies, and discuss and interpret findings with university academics is vital to collaborative action research. University faculty members win these conditions by honoring, respecting, and responding to the knowledge and skills of other action research team members and proving their competence in providing some kind of unique service to the team. University faculty participants in the research process must be comfortable in public schools, possess interpersonal and group process skills, be familiar with alternative research methodologies, and have the ability to capitalize on unanticipated events, serendipitous opportunities, and unsettling insights.

University faculty need to be especially sensitive to their role as members of a collaborative action research team, lest they unconsciously reproduce the "researcher-subject" relationship that has characterized traditional positivistic research. The unconscious "researcher-subject" relationship reinforces the role of university faculty members as "experts" who, without full realization of the consequences of "expert" status, could subliminally control the goals and the agenda of the research process. Consequently, the potential for teacher professional development through reflection can become compromised by:

1. A focus on helping teachers better reproduce practices suggested by university sponsored research, and neglect of the theories and expertise embedded in teachers' own practices;

2. A means-end thinking which limits the substance of teachers' reflections to technical questions of teaching techniques and internal classroom organization and a neglect of questions of curriculum and education purposes;

3. Neglect of the social and institutional context in which teaching takes place;

4. A focus on helping teachers to reflect individually referring to their own research thus avoiding critical dialogue with others about larger issues. (Gore & Zeichner, 1995, p. 204)

Unless university faculty remain sensitive to this issue of unconscious role, there is the danger and irony that in their efforts to have teachers function as researchers, positivist norms of research will prevail, teachers' expertise will be diminished, teachers will be relegated to secondary roles in generating knowledge about their own work, and action research will be colonized by the academic knowledge interests of teacher educators (Day, 1993). Ongoing critical self-reflection is required of university faculty to guard against academic imperialism and to ensure that teachers will function as authentic coresearchers in a genuine partnership of collaborative inquiry.

University faculty would need to recognize that their career and professional interests can be advanced by their active participation in field-based staff development as an effective entree into field-based research. Often, university faculty who have been educated to conduct research are reluctant or find it difficult to participate in school-based action research, viewing it as less rigorous and not up to par with more traditional paradigms of research; they choose not to do what they have the capacity to do to advance the ethos of collaborative inquiry. Rather than viewing on-site inquiry in schools as inconsistent with academic career development, faculty need to see there is much to gain personally and professionally from working with schools and communities in researching the problems of teaching, learning, curriculum, inclusion, classroom management, diversity, and equity. The opportunities for research in the field are limited only by the imagination. However, it may be necessary to provide professional development for university faculty so that they can become enthusiastic participants in the collaborative action research process. In the literature of professional development, it is interesting to note that the focus, even in university/school collaborative efforts, seems to zero in on K–12 teachers with an absence of any language suggesting that university faculty may need professional development experiences and preparation to work in schools. Some time ago, I interviewed a dean at a state university who had become actively involved with field-based teacher inquiry. He offered this advice for university faculty:

> Long-term systematic approaches to in-service education offer university faculty and classroom teachers the time and place to identify and explore natural problem situations for action research. To begin, deal with the problems confronting teachers in the classroom and help them to become researchers to solve their own problems. Next, work with them, formulate hypotheses, test them out in the classroom, and write down the results. Everyone should publish. An in-house journal or action research papers could be circulated among faculty colleagues, teachers, and parents in the community. Function as teams of inquirers and problem-solvers, bringing in-service and preservice teachers and university faculty together as research teams. Teachers should be encouraged to investigate problems regarding individualization, school climate, reading, and creativity. It is absurd that concurrently in one university, teacher education program preservice students will be writing term papers, teachers will be writing term papers or preparing projects for a graduate course or workshop, and some university faculty will be writing manuscripts—all in splendid anonymous isolation from each other. What intellectual excitement and what quality research would emerge if we could assemble these people, create action research teams, identify real problems, and have these teams do some real blood and guts problem-solving. We would break down the fragmented approach to teacher education, integrate preservice and in-service education, and produce useable knowledge. This is the best and most meaningful kind of professional development. (Pine, 1980b, p. 15)

❖ INCLUDING STUDENT AND PARENT RESEARCH PARTNERS

Students as Researchers

Whereas much of the literature on collaborative action research focuses on school-university partnerships and the engagement of university faculty and K–12 teachers, there are other constituents whose voices need to be heard in the collaborative action research process if an authentic knowledge democracy is to be achieved. The missing links are students and parents. Up to this point, I have focused on the relationships between university faculty and teachers in the formation of collaborative research, but I believe that a knowledge democracy cannot be fully realized without the active engagement of students and parents as researchers. In collaborative action research, there is an ethical obligation to involve students and parents as active participants in the process of inquiry. "To generate knowledge about persons without their full participation in deciding how to generate it is to misrepresent their personhood and to abuse by neglect their capacity for autonomous intentionality. It is fundamentally unethical" (Heron, 1996, p. 21). Unfortunately, students, children, and parents traditionally have been viewed as passive subjects of research and most often have been excluded from being active participants in the research process. But they often have compelling and profound insights into research problems. As members of a collaborative action research team, they bring local knowledge, personal views, and access to peer cultures that are beyond the reach of traditional researchers.

Student action research is defined by Rubin and Jones (2007) as

> research that (a) is conducted by youth, within or outside of schools and classrooms, with the goal of informing and affecting school, community, and/or global problems and issues and (b) contributes to the positive development of a variety of academic, social, and civic skills in youth. (p. 363)

The empowerment of students as researchers will generate different research questions, perspectives, and concerns. Adults do not see the world as students do.

> Adults simply cannot become children again because they cannot discard the adult baggage they have acquired in the interim and will always operate through adult filters, even if these are subconscious

filters. It would also be unwise to try and apply the principles of childhood from a generation ago to a contemporary childhood. Above all we need to be able to learn and understand about the lived experiences of children of today.... Children observe with different eyes, ask different questions—they ask questions adults do not even think of—have different concerns and have immediate access to peer culture where adults are outsiders. The research agendas children prioritize, the research questions they frame, and the way in which they collect data are substantially different from adults, and all this can offer valuable insights and original contributions to knowledge. (Kellett, 2005a, p. 5)

In addition to bringing different perspectives and knowledge to the research process, students derive many benefits from their participation as researchers. Participation as researchers helps students (Steinberg & Kincheloe, 1998, p. 240) move to a critical realm of knowledge, focus their attention on thinking about their own thinking, create an analytical orientation, learn to teach themselves, improve their ability to engage in anticipatory accommodation, cultivate empathy with others, and negate reliance on procedural thinking. For student-researchers, research becomes a way of life, a way of approaching the world.

How, then, can the voices of students and parents be engaged in the collaborative action research process? Here, I will focus first on the role of students as researchers. Thinking about students as researchers brings to the surface questions of power. Whose interest does action research serve? Who owns the research? For whom is the research conducted? In response to these questions, a number of initiatives have been launched in England, Australia, and the United States to demonstrate and document how students can be empowered to do the kind of research that makes a difference; such work enables students to create new knowledge, transform themselves and their peers, and shape educational outcomes.

For example, the Children's Research Center at Open University in Milton Keynes, England, was established in 2003 to empower children and young people as active researchers. Reflecting the principle that children are experts on their own lives, the center aims to promote student voices by supporting children to conduct research on topics that are important to them, giving them the research skills and tools, and enabling them to become active researchers. Diverse groups of children and young people are taught the vital aspects of the research process, followed by one-to-one support for implementing their research. The center assists young researchers in disseminating their research findings to other children, schools, and related agencies. Research topics have included a study on the gender differences in the computer use of fifth-grade students, the social nature of TV viewing among 9- to 10-year-old children, social relationships in the classroom, a study of teachers' and children's views of creativity, and the kind of environment children like for doing their homework. The goals, strategies, and work of the center are described in a book entitled *How to Develop Children as Researchers*, by Mary Kellett (2005b).

What does it take to get students involved in studying and improving their own schools? How can students become allies with their teachers in conducting collaborative participatory research that will make a difference in their school lives? With support from MetLife Foundation, What Kids Can Do (WKCD) has explored these questions for several years in an initiative called "Students as Allies." In Chicago; Houston, Texas; Oakland, California; Philadelphia; and St. Louis, Missouri, WKCD has collaborated with teams of students and teachers organized by a local nonprofit intermediary. The work in each city includes several parts: helping students conduct survey research about their own schools, supporting thoughtful dialogue and initiating constructive action around the research results, and nurturing youth leadership all along the way. Making students daily allies in improving schools requires patience and practice in inviting and asking questions, listening closely, building trust and respect, and taking action with students.

One of the unique features of Students as Allies is that, in each city, students were selected to represent the diversity of the school's student population, and concerted efforts were made to recruit students who were not academic or social stars as well as more traditional students. In one site, teachers thought about the many cliques operating in the student body and then recruited students who reflected this diversity. Students conducted research on many issues, including school discipline policies, student-teacher relationships, school climate and safety, student voice, sense of belonging, and teaching styles. Each of the student research teams presented its findings at a public summit of students, teachers, and administrators in each school district through the use of flip charts, Power Point presentations, skits, videos, and hip hop poetry.

Another program that actively engages students as researchers is the Youth Action Research Institute, which is affiliated with the Institute for Community Research in Hartford, Connecticut. The Youth Action Research Institute promotes the use of action research by children, preadolescents, and youth of diverse ethnic backgrounds as well as youth who have non-heterosexual sexual orientations. The institute trains children and adolescents to do ethnography-based action research for personal growth, group development, and community change. Teens train other teens, children, and youth to use action research for social problem solving and advocacy in a peer leadership program.

Among the institute's programs is the Education and Advocacy Project, which seeks to improve teaching and learning through student action research studies conducted by students in fifth- and sixth-grade elementary and middle-school classrooms in four Connecticut school districts. Through the action research process, students take an active role in designing their research as a group, choosing a research area of importance to them, the methods they will use to collect the data, and the means they will use to disseminate the results of their research. One of the major goals of the Education and Advocacy Project is to assess the impact of action research on student learning outcomes, school attachments, and teacher satisfaction.

"What happens when my students inquire about the issue of high school dropouts in their local community?" is an action research question that Erik Shager (2007, p. 30), a teacher in the Work and Learn High School in Madison, Wisconsin, posed for himself and his students. The alternative high school students in his class began their research with a single question: Why do students drop out of high school? Students wrote about the question in their journals, discussed what they had written, read and discussed articles written on the topic, and brainstormed their own hypotheses. Identifying three major themes to pursue, the students broke themselves into three research teams. They designed and administered surveys; collected, tabulated, and analyzed data; wrote and disseminated their findings and recommendations; and made presentations to groups of teachers and students about proactive steps that could be taken in schools to reduce dropout rates in urban schools.

Most recently, Cammarota and Fine (2008), in their book, *Revolutionizing Education*, extensively document a critical research methodology known as Youth-led Participatory Action Research, a process for engaging young people in defining research problems most relevant in their lives and acting on them. The chapters in this book describe the implementation of this process in addressing educational problems and bring together student writings alongside the work of major scholars. For example, Torre and Fine et al. (2008) describe how, over a period of 3 years, 100 young people from urban and suburban high schools in New York and New Jersey collaborated with researchers from the Graduate Center of the City University to study racial and class-based injustice in schools. The high school students participated in a series of "research camps" held for 2 days at a time in community and university settings.

Deconstructing who can do research, what constitutes research, and who benefits they were immersed in methods training and social justice theory. The students learned how to conduct interviews, focus groups, and participant observations; to design surveys and organize archival analyses. (p. 8)

Collecting and analyzing their data, students have written research reports, presented their findings to the National Coalition for Educational Activists, the Public Education Network, the Cross Cultural Roundtable, and their schools and communities. They have shared their findings and recommendations for de-tracking, for focusing on racial inequities in their schools, and for multiple forms of assessment rather than single high-stakes testing.

In summary, these examples represent a small random sample of the growing movement of initiatives to engage children and adolescents as student researchers (see Tables 7.1 and 7.2). It is clear that given time, trust, respect for their voices, and preparation, students can, through their research, bring compelling and relevant views, insights, and ideas to bear on significant issues in education such as academic achievement and educational inequality, as Wiggan (2007) contends. After examining major developments in achievement research over the past century, Wiggan concluded that there should be a major change in the power dynamics of research, with students sharing in the development and design of research studies. For Wiggan, student-based inquiry would be a major step in addressing quality instruction and school-climate issues.

Karen Hume (1998), a teacher at E. A. Fairman Public School, Durham District School Board, Ontario, reflecting on her experience in working with her students as coresearchers, celebrates the potential role of students in building knowledge communities:

When students become involved in knowledge building around action research issues they have the opportunity, likely for the first time, to experience the connection between knowledge and development, both individual and collective. I think that this cannot help but change their understanding of the nature of knowledge, helping them to recognize it as an object that can be continually improved through their active participation. When groups of students have this experience, the possibility exists for the creation of vital knowledge building communities which may, by example, transform the way we think about teaching, learning, and school. (p. 12)

Table 7.1   Publications on Students as Researchers

Alderson, P. (2001). Research by children. *International Journal of Social Research Methodology*, 4(2), 139–153.

British Youth Council. (2000). *Youth agenda: Involving young people in research* (Discussion Paper No. 11). Retrieved from http://www.byc.org.uk/images/Research.pdf

Egan Robertson, A., & Bloome, D. (1998). *Students as researchers of culture and language in their own communities*. Cresskill, NJ: Hampton Press.

Fielding, M., & Bragg, S. (2003). *Students as researchers: Making a difference.* Cambridge, UK: Pearson.

Goodyear, L. K., & Checkoway, B. (Eds.). (2003). Youth engagement in community evaluation research [Special issue]. *Community Youth Development Journal*, 4(1).

Groundwater-Smith, S., & Downes, T. (1999, November). *Students: From informers to co-researchers.* Paper presented at the Australian Association for Research in Education Annual Conference, Melbourne.

Kellett, M. (2005b). *How to develop children as researchers: A step-by-step guide to teaching the research process.* London: Paul Chapman.

Kirby, P. (1999). *Involving young researchers: How to enable young people to design and conduct research.* York, England: Joseph Rowntree Foundation.

SooHoo, S. (1993). Students as partners in research and restructuring schools. *Educational Forum*, 57, 386–393.

Steinberg, S., & Kincheloe, J. (1998). *Students as researchers: Creating classrooms that matter.* Bristol, PA: Falmer Press.

Warren, S. (2000). Let's do it properly: Inviting children to be researchers. In A. Lewis & G. Lindsay (Eds.), *Researching children's perspectives.* Buckingham, UK: Open University Press.

Worrall, N., & Naylor, A. (2004). *Students as researchers: How does being a student researcher affect learning?* [online]. Retrieved from http://www.standards.dfes.gov.uk/ntrp/lib/pdf/WorrallNaylor.pdf

---

Table 7.2   Web Sites Promoting Students as Researchers

Pupil Voice

http://www.pupil-voice.org.uk/

Located at the University of Nottingham, England, this Web site contains links to other Web sites, resources, publications, projects, and conference proceedings, which reflect a range of practices and research that can be identified as "pupil voice." The theme of the Web site is "engaging critically with pupil voice. Children and young people are viewed as partners in school and community change."

Sound Out: Promoting Student Voice in School

info@soundout.org

This is the Web site of Sound Out, a program of Common Action located in the state of Washington. Sound Out works extensively throughout the

(Continued)

Table 7.2 (Continued)

education system to promote student involvement in school improvement and to promote student voice. The Web site describes various projects and programs designed to engage students throughout the country, and it lists resources, tool kits, publications, and other Web sites that focus on student involvement and research in schools.

Students as Researchers

http://www.studentsasresearchers.nexus.edu.au

This is a Web site that reports the findings and experiences of students doing research within the Department of Education, Employment, and Training schools in South Australia. The site also includes accounts written by teachers describing their experiences in implementing a students-as-researchers approach in their schools.

WKCD What Kids Can Do

www.whatkidscando.org

Presents the lives, learning, and work of young people and their collaboration with adults in and out of school. Through the Web site, readers have access to Next Generation Press, which includes accounts of students as social documentarians, knowledge creators, and advisers to educators, peers, and parents. The Web site contains feature stories, short publications, a list of resources for promoting the voice of youth, and a comprehensive list of more than 120 annotated Web sites helpful to those who wish to work with adolescents in new ways.

Youth in Focus

http://www.youthinfocus.org

Youth in Focus works for social justice by preparing underrepresented youth and adult allies in Youth REP (Youth-led Action Research, Evaluation and Planning) to create conditions for social justice. Its Web site features, among many items, a project gallery that includes stories of Youth REP initiatives to improve public education. One such project is the Education Justice Initiative, which works to promote increased youth engagement in school improvement, leadership development, and decision making and to link youth work to local action in education equity.

The examples of student-researcher programs described here indicate that we need to turn up the volume of student voices and recognize that students must be fully empowered as researchers. Along with teachers, administrators, university researchers, parents, and other adults, they can and should actively participate in building knowledge democracies through the collaborative action research process.

Parents as Researchers

Increasingly, parents are becoming involved in educational research. Parent-U-Turn, a parent organization in Lynwood, California, and surrounding cities in Los Angeles County worked with UCLA researchers to gather information about quality schooling (Johnson, Munoz, & Street, 2003). Parents studied the history of education and the social reproduction cycle as well as approaches to doing research. They learned a variety of data collection procedures including audio-taping, interviewing, using parent checklists, videotaping, construct-ing surveys, and conducting focus group meetings. They gathered data about conditions in their schools, teacher quality, and quality educa-tion for students. The parent-researchers conducted focus group meet-ings in schools with students, parents, teachers, and principals and then expanded their research to shopping malls and centers to inter-view and conduct surveys with other parents about conditions and quality education issues in their children's schools. The research out-comes included the development of a school accountability report card (SARC) and the establishment of a Student Bill of Rights.

The Center for Popular Education and Participatory Research was created in 2000 in the University of California, Berkeley, Graduate School of Education to promote and support popular education and participatory research to strengthen the participation of everyday people—especially the poor, youth, immigrants, and people of color—in efforts for social justice. Participatory research is aimed at engaging members of the community as active researchers. The center features two videotapes produced by Mary Jo Bauen on her work with parent research teams in the Oakland public schools. One film documents parent research teams in the Melrose Leadership Academy as they systematically reviewed high school options for their middle-school children. The second video is about K-CAM, a parent leadership project with McClymonds High School, which formed as a result of a participatory research project with West Oakland parents.

Another example of parents functioning as researchers can be found in a study conducted on the impact of a United Kingdom Sure Start Program (Rowe, 2006). Sure Start is a government program that aims to achieve better outcomes for children, parents, and communities by increasing the availability of child care for all children, improving health and emotional development for young children, and supporting parents as parents and in their aspirations toward employment. Parents conducted a community survey to generate insights into the early impact of the Sure Start program and to inform program expansion.

Researchers were recruited from the local community and provided with a research-training program before working on the development of the research itself. Parents took a lead role in the development, data collection, analysis, and report writing of the survey and were actively involved in the dissemination of the findings. The parent-researchers reported that they developed new skills and understandings, and the research had a significant impact on themselves and Sure Start.

Other examples include a parent and teacher collaborative research project in which the researchers used three basic multiple baselines to study systematic reinforcement and punishment procedures in the classroom and at home (Hall, Cristler, Cranston, & Tucker, 1970); parent researchers conducting research on vouchers and public schools in Milwaukee (Van Dunk & Dickman, 2003); and parents researching child care decisions of inner-city and suburban mothers (Anderson, Jackson, Wailoo, & Peterson, 2003). It is clearly evident that the voices of parents must be heard—and are being heard—through their participation as researchers in education and the social sciences. Together with students, parents have proven to be important allies in conducting collaborative action research. To build knowledge democracies, their partnership as active researchers with teachers, administrators, K–12 students, and university faculty is essential.

❖ LEARNING HOW TO COLLABORATE

It is vital that all the members of the action research team be brought together initially to learn how to collaborate. This is seldom done. Too often, it is gratuitously assumed that collaboration will happen if people are brought together as members of a task force, team, or committee. In my judgment, it is imperative that participants concentrate right away on what collaboration is and what it demands. Teachers, university faculty, and other partners need to reflect, discuss, and think about how to collaborate and deal with significant questions about the process. What is collaboration? What does it involve? What does it cost? What are its risks? What are its benefits? Am I or are we ready to pay the costs and give up something to get the benefits that accrue from collaboration? How do we help each other in the process? What are the ground rules for making decisions?

Collaboration is a dialectical and dialogical process with a great deal of give and take, and its use in action research requires that university faculty, classroom teachers, parents, and students build trust and relationships and communicate and solve problems together from the beginning. Action researchers need to prepare themselves for dealing with the conflicts that naturally emanate from the interface of the different norms, behavioral regularities, and values of the university and the school. Collaboration is not achieved naturally. It is a sophisticated process that must be learned deliberately. It requires building trust and relationships over time and self-monitoring to ensure that the collaborative process is maximized.

The collaborative process is facilitated when members of the action research team can discuss, reflect on, and formulate their own principles of collaboration to guide their processes of communication, critical dialogue, collegial sharing, and support. Sachs (1999), in writing about collaboration between university faculty and teachers, makes the case for explicit discussion and negotiation:

> If cultures of collegiality and professional reciprocity are to be valued and practiced in the interactions between the two parties, then the ground rules for association must be negotiated, practiced, and renegotiated. . . . if the collaborative work is to continue then making public some of the taken for granted aspects of collaboration need to be made explicit. Goodwill, a commodity very often exploited in these types of research activities, may well run out and both academic researchers and practitioners will be the poorer for this failure. (p. 45)

For example, the following principles of collaboration were developed and used by a team of Boston College graduate students who were conducting action research studies as part of their teaching internship:

Principles of Collaboration

- Model what we expect in our own classrooms, that is, respect each other, listen carefully to everyone, provide constructive and honest feedback, and be careful not to dominate discussion.
- Rotate and assume different roles in the group as facilitator, prober, summarizer, recorder, and timekeeper.
- Value the perspectives, experiences, knowledge, and expertise that each person brings to the group. Allow time for each person to share his/her views. Actively listen to all points of view and address them before moving on to another point.
- Get to know each other. Develop a network of communication and support that can be tapped into during the week between team meetings, for example, an e-mail and phone list.

- Work consciously to develop a spirit of collegiality, sharing references, journal writing, and ideas and themes emanating from classroom observations and personal reflection.
- Begin each meeting by "checking in" to see where people are coming from.
- Stay on task, stay focused, and monitor process. Reflect on individual participation and the group's process following each meeting.
- Come to team meetings on time, prepared, accountable, and ready to participate.
- Build on each others' ideas; scaffold ideas.
- Have a good sense of humor, have fun, and bring some food.

Three Challenges in Developing Collaboration

In developing collaboration for inquiry, it is important to be mindful of how collaboration has the potential to go askew. Three challenges need to be addressed:

1. Collaboration is a powerful process for inquiry and learning, but inquiry groups can evolve into discussion and emotional support groups in practice, valuable to the morale and mental health of the participants but unlikely to create real change in their beliefs or knowledge. The challenge of developing authentic collaborative inquiry is found in the independent nature of teaching and a "make-it, take-it" approach to professional development (Huberman, 1995; Loucks-Horsley, 1998). In the research-engaged school, it is vital to bring all participants together to explicitly and continuously focus on inquiry and research. This will require an understanding of school culture and norms of behavior, patience, and a recurring reminder of the purpose of collaboration for inquiry.

2. Collaboration can be contrived, leading to inefficiency, inflexibility, and insensitivity to teachers' professionalism, leadership, and intelligence. In comparing *contrived collaboration* to *collaborative cultures*, Hargreaves (1994, pp. 186–211) notes that contrived collaboration is mandated, not voluntary and spontaneous; it is administratively regulated; teachers work together to implement the mandates of others; implementation is the focus rather than development; it is fixed in time and space; and it is designed to have relatively high predictability in its outcomes. In collaborative cultures, genuine collaboration is characterized by spontaneity; collaboration emerges from teachers as a social group and from teachers' perceived value of collaborative work. It is

development oriented: "Teachers work together primarily to develop initiatives of their own, or to work on externally supported or mandated initiatives to which they themselves have a commitment. . . . Teachers . . . initiate change as much or more than they react to it" (Hargreaves, 1994, p. 192). Collaboration is not scheduled or fixed. Although scheduled meetings may be part of the process, informal interactions and discussions and sharing of ideas and questions are integral to the process. Because "teachers have discretion and control over what will be developed, the outcomes of collaboration are often uncertain and not easily predicted" (Hargreaves, 1994, p. 193).

3. Collaboration can lead to *group think* (Janis & Mann, 1977). Group think is characterized by: illusions of invulnerability, in which members ignore obvious pitfalls and are overly optimistic; collective rationalization, in which members discredit and explain away any ideas contrary to group thinking; self-censorship, in which members withhold their dissenting views and counterarguments; illusion of unanimity, in which members perceive falsely that everyone agrees with the group's decisions and silence is seen as consent; pressure for conformity, in which members pressure any in the group who argue against the group's views and commitments, viewing such opposition as disloyalty; illusion of morality, in which members believe their decisions are morally correct, ignoring the ethical consequences of their decisions; and mind guards, in which some members of the group appoint themselves to the role of protecting the group from adverse information that might threaten the group's views and ideas.

Group think can be avoided, as I have noted above in discussing the conditions for building a culture of collaborative inquiry. Authentic collaboration thrives and group think is avoided in an atmosphere of facilitative confrontation, one that tolerates ambiguity and consistently recognizes the right of participants to make mistakes. In authentic collaboration, difference is good and desirable, ideas can be explored and confronted, there is space for unpopular views and perspectives, participants are active and assert leadership, and people are valued and respected.

❖ SUMMARY

Building a knowledge democracy through collaborative action research is a complex project. It requires a "work with posture," time to build relationships and conduct research, systemic and relational trust, resolution of inherent issues that confront university faculty and classroom teachers, active inclusion of students and parents as co-researchers, and explicit attention to the process of collaboration. Like most complex endeavors, developing a knowledge democracy through collaborative action research is worth the effort. When teachers, students, and parents work together in conducting caring inquiry in the classroom, school, and community and construct knowledge for meaningful change, they experience self-affirmation and self-renewal. They see themselves as making a significant difference in the transformation and construction of knowledge to improve teaching and learning. Their collaboration changes schools and advances social justice and educational equity. In summary, the rewards of collaboration are the worthy outcome of teachers, students, and parents working through the complexities of collaboration to build a knowledge democracy.

8

Creating Knowledge Democracies

Professional Development Schools

In this chapter, I introduce the concept of the Professional Development School (PDS) as a comfortable and inviting home for creating a knowledge democracy. I discuss how the formation of a PDS brings essential resources and precious time for collaborative democratic research. The distinctive features of the PDS as a knowledge-creating school are delineated, the development of a school research culture is examined, and the challenges of building a professional development school as a knowledge democracy are explored. The common elements of critical collegiality and the essential concrete requirements for establishing an embedded research culture are developed. The chapter concludes with a discussion of 11 conditions for facilitating collaborative inquiry and a presentation of the outcomes that emerge from a PDS-based knowledge democracy.

❖ THE NATURE AND CHARACTER OF A PROFESSIONAL DEVELOPMENT SCHOOL (PDS)

What organizational structure best supports the development of collaborative cultures of inquiry, knowledge communities, and consequently

knowledge democracies? Although many models of collaborative partnerships have emerged over the past 20 years to focus on knowledge
creation, the PDS is a significant and distinctive organizational model
that has attracted much attention and debate. PDSs have been promoted by a range of organizations: the Holmes Group (1986, 1990,
1995), the Carnegie Forum on Education and the Economy (1986), the
National Network for Educational Renewal (Goodlad, 1994), the
American Federation of Teachers (Levine, 1992), the National Education
Association (Robinson & Darling-Hammond, 1994), and the Ford
Foundation (Anderson, 1993).

What is a PDS? The Michigan Partnership for New Education
(1992) offers one view, which is helpful in moving to a useful, distinctive, and comprehensive definition:

> While a PDS is a site for schooling, it is not representative of the
> typical school culture; while it is a site for teacher education, it is
> not representative of the typical university culture; while it is a site
> for scholarly inquiry, it is not representative of the typical research
> culture. It is a unique social and educational institution in its own
> right; it will develop its own culture distinct from traditions of
> either schools, teacher education institutions, or research universi-
> ties. The Professional Development School is not, therefore, merely
> a bridge between school and university; it is, instead, a new com-
> munity of professionals and citizens committed to making educa-
> tion more effective and efficient to produce "higher order
> learning" for all children, youth, and adults. (p. xxx)

The perspective of the Michigan Partnership reflects the inherent
tensions and paradoxes embedded in a PDS and offers a contextual
framework for operationally defining a PDS. A PDS is a community of
partners: teachers, administrators, parents, teacher-interns, students,
and citizens, who over time collaborate in the design, development,
implementation, and evaluation of a school dedicated to the simultaneous improvement of education for all children and the professional
preparation and development of educators through a broad K–16
agenda focusing on:

Educational restructuring, K–16

Instructional/curriculum change and development

Research and development

Pre-service teacher education and induction into teaching

Professional development for all partners (including university faculty)

The Holmes Group (1986) envisioned PDSs as centers of inquiry

where people can seek to improve their practice in ways that are more diverse, subtle, substantive, broad gauged, and ongoing. . . . A certain amount of groping, improvisation, and serendipity should be part of any organization that is experimenting with new responses to complex problems. Thoughtful replication of and generalizations about innovations will be needed. (p. 45)

Reinforcing the central role of inquiry in professional development schools, Berry, Boles, Edens, Nissenholtz, and Tractman (1996) argue that

inquiry is (or must be) the sine qua non of PDSs. With inquiry emerges the possibility of quality assurance—when those who are responsible for delivering quality education

- use inquiry as a means to transform day-to-day teaching and learning
- engage inquiry in order to determine what works best (or doesn't) for students
- conduct inquiry on the effects of their efforts. (p. 2)

How then can professional development schools become centers of inquiry?

Clustering Resources

By clustering university undergraduate and graduate teacher-interns in teams, together with students studying in such professional preparation programs as educational administration, school counseling, reading, and early childhood, while at the same time placing university supervisors and faculty in selected school sites, local districts would have a critical mass of resources to work with in creating professional development and action research initiatives by redirecting existing resources, consolidating resources, and discovering mutually benefiting resources. Through teacher leadership, such initiatives could lead to the development of a knowledge democracy in which the school or school district would be permeated by open and ongoing inquiry and democratic knowledge construction. How would such a development occur in a single school?

In a PDS, the university and a local school district work out arrangements so that the following kinds of university students can be placed in a school:

One or two post-master's degree students in educational administration and supervision

Two master's degree students in administration

Three master's degree students in counseling

Three master's degree students in reading

An early childhood team of two master's degree students who could help staff an early childhood learning center (full year)

Ten master's degree teaching interns (full year)

The group would also include:

15 to 20 undergraduate students who were exploring teaching

Two or three university faculty assigned as on-site supervisors, with additional faculty coming to offer university courses and professional development assistance on site

In addition, a significant number of parents and students would actively participate as researchers.

A school would then have about 35 to 40 people available as additional external resources along with the school's teachers, parents, and students. There are endless possibilities with this kind of critical mass available to serve the interests and needs of all parties concerned. After 2 or 3 months of the internship, teacher-interns could begin to share responsibility for classroom instruction, thereby freeing up classroom teachers for part of the day, so that they could:

1. Plan and develop curriculum materials

2. Visit and observe teachers in other classes

3. Form collaborative action research teams

4. Participate in workshops or take courses on site

5. Participate in conferences and case studies of individual students

6. Design and plan approaches to individualize instruction

7. Meet with colleagues in a relaxed atmosphere to share ideas

8. Assume responsibilities for staff development activities

9. Collaboratively and formatively evaluate instruction and learning

Over time and after demonstrating their teaching skills, interns could release a cadre of experienced, knowledgeable, and effective teachers to help mentor and assist the less experienced and the newer members of a teaching staff ("teachers teaching teachers").

Meanwhile, counseling and reading interns could provide support services for meeting the special emotional and intellectual needs of students. Post-master's degree administration interns and master's degree students could take on specific and substantial leadership assignments and problems of the kind that would support the school's leadership in building a culture of collaborative leadership. Undergraduate students who are exploring teaching as a possible career could provide tutorial help to children and offer individual attention to children who need it.

Through the cluster placement of interns, the principal, teachers, and support staff would have additional resources that would enable them to gain flexibility in scheduling and offer increased opportunities for differentiated staffing, individualization of instruction, and staff and curriculum development. On-site university faculty could offer courses or a series of workshops for school staff, coteaching with class-room teachers. Working together, school staff and interns could collect data for ongoing needs assessments, instructional and curriculum planning, and the evaluation of programs. A library of instructional modules, action research studies, curriculum materials, assessment tools, and other resources could be developed.

Collaborative action research teams consisting of undergraduate students, interns, classroom teachers, parents, K–12 students, and university faculty could be formed. These teams would identify specific problems to be researched. Decisions would be made and responsibilities assumed for literature searches, documentation, observation, evaluation, data collection and interpretation, and implementation of alternative problem solutions. Results of the action research would be written by the partners in the research teams. A series of action research reports would be published in-house and disseminated to everyone in the school. Reports could be submitted to professional journals for publication and to professional conferences for presentations.

The interests and needs of the university and local school district would be well served. The school's K–12 students would learn in an environment of intellectual inquiry and would conduct their own studies on teaching, learning, and curriculum. Interns would have meaningful learning experiences to test and apply theory, to acquire and extend professional competencies, and to learn and grow in the real world of education. University faculty would interface more frequently with teachers on the front line of education and in the crucible of the real world of teaching, expand their perspectives on the teaching and learning process, and generate new hypotheses for research. Teachers would be empowered as action researchers, giving them greater confidence in their ability to individually and collectively promote change and to create knowledge. They would gain knowledge and skill in research methods and applications, become more critical and reflective about their own practice, and attend more carefully to their methods, their perceptions, their understandings, and their whole approach to the teaching process. A richer and greater variety of human resources would be available to facilitate student learning and development. The sites that would be available for the cluster assignments of interns would offer a wide range of experiences, making university supervision more efficient and effective.

While PDSs cannot be implemented overnight and require long-term commitment, sustained effort, democratic leadership, careful planning, and reallocation of resources, they demonstrate that in the final analysis, in addition to financial support, what is required for the integration of research and practice are imagination and will.

Becoming Knowledge Democracies

Such professional development schools would become more than teaching centers and centers of inquiry: They would truly evolve as knowledge democracies—places where administrators, teachers, interns, parents, K–12 students, and university faculty could share ideas and grow together through a sustained program of systematic, open, and intentional inquiry to improve and advance the quality of learning for everyone. In summary, these knowledge democracies would be characterized by a number of distinctive features (Hargreaves, 1999).

- Enthusiasm for continuous improvement
- Awareness of external environment
- Sensitivity to students, teachers, parents, and administrator interests

- Coherent flexible institutional planning
- Flat hierarchies and devolved power
- Recognition of teacher, student, and parent expertise
- Informal staff relationships with the accent on expertise and not status
- High volume of internal debate and professional networking
- Knowledge creation seen explicitly as a whole-school regular process
- Regular opportunities for reflection, inquiry, and dialogue
- Internal hybridization (job rotation, cross-functional teams)
- Use of temporary developmental groups
- Culture of "no blame" experimentation and challenge
- Encouragement of diversity and deviation from the norm
- Partnerships
- Positive tension between control and liberty, freedom and responsibility

❖ THE CHALLENGES OF BUILDING A PDS AS A KNOWLEDGE DEMOCRACY

The process of building a PDS as a community of inquiry is not a straight-line process but a series of hills and valleys. The process is circular, iterative, and sometimes discontinuous. It involves an ongoing process of renegotiation and reformulation between individuals, groups, and the larger context of a collaborative. Collaboration for inquiry in a PDS is not a mere mechanical matching of needs and capabilities followed by a definition of objectives and a working plan and schedule. It is, more important, an exercise in mutuality where understanding and shared values are more important than contracting, where personal contacts outweigh administrative mechanisms, where there is a climate that addresses differences as they arise, and where there is a desire to arrive at solutions in spite of the obstacles that may present themselves.

That is not to suggest that structure and ground rules are not important. Improving communications, developing positive norms, and promoting interpersonal goodwill are necessary but not sufficient conditions for successful collaboration in building a knowledge democracy. Attempting to promote collaboration only by adding a human relations overlay onto existing management structures and systems can consume even the most determined of collaborative processes. PDS collaboration can best be achieved by the design of creative, fluid, and flexible structures that remove institutional barriers and promote interdependence, reciprocal relationships, and permeable organizations.

PDSs operate more effectively when all participants recognize that concerns and objections usually flow from different experiences, goals, expectations, obligations, and values. Mutually derived resolutions of problems and challenges cannot happen until participants in the PDS accept each other's good faith and attempt to understand the experiences and premises from which each participant is operating. An intellectual and affective appreciation of the added value provided by authentic collaboration can offer the motivation to show patience even when the reservoir of patience appears empty. Finally, it should be noted that

> At the heart of democratic life is acceptance of uncertainty. The school should be an area of uncertainty. The goal is to learn to live with uncertainty, to live with it productively. And always there is the relationship with people. (Holmes Group, 1990, p. 3)

In summary, then, it is by addressing the challenges of building a professional development school characterized by mutuality, authentic collaboration, and a fluid and flexible organizational context that the evolution of a school research culture gains enabling traction.

Developing a School Research Culture

Ebbutt (2002; Ebbutt, Robson, & Worrall, 2000) has identified three kinds of school-based research cultures: *emergent, established,* or *established-embedded.* In an emergent research culture, the history of school-based research is fragmented and discontinuous. Teachers experienced and expert in school-based research are few, and the main focus is to get research started. In an established research culture, more teachers are willing, experienced, and capable of conducting research; there is a long-term plan of research; research is viewed as contributing to the development of the school; and groups of teacher-researchers work together on a similar idea or a range of ideas. In an established-embedded research culture (sometimes referred to as a *research-engaged school*), "staff accept the potential link between research and pedagogy for the enhancement of student learning and for the professional learning of teachers," and research "is seen as a pervasive and inclusive activity to be undertaken by the many, regardless of role (staff or students), status, or curriculum specialty" (Ebbutt, 2002, p. 134).

Features of a Research-Engaged School

Drawing on Ebbutt's work, the Essex Forum for Learning and Research in England has published a paper that identifies the features of a research-engaged school (Handscomb & MacBeath, 2003). As a culture of collaborative inquiry evolves over time, the PDS evolves into a research-engaged school where research and inquiry are at the heart of the school, its outlook, systems, and activities. What features define the PDS as a research-engaged school?

1. The research-engaged school has a "research rich" pedagogy.
   - There is a focus on learning throughout the school.
   - Research is driven by teaching and learning needs.
   - Students use and apply research.
   - Staff, together with their pupils, understand and apply research.
   - Risk taking is welcomed and encouraged.
   - There is an impact on pupil learning.
   - Unexpected and unwelcome outcomes are allowed and valued.

2. The research-engaged school has a research orientation.
   - There is a shared recognition of the value of research.
   - Research activity is "owned" and not imposed.
   - The benefits of research are widely understood and frequently modeled.
   - There is an improvement focus.
   - The culture is one of "learning how to learn."
   - Classroom practice is characterized by continuous evaluation.
   - Teaching and learning are evidence based.
   - Participants are both ready and confident to engage in and with research.
   - Research engagement is built into school processes and planning.
   - Research infuses continuing professional development.

3. The research-engaged school promotes research communities.
   - Research engagement runs throughout the whole school.
   - There is a belief in the potential of all staff (teachers, administrators, counselors, etc.) to make a valid contribution.
   - Ways are found of exploiting and enriching professional expertise.

- People in different roles and with different backgrounds all play a part.
- The widespread nature of activity produces a critical mass of research activity.
- There is a full commitment to the engagement of students and parents with research.

4. The research-engaged school puts research at the heart of school policy and practice.
   - Research engagement is built into school improvement planning.
   - Activities are clearly planned, timed, and implemented.
   - There is clarity of tasks and roles.
   - There is a diversity of projects, well tracked and well managed.
   - People are equipped with research "tools" through workshops and mentoring.
   - Advice is given for shaping tasks and projects.
   - Attention is given to robust research approaches and methods.

How can these features evolve over time? Ebbutt (2002) argues that differences between the research cultures of schools can be viewed as a series of developmental stages along an evolutionary path. If schools wish to develop an embedded research culture (or emerge as a research-engaged school), they will need to evolve through prior stages of: *no research culture → emergent research culture → established research culture → established-embedded research culture*. It seems to me that at this last stage of development, one would find in an established-embedded research culture the practice of "critical collegiality" through which the link between research and pedagogy to improve student learning would be made. Critical collegiality or "critical colleagueship" includes six common elements (Lord, 1994, pp. 192–193):

1. Productive disequilibrium, which "depends on difference and conflict as driving forces" (p. 194). Reflection, debate, and critique are fundamental processes. There is a perspective that things are not quite right, combined with the belief that they can be made better. Teachers feel that there is always room for improvement in their practice and persist in believing that their craft is not yet as it could be.

2. The embrace of fundamental intellectual values such as openness to new ideas, willingness to reject weak practices and flimsy arguments, and acceptance of responsibility to use information relevant to teacher-researchers' arguments.

3. A willingness for teacher/university researchers to be empathetic with colleagues, crawling under the skin of other people to see the world as colleagues do, to put themselves in the shoes of their colleagues; seeking a way to move beyond their personal experiences to seeing and understanding the experiences of others, to understand their perspectives.

4. An increase in the skills of negotiation, communication, and problem resolution. Negotiation is fundamental to discussions that have no right answers. Negotiation skills and the willingness to resolve differences in ideas and opinions are connected by the desire for teacher/university researchers to listen deeply and empathically to each other.

5. An increase in researchers' comfort with ambiguity and uncertainty, acknowledging that teaching and learning are inherently ambiguous: There are always competing concerns and paradoxes.

6. The achievement of collective generativity: knowing how to go on, knowing that more can be done, that collaborative research involves lifetime inquiry, that collaborative action research generates new questions and issues that need to be addressed in the future.

To arrive at an established-embedded research culture, which includes the practice of critical collegiality, I believe that certain necessary concrete conditions need to be built into the working environment of the schools. If teachers are going to function as researchers in partnership with colleagues, students, parents, or university faculty in an embedded research culture of support and inquiry, then these facilitative conditions need to be present in the school and the school district:

- School leadership is committed to and supportive of teachers, students, and parents as researchers and to the concept of research as a form of teacher professional development.
- Time is made available as part of the teacher's regular teaching load for discussion, reflection, investigation, and speculation. Principals and teachers work together to restructure school schedules to build in time for teachers and principals to reflect, dialogue, and conduct action research studies.
- There is an atmosphere of trust. Teachers have the freedom to identify and initiate their own problems for inquiry, to express their ideas and develop their ideas into researchable questions, and to share and defend their ideas with administrators and colleagues.

- Technical assistance, support, and consulting services are provided when necessary to help teachers (and university faculty) learn field-based research processes.
- Universities offer documentation and reflective writing workshops for principals and staff.
- School districts use professional development funds to offer mini-grants to initiate and support action research projects.
- Universities provide opportunities for teachers to present their work in university courses and conferences.
- School districts sponsor annual teacher research conferences.
- An in-house journal of teacher research is published and supported by the school district.
- Universities, school districts, principals, and teachers encourage teacher-researchers to publish. A product emerges from the research process (article, paper, report, curriculum, videotape, exhibit, conference presentation), and it is shared publicly.
- Through professional development, principals and teachers learn how to create open, trusting, and collegial school environments where risk taking and inquiry are encouraged.
- Adequate resources and materials are provided in schools to support action research studies.
- Opportunities are provided for teacher-researchers to build internal consulting teams that network with teaching staffs in schools throughout the district in supporting teacher research.
- Opportunities are provided for extended conversations among all parties on how norms and values of inquiry, experimentation, sharing, risk taking, and collaboration can become embedded in the school culture.

Conditions for Facilitating Collaborative Inquiry

Translating the principles and characteristics of a school research culture into operational meaning and action in a school requires the facilitation of collaborative inquiry to support reflection and critical dialogue and advance the collaborative action research process. Collaborative inquiry is the sine qua non of a school research culture. Underlying the following conditions for collaborative inquiry is the foundational principle that inquiry is a lifelong process of problem posing and not a discrete, isolated "project" of problem answering.

Condition 1. Collaboration for inquiry is facilitated in an atmosphere in which positive interpersonal relationships are prized and valued. It takes time to build effective interpersonal relationships and requires consistent attention in exercising strong communication skills. For example, members of the Communities of Learning, Inquiry, and Practice at Bakersfield College (Parsons, 2007) report that the communication/relationship practices that made a difference in attaining successful outcomes in their work were the value of listening to one another; appreciating different perceptions; using brainstorming techniques (rather than debating point of view); negotiating with one another; respecting each other; creating a safe, trusting environment; discussing common problems; paying attention to group dynamics; taking time to meet on a regular basis; and working collaboratively. As a result of developing strong interpersonal relationships with each other, members of the CLIP gained greater respect for colleagues and for the value of diverse feedback, established shared goals, made shared decisions to enhance the quality of instruction, engaged in meaningful and productive discussions about teaching and learning, and improved communication across disciplines and departments. Within this context of effective interpersonal relationships, the members of CLIP learned how to conduct focus groups, use various approaches for interviewing, construct surveys, analyze qualitative and quantitative data, and fine-tune their focus in conducting a study.

Condition 2. Collaboration for inquiry is facilitated in an atmosphere that encourages participants to be active and assume leadership roles. The collaborative process thrives when there is less domination by formal leadership and more faith that participants in the collaboration can find alternatives and solutions that address problems in the collaboration and that are satisfying to the participants. Listening to members of the collaboration, and enabling them to tap the collaborative team or group as a resource, facilitates the active exploration of ideas and possible solutions to problems that inevitably arise in any authentic collaboration. Participants in a collaboration are more engaged when they feel they are a part of what is going on, when they are personally involved, and when they have the opportunity to actively participate in determining the goals and the research agenda of the collaboration.

Condition 3. Collaboration for inquiry is facilitated in an atmosphere in which difference is good and desirable. Collaboration that emphasizes the "one right strategy for change," the "magical solution," or the "one good way" to act, or think, or behave limits exploration and limits discovery. If participants are to advance the goals and purposes of collaborative action research, they must have frequent opportunities to look at themselves, at others, and at ideas openly and reasonably, and they must have the opportunity to express their opinions, no matter how different they may be. This calls for an atmosphere in which democratic dialogue thrives and different ideas can be accepted (but not necessarily agreed with). Differences in ideas must be accepted if differences in people are to be accepted and the tensions of collaboration addressed.

Condition 4. Collaboration for inquiry is facilitated in an atmosphere that consistently recognizes the participants' right to make "mistakes." A collaboration that does not accept "mistakes" severely limits the freedom and willingness of the participants in the collaboration to make choices and decisions. The collaborative research process involves the challenge of meeting new and different experiences and, therefore, necessarily involves making mistakes. If the collaborative process is to be advanced and fruitful, the members of the collaboration need the opportunity to explore the unknown without apprehension of being penalized or punished psychologically or socially.

Condition 5. Collaboration for inquiry is facilitated in an atmosphere that tolerates and works through ambiguity and uncertainty. In contrived collaboration, participants feel they cannot take time to look at many possible alternatives and solutions. They feel uncomfortable without answers and ready-made solutions to complex problems and issues. Open and fearless exploration of thorny issues through problem-solving and conflict resolution processes calls for time to explore alternatives without feeling pressure for immediate answers. In every educational institution, there are forces working for and against change. A deliberative analysis of these forces, of the tensions inherent in the collaborative process, and of the institutional and community contexts of collaboration requires tolerance for the discomfort of ambiguity and uncertainty.

Condition 6. Collaboration for inquiry is facilitated in an atmosphere in which participants feel they are respected and valued. When high value is placed on the individuality of the members of the collaboration and on the collegial relationships that exist within the collaboration, participants feel they are cared for. A caring atmosphere generates a climate of safety in which people can explore ideas, confront differences, and work out solutions without any feeling of threat. Confrontations and differences of opinion become constructive forces in collaboration when participants know they are respected as people.

A caring and respectful atmosphere and a sense of community need not exclude personal confrontations; they are often effective catalysts for resolving problems and advancing the agenda of the collaboration.

Condition 7. Collaboration for inquiry is facilitated in an atmosphere of facilitative confrontation. A nonthreatening climate that encourages free and open communication allows the unique self of each participant to be expressed. It is inevitable that individuals and groups will confront each other and that ideas will challenge ideas. Confrontations can facilitate and strengthen collaboration; they provide opportunities for participants to see their ideas and themselves from the perspective of other participants and groups. No one learns and grows in isolation from other people. Knowledge begins in human interaction. Behavior is changed and ideas are modified on the basis of feedback and challenge from other people. Facilitative confrontation is based on an ethic of caring, respect, and engagement. Such confrontation strengthens collaboration by allowing participants to test, synthesize, and discover new ideas; to change behaviors, structures, and practice; and to forge agreement out of disagreement.

Condition 8. Collaboration for inquiry is facilitated in an atmosphere that encourages openness of self rather than concealment of self. Problem posing, problem solving, and learning require that personal feelings, attitudes, ideas, questions, and concerns be brought to light and examined openly. To the degree that an idea, a thought, a feeling, or an attitude related to the topic or question at hand is held back and not openly expressed—to that degree are the processes of learning and discovery inhibited. Participants on a collaborative action research team need to feel that they can try something, that they can fail if necessary without being humiliated, embarrassed, or diminished as people. Openness of self occurs in an atmosphere free from psychological threat. Members of the action research team can invest themselves fully and openly in the collaborative and interactive process of inquiry when they know no matter what they say or express, it will not result in psychological punishment, deflection, or diminution. Consequently, previously silenced or subjugated knowledge will emerge, becoming a rich resource for facilitating the process of collaborative inquiry.

Condition 9. Collaboration for inquiry is facilitated in an atmosphere in which participants are encouraged to trust in themselves. Participants become less dependent on external research authority when they open up to the self and feel that they are a valuable resource for inquiry. It is important for people to realize that they have something to bring to the inquiry process. Inquiry is not the acquisition of facts and knowledge passed on by some external agent for use in solving a problem. Participants become active inquirers when they begin to see themselves as the wellsprings of ideas, questions, and alternative ways of looking at problems. Inquiry improves when people begin to draw ideas from themselves and others rather than relying on the external research expertise.

Condition 10. Collaboration for inquiry is facilitated when participants in the collaboration recognize, understand, and are prepared to work through the informal systems of the partnership institution. Every educational institution has informal norms and values, groups and cliques that can have a significant bearing on the way formal structures and processes function. Informal relationships and communications systems should be carefully considered in planning and implementing collaborative research. The informal features of an organization, such as the amount of liking members have for one another or their willingness to help and support each other, can be positive and facilitating processes that can be drawn on in planning and implementing collaboration. However, these same processes can also constitute a powerful restraining influence effectively blocking collaboration. For successful collaboration, it is essential to analyze each partner institution's informal structure and work with that structure in planning and implementing collaboration. Gaining the support and the cooperation of informal groups often requires the highest levels of human relations skills and the recognition that the sine qua non of successful collaboration are tenacity, trust, and sustained commitment to the goals and processes of collaboration.

❖ SUMMARY

This chapter documents that building a knowledge democracy, even in a congenial setting such as a PDS, is a complex and challenging proposition. It requires time, patience, and participants' willingness to deal with ambiguity, uncertainty, and conflict. It requires democratic administrative leadership that is supportive of active teacher, student, and parental involvement in the construction of knowledge about every facet of the school and its educational process. It requires teacher leadership and commitment to the action research process. And, finally, it requires the embedded features and conditions that characterize a research-engaged school centered on collaborative inquiry. Practicing democracy in any culture, context, or organization has never been easy, but the outcomes of democratic participation in knowledge creation can revolutionize the quality of student learning and teacher development. These outcomes include:

- An authentic integration of research and practice occurs.
- Knowledge construction supports the improvement of teaching and learning.
- An "inside out bottom up" approach characterizes knowledge creation.
- Teacher, student, and parental experiences and expertise are actively employed in democratic problem solving.
- The voices of the "silent and the silenced"—teachers, parents, and students—are raised, heard, valued, and used in problem identification and problem solving.
- Knowledge is a vital resource that affects decisions and actions in the school.
- Knowledge is publicly shared, debated, and jointly used.
- The school is a living democracy.
- Research permeates every aspect of the school's organization, programs, activities, and culture.
- The development of research skills for all participants is built into the school's professional development program.
- An effective system of dissemination ensures transmission and application of research outcomes in the school's classrooms.
- Dissemination of research studies includes full details of the context of the research and the way in which it was conducted so that others can make fully informed judgments about relevance to their own situation.
- Teacher leadership is evident throughout the school's programs and activities.
- Student learning and classroom teaching are significantly advanced and continually improving.

Part III

Practicing
Action Research

Chapters 9, 10, and 11 deal with the practical aspects of conducting individual or collaborative action research. These chapters are intended to illuminate the practice of the action research process, but they must be considered within the context of the preceding chapters on the power of action research to build knowledge democracies. Although practice is the focal point of these chapters, the philosophical and theoretical bases of practice are examined.

9

Fundamental Practices for Teacher Action Research

C hapter 9 focuses on fundamental practices for conducting teacher action research, including reflection, documentation, observation, writing, journaling, and dialogue. In this chapter, I emphasize that although these can be treated as discrete practices, they ought to be considered as intersecting processes of study—mental dispositions and behaviors that interactively nurture lifelong inquiry. The interaction of these practices is explored, and concrete steps for their implementation are described. At the end of the chapter, I pose a series of questions to facilitate reflections about teaching and learning experiences and to offer focal points for observation, journal writing, and reflection.

❖ REFLECTION

Dewey (1933) defined reflection as a specialized form of thinking that is precipitated by a state of doubt or perplexity, leading to active and purposeful inquiry. The purpose of reflection is "to transform a situation in which there is experienced obscurity, doubt, conflict, disturbance of some sort, into a situation that is clear, coherent, settled, harmonious" (pp. 100–101). It begins with observations made by one-self or others in a directly experienced situation. These observations, in turn, suggest possible courses of action. Together, data (observations) and ideas (suggested courses of action) constitute "two indispensable and correlative factors" of reflection (Dewey, 1933, p. 104). The paradox of reflection is that while observing situations puzzles us, causing suggestions for action, immediate direct action is withheld until the suggested actions are treated as hypotheses to be tested by mental elaboration or reasoning before action is taken. The paradox is "that one cannot know without acting and cannot act without knowing" (Grimmett & Erickson, 1988, p. 6).

To conduct inquiry on practice and to change practice requires reflection, which eventually leads to understanding and the teacher's construction of new knowledge about practice (see Osterman & Kottcamp, 2004; Reagan, Case, & Brubacher, 2000; Taggart & Wilson, 2005; York-Barr, Sommers, Ghere, & Monte, 2006). "If we don't reflect, we are teaching in the dark without knowing if we are effective and if we should modify our teaching" (Hart, Sorensen, & Naylor, 1992, p. 10). Donald Schön's (1987) seminal work on reflection has generated new understandings about the process of teacher reflection. Central to his conceptualization of reflection is his distinction between two ways in which teachers reflect on practice: reflection *in* action and reflection *on* action.

Reflection in action refers to "reflection on one's spontaneous ways of thinking and acting, undertaken in the midst of action to guide further action" (Schön, 1987, p. 22). Reflection in action may be described as thinking on our feet and is dependent on the "action-present," when action is possible within the time frame of the reflection. It involves spontaneous and tacit analysis of one's experiencing, making connections with feelings and thinking, and attending to "theories in use." In Schön's (1987) words,

> It involves a surprise, a response to surprise by thought turning back on itself, thinking what we're doing as we do it, setting the problems of the situation anew, conducting an action experiment on the spot by which we seek to solve the new problem we've set, an experiment in which we test both a new way of seeing the situation, and also try to change the situation for the better . . . my favorite example of reflection in action is jazz. (p. 4)

The key elements that capture the concept of reflection in action are that it (1) occurs during ongoing activity, (2) arises spontaneously from the activity, (3) produces a decision during the activity, and (4) is usually intuitive and tacit (Louden, 1991). What makes reflection in action difficult is that life in classrooms is contingent, dynamic, ever changing: Every moment, every second is situation specific. Moments of teaching are ongoing incidents that require instant actions.

> Teachers practice an art. Moments of choice of what to do, how to do it, with whom and at what pace, arise hundreds of times in a school day, and arise differently every day and with every group of students. No command or instruction can be so formulated as to control that kind of artistic judgment and behavior, with its demand for frequent, instant choices of ways to meet an ever varying situation. (Schwab, 1970, p. 245)

Reflection on action refers to reflection that occurs after the action or event. It is a postmortem of the action. Reflection on action involves taking time to consider any number of questions after the action in the classroom has been completed. Why did I take the action? What was going on in the classroom? How did the students respond? What was I feeling and thinking about? Would I do anything differently the next time around? In reflection on action, teachers look for patterns and contradictions and critically examine beliefs and ideas that frame or have informed the completed action. Reflection on action enables us to think back on what we have done in order to discover how our knowledge in action may have contributed to an outcome, expected or unexpected. The key elements that distinguish reflection on action are that it (1) occurs out of the immediacy of practice, (2) involves conscious deliberation knowingly engaged in, and (3) produces a decision about practice (Airasian, Gullickson, Hahn, & Farland, 1995).

Models of Reflection

Expanding Schön's typology of reflection, van Manen (1991a, 1991b) and Killion and Todnem (1991) have added the concept of *anticipatory reflection* or *reflection for action*. Reflection for action is a way of framing an anticipated problem, considering possible alternatives, formulating a course of action to be tested, and thinking about the outcomes that may emerge from planned actions. It enables us to consciously, carefully, and systematically think through anticipated situations and thoughtfully prepare actions for testing in the classroom.

A useful typology for understanding and practicing reflection is offered by Valli (1997), who delineates four different kinds of reflection:

reflection in/on action, which focuses on the teacher's personal teaching performance; *deliberative reflection,* which focuses on a range of teaching concerns, including students, the curriculum, teaching strategies, the rules, and the organization of the classroom; *personalistic reflection,* focusing on one's own personal growth and relationships with students; and *critical reflection,* in which the social, moral, and political dimensions of schooling are examined. Valli's typology of reflection is somewhat similar to van Manen's (1977, pp. 205–208) concept of levels of reflection, which was developed prior to Schon's catalytic work. Van Manen postulated three levels of reflection:

Level 1. *Technical reflection* focuses on basic technical skills (instructional skills, classroom management skills, subject matter content) required to reach a predetermined goal. Teachers center on applying knowledge to reach predetermined ends and objectives, which are not questioned. Educational practices are evaluated according to the criteria of effectiveness, economy, and efficiency.

Level 2. *Practical reflection* advances to a critical analysis of the rationale for the educational practices being used to reach goals, of the goals themselves, and of the contexts that affect the achievement of the goals. Teachers focus on studying, questioning, and clarifying the end objectives and the assumptions undergirding teaching practices to achieve the objectives.

Level 3. *Critical reflection* involves making connections between what happens in the classroom and the wider moral and social structures that affect what goes on in the school and the classroom and considering the moral and ethical implications and consequences of teachers' beliefs and practices on students.

Another construction of reflection is offered by Rearick (Rearick & Feldman, 1999, as cited in Feldman, 2003), who identifies three forms of reflection: *autobiographical reflection,* in which action researchers examine the metaphorical meanings of their stories to understand and explain practice; *collaborative reflection,* in which participants share personal theories, ask questions, and seek answers beyond the self; and *communal reflection,* in which action researchers examine the social construction of the self and the situation within cultural, historical, and institutional contexts, addressing such questions as the meaning of democracy, freedom, and social justice. Located within these forms of reflection is *existential reflection.* Feldman (2002), in proposing a case for the concept of existential reflection, reminds us that because we are conscious beings, we all engage in reflection; there are various forms of reflection that can include others in multiple ways, he asserts. The goals of existential reflection, Feldman (2002) says, are to "illuminate assumptions about oneself as a teacher; bring to light assumptions, theories, and myths about the outside systems that affect learning; and work towards a transformative and transcendent experience and emancipation" (pp. 247–248).

Mark Cooper (2008), coordinator of the Volunteer Action Center at Florida International University, has identified three levels of reflection that serve as guides for all modes of reflection to shape one's thinking and to make sense of one's experience:

The Mirror: The Self Becomes Clearer. Reflection as a mirror helps you to understand yourself, your values, your assumptions, and your biases, and to see how your experience has helped you learn more about these dimensions of yourself.

The Microscope: A Small Experience Becomes Larger. Reflection as microscope helps you to understand how your individual activities impact your students, other people, yourself, and your work as a whole. It facilitates reflection on events that occurred, your role in them, and their impact.

The Binoculars: The Distance Becomes Closer. Reflections as binoculars help you identify larger issues that surround the work in which you are engaged. It can expand your vision and understanding of overarching issues, causes, effects, and impacts and help you to envision future developments and to change future behaviors, attitudes, and decisions.

Zeichner and Liston (1996, pp. 44–47) maintain that all teachers pedagogically behave in their classrooms according to the personal theories they hold; that these personal theories, by and large, are not conscious; and that through the process of reflection, teachers' personal theories can be brought to the surface, examined, and questioned in terms of how they affect teaching practice. They suggest a five-level approach for reflection to help teachers make their personal theories explicit:

- Rapid reaction: Something happens, and a teacher reacts instinctively. The teacher's response is immediate in reflection and action.
- Repair: The teacher pauses to think about what happened and may try to repair the situation.

- Review: The teacher takes time out (hours or days) to assess the situation.
- Research: The teacher systematically researches the situation in all its forms.
- Retheorize and research: The teacher rethinks the situation in view of what the teacher discovered in the previous four levels of reflection and engages in long-term reflection while looking at what others have done.

Four processes have been identified as essential to becoming critically reflective: assumption analysis, contextual awareness, imaginative speculation, and reflective skepticism (Brookfield, 1988, 1995). Brookfield indicates that we engage in *assumption analysis* when we bring to conscious awareness beliefs, values, cultural practices, and social structures regulating behavior and assess their impact on our daily activities. Assumptions structure our way of seeing reality, govern our behavior, and describe how our relationships should be ordered. As a first step in the critical reflection process, assumption analysis makes explicit our taken-for-granted notions of reality. We become *contextually aware* when we realize that our assumptions are socially and personally created in a specific historical and cultural context. Through *imaginative speculation*, we challenge prevailing ways of knowing and acting by imagining alternative ways of thinking about phenomena. The end result of assumption analysis, contextual awareness, and imaginative speculation is *reflective skepticism*, the questioning of any universal truth claims or unexamined patterns of interaction.

Reflection and Phronesis

Regardless of the conceptual approaches to reflection one uses, reflection is not easy. As we progress through multiple levels and forms of reflection, the challenge resides in the problem of how we extract complex meaning from experience. Reflection is multidimensional and multilayered and requires conscious, deliberate, and purposeful effort and time for: asking questions, engaging in introspection, having internal and external dialogues, synthesizing experiences, integrating knowledge, finding patterns, and bringing together discrepant variables, as well as observation, reading, and writing. Dewey (1933) believed that this kind of qualitative reflection required three attitudes: open-mindedness, a willingness to hear what is really happening, to consider multiple perspectives, and to entertain solutions that might be different from one's own; wholeheartedness, a disposition of single-mindedness and attentiveness directed unflinchingly toward a problem; and responsibility, intellectual and moral consciousness regarding one's own actions.

Reflection, then, is more than a form of knowledge or a process for creating knowledge. Van Manen (1991b) treats pedagogy as a form of virtuous action similar to the Aristotelian concept of phronesis: an intellectual virtue and mode of judgment about living the moral life. As he sees it, the basic core of teaching is not reflection before or after action or reflection on reflection. Reflection of this kind is limited in that it involves an attempt to distance us "from situations in order to consider the meaning and significance embedded in those experiences" (1991b, p. 100). He views the essence of pedagogy as the habit of acting "mindfully" in a teaching situation because our entire relationship to students is imbued with "pedagogical thoughtfulness" and is normative, oriented toward doing what is right and appropriate. Van Manen calls such thoughtful, student-oriented action "tact." Tact "differs from reflective action in that it is thinkingly attentive to what it does without reflectively distancing itself from the situation by considering or experimenting with possible alternatives or consequences of the action" (p. 109). Van Manen, whose concept of pedagogy embraces not only teaching but parenting, counseling, and other practices where "adults are living with children for the sake of those children's well-being, growth, maturity, and development" (p. 28), holds the thoughtful enactment of pedagogy to be a virtue or excellence of action rather than simply the intelligence of a pedagogical action as determined by intellectual understanding or analytic knowledge.

For Van Manen, then, reflection is more than a process of thinking; it is a virtuous and moral way of being. Phronesis is deliberation connected to praxis. The praxis of teaching is guided by a moral disposition to act truly and rightly and to advance human well-being and the good life. Reflection supports rather than determines this habitual moral orientation to the good of students by helping us both to plan our actions and also to interpret their significance after the event. A teacher using phronesis deliberates about ethically correct teaching behaviors in a particular situation. Without phronesis, reflection becomes a mere intellectual exercise, and good practice becomes a clever application of techniques (Carr, 1987).

Through reflection with phronesis, reflective teachers study what they are doing; examine pedagogy, curriculum, and student learning; reconstruct their professional and personal knowledge bases; and at the same time make judgments to adapt their practice to best meet the needs of their students. They go beyond the technical aspects of teaching to consider the personal, political, and ethical aspects of teaching, recognizing that reflection is about social justice, equity, and change. They review, reenact, and systematically and critically analyze their own teaching and the learning of their students and formulate explanations with evidence (Shulman, 1987). They

> consistently articulate their current beliefs and examine their underlying assumptions; compare the substance of their beliefs to those held by others; think about the origins, implications, and consequences of those beliefs; and think about the consequences for self and others of holding any particular beliefs. (Grant & Zeichner, 1984, p. 63)

Through reflection teachers find their "inner voice," make the invisible visible, and consciously focus on the processes of teaching and learning to improve teaching and learning. Capturing this spirit of reflection, Palmer (1998) writes:

> As I teach, I project the condition of my soul onto my students, my subject, and our way of being together . . . teaching holds a mirror to the soul. If I am willing to look in that mirror and not run from what I see, I have a chance to gain self-knowledge—and knowing my self is as crucial to good teaching as knowing my students and my subject. (p. 2)

Reflection, as Palmer implies, is not solely an intellectual process. Supporting this view, Leitch and Day (2000, p. 179) argue that reflection is more than an intellectual cognitive process and suggest that "more attention needs to be given to the importance of the role of emotion in understanding and developing the capacities for reflection which facilitate personal, professional, and ultimately system change." They contend that a more integrative model of thinking, feeling, and acting must be embraced by the concept of reflection to escape the linear hierarchical mode of reflection that characterizes much reflective practice. Emotions and thinking are inextricably bound to each other, and access to the emotional aspects of thinking leads to a richer and deeper understanding of self, practice, values, and purposes.

Learning to become critically reflective requires developing a plan and following it until reflection becomes integral to one's everyday behavior. Zehm and Kottler (1993) suggest a process and plan for preparing to become more deeply reflective:

- Develop the conviction that regular involvement in reflection is worth your time and energy. Without such a conviction, deliberate and regular reflection will not occur.
- Make time for reflection when you can be alone to examine and review, collect and connect your reflections. Try to set aside a half hour a day for reflection. Find a quiet place for reflective activity where you will be uninterrupted.
- Record your reflections in a journal or through some other form of documentation.
- Try to assess the effectiveness of regular reflection to your personal and professional life, identifying the benefits you derive from your commitment to reflection. (pp. 116–117)

Although such a plan is a good first step in becoming critically reflective, I believe more is needed to achieve the quality of reflection embodied in the work of Dewey, Palmer, Schön, and van Manen.

❖ DIALOGUE

In my judgment, collaboration and critical dialogue are foundational for reflective practice. "The Socratic admonition to know thyself may not lead to self transformation" or to any "measurable change or good to others or oneself" (Boler, 1999, p. 178). Three limitations are likely to emerge from individual reflection: "reflections that focus on personal impressions as opposed to data; reflections that are done in isolation minus other perspectives; and reflections that are limited to superficial consideration of what works and what doesn't" (Fullan & Hargreaves, 1996, p. 36). Elliott (1991, p. 55) is concerned that teachers who reflect in isolation from each other are more likely to reduce action research to a form of technical rationality. He contends that through collaborative reflection, teachers are empowered and enabled to critique the structures that shape their practice and to change them. Brookfield (1995) warns that reflection can be used to reject outside ideas and may affirm what we already know:

To some extent, we are all prisoners trapped within the perceptual frameworks that determine how we view our experiences. A self-confirming cycle often develops, in which our uncritically accepted assumptions shape actions that then serve to confirm the truth of those assumptions. (p. 28)

Ogusthorpe (1999), arguing that reflection is more than the individual thinking about his or her practice in isolation, makes the case that collaborative reflection is a powerful and effective medium for deeply exploring ideas and practice. Collaborative reflection involves two or more people engaging in conversation about their practice, raising questions, providing feedback, sharing opinions and perspectives, raising awareness, challenging personal beliefs, and searching to advance their knowledge and understanding. Collaborative reflection is a prerequisite for developing and sustaining a culture of inquiry. Ways to foster collaborative reflection include participants building trust, making time for reflection, nurturing questions, forming their own groups, taking risks, being patient, giving the gifts of what each one is learning, accepting offerings of learning, and recognizing the results of collaboration.

Weblogs ("blogs") offer a significant means for supporting collaborative reflection. Sessums (2005) has identified several key elements of blogs that make them effective in facilitating collaborative reflection. He notes that blogs are convenient, support self-expression and "voice," provide access and links to many appropriate resources, offer multiple communication channels, foster efficient collaboration and connectivity, promote viewing peers as constructors of knowledge, and offer a connectivity that transcends formal classroom and organizational structures. A blog can be thought of as an online journal that can be continuously updated as well as an interactive resource where readers can dialogue with each other and add pictures or audio to enhance communication (Shih-hsein Yang, 2005).

Whether through blogs or other means, it is clear that the great strength inherent in collaborative reflection is its requirement for dialogue. Without dialogue, there is no collaborative reflection. As I have noted before in this text, the beginning of knowledge lies in human relationships and interactions. Dialogue with others is essential to critically examine one's ideas, beliefs, values, and performance. Dialogue is more than conversation and discussion. It is a process of "meaning making and knowledge construction through words" in which "group members inquire into their own and one another's beliefs, values, and mental models to better understand how things work in their world" (Garmston & Wellman, 1998, p. 31). In discussing conversation as inquiry and as research, Feldman (1993) describes conversation as dialogue:

Conversation is a dialectical process as the participants share knowledge, views, understandings, and feelings while relating to all contexts and contingencies of personal and political history. It can range over many subjects and include a variety of voices. It can lead in directions not thought of, and answer questions not asked. Participants in conversations can come close to one another, "to what they know, desire, imagine, and believe in" and can reveal to them their "power of mind, good sense, and moral sentiments" (Buchmann, 1983, p. 23). (p. 9)

Dialogue is different from argument in that argument is a process in which we communicate our opinions and counteropinions in an atmosphere of "one upsmanship," whereas in dialogue we engage each other empathically, genuinely striving to understand others' perceptions, feelings, and perspectives; to listen attentively to others' intentions, values, and ideas; and to allow, indeed to create space, for other voices as well as our own (Bohm, 1996). Dialogue begins when participants meet together to listen openly to others and to themselves. As past thoughts are suspended, a desire to examine new ideas emerges. Suspension of one's thoughts, judgments, feelings, and impulses is essential for dialogue. While suspension involves attention, listening, and exploration with others, it also involves listening to yourself examining your own feelings and reactions so they can be seen by you and also be reflected back to you by others in the group. Through this process of examination, differences in ideas surface, sometimes leading to conflicts and a sense of discomfort. As different ideas and concepts are analyzed, new and shared conceptualizations develop. Seemingly diverse perspectives are integrated, and shared meanings are articulated. New understandings emerge. New words express new ideas, and a common language celebrates creative, collaborative new power.

Through dialogical conversation, participants engage in and make sense of their experience through patterns of learning known as streams of meaning making:

Stream 1—*Resonating and Reflecting*

Gaining understanding of the meaning of one's own experience and/or others' experiences through resonating and reflecting in and through conversation.

Hearing Others

Stream 2—*Expressing and Interacting*

Gaining understanding about one's own perspectives and feelings through expressing them, and feeling and hearing others resonate and respond during the course of conversation.

Heard by Others

Stream 3—*Attending and Appreciating*

Gaining understanding of specific others and self through attending to and appreciating the interaction in the "here and now" of the conversation.

Aware of Others

Stream 4—*Interacting and Conceptualizing*

Gaining understanding of one's own and others' perspectives and feelings through interacting in conversation with others who hold and express different perspectives.

Differ With Others

Stream 5—*Listening and Analyzing*

Gaining understanding of others' perspectives and feelings about the topic of conversation through listening and interpreting others' interaction in the conversation.

Compare With Others (Jensen & Kolb, 2002, p. 127)

❖ DOCUMENTATION

Documenting is a process of observing, recording, describing, and analyzing human action; a way of monitoring, observing, and defining what takes place in ongoing processes (Carini, 1975, 1986; Ianni, 1978). One of the fundamental tools of action research is documentation. It subsumes an entire gamut of activities concerned with information (Mertens & Yarger, 1979), including collecting, generating, organizing, synthesizing, analyzing, interpreting, and using information to construct knowledge.

Reflective documentation is a most productive approach for examining the wide range of contextual and multidimensioned variables that impinge on teacher and student development; it provides a sound action research base for generating new questions about student learning and growth. The purpose of documentation is to develop an ongoing record, an ongoing process, and a continuous form of assessment. Carini (1986) describes documenting as a "process of selecting and juxtaposing recorded observations and other records of phenomenal meaning to reveal reciprocities and, therefore, to approach the integrity of a phenomenon" (p. 27). Documentation is the sine qua non for evaluation and action research. The only adequate way of describing what takes place in any social or behavioral situation is to be there, to be a participant, to observe continuously, and to become intellectually and emotionally involved in what takes place.

In other words, action research requires that an open field rather than controlled laboratory perspective be taken. Educational research traditionally has been a process by which preexisting ideas are vindicated or validated. However, in action research, teacher-researchers are actively involved in the process and milieu of the classroom and give feedback that allows individuals to change their actions and practice and to change their objectives, when appropriate and possible.

Observation and Documentation

An analytical process essential to documentation and the study of classroom life is observation. Ongoing keen observation is fundamental for effective teaching, for teacher decision making, and for making judgments. As a process for informing and improving teaching practice, observation is used to collect data about students, to document learning and growth, to individualize instruction, to address special needs of learners, to evaluate instructional planning, to study the classroom learning environment, and to assess one's own professional growth. More significant, observation is a process for discovering the hidden side of classroom life, where everyday practices become so ordinary and so routine, they often become invisible. These implicit and subliminal practices become accessible through observation, which is central to conducting action research (Frank, 1999).

Historically, observation has been a foundational process for scientific inquiry in developing speculations, building and confirming theories, and generating knowledge. Observation is critical in acquiring information, developing inferences, and defining problems. Within the action research framework, the power of observation lies in the study of observable phenomena as they naturally occur in the classroom, in the school, and in the community.

To sharpen teachers' classroom observations, increase their skills in reflection, and help them see in more nuanced ways, Carol Rodgers (2002), inspired by Dewey's concept of reflection, has developed an observational framework that she describes as a reflective cycle. It has four phases: Learning to See, Learning to Describe, Learning to Think Critically, and Learning to Take Intelligent Action.

Learning to See means that the teacher is fully present in the here and now of the classroom and open to indications of students' learning that facilitate informed and responsive action. The emphasis in this stage is on the process of observational description without judgment or evaluation. When teachers closely attend to what and how their students strive to learn, and when they adjust their instruction to their students' efforts, they are "present to learning."

The *Learning to Describe* phase involves discussions of videotaped lessons, case studies, and student work. Participating teachers are introduced to the "I, Thou, It" paradigm, a way of looking at teaching and learning developed by Hawkins (1974) and adapted by Rodgers. Using this lens, teachers describe a student or event from their own classroom that concerns or puzzles them, shaping their description with reference to the teacher ("I"), the learners ("Thou"), the subject matter ("It"), and the context. Members of the teacher inquiry group then pose clarifying questions and elicit relevant stories to illuminate the subject from a variety of different perspectives. The emphasis is on thoughtful description and not interpretation. Teachers focus on close descriptive examination of a situation, consider the possibility of alternative viewpoints, and keep the student's point of view and the complexity of the situation in mind.

In the *Learning to Think Critically* phase, teachers examine the evidence they have collected with respect to four different but interrelated facets of analysis. First, they look closely at the descriptive data for contrasts or other patterns of behavior that enable a thoughtful interpretation and thoughtful action. Second, they work toward developing a shared language by clarifying terms and probing meanings to ensure common understandings about teaching and learning. Third, they encourage one another to question their assumptions about their practice, theories, and the intersection of the two. Finally, they turn to professional reading for other paradigms and frameworks that will help them to name, understand, and test their emerging theories.

In the fourth phase of the reflective cycle, *Learning to Take Intelligent Action*, ideas for action that emanate from the first three phases of the cycle are tested in action. Having strengthened their capacities in the first three phases to look closely at learning, teachers are better equipped to see its impact when ideas are put into practice. Their actions then become the text of a new experience on which to reflect.

Just as important as the observations themselves is the recording of those observations, continuously and immediately after each observation has been made. Immediate documentation of observations is helpful in capturing the rich context of an interaction or event. Teacher-researchers also need to record their own impressions following an event. Using a tape recorder during the observation is particularly helpful in capturing the "here and the now" of a specific teaching/learning situation. It is good to bear in mind that documentation aims to reveal a multiplicity of meanings and does not strive to exhaust the singular meaning of an event.

Video- and audiotape recordings offer one of the most appropriate and useful means for capturing the teacher/student relationship and generate a richness of observational data unequaled through any other procedure. Only on the video recording can teachers observe the authenticity of the interaction between students, between students and teacher, as well as the dynamics and fluidity of teaching and learning, personality, and behavior; intellectual communications; and the varied other dimensions and dynamics of the classroom. From tapes, teachers can begin to explore such questions as: Is that me in the classroom? Am I real with my students? Do I play a role? Am I accepting of students? How do I facilitate learning? Are students learning? Am I using appropriate questioning strategies? How well am I responding to students? Through tape recordings, teachers can determine the quality of students' responses to themselves both as teachers and people. By asking colleagues to listen to and critique recordings of their teaching and their interactions with students, teachers learn what impact they have on students and, through peer feedback, how they can advance the quality of their teaching. Such learning fosters self-discovery, personal confrontation, and challenge within teachers to stretch their thinking and enables them to become more sensitive and attuned to their students and peers as people.

Observation is not totally objective; there is an interdependence between the knower and the known. The observer needs to be vigilant in avoiding "observer bias" (Gay & Airasian, 2000), in which the observer filters observational data according to personal assumptions, beliefs, and understandings. Observations of events, situations, behavior, and actions are not decontextualized. Observations are actively interpreted by the observer as a function of the meaning context available. Such contexts of interpretation include the observer's knowledge, experience, assumptions, and perceptual framework. The observer affects the observed, and the observed affects the observer; thus, the observer cannot escape being a participant in the process or the event observed. It is through the observer's encounter with the event that multiplicity of meanings emerges. Subsequent reflection on documented observation can generate a richer understanding of the multiple meanings found in the situation.

No standard format for collecting observations would be appropriate for different settings, contexts, and purposes. A variety of procedures can be used including graphs and charts of students' activities in various classroom spaces, records of interaction patterns among students, time and event sampling, teachers' notes, interviews, student products, teacher and student journals, logs/diaries, questionnaires, surveys, video and audio recordings, drawings, running records, and other devices aimed at recording perceptions, ideas, questions, concerns, and trepidations—everything that takes place in a classroom—from as many perspectives as possible.

> The process of documenting can move through several levels, which are not so much steps to be taken one after another but rather represent a movement toward a fuller understanding of the multiple meanings of the phenomenon, that is, of its coherence, durability, and integrity. (Mishler, 1979, p. 10)

Documentation enables teachers to underwrite and to validate what is taking place in a particular classroom. Documentation should not be viewed as simply a matter of collecting and keeping sterile quantitative records. The qualitative issues—the values that are inherent in a classroom—can be described only through careful documentation. In this respect, then, documentation can be regarded as a phenomenological tool, for it records perceived reality as well as objective reality. It records feelings and personal experiencing, and through the documentation process, teachers can describe and interpret their intentions as well as students' intentions, probe the realms of their lived experience, and explore the boundaries of their awareness, which form their horizons in the classroom and in the school. Documenting feelings, personal observations, perceptions, and the context in which they are experienced helps to define action research as a vital process that captures the pulse, the vitality, and the fibrous nature of life in the classroom.

Writing and Journaling

In my judgment, writing is one of the most powerful tools we have for learning, for professional and personal growth, and for critical reflection. Writing is a form of reflection; it is conversation thought out and written down. When we write, we become more aware of who we are and what we are about. Words become the tools for making meaning and for discovering and generating personal knowledge (Polanyi, 1962). Consciousness is created by the act of writing. Writing mediates reflection and action, fixes thoughts on paper, constantly seeks to make external what is internal, and focuses our reflective awareness. To write is to measure our thoughtfulness. Writing separates us from what we know, and yet, it unites us more closely with what we know (van Manen, 1991b). "When we write we become more responsible for our words, and ultimately we become more thoughtful human beings" (Barth, 2001, p. 67).

Writing to record our thoughts, observations, and reflections is promoted through journaling. Journal writing is closest to natural speech, and writing can flow without self-consciousness or inhibition. A journal offers personal and private space to record honestly what is happening in the classroom, in the school, and in the teacher's life. It is a place of safety where we can talk to ourselves and experiment with new ways of thinking and feeling. A journal is a willing ear and a confidant with whom our questions, concerns, anxieties, and joy can be shared. The primary audience for a journal is the person writing the journal. A journal is not maintained for colleagues, friends, supervisors, and professors. If it is written for external audiences, then our true thoughts and feelings about teaching will be mitigated. It is important that we write for our own reasons and not to meet the expectations of others. The maximum benefits from journaling accrue when the first audience is ourselves.

Journaling offers a rich means for describing practice; for recording and examining beliefs, assumptions, questions, and challenges; and for expressing feelings and identifying problems. A journal can be a place for releasing tensions and clarifying feelings. A journal also can serve as a historical document providing opportunities to review journal entries written at different times and places in one's teaching and to honestly assess how challenges and problem situations were confronted then and how they might be handled now. Journal entries can be helpful in planning future actions, generating research questions, developing new insights about teaching, making connections between thought and action, making connections between the classroom situation and broader frameworks, assessing the effectiveness of teaching strategies, and determining how well students are learning.

Journaling also promotes the discovery of the teaching self. A journal is a rich and personal data source for finding out more about who we are and how our identity and integrity are expressed in the classroom and for finding personal meaning in teaching. Journaling helps us to discover the wisdom we already possess and to transform our voice. Journaling can provide tangible evidence of mental processes, revealing thought processes and mental habits, facilitating memory, and providing a context for healing and growth. Journaling both affirms and challenges your beliefs about yourself. Journals offer place and space to practice ways of knowing and to envision new ways of thinking and responding to reading and experiences in the classroom and school. In essence, journaling offers opportunities for discovery and rediscovery of the self, of ideas, of meaning, of one's voice.

One of the major difficulties teachers and particularly teacher-interns have in writing reflective journals is in unlearning writing conventions that they have internalized over time as they progress through the educational system. They have been taught to deny the personal voice, the pronoun "I" is banned. They have become disembodied from their writing. They have learned to write in the third person, in a passive objective voice, and to cite academic authorities and experts rather than personal opinions or feelings. They have become inhibited by their "internal editor" or how their imagined audience might respond. There is no room for the subjective experience. Their writing focuses on outcomes rather than the struggle to achieve them (Kember, 2000, p. 215).

Catherine Battaglia (1996), a classroom teacher writing about her experience in conducting an action research study, says this about journaling:

> We are often taught to appeal to "those who know better"—the experts, the research, the authorities. This process (action research) taught me to trust my thinking and my ideas more . . . not in an arrogant way, but in a professional way. Journal writing and audio taping were powerful sources of data; the simplest ideas had a way of growing once I reflected on them later. I emerged seeing the journal as a "greenhouse for ideas to be stored," until I could later use the "energy of reflection in order to help them germinate and grow." (p. 91)

For journaling to work, it is essential to make a conscious commitment to writing regularly. Making daily entries would be desirable but may not always be possible. On the other hand, if journaling is not done on some regular basis, then its potential for facilitating teacher reflection, action, and growth is lost. It would seem that writing three or four times a week would be a reasonable schedule for recording journal entries. When I have surveyed teachers and teacher-interns about how they journal, I find there are as many different ways of journaling as there are people. Some journal daily at a specific time during the day, often in the afternoon just before leaving school, to reflect on the day's events. Some journal during the day, recording events and thoughts on Post-it Notes to capture the immediacy of an experience or idea. Others make entries in the evening, when there is quiet time for thinking about the day. Still others find time in the morning after a good night's sleep as the best time to pull their thoughts together. Small spiral notebooks, a pad of Post-its, clipboards, three-ring notebooks, diaries, leather-bound journals, scraps of paper, livejournals, electronic recorders—there are many different kinds of journals.

I find that audiotaping is a particularly useful mechanism for facilitating reflective journaling. For me, it is less cumbersome and difficult to consistently audiotape than videotape. Audio recordings enable us to capture moments in the classroom as they occur. We can also use audiotaping to interview students on the spot. The sights, sounds, and data we record can later be used to prompt creative and reflective writing in our journal. Audiotapes can be used to transcribe dialogue between teacher and student/s or between teachers to create a record of the dynamics of teaching and learning in the classroom. In addition, audiotaping provides a means for composing a journaled script of the teacher's day—complete with a timeline and a description of key events.

Incorporating artwork in the journaling process—drawings, photographs, and sketches, for example—can encourage discovery of deep feelings and thoughts. When words seem to fail or to be hiding, sketching or working with an image can be a starting point for exploring feelings, impressions, and ideas in new and different ways. Many teacher-interns use drawings as intellectual and creative nutrients to enhance, clarify, and expand reflection in their journals.

Where we write can be a factor in contributing to the regularity of journaling. The classroom, a home office, another room in the home, a table at a coffee shop, and the school library are venues that are often cited as places where teachers journal. I know one teacher, an itinerant special needs teacher, who uses a small tape recorder regularly to dictate her impressions and ideas of the day in her car as she drives from school to home.

Journaling is a personal process, so there is no standard format for journaling. While there are no specific guidelines, Kochendorfer (1994) offers a few suggestions for making writing meaningful:

- *Letter to yourself.* Write the entry as a letter from the present you to the future you.
- *Unsent letter.* Write a letter that you would never send. . . . An unsent letter can help you realize what you really believe and what you really want.

- *Feeling focus.* Begin the entry with a report of intense feelings you have at that moment or had earlier in the day. Include the primary and the secondary feelings, the overt and the subtle, the pleasurable and the aggravating. . . . Write a dispassionate account of the events that preceded this moment of intense feeling.
- *Snapshot.* Record significant moments. Do not limit your choices to problems. Include incidents that seem to pop out. . . . Jot down key words that will help you remember what happened. Later, describe the event in your journal in some detail.
- *Conversation.* Frame the entry to take the form of a script recording a conversation between yourself and another person, or between your different selves, rational and emotional, free and restrained, or teacher parent.
- *Insight notes.* Begin your sentences with phrases like "I wonder if. . . ." "Could it be that. . . ." "I noticed. . . ." or "It seems to me that. . . ."
- *Free writing.* Start with a topic and let the writing flow. Do not stop or be concerned whether what you write makes sense. Just let thoughts and feelings pop into your head and immediately out of the blue. (p. 42)

Writing Stories

Writing accounts and stories of our teaching experiences is a powerful way of discovering our voice and finding and making meaning of teaching. Every teacher has stories to tell—a teacher is a book waiting to be written. Through teacher narratives of events and experiences in the classroom, through teacher stories of children, schools, and the complexities and richness of the lives we live, and through personal accounts, autobiographies, and histories, we can come to a deeper and richer understanding of teaching and learning (Bolton, 2006; Clandinin et al., 2006; Connelly & Clandinin, 1996, 2000; Czamiawska, 2004; Elliott, 2005; Heikkinen, Huttunen, & Syrjala, 2007; Riessman, 2008). Teacher narratives liberate our creative capacities for changing ourselves, for changing teaching and improving student learning, and for initiating both classroom and school change. They can draw out and develop the ability to see and understand the complexity, mystery, and richness of teacher and student lives. Authentic teacher stories are a means for finding and giving professional voice, stimulating critical dialogue, exploring underlying principles of practice, communicating beliefs and ideas to a wider audience, building self-confidence in confronting professional dilemmas, describing and documenting professional experiences, developing insight into teacher-student relationships, and contributing to the overall wisdom of practice (Jalongo & Isenberg, 1995, pp. 26–27).

In writing her own story about her collaboration with an educational consultant in the implementation of a new curriculum that focused on the learner as inquirer, Beattie (1995) justifies the claim for the use of teacher narratives in action research:

> It was during the process of writing that I came to understand that these stories of change focusing on learning, growth, and professional development are all fundamentally about voice—the discovery and rediscovery of voice, the development of increased capacities to listen to one's own voice and the voices of others, and the expression of self through practice and writing. It was through the writing that I have come to see that it is through the telling and retelling of our stories of practice that we construct and reconstruct our understandings of who we are, can create new and more significant versions of ourselves, and can thus transform ourselves. (p. 140)

What constitutes a meaningful teacher narrative? Teacher narratives offer a way of engaging in the discourse of teaching. They can accommodate ambiguity, contradiction, emotional struggle, and dilemma. They can be written to process a disappointing experience when mistakes are made in the teaching/learning situation; to examine anger, frustration, and anxiety when students don't do their assignments or act out in the classroom for no apparent reason; to record meaningful and touching interactions when students "teach the teacher" or give a gift of love, appreciation, or kindness; to assess the dynamics of one's interactions with students, parents, and colleagues; to explore more deeply the power of a lesson gone well; to understand why a specific situation unfolded as it did; or to discover personal patterns of emotional responses and habitual ways of interacting.

Good teacher narratives capture authentic teacher knowledge. Teacher knowledge can be represented through three forms of stories: the sacred story, the lived secret story, and the cover story (Connelly, Clandinin, & He, 1997). The sacred story consists of dictates from above, such as researchers' theories and policymakers' rules and regulations. The secret story is what the teacher really thinks and does. The cover story is what teachers tell administrators or other teachers about what they do or what they think other people want to hear. Fieleke

(2002), in his study of teacher talk, found that teachers connected constructions of purposes, subject matter, and pedagogy primarily with secret stories and not with the sacred story. He found that "the sacred story of positivistic research findings, prescriptions, and public policy mandates undermined the participants' experiences of teaching as meaningful" and concluded that "research on teaching must provide edification and build up the soul of teaching through affirming constructions of what it means to teach" (pp. 182–183). These affirming constructions are located in teacher narratives.

The process of writing a teacher narrative involves exploring the specific details of a particular teaching or learning situation. The context, including the people involved and the point of view of the teacher, are all taken into account. The process of writing the narrative often clarifies a problematic situation. The teacher's awareness may expand, interpersonal connections may be realized, and the truth of a situation may be understood. Narrative writing can help teachers process the intense and stressful aspects of teaching because writing can be a catharsis, bringing a sense of relief and renewal. Writing makes sense of confusion and gives voice to the teacher's wisdom while acting as a forum for new ideas and solutions. Writing for the purpose of self-reflection and to gain self-knowledge is a way to bring more satisfaction to one's teaching, to continue personal and professional growth, and to decompress what others cannot know.

A teacher narrative can be considered as a crucible in which experience and ideas meet, where feeling and emotion are transmitted as the narrative shows us worlds we do not know or changes our perspectives toward the world we know all too well. By sharing narratives with each other, teachers can develop a feeling of connection to the larger world of education and an understanding that many experiences are universal even if the details are different.

A good teacher narrative is characterized by four elements (Jalongo & Isenberg, 1993):

1. It is genuine and true. It is not contrived to be cute, sensational, or to show the teacher in the best possible light. It is real and authentic and resonates within each of us.

2. It invites reflection and discourse, which are fundamental to reflective practice. It invites discussion of critical issues and stimulates dialogue. It invites us to respond.

3. It is interpreted and reinterpreted, looking beneath the surface to discover underlying meanings. Although the account of the

particular experience does not change, the concepts and themes used to interpret it can change, that is, the same story can be viewed from different angles.

4. It is powerful and evocative, eliciting strong emotions, challenges, and responses.

Getting started in writing a narrative about our teaching and learning is not easy—there are no magical formulae to tell us when to start writing or how to start writing. As Bogdan and Biklen (1982) suggest, beginning writers are procrastinators who find numerous reasons for not getting started and who always seem to find diversions to deflect their time and energy away from writing. They advise that "you are never ready to write; writing is something you must make a conscious decision to do and then discipline yourself to follow through" (p. 172).

One way to get started is to write in response to some cues that can trigger memories and ideas. Here are some cues that may be helpful in stimulating recollections and reflections about specific experiences and events:

I recall:

A time I was surprised how one student responded to me

A time I was surprised how an entire class reacted

A class period I wish had never happened

An incident that was my baptism of fire

The day I lost my innocence

A time I was forced to change

A time I felt strong conflict between teaching and the rest of my life

A time I felt a strong connection between my teaching and the rest of my life

My shining hour (Kochendorfer, 1994, pp. 24–26)

Writing an Autobiography

The cues listed above suggest that autobiographical writing can be an exciting and illuminating journey for self-discovery and self-reflection. Autobiographical writing is a form of first-person research.

At any given moment, we live in a "biographic situation" (Pinar & Grumet, 1976, p. 51). Each of us is located in historical time and cultural place and brings our lived meanings about teaching and learning that follow from past experiences and contain "unarticulated contradictions of past and present as well as anticipation of possible futures" (Pinar, 2004, p. 36). Through autobiographical writing, we can discern personal values, worldviews, and assumptions. Writing an autobiography facilitates the discovery of significant experiences that affect current goals and dispositions. It also offers the opportunity for each of us to write a new story of who we are as people, why we are here, and why we are in education. An autobiography can be seen as a new beginning—a way of exercising our uniqueness while at the same time finding our common humanity and connections with others.

Action research itself is a form of autobiography:

Autobiographical writing is common in accounts of action research. Researchers make frequent use of diaries, logs, and journals as part of the action research "tool kit." The final report often contains references to the writers' own lives: their professional development and personal experiences. Indeed, it would be odd if it were not so. One way of describing an action research report is that it is an autobiography—writing about one's own story. Action research is, inevitably, a narrative: it is research into one particular situation, in one particular time and place. Moreover, it is research carried out into the researcher's own situation. Finally, it is research in which the self of the researcher is itself at issue. (Griffiths, 1994, p. 72)

The word *autobiography* means self-life-writing. *Auto:* the self. What do we mean by the self? How have my conceptions of self changed over time? How do I conceive of my self as a person? Learner? Teacher? *Bio*: life. Beyond physical existence, what do we mean by life? How do I measure, describe, and evaluate my life? What do I want my life to be as a person? Teacher? *Graphy:* writing. What will be the effect of transforming my life into text? How do I want to represent my life in text? How do I want to explore my life through text?

When we enter the classroom, we bring who we are as people—our gender, race, ethnicity, worldview, beliefs, ideologies, assumptions, values, perceptions, past experiences, personal history, biases, and attitudes. We cannot escape who we are, nor can we keep who we are out of the classroom.

Many of the moral meanings evident in classroom teaching are unintended because they result from the enactment of what the person is, which is more than their conscious intentions realize. So how can the teacher control, much less dictate, the impact they have in educational contexts without self-knowledge and understanding? (O'Hanlon, 1996, p. 85)

Autobiography offers us the opportunity to come to a deeper understanding of who we are and the chance to change aspects of who we are, if such change is needed. Autobiography also provides a framework for teacher development in that it can raise consciousness about unexamined beliefs and values that affect teaching, student learning, and the professional life of the teacher. By surfacing and confronting unarticulated beliefs, values, and assumptions and their origins, we can then begin to understand who we are as teachers, how we affect student learning, and how we can advance our own growth. As a form of self-inquiry, then, autobiography fosters an inquiring approach to the way we live and teach and enables us to act with awareness and with choices.

Doing action research requires self-reflexivity and attention to our own practice. Through autobiography, we can give voice to the silenced parts of our lives, discover what sustains and supports us, learn about self as constant and changing and who we are as the people behind the research we do. One form of autobiography that lends itself to learning about the self in relation to others is the **autoethnography** (Ellis & Bochner, 2000; Menley & Young, 2005; Reed-Danahay, 1997), in which researchers study their own life experiences within a social context. An autoethnography is an analytical personal account about the self as a part of a group or culture—an attempt to see the self as others might—an opportunity to explain differences from the inside; it is written for others as the major audience. Autoethnography turns "the ethnographic gaze inward on the self, while maintaining the outward gaze of ethnography looking at the larger context wherein self experiences occur" (Denzin, 1997, p. 227). Cunningham and Jones (2005) put it another way: Autoethnography casts the researcher as both the informant-insider and the analyst-outsider. Autoethnographers may vary in their emphasis on *graphy* (i.e., the research process), *ethnos* (i.e., culture), or *auto* (i.e., self) (Reed-Danahay, 1997). Two good examples of autoethnography are *Inside Stories: Qualitative Research Reflections* (de Marrais, 1998), a collection of personal stories written by qualitative researchers in which they delineate ethical issues, power relations, and the "messiness" they experienced inside the field of qualitative research; and *Rewriting Narratives* *of Self: Reflections from an Action Research Study* (James, 1999), in which the author traces the learning and transformation of an action researcher through a particular project and explores the influence of researcher autobiography on the processes and outcomes of the research.

I have found that writing an autobiography of learning has resonated with teachers and teacher-interns, evoking powerful images and deep discoveries of personal experiences in learning that have impacted their teaching as well as their personal lives. The autobiography of learning is also the beginning point for self-inquiry, which eventually leads to collaborative inquiry. Here is how I frame the autobiography of learning assignment for graduate students and teachers enrolled in my inquiry course:

Autobiography of Learning

We bring to our teaching and to any form of research and inquiry who we are as people—our assumptions, values, history, experiences, attitudes, ideas, knowledge, understandings, biases, and where we are in the moment of our development. Writing about our history of learning can be helpful in illuminating our current situations in learning to become a teacher and surface issues and questions we might wish to explore further in studying our own classrooms and the ways we teach and students learn in our classrooms.

After taking notes on the following points, write a biographical essay that synthesizes these experiences, draws out their major themes, and gives a clear picture of how you currently think about teaching, the nature of learning, and the purposes of education and how that has changed over time. Write an autobiography of your experience in learning (or not learning), focusing on how you were thinking about the purposes of education and the nature and quality of your learning experiences. Try to capture the first day of school. Some questions you might address are:

Why did you want to go to school? Or did you? What did you think would happen there?

How were you feeling as you entered school? Consider your experience of school, how school felt, and how you best learned and when you felt most valued and at peace—or least valued, most disconnected, and most at war with yourself and school.

Try to recapture important educational moments and events throughout your learning life: fourth grade, sixth grade, high school, university, graduate school, and other learning venues.

Did any of these events have a lasting impression on your ideas about school, teaching, and learning? Explain these fully. Consider the contextual,

(Continued)

> (Continued)
>
> environmental, and psychological influences that shaped your concept of school, education, and teaching/learning. Friends, family, church, media, community, teachers, geography, neighborhood, school.
>
> Why did you decide to become a teacher? What do you hope to accomplish as a teacher? What do you want students to learn, think, and be able to do as a result of their interactions with you?
>
> What impact has the prepracticum experience had on your thinking about teaching and learning and the purposes of education? How does the prepracticum experience fit with your personal history of learning, aspiration, and development?
>
> Reflecting on your autobiography of learning, how might it inform your inquiry about teaching and learning? What questions are you struggling with now at this point in your history?

A Final Note on Writing

The best perspective on writing, one that has guided my own writing over the years, is provided by Don Murray, Pulitzer Prize winner, columnist, professor emeritus of English at the University of New Hampshire, and author of numerous books and hundreds of articles dealing with the art of writing. Here I would like to share with you, the reader, some of Murray's observations and thoughts about writing, drawn from three of his books. I hope his thinking about writing will encourage and support you in your own writing.

1. *Nulla dies sine linea:* "'Never a day without a line'—Horace (65–8 BC). Writing, like jogging, has to become a habit. I write when I have nothing to say, when I don't feel like writing, when I cannot write anything worth reading" (Murray, 2002, p. 153).

2. *Expectation:* "I expect to write, my attitude predicts my performance. The swimmer who goes to the starting block prepared to lose will lose; the writer who does not expect a draft will not write one. I have to recall when I have written easily before to expect that the draft will come" (Murray, 2002, p. 42).

3. *External:* "Ripeness is a product of a deadline. Without a deadline I do not begin to write and finish what I am writing. I have yearly, monthly, and weekly deadlines but the most important one is tomorrow morning's deadline" (Murray, 1996, p. 17).

4. *Internal.* "I also have an internal demand. . . . I write to discover who I am and what the life I am leading must mean. The

surprise of saying what I do not intend keeps me returning to my writing desk" (Murray, 2002, p. 42).

5. *Rehearsal.* "Most times I come to my desk having rehearsed what I may say, the way I would rehearse an employment interview. . . . I talk to myself, I dream, I imagine what I might say, sometimes making notes, often just letting the random fragments of writing circulate through my mind. It is all brought together as I start to draft" (Murray, 2002, p. 43).

6. *Forgiveness.* "To write I have to write as well as I can write today, accepting the fact that I cannot write as I'd like to or as well as other writers are writing" (Murray, 2002, p. 43).

7. *Velocity.* "To discover your voice, write fast and write out loud. Velocity will drive you into naturalness and allow you to out-run the censors—teachers, classmates, colleagues—that inhibit you and make you want to write in someone else's voice. You will begin to sound like yourself" (Murray, 1996, p. 43).

8. *Failure.* "Failure is essential to effective writing. It is the failure that instructs the chemist, the football coach, the defense attorney, the entrepreneur, the writer. An attempt is made. It doesn't work. But the way it fails instructs. I fail. Failure is necessary and instructive. I find out what I need to write by not yet being able to write it" (Murray, 2004, p. 91).

9. *Write out loud.* "We learned to speak before we wrote, and, even if we are writers, we speak thousands upon thousands of words more than we write in a day. When we write, we speak in written words. The magic of writing is that readers who may never meet us hear what we have written. . . . We call the heard quality of writing *voice* and it may be the most important element in writing" (Murray, 2004, pp. 51–52).

10. *Writing is editing.* "It is not an admission of failure when you have to edit. It is a normal part of the process of making meaning with language. Editing is not punishment, but opportunity" (Murray, 2004, p. 220).

❖ FOCAL POINTS FOR OBSERVATION, JOURNAL WRITING, AND REFLECTION

These questions are posed to stimulate individual or group reflection about the subtleties and challenges of teaching/learning situations.

They have the potential to generate meaningful dialogue, journal entries, narrative reflective essays, or research studies. The listed questions are not meant to constitute a checklist for reflection. One question may be more than enough in nurturing critical dialogue and writing. These are but a finite number of questions about the complexities of teaching and learning. The complexity and challenges of teaching and learning suggest that there are an infinite number of questions that cry out for exploration.

Instruction

- What were my attitudes and mental disposition prior to teaching? As I began teaching? While teaching? When I concluded teaching?
- What did I first see or hear or sense in my classroom: enthusiasm, raw energy, controlled energy, rowdiness, receptivity, eagerness, anticipation, noise, passivity, comfort, discomfort, defiance?
- What was the manner or attitude of students as they entered the room or before I began to teach? Which students greeted and/or interacted with one another warmly, with antagonism, or not at all?
- How did I react to inappropriate student behavior? How did I respond to positive student behavior?
- How did I establish seating arrangements in my classroom? What was my rationale? How have I configured space in my classroom to enhance learning?
- How did I plan and pace my instruction? What did I do to prepare for this class?
- Exactly how did I begin my instruction?
- What was the sequence of teaching and learning events? Was there a variety of learning experiences and activities?
- How did I engage students in learning activities? What did I do to help students reflect on their own learning? What strategies did I use to encourage students' critical thinking?
- How long did each learning activity last? How did I transition from one learning activity to another?
- How did my instruction accommodate students' different learning styles?
- What was the most effective part of my teaching? Where did my teaching "peak"? Where did student learning peak?

- How did I check for student comprehension and understanding? How did I frame questions to facilitate student comprehension and learning?
- How much of the material could have been learned without me (for example, by handouts, homework, independent study, small-group discussion, guided reading, video tapes, online Web sites)?
- To what extent did the sequencing of my instruction anticipate probable student responses?
- To what extent did I help students connect new learning with their prior knowledge and experiences? How did I build on students' life experiences? How did I help students make connections between the content and their lives and experiences?
- How did I help students assess and evaluate their own work?
- How did I create and deliver instruction to accommodate cultural diversity, varied abilities, and linguistic differences among my students?
- Were there student questions or responses that were totally unexpected? How did I handle them? How did I facilitate and encourage student questioning to advance their learning?
- To what extent did I provide meaningful and useful feedback to my students to advance their learning?
- What instructional approaches worked well with a wide variety of students? What approaches led students to produce high-quality work?
- Exactly how did my instruction end?
- Was it clear what would or should happen next (tomorrow, next week)? Were my goals for instruction consistent with the students' learning needs, interests, and abilities?

Dynamics of Grouping

- How were student groups chosen? How were they structured? Why?
- Where were the groups situated?
- When and how were instructions for group work given?
- Which group did I assist first? Why?
- How did I decide which group to help next?
- How did I monitor the groups I wasn't working with?
- What did I do when I wasn't working with any of the groups?
- How long did the groups work effectively? What factors determined the length of time on task?

- Were all of the members of each group actively engaged? Were there group leaders? Were some members letting others do all or most of the work?
- How did I determine whether or not the groups did their work?
- Did the class regroup as a whole by the end of the period? Did each group report back to the rest of the class? What were the seating arrangements?
- Could this work have been better accomplished in some other form (for example, lecture, homework, independent study)?

Assignments

- Were directions and expectations for homework or assignments for the next session clear?
- What was the purpose of the homework assignment? How meaningful was the assignment for students? Did it promote learning? How?
- How did the homework fit into the next day's class work?
- What was my rationale for the assignment? Would the assignment make a difference in advancing student learning? Was the assignment necessary to promote learning?
- Did the assignment encourage students to use a variety of learning resources?

Student Reaction to My Teaching

- Did students sense that my questions were real or only rhetorical?
- Were students encouraged to generate their own questions? Did they actively participate in their learning? What kind of questions did students raise?
- Did students respond to each other or just to me?
- How did students know whether or not their responses were on target?
- Were students confused by any part of my teaching? Did I anticipate this? How did I handle it?
- What was the nature of student interaction in my classroom? How did I encourage and facilitate quality interaction among students?
- Were there cliques in the room? If there were, how did I deal with them?
- Was there a struggle for power or attention among the students? Who were the student leaders?

- Did any one student dominate the discussion? If so, how did the other students feel about this? How did I handle this situation?
- Was any student excluded? If so, how did I respond to the student?
- Which student (or students) was/were the most: bored, engaged, enthusiastic, confused, bright, disturbed, cooperative, angry, cheerful, humorous, indifferent, judgmental, helpful, sensitive, obstinate, defiant, vociferous, silent, caring, kind? How do I know?
- How did I influence student interaction?
- How well did I listen and attend to students?
- To what extent did I use student responses to encourage or to bring others into the class discussion?
- How did the students feel about being in my classroom?

Teacher Action and Reaction

- To what extent did I enjoy this class? What aspects of this class did I enjoy most? Least?
- What was I feeling in this teaching/learning situation?
- What does it mean for me to feel the way I did?
- What do I think students were feeling?
- How am I feeling now as I reflect on this teaching/learning situation?
- As I reflect on the teaching/learning situation, what advice would I give myself?
- What were my teaching objectives? Did they change as the teaching/learning situation evolved? How do these objectives fit with my long-term instructional goals?
- How did I involve my students in learning? What evidence do I have that students learned?
- What part of the teaching/learning situation did I find the most difficult?
- Did I favor some students over others? To what extent did I develop a climate of mutual respect and trust among my students?
- How much individual attention did I give to students? Could I have given more? Would more be useful?
- How did I handle attendance, notices, classroom interruptions, discipline, lateness to class, late work, homework assignments, grades?
- What approaches did I use to provide immediate feedback to students to facilitate their learning?

- How did I make transitions between ideas, topics, and learning activities?
- How did I promote student assessment of their own work?
- To what extent did I role-model learning behaviors such as questioning, inductive and deductive thinking, dialogue, explaining, and reflecting?

Overall Impressions and Assessment of Teaching

- What were the essential strengths of my teaching?
- What, if anything, would I change about my teaching? What would I do differently? What was problematic about my teaching?
- Do I think my teaching was effective in promoting student learning? Why or why not?
- Did I know whether or not my instruction had been understood?
- What conditions were important to student learning?
- What, if any, unanticipated learning outcomes resulted from my instruction? Were there any unintended consequences that affected students?
- Can I think of another way I might have taught this material or concept? Can I think of other alternative pedagogical approaches to teaching this material to improve student learning?
- Was the content covered relevant and important to students? Did my teaching process facilitate learning?
- What moral, ethical, and political issues were involved in this teaching/learning situation? How did I handle the issues?
- How did I try to determine whether or not the students "got" the lesson?
- If I were asked, what would I probably say was the purpose of the lesson? What would the students say?
- Was my instruction successful? Were instructional goals and objectives achieved? Why or why not? How did I assess the outcomes of my teaching? How did I assess student learning? What kinds of assessments did I use during and after the lesson?

❖ SUMMARY

Zeichner (1996) reminds us that "there is no such thing as an unreflective teacher." In our attempts to advance teacher reflection through observation, journaling, dialogue, and writing, we may be assuming that teachers are not reflective unless they practice the specific techniques promoted by researchers. It is ironic that the rhetoric about reflective practitioners focuses on empowering teachers, but the requirements of learning to be reflective are based on the assumption that teachers are incapable of reflection without direction from expert authorities. (Fendler, 2003, p. 23)

This chapter acknowledges that the vast literature on teacher reflection may be based on such assumptions. On the other hand, like all things in life, the systematic and deep exploration of ideas and concepts of reflection may lead us to more profound understandings of the nature and character of reflection and how we can collaboratively optimize its practice. University faculty and teachers need to be mindful of any hidden assumptions, particularly in regard to power relationships, buried in their work, whether it be in practicing reflection, observation, journaling, or writing, but they also need to be careful not to ignore or to deflect the rich literature supporting these practices.

10

Case Study and Teacher Action Research

In this chapter, I discuss the nature and role of the case study in teacher action research. The advantages of using the case study as a research methodology are described, along with different types of case study approaches. The nature and character of different kinds of individual and program case studies are featured. Assumptions underlying the case study are explored. The chapter concludes with a detailed discussion of three major case study approaches: appreciative inquiry, the cultural inquiry process, and the descriptive review.

❖ WHAT IS A CASE STUDY?

"Almost by definition, teacher research is case study: The unit of analysis is typically the individual child, the classroom, or the school" (Cochran-Smith & Lytle, 1993, p. 59). Within the action research paradigm, the case study is a powerful research methodology for sparking interplay between thought and action, helping to develop increased capacities of analysis, which make educational change actions possible (Abramson, 1992; Hancock & Algozzine, 2006; Merriam, 1998; Stake, 1995; Yin, 2008). The case study is an empirical approach that studies a contemporary phenomenon within its real-life context and when the boundaries between phenomenon and context are not clear; it uses multiple sources of evidence (Yin, 2008). The case study is more than an empirical approach, however.

> Case study is the way of the artist, who achieves greatness when, through the portrayal of a single instance locked in time and circumstance, he communicates enduring truths about the human condition. For both scientist and artist, content and intent emerge in form. (McDonald & Walker, 1975, p. 3)

The history of the social sciences is filled with dramatic and artistic conceptual breakthroughs that have emanated from the use of the case study. The intellectual contributions of Freud, Piaget, Maslow, Erickson, Jung, Adler, and Rogers are examples of profoundly influential thinking and seminal ideas that were born and nurtured through the case study approach. When we look at other professions, we find that the research literature of law, for example, is the deliberate elaborate analysis and explanation of cases, that the research literature of medicine is the deliberate explanation of cases or clinical research, and that case study research is the predominant teaching resource in MBA programs across the country. The case study is a congenial approach for people of action, for professionals who engage life, who try out ideas, reflect on their implementation, and try again. The cycle of thought-action-thought finds comfortable embrace in the case study, a basic methodology for action research.

Case studies can be characterized by a concern for rich and vivid description of events, a chronological narrative of events, an internal debate between the description of events and the analysis of events, a focus on particular individuals or groups of people and their perceptions, a focus on particular incidents within the case, the integral involvement of the researcher in the case, and a way of presenting the case that captures the richness of the situation (Hitchcock & Hughes, 1995, p. 317).

Advantages of Using the Case Study Approach

There are several advantages in using the case study approach:

- Case study data, paradoxically, are strong in reality but difficult to organize. In contrast, other research data are often weak in reality but susceptible to ready organization.

- Case studies allow generalizations either about an instance or from an instance to a class. Their peculiar strength lies in their attention to subtlety and complexity of the case in its own right.
- Case studies recognize the complexity and embeddedness of social truths. By carefully attending to social situations, case studies can represent something of the discrepancies or conflicts between viewpoints held by participants. The best case studies are capable of offering some support to alternative interpretations.
- Case studies, considered as products, may form an archive of descriptive material sufficiently rich to admit subsequent reinterpretation.
- Case studies are a step to action. They begin in a world of action and contribute to it. Their insights may be directly interpreted and put to use.
- Case studies present research or evaluation data in a more publicly accessible form than other kinds of research reports, although this virtue is to some extent bought at the expense of their length. (Adelman, Kemmis, & Jenkins, 1980, pp. 59–60)

Types of Case Studies

The case study is the traditional approach of clinical research and lends itself extremely well to action research. It is the preferred method of practitioners who are concerned with complex interrelationships among many variables and whose subject matter (i.e., complex, changing, and situation-specific programs involving human beings) makes experimental manipulation difficult and often impossible (Bolgar, 1965; Merriam, 1998; Stake, 1995). Case studies can be single or multiple in-depth, detailed, and focused studies of individuals, events, programs, organizations, processes, interventions, schools, classrooms, and school districts. *Intrinsic case studies* (Stake, 1995, p. 64) focus on a specific situation or case in which the researcher seeks to understand the case as a holistic entity as well as to understand its inner workings. Much attention is given to understanding the contexts of the case. In *instrumental case studies* (Stake, 1995, p. 64), the case is viewed only as a means to an end in which the researcher seeks to make conclusions that go beyond the specific case. The goals of the study are less specific and more broad. While certain contexts may be important, other contexts are of little interest to the study. In a *collective case study,* the researcher studies many cases to gain greater insights, with the cases usually studied instrumentally rather than intrinsically. Several cases can be compared for similarities and differences, and the researcher is more able to generalize results from many cases than from a single case.

Another typology of case studies is suggested by Jensen and Rodgers (2001):

1. *Snapshot case study,* which is a detailed objective study of one research entity at one point in time.

2. *Longitudinal case study,* which is a study of one research entity at multiple time points.

3. *Pre-post test case study,* which is a study of one research entity at two time points separated by a critical event.

4. *Patchwork case study,* which is a set of multiple case studies of the same research entity, using snapshot, longitudinal, and pre-post designs.

5. *Comparative case study,* which is a set of multiple case studies of multiple research entities for the purpose of cross-unit comparison. (pp. 237–239)

All of these approaches to the case study can be applied in the classroom. Every teacher's classroom is a case, and every teacher's experiences inside and outside the classroom also can be considered as cases for study. Case studies could focus on the process of designing a curriculum, the design and implementation of an instructional unit, classroom management issues, evaluation of instruction, assessment of student learning, individualized instruction, student self-assessment, multicultural curriculum, or an individual child, for example. The number of issues that could be studied in one teacher's classroom is virtually infinite.

When an inquirer approaches a new area in which relatively little is known, the case study is a desirable methodological choice. The true power of the case study lies in its ability to generate hypotheses and discoveries; its focus on the individual, program, or event; its flexibility; and its applicability to natural settings. Case studies typically examine the interplay of all variables to provide as complete an understanding of an individual, event, or program as possible. This type of comprehensive understanding is arrived at through a process known as *thick description* (Geertz, 1973), which involves an in-depth description of the individual, the intervention or program, the circumstances and context in which people function, the nature of the community and school, and the interpretation of demographic and descriptive data such as cultural norms and values as well as individual attitudes, motives, expectations, and assumptions.

> A thick description. . . . does more than record what a person is doing. It goes beyond mere fact and surface appearances. It presents detail, context, emotion, and the webs of social relationships that join persons to one another. Thick description evokes emotionality and self-feelings. It inserts history into experience. (Denzin, 1989, p. 83)

In addition to "thick description," the case study is also distinguished by grounding through experiential, holistic, and realistic (life-like) perspectives; it uses a simplified range of data without losing its integrity and illuminates meaning; it has more in-depth communication than propositional language can provide (Guba & Lincoln, 1981).

The procedural requirements for a case study lend themselves to the solution of problems relevant to teacher-student interactions. Case studies can assist in the identification of educationally relevant variables and the conditions under which they are effective. Case studies are intended for natural settings and contain data collection procedures that can help teachers in their decision making. The collection of data and the procedures required for case studies are compatible with instructional purposes. The inherently flexible nature of the case study approach, the search to identify sources of variability, and the requirements for data-based feedback for decision making are components necessary for the improvement of teaching and the design of situation-specific programs.

The great strength of the case study approach is its ability to describe in a holistic way the program "treatment" and its effects on students; it does not focus on narrowly defined outcome variables but instead includes much descriptive information. The case study synthesizes vast amounts of information about individuals, their instructional programs, and their teaching/learning contexts, and presents it in a form that can be interesting and easily understood. Information sources including background data, test scores, affective measures, self-reports, peer reports, staff reports, parent observations, student products, anecdotal data, and evaluator observations are considered essential for the case study.

Bassey (1999, p. 63) indicates that, in a good case study, sufficient data are collected for the researcher to:

- Explore significant features of the case
- Create plausible interpretations of what is found

- Test for the trustworthiness of these interpretations
- Construct a worthwhile argument or story
- Relate the argument or story to any relevant research in the literature
- Convey convincingly to an audience this argument or story
- Provide an audit trail by which other researchers may validate or challenge the findings or construct alternative arguments

Of special importance is the development of chronological case histories in which data are collected at different points in time. The integration and cross-validation of this information adds strength to the final case study report. Direct contact and extended observation of the students themselves are necessary to reach conclusions related to variables involving the academic and affective behaviors of children. Through the case study, we can examine not only pre- and post-test data, but also the intervening events, forces, and activities affecting the life of each student and the interventions that do or do not influence cognitive and affective changes. Studies of this kind are needed to investigate the developmental histories of different student populations targeted by reform initiatives and innovative programs in relation to a particular project's objectives.

❖ CASE STUDIES OF PROGRAMS

As an approach for studying the effects of an intervention or program, case studies can be classified into six different types (Datta, 1990; Davey, 1991):

> *Illustrative case studies* are descriptive; they use one or two instances to show what a situation is like. This helps interpret other data, especially when there is reason to believe that readers know too little about a program. These case studies serve to make the unfamiliar familiar and give readers a common language about the topic in question.
>
> *Exploratory case studies* are condensed case studies undertaken before implementing a large-scale investigation. Where considerable uncertainty exists about program operations, goals, and results, exploratory case studies help identify questions, select measurement constructs, and develop measures.
>
> *Critical-incident case studies* examine one or more programs either to examine a situation of unique interest with little to no interest

in generalizability or to call into question or challenge a highly generalized or universal assertion. This approach is useful for addressing cause-and-effect questions.

Program implementation case studies help determine whether implementation is consistent with its intent. These case studies are useful when questions arise about implementation problems. Extensive longitudinal reports of what has happened over time establish a context for interpreting findings regarding implementation variability.

Program effects case studies determine the impact of programs and provide reasons for success or failure. Like the program implementation case studies, evaluation questions require extensive longitudinal reports of what has happened over time.

Cumulative case studies aggregate information collected from different sites (classrooms, schools, etc.) at different times. The cumulative case study can be retrospective, collecting information across studies done in the past, or prospective, structuring a series of studies for different times in the future. The techniques for ensuring sufficient comparability and quality and for aggregating the information are what constitute the cumulative part of the methodology. Two features of the cumulative case study are the case survey method, used as a means of aggregating findings, and backfill techniques. The latter are helpful in retrospective cumulation as a means of obtaining information from a variety of sources that permits the use of otherwise insufficiently detailed case studies.

Appreciative Inquiry

An interesting and promising case study approach for changing a program or organization such as a department or school is *appreciative inquiry*. Appreciative inquiry is a case study and contextual method developed by Cooperrider and Srivastva (1987) as a revision of action research that explicitly seeks to isolate, magnify, and document the life-giving forces involved in the cooperative action and collective existence of any human system (families, schools, communities, organizations, departments, programs). It is a way of seeing that is selectively attentive to and affirming of the best and the highest qualities in a system, situation, or another human being: an appreciation for the "mystery of being" and a "reverence for life." A process of collaborative inquiry primarily based on interviews, it sets out to identify the elements and factors in a system (unit, situation, organization, etc.) that enabled it to achieve success in the past in order to build on the best of what is and has been to enable the system to pursue dreams and possibilities of what could be to create inspired change and a positive future for the system. In an educational setting, the focus of appreciative inquiry would be not on the problems of the school, department, or program but rather on a unit's gifts—its building blocks—including ideas, beliefs, values, structures, practices, and procedures. The possibility-focused orientation of appreciative inquiry is vividly described by Cooperrider and Srivastva (1987):

> The spirit of Appreciative Inquiry is to be found in one of the most ancient archetypes or metaphorical symbols of hope and inspiration that humankind has ever known—the miracle and mystery of being. . . . In the same way that the birth of a living, breathing, loving, thinking human being is an inexplicable mystery, so too can it be said in no uncertain terms that "organizing is a miracle" of cooperative human interaction, of which there can never be final explanation . . . the action researcher is drawn to affirm, and thereby illuminate, the factors and forces in organizing that serve to nourish the human spirit. (p. 130)

Assumptions of Appreciative Inquiry

Appreciative inquiry reflects several assumptions about reality, organizations, and inquiry:

- *Constructivist principle.* We co-construct realities based on our previous experiences through our language, thoughts, images, and beliefs about reality so our knowledge and the destiny of the system are interwoven.
- *Principle of simultaneity.* Inquiry and change are simultaneous. The act of asking a question influences the system's reality in some way. Questions are a form of intervention.
- *Poetic principle.* The story of the system is constantly being coauthored, and it is open to infinite interpretations.
- *Anticipatory principle.* What we anticipate determines what we find. The types of questions we ask determine the types of answers we receive. The seeds of change are in the very first questions we ask.
- *Positive principle.* We manifest what we focus on, and we grow toward what we persistently ask questions about. As an image of reality is enhanced, actions begin to align with the positive change.

Operating Principles

Emanating from these assumptions are four operating principles of appreciative inquiry as a form of action research (Barrett & Fry, 2005; Clarke, Egan, Fletcher, & Ryan, 2006; Cooperrider, Sorenson, Whitney, & Yaeger, 2000; Cooperrider & Srivastva, 1987; Cooperrider & Whitney, 1999, 2005; Cooperrider, Whitney, & Stavros, 2003; Fry, 2002; Reed, 2006; Stavros & Torres, 2005; Thatchenkery, 2005; Van Tiem & Rosenzweig, 2006; Watkins & Mohr, 2001; Whitney, Trostem-Bloom, Cherney, & Fry, 2005):

- *Appreciative.* Every social system works to some degree; it is not in a complete state of entropy. The primary task of research is to discover, describe, and explain those social gifts, talents, and innovations that give life to the system and activate members' competencies and energies.
- *Applicable.* Appreciative inquiry is pragmatic. Its results are concretely beneficial to the system. An applicable system analysis leads to new understandings that can be used, applied, and thereby validated in action.
- *Provocative.* Appreciative inquiry holds that any system is an open-ended, indeterminate system capable of becoming more than what it is at any given moment and of learning how to take active part in guiding its own evolution. Appreciative inquiry can be both pragmatic and visionary.
- *Collaborative.* Members of the system need to be viewed as coresearchers. Every step in the research is done as collaboratively and consensually as possible. By conducting the research as a collaborative process of inquiry, the other three principles are more possible to fulfill.

Implementation Phases

There are four phases involved in the implementation of appreciative inquiry:

Discovery. The core task in the discovery phase is to appreciate the best of what is by focusing on peak times of community excellence—when people have experienced the community in its most alive and effective state. Participants then seek to understand the unique factors that made the high points possible, such as leadership, relationships, values, and capacity building. In the discovery phase, the first step for a school or program would be to choose the central issue of inquiry.

What we study becomes our reality. The topic that will most effectively move the educational unit (school, department, program, etc.) to achieve the desired outcome is chosen. Examples of topics might be increased student learning, collaboration across grade levels, and parental involvement.

The second step is to create the question. The more positive the question, the greater the chance of affirmative change. Examples of such questions include:

1. Describe a time when you were involved in a project or situation where you successfully joined with others to accelerate student achievement, a time when you felt most alive and most effective; tell the story.

2. Without being humble, describe what you value most about your self, your work, and your school community.

3. Project yourself 5 years into the future. The student achievement initiative has been unbelievably successful. Describe what is in place in our school community.

The third step is to conduct appreciative interviews with all the stakeholders in the school, department, or program—including students—to inquire on the chosen topic and to gather responses. The responses are transformed into information. Themes, common threads of success, and knowledge about the positive core of life-giving forces on which to build future change are identified.

Dream. The status quo is challenged by envisioning more valued and vital futures. Participants think about and create possibility statements and provocative propositions in addressing the question of what might be. The possibility statement is a vision that is grounded in history, tradition, and the stories that emerged from the interviews. It is easier to move to the future when you take the best of the past.

Design. In the design phase, participants create a strategy to implement their possibility statement and their provocative propositions. They do so by building a social architecture for their school community that might, for example, redefine approaches to leadership, governance, participation, or capacity building. Often the design phase involves a 2- to 3-day appreciative inquiry summit that brings teachers, staff, students, parents, and community members together in the design of the new system.

Destiny. The final phase involves the delivery of new images of the future and is sustained by nurturing a collective sense of destiny. It is a time of action, continuous learning, adjustment, and improvisation in the service of shared school community ideals.

These four phases of appreciative inquiry constitute an iterative recursive process of inquiry and action. The process has been employed by the West Springfield Schools in Massachusetts, three Catholic high schools in Philadelphia (Van Buskirk, 2002), the Shaw High School in Ohio, and a number of community colleges around the country (Henry, 2003).

❖ RETROSPECTIVE CASE STUDIES OF CURRICULUM

One of the significant ways in which the case study approach can be used to explore the phenomena of the classroom and the school is through retrospective studies of curriculum development. The retrospective case study has a rich history, beginning with the work of Schwab (1975), who suggested that in classroom situations, there are five commonplaces: teachers, students, subject matter, curriculum decisions or policy, and milieu/context. The interactive impact of these forces, in fact, constitutes the curriculum. Curriculum, used in this way, can become a primary focus of educational research (Schubert, 1980). Wise (1977) argues that if developing good curricula is a central concern, then personal accounts of such attempts should be emphasized in professional discussions, and a literature of curriculum practice should become integral to teacher preparation and practice. Retrospection is, therefore, a legitimate form of inquiry into curriculum development practice.

Productive forms of personal inquiry into curriculum development include historical case studies developed through documentation analysis and retrospective case studies (Purves, 1975; Regan, 1971). As a form of inquiry, retrospection is unique, including both introspection and observation as sources of data. Recently, this approach has been applied to segregation (Gersti-Pepin, 2002); technological advancements in special education (Jeffs, Morrison, Messenheimer, Rizza, & Banister, 2003); methods used in urban schools to improve student achievement (Snipes, Doolittle, & Herlihy, 2002); and retrospective versus prospective analyses of school inputs affecting student learning (Glewwe, Kremer, Moulin, & Zitzewitz, 2004).

Retrospective accounts of curriculum development offer "our most precious source of knowledge about our field—our own experience"

(Wise, 1977, p. 2). Such case studies recognize curriculum development as a personal, human, particular, and often episodic process. The human particulars of curriculum development make practice what it is, and it is those particulars with which the field is out of touch (Schwab, 1975; Wise, 1977). Retrospective case studies grasp the contexts, nuances, personal realities, and situational specifics of what happens when a teacher tries to implement new ideas and approaches. As personal accounts, they describe logic in action as demonstrated in classrooms, as opposed to *reconstructed logic*—the manner in which personal experiences are presented as knowledge (Kaplan, 1964). Curriculum theorists (Eisner, 1975; Fox, 1971; Schwab, 1970; Walker, 1975; Wise, 1977) indicate that the major problem of curriculum theory is that personal experiences have been reconstructed into a knowledge that does not reflect actual practice. The aim of retrospective studies is to capture the practical sense and concrete reality of the classroom world and to share these with colleagues. Summarizing the case for retrospective studies as a form of action research, Wise (1977) observes:

> Our literature about curriculum development does not now indicate much in the way of accumulated practical sense. We do not have a rich store of studied and catalogued accounts of curriculum development practice in which what happened and how well it happened are presented. We do not recount for others the problems we faced in development, the problems solved, the solutions discovered, the solutions failed. We do not recapture and report strategies of thinking that have led us to good decisions. We do not distill from our experience what manners of imagination, judgment, arguments or brainstorming helped or hindered our work. We ought to be reflecting on our experiences in curriculum development, recounting them to ourselves, analyzing them, and presenting their accounts to our colleagues in a form that helps them to understand the significance of the experience, the lessons of the experience. (p. 4)

❖ CASE STUDY OF THE INDIVIDUAL

The case study offers an in-depth approach to studying the impact of a program or intervention, however, the greatest use of the case study by the teacher-researcher would probably be in the study of the individual. In a profession where there is a basic commitment to teaching and understanding individual students and situations, case study research devoted to the full study of individuals offers a comfortable and rewarding action research approach for teachers and university faculty. The full study of individual students enables teachers and university faculty to function as clinical researchers in examining the wide range of contextual and multidimensional variables that impinge on student learning and development. The case study provides a sound action research base for generating new hypotheses about student learning and growth. Among the many formats for conducting case studies of individuals, there are two unique and in-depth collaborative approaches that warrant greater discussion: the cultural inquiry process and the descriptive review.

Cultural Inquiry Process

Our ideas about the concept of culture are clearly changing and are constantly being contested. The concept of culture is much more complex than heretofore understood and requires that we move away from broad generalizations about culture and focus more specifically on individual students and families. The context for this personalization of culture is informed by the following, sometimes conflicting ideas:

- Culture is not tightly bounded for many contemporary urban groups. In urban areas, cultural borderlands—areas where several cultural groups live side by side—are more the rule than the exception.
- Within any given cultural group, there is significant variation according to gender, age, status, occupation, and many other factors.
- Living cultures are constantly changing. Culture is not static but is always being actively constructed.
- Much of our cultural knowledge is implicit. Culture can be so all encompassing that we take it for granted. Our implicit understandings and knowledge of our own culture become more explicit from the internal conflict experienced when living in another culture or with someone who has a markedly different cultural background.
- Some aspects of culture exist inside people, primarily in the meanings and interpretations they bring to their experiences living in the world.
- Other aspects of culture exist in everyday lived practices rather than as meanings inside people's heads.

- Anyone who studies cultures brings certain assumptions, lenses, and biases to the task, and it is important in working with students and their parents that these biases are surfaced and made explicit so they don't get in the way of cultural understanding. (Henze & Hauser, 1999, p. 4)

Assumptions of the Cultural Inquiry Process

These ideas about culture are implicit in the cultural inquiry process (CIP), which has been developed by Evelyn Jacob (1995) and Jacob, Johnson, Finley, Gurski, and Lavine (1996) and can be explored on the CIP Web site (http://classweb.gmu.edu/cip/g/g-top.htm). Their goal is to improve the education of culturally diverse students by marrying principles and perspectives of educational anthropology to reflective practice and classroom inquiry. Jacob (1995) believes

> that (1) anthropological concepts such as culture, context, social structure, and power provide productive ways of understanding culturally diverse classrooms; (2) that anthropological methods such as observation, open-ended interviews, and artifact analysis can contribute useful information; and (3) that by drawing on these concepts and information, educators can develop successful interventions. (p. 460)

Jacob (1995, p. 455) observes that schools are sites of cross-cultural encounters; that the routines and practices of schools reflect cultural assumptions and values; that both teachers and students bring to the classroom their own cultural meanings and behavior patterns influenced by their ethnicity, social class, gender, and degree of acculturation; and that culture is not static but continually evolving. She asserts that the CIP can help teachers identify and build on the strengths of cultures, recognize the variations and fluidity within cultures, and develop their cultural sensitivity to create opportunities for the improvement of student learning and development in culturally diverse classrooms.

Implementation Steps

The CIP is implemented by a team of teachers, initially working with an educational anthropologist, who focus their inquiry on a student or small group of students. CIP involves six basic steps, and various courses of action are possible for each step.

In the first step, the team selects as its focus one or more teachers identifying "puzzlements" about the student(s). Puzzlements include student performance that a teacher does not understand, whether the performance is considered positive, neutral, or negative. A puzzlement need not be cultural, but the CIP focuses on puzzlements that may have cultural roots. By treating a puzzlement as an opportunity to explore cultural influences on a student's performance in educational settings, teachers increase the likelihood of developing appropriate interventions.

In the second step, the team summarizes what is known about the focus student and the context. Information about the student could include a description of the individual's performance or behavior in class and other contexts, as well as discussion of the student's gender, social class, and cultural background. Information about the context might include reflections on the teachers' own gender, social class, and cultural background, along with contexts of the student and his or her family.

The third step involves considering alternative cultural questions and selecting one of them to explore. Teachers are asked to consider carefully the following questions and their subquestions before deciding on a focus for exploration.

- How might your beliefs or values, or those of other educators, be contributing to the puzzling situation?
- How might the school's culture(s) be contributing to the puzzling situation?
- How might cultural mismatches be contributing to the puzzling situation?
- How might the student's experiences and meanings be contributing to the puzzling situation?
- How might individual students' cultural negotiations be contributing to the puzzling situation?

The cultural questions draw attention to influences from ethnic and racial cultures and cultures associated with other socially constructed groups, such as those based on gender, social class, peer groups, and schools. Because language is such an important part of all cultures, language and second-language acquisition are also included within the scope of the cultural questions. Cultural questions also examine the influences of historical events and of larger socioeconomic and political structuring.

The cultural questions organize issues around aspects of culture that teachers encounter directly in their work; larger cultural questions are treated within the main questions listed above. The questions begin with a focus on cultural influences from individual teachers, move to consider various extraindividual influences, and end with a focus on individual students' negotiations of cultural influences. The order and scope of the questions are designed to encourage questions and discussion about a wide range of cultural influences before viewing the puzzlements from the perspectives of individual psychology or family dynamics.

The cultural questions selected as a focus are viewed as the starting point for explorations. Although the questions listed above are listed separately, the issues they represent are interrelated.

In the fourth step, the team gathers and analyzes relevant information about each of the questions raised in the previous step, in other words, information about:

- personal beliefs or values, or those of other educators
- the school's culture(s)
- cultural mismatches
- students' experiences and meanings
- individual students' cultural negotiations

Once information is collected, patterns in the information that occur across various sources of information are identified and then analyzed in relation to the cultural questions that were examined. What does the information indicate about possible cultural influences on the puzzlement? Discussion of the possible answers to this question provides the basis for developing interventions in the fifth step, where interventions are developed and implemented as needed. Interventions are informed by the analyses of the information gathered. Should the evidence indicate that cultural influences are relevant to the puzzlement being studied, the intervention(s) might include efforts related to these cultural influences. Possible interventions could be constructed based on the following ideas:

- Your beliefs or values, or those of other teachers, seem to be contributing to the puzzlement.
- The school's culture(s) seem to be contributing to the puzzlement.
- Mismatches between a student's culture(s) and the school's culture(s) seem to be contributing to the puzzlement
- Student experiences and meaning seem to be contributing to the puzzlement.
- Individual students' cultural negotiations seem to be contributing to the puzzlement.

In the final step, the team monitors the process and the results of interventions over time. Based on the feedback they receive, they may revise their interventions or return to a previous step to reconsider the information gathered or to revise their cultural questions.

The CIP offers a unique way to view students, and it comes at a critical time in education. Public school enrollment at the beginning of the 21st century is more diverse than ever before. Currently, white students constitute only 60% of the school enrollment in the United States, compared with 80% during the civil rights era of the 1960s and 1970s. It is predicted that, within the next few decades, fewer than half the students in our nation's public schools will be white.

But teachers often feel they are unequipped to be effective in dealing with cultural diversity. In a 2000 National Center for Educational Statistics survey, only 32% of the participating teachers indicated they were well prepared to teach in a culturally diverse setting. The cultural inquiry process addresses this issue, offering an opportunity for teachers to become more comfortable with and knowledgeable about cultural diversity in serving the needs of individual students or small groups of students.

Descriptive Review

Characteristics of the Descriptive Review

A dynamic form of the case study of the individual is the descriptive review, a process of oral inquiry developed by Carini and her colleagues at the Prospect School in Bennington, Vermont (Carini, 1975, 2000; Himley & Carini, 2000). The descriptive review process has been adopted as a protocol for looking at student work by the Coalition for Essential Schools, for sharpening teacher observations (Rodgers, 2002), and for whole school inquiry (Traugh, 2000, pp. 182–198).

The descriptive review emphasizes oral inquiry through collaborative inquiry focused on one child. It is a structured conversation about a child guided by one or two focusing questions, for example: How can I help Scott recognize feelings, what they mean, and reasons for these feelings in the classroom? How can I help Billy to become more independent? How can I help facilitate Tavis's expressive language development in my preschool classroom? What teaching strategies can I use to increase Paige's reading comprehension? How can I help Mary become more involved in school life? *Descriptive* is the key word meaning that the writing and the discussion are to be free of judgmental and evaluative language. Indeed, the power of the descriptive review lies in the learning that takes place when teachers take the time to look at a child deeply, using descriptive rather than evaluative language.

The descriptive review is a layered collaborative narrative account built up over time through an inductive and deliberate process. The focus of the descriptive review does not have to be a major problem or concern. The presenting teacher may just want to get to know a particular child better. To fully portray the child in all realms of the classroom, a description of the child is written up according to five headings of the descriptive review. In writing the descriptive review, illustrative examples are given under each heading whenever possible.

Five Headings for the Descriptive Review Presentation

The five headings for the Descriptive Review of the Child presentation and the kinds of questions or specific observations that might come within each heading include the following (Carini, 2000):

1. *Physical presence and gesture:* What are the child's size and build, style of dress, color preferences, prized possessions; how does the child move, enter the classroom, position him- or herself in a group; what does the child like to do outdoors and indoors; where does the child seem most at ease and least comfortable; what is the child's voice, volume, and rhythm; what is the child's characteristic ways of speaking; how does the child use eyes, hands, and mouth for expressiveness; what are the pace and gestures of the child in quiet occupations of reading, drawing, observing, and conversing.

2. *Disposition and temperament:* How does the child greet the world, what are the child's typical attitudes toward life, what stirs deep feeling in the child, what does the child care for deeply, what goes against the child's sense of honor and justice, how does the child display feelings, what moves the child to laughter, what moves the child to tears, what are the strong personal commitments of the child.

3. *Connections with children and adults:* In the classroom or in the community, how does the child go about making a place for him- or herself, move into a new group, respond to unfamiliar children; with what children has the child formed close and enduring relationships; how does the child act in loosely connected groups that form around games or other classroom or neighborhood activities; what is the child's role in friendships and small groups, with brothers and sisters or other close relatives, and within larger groups; when does the child prefer to be alone; how does the child respond if difficulties arise in a

group; what adults does the child seek out; how does the child greet familiar adults; what are the child's preferred ways of being with adults; what makes the child feel safe, trusted, respected, and secure with adults (or not); how do adults tend to welcome the child and generally respond to him or her; what adult responses and interests hold the child's interest; what kind of adult response or attitudes put the child off or lead to conflict.

4. *Strong interests and preferences:* What are the things the child likes (particular foods, colors, people, animals, places [indoors or outdoors]); what are the things the child dislikes or finds repellant; what are the questions, wonderings, and curiosities that stir the child's mind and imagination; which of these persist or are recurrent; how are the child's questions and interests expressed in play, in choices of books or films, in conversation, in drawing, or in construction; what are the media and the play that most capture the child's attention; what does the child prefer to do if she or he has choice and plenty of time; what are the child's favorite books and stories, television programs and movies, games and activities; what role does the child assume in keeping group play and activities going; what makes play go right for the child; what spoils it; what are the favorite themes or topics featured in the child's play—superheroes or knights or battles or space or dinosaurs or ninja turtles or disasters or fairy tales.

5. *Modes of thinking and learning:* What things, ideas, or media does the child seem to have an inner sense or feel for (machines or music or language or people or animals or drama or numbers or throwing a ball); what does the child do with great ease; how does the child internalize knowledge and figure things out; how does the child position him- or herself as a learner; does the child plunge right in or take some other "I'll do it myself" approach, or does the child want a lot of time to observe and practice privately; what are the child's responses when mistakes or accidents occur, when there are interruptions, when the situation is highly competitive; what specific skills has the child easily mastered and what skills have been more difficult to acquire; what subject matter or fields of study does the child gravitate to; what makes these areas of learning attractive, and how does the child engage with these modes of thinking and learning; what disciplines does the child find boring or actively dislike; what standards does the child hold for him- or herself, and how do these vary depending on circumstances; what are the times and places of work that have been pleasing or displeasing to the child;

what influences the value the child accords to his or her own work when the work and learning are the child's choice.

Procedures for Conducting the Descriptive Review

Each team has a chair who facilitates the descriptive review process and a person who is designated as note taker. The note taker is responsible for recording the major themes emanating from the description of the child and the recommendations that emerge from the descriptive review. Meetings are planned by the chair and the presenting teacher in collaboration; they select focus or theme words and questions to drive the process. The group first reflects on a key focus word because it offers some insight into the questions the presenting teacher will ask. In the first round, the members of the team may ask any questions and make comments but offer no solutions. The chair of the team makes sure that members of the group are seated in a circle so that everyone is face to face and invited to participate. The chair emphasizes confidentiality in the process and respect for the child. Participants speak descriptively and provisionally. They avoid speculations about the family and any

> heavily judgmental language and diagnostic or other categorizing labels such as "hyperactive" or "learning disabled" or "developmentally delayed.". . . The chair stresses that what is most important is to ground language used to describe a child in examples and illustrations so that language is well rooted in observation. (Carini, 2000, p. 14)

The guiding question and the descriptive review are presented by the presenting teacher to the team of teachers and/or resource people for the structured conversation. The child's art works, writings, and projects are available on a low table so that the presenting teacher can refer to them as he or she makes the presentation. The team then focuses on the child, using the guiding question to focus the conversational inquiry. Members of the team discuss the child from various angles and through oral inquiry develop a full picture of the child, gaining insights to illuminate the guiding question. Although there is a note taker, everyone in the group writes notes to track questions and observations that arise during the presenting teacher's description of the child. The chair identifies main threads and themes making "integrative restatements," summarizes questions and comments, and invites recommendations. In Round 2, recommendations are offered to the teacher-researcher, but the researcher does not respond to the recommendations. Following the second team session, the teacher-researcher reflects on the conversation and the recommendations, then revises the descriptive review. At the conclusion of each meeting, participants evaluate the process, making sure that the process has reflected respect for the family, child, and teacher. The descriptive review is a powerful form of inquiry that leads to a deeper understanding of the child and the ways in which the child's learning and development can be advanced.

Kanevsky (1993), in sharing her experience carrying out a descriptive review, delineates the values that underlie the descriptive review process:

- We value the teacher's role as the observer in the classroom.
- We value description and context. We describe a child's experience in the classroom setting at the present time. We use specific details grounded in everyday classroom activities.
- We value plain nonjudgmental language. We try not to use jargon.
- We value collaboration—active and attentive collaboration.
- We value the child's point of view. We ask what arouses a child's wonder, curiosity, what sustains interest. We try to see the child's world.
- We value what a child and a teacher can already do and build from the strengths we see.
- We value the teacher's judgment to choose recommendations that he or she thinks are useful.
- We value what we do. One of the participants takes notes, and we save the notes in three ring notebooks. (p. 162)

Watkins (2001) observes that the careful and caring attention given to the individual learner in the descriptive review cultivates habits of mind that carry over to a way of regarding other children; a changed attitude about children as learners and people; a way of working with children that is deeper, more connected to the child, and more respectful and honoring of the individual child; and a way that makes us more humble about what we think we know about children. Carlina Rinaldi (2003), professor at the University of Modena and Reggio and pedagogical consultant to Reggio Schools in Italy, captures the soul of the descriptive review process when she says:

Children can give us the strength of doubt and the courage of error. They can transmit to us the joy of searching and researching . . . the value of research, as an openness toward others and toward everything new that is produced by the encounter with others.

❖ SUMMARY

The use of the case study has yielded significant conceptual and theoretical breakthroughs in the social sciences, as reflected in the work of Rogers, Piaget, and Maslow. It has been widely used as a teaching and research tool in schools of business, medicine, and law. The case study is a detailed, in-depth, holistic, and multifaceted approach for the intensive study of an individual, a group, programs, processes, organizational units, or an issue. The advantages of the case study are that it recognizes and captures the subtlety, complexity, and embeddedness of social truths; grasps reality; is a step to action; presents data in a more publicly accessible form; allows for alternative interpretations; synthesizes vast amounts of information; and deals with the complex interrelationships among many variables. Three major case study approaches for use in education are appreciative inquiry, the cultural inquiry process, and the descriptive review.

11

Conducting Teacher Action Research

This chapter describes a process for conducting a teacher action research study. The suggestions offered here have emanated from my reading in the action research literature and my personal experiences and engagement in a variety of collaborative teacher action research studies during the past 40 years. My pedagogical voice permeates the chapter, but I hope it does so in a way that establishes meaningful contact with you the reader. I have tried to capture in this chapter the realities, complexities, and challenges of conducting teacher action research. In several places in the chapter, I emphasize the importance of the critical process that recursion represents in the conduct of action research, particularly as recursion affects research questions and the processes of data collection and analysis. I hope this chapter will be a meaningful resource and foundation for you as you conduct your own research and that it will give you all the rudiments of practice you need to become a lifelong researcher.

❖ MODEST BEGINNINGS

Action research is demanding, complex, and challenging because the researcher not only assumes responsibilities for doing the research but also for enacting change. Enacting change is not easy—it requires time, patience, and sound planning, communication, and implementation skills. So, in establishing a foundation for conducting action research, I believe that modest beginnings are no disgrace and are in most respects preferable to more ambitious ones. The visibility and impact of early efforts may be small, but it is advisable to consider carefully the relative merits of simple versus more intricate research plans and data analysis procedures. It is likely that by adopting the strategies of a methodological miser, there is more to be gained than lost. In the conduct of action research, just as in the interpretation of its results, the law of parsimony is recommended. Modest beginnings can serve to build step-by-step an action research tradition of dealing with real problems that already have a natural and interested audience.

By selecting and pursuing questions that focus on the immediate and imperative problems of the classroom and the school, teacher action research can attract the greatest attention at the most opportune time (when there is something substantial to report), for the best reason (because some progress has been made, either in terms of increased understanding or approaches to dealing with a problem), and probably for the appropriate audience (those who have a preexisting interest and investment in the problem and its solution). A mounting record of visible accomplishment is an excellent way to dispel the initial anxiety teachers may experience in undertaking action research.

❖ FINDING CRITICAL FRIENDS

As a member of a collaborative action research team, whether pursuing an individual research study or a team study, it is important to engage colleagues in a process of collaborative inquiry to advance the developing research effort. Particular colleagues may be enlisted at the beginning of the research for a variety of reasons—because they are especially sensitive to emerging problems, or are creative and have ideas about how educational issues might be addressed, or are skilled in problem definition, or are greatly interested in a particular issue.

Whatever the reason, it is extremely helpful to have a circle of "critical friends" who will work with you to help define the research problem, formulate the questions, collect and analyze the data, and discuss the data and outcomes of the study (Bambino, 2002; Cushman, 1998). To facilitate critical collegiality, it is helpful to consider the norms developed by the Bay Area Coalition of Essential Schools, which are paraphrased here:

- In collaborating with a group of critical friends, you and the members of the group describe only what you see; you don't try to describe what you don't see; you learn to express what you don't see in the form of questions.
- Together, you resist the urge to work on solutions until you are comfortable with what the data say and don't say.
- The perspectives and experiences of each member of the group are brought to the analysis.
- Everyone seeks to understand differences of perception before trying to resolve them, recognizing that early consensus can inhibit depth and breadth of analysis.
- In this critical process, members raise questions with each other when they don't understand ideas or what the data are saying.
- Members surface assumptions and use data to challenge them, actively searching for both challenges and support for what they believe is true.

This kind of process exemplifies critical collegiality, which is essential in dealing with the complexities and changing circumstances of any action research project.

It is good to remember that action research can be messy. Cook (1998) and Mellor (2001), in writing about the importance of "mess" in action research, discuss the problems and overwhelming amount of data or possible areas that one can examine in doing action research. They describe their personal experiences in conducting classroom action research projects and provide insights into some of the pitfalls, issues, and other concerns you might have before initiating your own action research study. Here again, the need for a circle of critical friends to deal with the "messiness" of action research seems apparent. Critical friends share a commitment to inquiry, offer continuing support throughout the research process, and nurture a community of intellectual and emotional caring.

❖ A FEW PRINCIPLES FOR CONDUCTING ACTION RESEARCH

Action research takes place in a context of discovery and invention as opposed to a context of verification. Discovery and invention, the main business of human science, have little to do with experimental designs. What one does to discover and invent a new way of teaching or a different approach to assessment, for example, is a completely separate activity from the strict procedures of classical experimental design.

Some basic principles for conducting action research can be found in Gregory Bateson's "Rules of Thumb" for doing research:

- Study life in its natural setting, being careful not to destroy the historical and interactional integrity of the whole setting.
- Think aesthetically. Visualize, analogize, compare. Look for patterns, configurations, figures in the rug.
- Live with your data. Be a detective. Mull, contemplate, observe, and inspect. Think about, through, and beyond.
- Don't be controlled by dogmatic formalisms about how to theorize and research. Avoid the dualisms announced and pronounced as maxims by particularizing methodologists and theorists.
- Be as precise as possible, but don't close off possibilities. Keep your explanations as close to your data and experience as possible.
- Aim for catalytic conceptualizations; warm ideas are contagious. (as cited in Bochner, 1981, pp. 76–77)

Identifying the Research Question

By studying life in the natural setting of the school and the classroom, by looking for "patterns in the rug," and by mulling, contemplating, and closely observing authentic events in teaching and learning situations, one can identify a research question that will enlist personal passion and energy. "A teacher researcher, among other things, is a questioner. Her questions propel her forward" (Hansen, 1997, p. 1). Meaningful questions can emerge from: conversations with your colleagues; professional literature; examination of your journal entries and teaching portfolio to identify, for example, patterns of teacher/student behavior or anomalies, paradoxes, and unusual situations; dissonance between your teaching intentions and outcomes; problematic learning situations in your classroom that you want to resolve; a new teaching strategy you are eager to implement; an ambiguous and puzzling classroom management concern; or your curiosity about testing a particular theory in the classroom.

Cindy Meyers, a teacher of writing, discusses how the process of research in her classroom is clarified and informed by her field notes:

Every year when I start research by keeping field notes, I keep thinking that this is an exercise, and I'm just writing down what's happening and I'm not getting anything out of it. It seems like a bland kind of thing. But when I keep doing that, all of a sudden I'll hear the kids say something that shows they've changed in some way, and I'll put that down too. And then things start to pull together. It's almost like the field notes that I keep and through what I see happening—out of those field notes—the classroom becomes more alive. (Goswami & Stillman, 1987, p. 3)

Sometimes it helps to use a variety of questions as starting points to identify an issue you would like to research (Caro-Bruce, 2000):

I would like to improve _____

I am perplexed by _____

I am really curious about _____

Something I think would really make a difference is _____

Something I would like to change is _____

What happens to student learning in my classroom when I _____?

How can I implement _____?

How can I improve _____?

Classrooms are complex environments in which teachers engage in as many as 1,000 interpersonal situations during a stretch of 6 hours with as many as 200 or 300 interpersonal exchanges in an hour (Jackson, 1968). An almost infinite number of research questions are inherent in the context of the classroom, the context of teaching, and the context of learning.

Identifying a good research question from these possibilities requires reflection, observation, conversation, and study of the natural life of the classroom. It is important to remember that the first question propelling an action research study may change as the research is under way. The recursive, iterative, and spiraling nature of action research suggests that a research question may change and be refined as new data and issues surface in the research study.

Passion is integral to doing action research and can be a resource for identifying a research question, as indicated by Dana and Yendol-Hoppey (2008, pp. 15–48). After analyzing more than 100 teacher classroom research studies, they identified eight passions as possibilities for finding a research question:

1. Helping an individual child

2. Improving and enriching curriculum

3. Developing content knowledge

4. Improving or experimenting with teaching strategies and techniques

5. Exploring the relationship between your beliefs and classroom practice

6. Exploring the intersection of your personal and professional identities

7. Advocating social justice

8. Understanding the teaching and learning context

Characteristics of Good Research Questions

What constitutes a good teacher research question? (See examples in Table 11.1.) A good classroom action research question should be meaningful, compelling, and important to you as a teacher-researcher. It should engage your passion, energy, and commitment. It has to be important for your personal and professional growth; it should stretch you intellectually and affectively. You should love the question.

A good research question is manageable and within your sphere of influence. It is consonant with your work; you can address it within the confines of your classroom. It is focused and not so ambitious, big, or complex that it requires extraordinary resources, time, and energy.

A good research question should be important for learners. A good research question benefits your students by informing your teaching and the curriculum, by providing new insights about students and their learning, by broadening and deepening your perspectives, or by improving practice.

A good research question leads to taking an action, to trying something out, to improving a teaching/learning situation, to implementing actions that can make a difference in the lives of students. "No action without research—no research without action." Even in those situations in which the goal of the research is to gain deeper knowledge and understanding of a student, such as in a case study or a descriptive review, it is assumed that the ultimate goal of such acquired knowledge and understanding is the improvement of one's teaching or the advancement of student learning and/or development.

Table 11.1   Examples of Teacher Action Research Questions

- What happens to the quality of student writing when we implement peer editing throughout our ninth-grade English classes?
- How does the use of computers affect the student writing process in our fourth-grade classrooms?
- What happens to student understanding of specific geometrical concepts when I incorporate exploratory exercises into the teaching of geometry in my classroom?
- What happens to students' academic performance in our sixth-grade classrooms when we assign heterogeneous groups for cooperative learning activities?
- How is student time on task affected when I assign middle-school students to co-ed groups in my classroom?
- How can I use small-group activities and "recorders" to improve attentiveness during the presentation of new information in a class of students with behavioral problems?
- What happens to my student's academic performance in history when I give daily quizzes on homework assignments?
- What happens to student behavior in my classroom when I start my class with a short meditation, mind-relaxing activity?
- What happens to the Massachusetts Comprehensive Assessment System (MCAS) scores of the students in my classroom when I don't teach to the test?
- What happens to the reading comprehension of the students in our third-grade classrooms when we systematically differentiate instruction?
- How can I use cooperative learning in my high-school mathematics class to improve student learning?
- How can we use learning centers to help the children in our second-grade classrooms improve their writing?
- What happens to student learning in my classroom when I use a project-centered approach to teaching the geography of Egypt?
- How can we improve students' interpersonal relationships in our classrooms through regularly scheduled small-group meetings?
- How can I use cooperative learning to increase student translation fluency in my ninth-grade Latin class?
- How can I help non-English speakers transition into my classroom of English-speaking kindergartners?
- How can I help facilitate Tim's expressive language development in my preschool special-needs classroom?
- How can I construct and use student feedback to improve my instruction in English?
- What happens to student attitudes about mathematics when we daily emphasize functional math in our classrooms?
- How can I construct and use student feedback to improve my instruction in English?
- What strategies can I use to build productive learning relationships in mathematics with the middle-school students in my classroom?
- What happens to EC's learning of mathematics when I make the Everyday Mathematics program more accessible to her?

A good research question is authentic—you have to own it. You are not disembodied from the research. That is why I encourage the use of the personal pronouns *I* or *we* and phrases such as "in my classroom" or "our students" in the statement of the research question. When you own the question and acknowledge your subjectivity, you are more likely to invest yourself in the research.

A good research question doesn't lead to a yes or no answer. It is specific but sufficiently open-ended to facilitate meaningful exploration and to provide opportunities for deep and rich understandings of teaching and learning in the classroom. The question needs to be "open-ended enough to allow possibilities to emerge" (Hubbard & Power, 1993, p. 23). Responding to the more open-ended research question will more often than not generate multiple directions and further research questions. On changing questions, Catherine Battaglia (1996), a classroom teacher, offers this advice from her experience with the action research process:

> Change questions! The questions I ask regarding my practice keep changing. Action research involves refining questions until you feel you have landed upon the right ones. I now see that the way you frame questions will, inevitably, determine the methodology you plan to study them. Differentiated solutions and subsequent understandings will be generated by the way questions are posed. . . . Action research is so much a matter of "seeing" that it is a good idea, I found, to develop a little intellectual schizophrenia. Be your own arbiter. Wear another hat, use a different lens, try to unpack your thinking in a different way. . . . Don't fall in love with an idea when it is the only one you have. Have the courage to kiss them goodbye. (p. 91)

And McNiff, Lomax, and Whitehead (2006) make clear that cyclical changes in questions and issues are integral to action research:

> People change all the time and their social situations change with them. This is one of the delights of working in action research . . . because you can see how one research question can transform into another and also how one issue can act as grounds for new issues to emerge. Nothing is ever static. We are constantly changing ourselves and our contexts. This kind of transformation of existing issues and questions into new ones can help your ideas and practices as ongoing cycles of action and reflection. (p. 117)

Framing the Research Question

In our eagerness to begin a research study, there is sometimes a tendency to try to state the question as soon as possible. It is advisable not to hurry the question. Identifying and framing the research question should be done carefully after mulling over and contemplating many different angles of the issues confronting you. As you reflect on the teaching and learning situations in your classroom let ideas percolate, brainstorm questions and play around with them, talk about your questions with colleagues, and let the questions emerge over time until you feel ready to frame the question that will guide your inquiry. Begin with "grand tour questions" (Spradley, 1979) such as: What is happening here? What problems are most salient about my teaching situation? What might happen if I change something in my teaching situation?

Once you have narrowed down the question, it should be framed so that the issue you are investigating is clearly and concisely stated. The action or intervention you intend to implement needs to be clearly stated. The question should be free of jargon and value-laden terms. Research questions beginning with *what, why,* or *how* are usually broader and get at explanations, relationships, and reasons. In discussing her experiences as a teacher-researcher, Carol Avery (1990) describes how framing her questions with *what, how,* and *why* changed her way of seeing children:

> As a teacher researcher I became a learner in the classroom concerned with what my students were learning and how they were learning. I experienced the classroom as a collaborative venture and examined not only how I functioned but also how we worked together and why strategies did or did not work. Asking questions of how and why led the way for me to delve into children's individual learning patterns, to see children in the context of their unique situations, and to understand and value the richness of their differences. I developed a responsive mode of teaching; I became more flexible in dealing with the children. (p. 37)

I recommend that the personal pronoun *I* or the collective personal pronoun *we* appear in the research question, asserting your ownership of the question and your personal agency in addressing the research problem. The use of the personal pronouns *we* or *I* also acknowledges that in all research, "subjectivity is invariably present," and "researchers should be meaningfully attentive to their own subjectivity" (Peshkin, 1988, p. 17). I cannot emphasize too much how important I believe it is to put the *I* (or *we*) at the center of the research question. The rationale for the inclusion of the personal pronoun is succinctly and eloquently stated by McNiff, Lomax, and Whitehead (2006):

How do "I" fit into the **research**?
- I am the subject and object of the research.
- I take responsibility for my own actions.
- I own my claims and judgments.
- I am the author of my own research accounts.

How do "I" fit into the **action**?
- by seeing my own practice as the central focus of my research through critical reflection and self-study
- by encouraging others to participate is a negotiated definition of shared practices
- by showing respect for other ways of doing things
- by showing humility and exposing my vulnerability
- by being open to argument
- by being willing to accept that I could be wrong
- by owning my mistakes
- by standing my ground when my principles are at stake. (p. 17)

In framing the research question, it helps to consider the wide range of variables that can affect your study. One of the exercises I ask teachers and teacher-interns to consider is to identify all the variables that could influence teaching and learning in their classrooms. They brainstorm lists of variables, including student variables, teacher variables, classroom variables, schoolwide variables, parent variables, and community variables (see Tables 11.2, 11.3, 11.4, and 11.5). A number of outcomes emerge from this exercise. As they examine and discuss the relevance of the variables to their work, teacher-researchers begin to develop a deeper appreciation of how complex teaching and learning are and a much richer understanding of how contextually circumscribed the classroom is. They also begin to realize that there are many factors over which they have no control in their teaching and in their research; to frame a manageable question, they must focus on those variables they can control. Finally, they begin to value the open-ended question that focuses on their classrooms

(*Text continues on page 247*)

Table 11.2   Student Variables That Can Affect Student Learning

- Gender, race, and/or ethnicity
- Prior education
- Prior knowledge and experiences
- Health
- Physical disabilities
- Age
- Socioeconomic status
- First language
- Learning styles
- Peer relationships
- Special talents
- Emotional health
- Size and stature
- Athletic ability
- Personality
- Interpersonal skills
- Nutrition
- Sleep
- Special needs
- Intellectual impairments
- Intellectual strengths–multiple intelligences
- Self-concept
- Hobbies and interests
- Behavioral issues
- Motivation to learn
- Level of participation in class
- Reading comprehension and skills
- Language skills
- Physical appearance
- Attitudes and dispositions
- Family mobility
- Single-parent versus two-parent family
- Social skills
- Values
- Home life
- Student culture
- Afterschool activities

Table 11.3   Classroom Variables That Can Affect Student Learning

- Size and configuration of classroom space
- Light
- Temperature
- Seating arrangements
- Availability of curriculum resources and learning materials
- Availability of computers and other instructional technology
- Class size: number of students
- Classroom décor: displays of student work, displays of commercial materials, few or no displays
- Carpeting

- Number of adults in the classroom
- Number of children with special needs
- Transition times
- Access to manipulatives
- Location of classroom in the building
- Age-appropriate environment
- Class schedule of learning activities
- Attractiveness and stimulation of physical environment
- Classroom pacing
- Classroom disruptions
- Classroom rules (where do they originate and how are they communicated)
- Classroom culture
- Class climate: student centered or teacher centered?
- Pathways in classroom; traffic flow
- Classroom routines

- Teacher's desk arrangements and location
- Configuration and location of student desks or work stations
- Noise levels, acoustics
- Supportive or nonsupportive learning environment
- Student responsibility and leadership in class
- Patterns of classroom interactions
- Availability of music and art materials, displays of student art
- Classroom safety
- Modular age-appropriate furniture
- Ventilation
- Blackboards and other similar equipment
- Emotional and affective climate
- Availability of print materials
- Greeting of students each day
- Snack time

Table 11.4   Teacher Variables That Can Affect Student Learning

- Professional preparation
- Content knowledge
- Knowledge and understanding of children
- Philosophy of education
- Motivation to teach and commitment to teaching
- Knowledge of pedagogy

- Personality
- Prior experience
- Classroom management effectiveness
- Collegial and administrative support
- Teaching style and specific instructional approaches

(Continued)

Table 11.4 (Continued)

- Enthusiasm
- Gender, race, and/or ethnicity
- Ability and commitment to individualize instruction
- Emotional disposition
- Interpersonal and social skills
- Health and energy level
- Expectations and assumptions about student learning
- Patience
- Hobbies and interests
- Level of education
- Age
- Size and stature
- Physical appearance
- Motivation skills
- Knowledge of curriculum
- Approaches to assessment
- Self-concept
- Attitudes about teaching, learning, and children
- Professional and personal confidence
- Authenticity
- Knowledge of and skill in cooperative learning
- Ability and motivation to team-teach
- Practice of reflection and self-assessment
- Participation in professional development
- Sense of identity and integrity
- Physical disabilities
- Commitment to diversity and social justice
- Knowledge of multicultural pedagogy and curriculum
- Involvement and experience in writing individualized educational programs or plans (IEPs)
- Skills and attitudes about collaboration
- Teacher culture
- Organizational and leadership skills

Table 11.5   School Variables That Can Affect Student Learning

- School culture
- Principal's leadership
- Parental involvement and parent-teacher organization (PTO)
- School mission and academic programs
- Formal curriculum
- Hidden curriculum
- School philosophy of education
- Organization and structure
- Size and configuration
- Budget and resources
- Student culture

- Extracurricular activities
- Athletic program
- School schedule and traffic patterns
- Staffing arrangements
- Demographic composition of student body
- Physical appearance of the school
- Resources (learning, curriculum, and technology resources)
- Special facilities (library, computer labs, gym, cafeteria)
- Philosophy of discipline
- Teacher and staff demography
- Partnerships with other institutions
- Transitions between classes
- Student leadership and engagement
- Student activities, clubs, and organizations
- Before- and afterschool programs
- Teacher/student ratio

- Class sizes
- Heterogeneous or homogeneous grouping
- Elementary, middle school, or high school
- Formal and informal communication systems
- Public/private/parochial
- Teacher culture
- District regulations
- Dress code
- Support programs available (counseling, reading, special education)
- Commitment to diversity, inclusion, and social justice
- Learning priorities
- Opportunities for professional development
- Community support
- Teacher leadership
- Safe environment

because they sense they can engage a wide range of variables without compromising the outcome of their inquiry; by such engagement, they can capture in their research the fibrous complexity of teaching and learning.

It is appropriate to close this discussion regarding finding and framing the research question with the words of Denise Dabish (2001), who teaches Spanish at Gilbert High School in Gilbert, Arizona:

In the end, I feel I have learned a great deal more than the answer to my research question. I believe that by becoming a teacher researcher I have rediscovered my desire to teach and my quest for improving how I teach. When I think about the path I took to become a teacher researcher I am no longer scared of being a teacher who conducts research. I kept wondering how my research was going to take shape. . . . I had to trust what I was doing was going to point me in the right direction. Now I know that simply starting with a question is all the information one needs to embark on an incredible journey of teacher discovery and research. Already I find myself wondering about what intriguing, important questions I will "live" next year as my students and I learn and grow together. (p. 5)

Conducting a Literature Review

Hart (1998, p. 27) suggests that a good literature review serves several purposes in facilitating the inquiry process, including helping the researcher to: distinguish between what has been done and what needs to be done; understand the structure of the problem; discover important variables relevant to the study; identify relationships between ideas and practice; identify areas of controversy in the research; establish and define the social, educational, or cultural context of the problem or question; identify methodologies and research approaches that have been used and could be employed in conducting the research; and place the research within an historical context.

In doing a literature review, it is critical that the teacher-researcher be mindful of the potential limitations of a review. Onwuegbuzie and Leech (2005) and Wolf (1986) cite a number of factors that limit the appropriateness, comprehensiveness, and representativeness of material included in a review:

- Selective inclusion of studies, often based on the reviewer's own subjective assessment of the quality of the underlying studies
- Failure to examine the characteristics and attributes of the studies as potential explanations for consistent and contradictory findings across studies
- Failure to consider the context under which each of the studies took place
- Differential subjective weighting of studies in the interpretation of a set of results
- Misleading interpretations of study results
- Confirmation bias

- Overreliance on findings from either qualitative or quantitative studies
- Failure to examine moderating or mediating variables in the underlying relationships

Among teacher-action-researchers, I have found there are mixed feelings and attitudes about the role and the timing of the literature review in conducting classroom or school research. Some teacher-researchers have told me that they have found themselves unconsciously bowing to the "expertise of the printed word," deferring to the authority of the printed text, and becoming unduly influenced in an unproductive way and intellectually deflected from their work by research approaches, conceptual frameworks, and theories generated mainly by university faculty. Consequently, they begin to doubt and lose trust in their own thinking and work. Other teacher-researchers have expressed concern that, in conducting a local classroom-based study, a review of the literature is not worth the time and energy required to do it; they point out that many published teacher research studies do not include literature reviews. Other teacher-researchers have demonstrated their skepticism and resistance to "truth coming down from on high," whether from research institutes, think tanks, universities, or what they perceive as arcane research publications; they have no trouble designing studies to address their classroom issues without a literature review.

However, based on my experience in working with classroom teachers and teacher-interns doing action research studies, I believe that a review of the relevant research literature is essential. (Indeed, this book is a case study of a literature review writ large.) A good literature review can help in focusing your research question, developing your research methodology and data collection procedures, identifying a conceptual framework for your research, making you more critical about your assumptions, situating your inquiry within context, identifying gaps in previous studies, identifying flawed methodologies or theoretical approaches, and identifying controversies in the research literature. A literature review also provides a check for testing your findings and conclusions and helps you to make meaning out of your findings.

Because of the recursive, iterative, spiraling, and cyclical nature of action research, it is imperative to recognize that, as new questions and issues emerge, you may find that you are reading a different literature than the one you had anticipated at the beginning of your study. Often, the relevant literature is identified by emerging data and your interpretation of the data. In action research, then, the literature review can be considered not a static collection of literature but rather an evolving, shifting, and changing body of work that is in a reciprocal relationship with the dynamics of the action research process. The iterative and recursive nature of the research affects the literature review, and the changing literature review affects the conduct and direction of the research.

Based on their experience in working with action researchers over the years, Holly, Arhar, and Kasten (2005) suggest several ideas for consideration in doing a literature review:

- Read broadly and generally, at first, then read more narrowly.
- When you are researching a novel topic that seems to have few resources, look for related topics and then synthesize them.
- Consult primary resources where possible. . . . The rule of thumb is use as many primary resources as is possible and feasible, and to check secondary sources to make sure that the information quoted is accurate.
- Ask for help. A few well placed questions to a librarian, media specialist, and colleagues can be helpful.
- Read enough to get started, but not so much that you become too exhausted to conduct your study.
- Read with a critical eye. . . . What are the theories, assumptions, and frameworks of the researchers? Are they plausible? Are they consistent with what you know? What is explained? What is left for interpretation? (pp. 114–115)

The information sources for conducting a literature review are varied and many, including books; professional journals; official government publications; research reports issued by foundations, professional organizations, and government agencies; theses and dissertations; and Internet resources such as blogs, podcasts, wikis, and Web sites. (For additional information about using the Internet as a teaching and information resource, see Green, Brown, & Robinson, 2008; Nelson, 2008; Richardson, 2006.) Appendix B provides an annotated list of teacher action research Web sites, and Appendix C lists the Web sites of leading professional educational and research organizations—rich resources for searching and finding information to support a literature review.

Identifying Data Sources

The biggest challenge in conducting action research is to collect and analyze data while you are in the midst of taking an action. As you are implementing an intervention to improve student learning or to make a change in your teaching practice, you have to be mindful of the details that will make the intervention successful while at the same time remembering to carefully collect and analyze data that will determine the degree of success or the need to modify the intervention.

Data are everywhere. An abundance of data can be found in classrooms, schools, and communities; data are all around the educational environment. Data collection should be a thoughtful, planned, and purposeful process. A good data collection plan will help participants think through important questions for data gathering, facilitate coordination of resources and timelines so that data are gathered by design rather than by chance, and bring clarity so that data are collected right the first time. A good data collection plan addresses the following questions:

- Why are we collecting the data?
- How are the data related to the research question?
- What will the data tell us about the research problem?
- What kind of data will yield the best information? What counts as data?
- What data will we collect? How much data will we collect? Will data be easy or difficult to collect?
- Who will be using the data? Who will be seeing the data?
- What data sources will we use to collect information?
- When will the data be collected?
- Who will collect the data?
- How will the data be collected and analyzed? How systematic will data collection be?
- How will the data be organized? How will the data be displayed?
- What criteria will be used to analyze the data?
- How will the data be recorded and shared?
- Where will the data be housed?

Schools include innumerable data sources; data can be found in every classroom. An exercise I ask of teachers and students who are involved in designing and conducting action research studies is to gather in small groups and brainstorm as many data sources as they can. When the groups come together to share their work and develop a common master list of data sources, the large number of resources available for generating data to address their research questions often surprises them. Table 11.6 is a list of more than 50 different sources for gathering data that was brainstormed by one group of teacher-researchers. These data sources can be grouped into three categories:

Existing archival sources are those items currently available in the files or archives of the school or of individual staff members. The collection of data from these sources requires little effort and time. Data include: student grades, attendance patterns, number of referrals, retentions, number/percentage of students in special programs, standardized test results, school mission statements, staff development plans, meeting agendas, discipline records, counseling service referrals.

Conventional sources are items that require communication, observation, or follow-up with members of the population and that often require instrumentation to standardize the information collected. Conventional sources include simple interviews, surveys, number of books read, writing samples, variety of materials used, observations, and journals.

Inventive sources are usually more creative, complex, and deep. We use these sources when we want deeper or qualitatively different information than we can gain from existing and conventional sources. Inventive sources include authentic assessment, performance assessment, exhibits, portfolios, expositions, videotapes, photography, and children's drawings.

Whatever data sources are used, it is important to collect data as you go along. As one teacher-researcher, Phillip White (1998), a third-grade teacher at McElwain Elementary School in Denver, Colorado, advises:

I cannot stress too strongly the need to make sure that you are gathering all the data at the moment it is there. When I went back to check my field notes on the class time that I described in this essay, I discovered to my chagrin that I had not documented what I had written on the dry erase board. After the

Table 11.6   Data Sources for Classroom/School Research

- Physical configuration of classroom
- Running records
- Individual Educational Plans
- Formal teacher evaluations
- Curriculum materials
- Lesson plans
- Classroom tests and quizzes
- Formal assessments
- School mission and goals statement
- School and district organizational and informational materials
- Local community newspaper
- School, school district, and teacher association newsletters
- Reviews of professional literature
- Class sociograms
- Student progress reports
- Student assessment of teaching
- Pre- and posttesting of students
- Fieldnotes
- Teacher planning materials/teacher plan book
- Professional journals
- Observational checklists
- Views and opinions of before- and afterschool providers
- Standardized tests
- Student work samples
- Professional development plan
- School-community demographic data
- Shadowing of students
- Meeting agendas
- Handouts from curriculum and professional development workshops
- Exhibits
- State assessment testing data
- Student suspension, expulsion, and dropout rates
- Student autobiographies
- Teacher and student journals
- Surveys of parents, teachers, and students
- Interviews with parents, teachers, and students
- Focus group interviews with parents, students, and colleagues
- Photographs
- Video- and audiotape recordings
- Informal feedback and informal assessments
- Observations of teaching by teacher and/or colleagues
- Tally sheets/checklists to record specific behaviors
- Student and teacher portfolios
- Student self-assessment
- Conferences with teachers and parents
- Report cards

(Continued)

Table 11.6 (Continued)

• Collaborative dialogue sessions with colleagues and specialists	• Number and percentage of students in special programs
• Curriculum-based assessments	• Student referrals to counseling
• Records of attendance and student participation	• Student discipline and retention records
• Student cumulative records	• Expositions
• Self-evaluations of teaching	• Norm-referenced testing data
• Student drawings and artwork	• Teacher/student ratios
• Internet sites for action research and education	• Teacher attendance rates
• Student writing and stories	• Blogs

class left, I was tired and the next class was coming through the door, along with the instructor. I looked at the board, at all that was written, and thought, "I don't need to write that down. I'll remember." But, I didn't. Happily, when I began writing this essay I was able to contact members of the class and use their class notes for documentation. But, I've learned my lesson. Save as much documentation as possible. It will be valuable in the future. (p. 6)

Collecting and Analyzing Data

Power (1996); Stainback and Stainback (1988); MacLean and Mohr (1999); Shea, Murray, and Harlin (2005); and the Madison Metropolitan School District Web site, *Classroom Action Research* (http://www.madison.k12.wi.us/sod/car/carhomepage.html) recommend several ways teacher-researchers can analyze the data they have collected. Their recommendations serve as "rules of thumb" and are not meant to be construed as prescriptions. Always keep in mind, as you proceed with the analysis of data, that action research is a recursive, dynamic, and cyclical process of inquiry.

Inquiry cycles are messy and are not necessarily discrete or linear. They can move much more fluidly, double back on themselves, and take unpredictable routes. Moving from fog to clarity, and back to fog can be part of the process. Just because the inquiry is making less sense does not necessarily mean you are going in the wrong direction. (Ladkin, 2004, p. 125)

These rules of thumb are not meant to be viewed as linear steps to be followed in a sequential manner. For example, as you begin to collect data, you may find that your analysis of the data suggests a significant modification in your research question. When you modify the question, it then may lead to collecting new data. This is the process of recursion.

1. Triangulate the data (see Table 11.7). Study the research question from at least three separate pieces of data and three points of view. I usually advise teachers and teacher-interns, in constructing their action research studies, to use mixed research methods, a combination of quantitative and qualitative approaches, for purposes of triangulation. I encourage them to identify five different data sources. For example, those five data sources might be your journal observations, recorded comments by a student or students, survey data collected from parents, student test data, observations and feedback from colleagues, and samples of student work. As you collect your data, ask yourself if the research question still fits the data that are emerging from the study.

2. Sift through and put into order everything you have collected, making notes as you go. As you examine the data, continually compare the data that were collected earlier in the study with data collected later in the study. Use different bases for comparison. For example, if you have conducted a study on the impact of student learning centers on reading comprehension, you might compare what the students did in October with what they did in May or June, or you might try comparing students' written work with their oral work or a combination of both.

3. Design a systematic approach to analyze your data. This may develop as you become more comfortable with what you are learning. Categorize and clarify the data and determine how to arrange the data findings, organizing the data chronologically, by importance, and by frequency (how often an incident occurs), for example. Organize the data based on what you are really learning from the

Table 11.7 Triangulation Matrix

Research Question	Data Source 1	Data Source 2	Data Source 3	Data Source 4	Data Source 5
1. What happens to my students' learning when I introduce primary sources into our history curriculum?	Daily teacher journal entries	Student narrative feedback	Samples of student work	Records of student grades, teacher assessments, and attendance	Supervisor feedback
2. How do the various assessment strategies of a new science curriculum and those that I design meet the learning and emotional needs of my students?	Surveys of students	Test scores from three different tests	Student journals	Small group-focused interviews of students	Individual interviews of students
3. What happens to my students' behavioral engagement in class when I use a variety of strategies to teach English?	Teacher journal entries and classroom observations	Student self-assessments	Teacher and student surveys	Student grades	Student attendance
4. How can I use student feedback to improve my instruction?	Student questionnaire	Informal and formal assessments	"Exit tickets" at the end of each lesson to gather student feedback	Observations of other teachers and interns	Performance on essays and quizzes
5. What happens to my second-grade students' reading comprehension abilities when I use drama activities to interpret texts?	Teacher journal entries	Student artifacts and classroom work	Running records	Developmental Reading Assessments (DRA)	Video recordings
6. What happens to kindergarten students' learning of sight word vocabulary when I use guided reading with a balanced literacy approach?	Marie Clay letter identification assessment and the Marie Clay word vocabulary dictation	Ohio Word Test	Student interviews	Home survey concerning literacy habits	Samples of student work

data, not on any assumptions you brought with you to your analysis. Develop charts, columns, outlines, and ways of counting occurrences. Coding your findings will help categorize the data. You can make up different categories that fit the teaching situation(s) or use categories developed by another researcher. Watch for ways that the data develop into categories different from what you expected, and explore those differences.

4. Review your information after it is coded to determine if there is a frequency of certain phenomena or powerful, unusual comments, events, or behaviors that particularly interest you. One occurrence may give you a new insight while another may be most important in helping you to reframe your research question.

5. Let the data influence you. Do not be afraid to let the data influence what you are learning as you go deeper with your analysis. Look for what doesn't fit the assumptions or theories of other researchers, and note what stands out or goes against the grain. Don't censor the data, even if you don't like what you are learning.

> As a human you cannot help but be influenced by the data you collect. It is common, therefore, to change a particular teaching strategy, the sources of data, or even the focus of the study as you are collecting data. This is acceptable as long as you let the reader know what you did and why you did it. (Johnson, 2008, p. 63)

Include data that don't necessarily reflect change or growth. Jot down ideas for actions you will take as a result of what you are learning. As you study the data keep in mind the reciprocal relationship between context and action—where action is a product of context, and context is a product of action.

6. Examine and study your data several times. New ideas will occur to you with a fresh perspective. Speculate. Identify repetitive words, phrases, ideas, beliefs, or values, as well as similarities and differences. Identify points that occur more frequently and are more powerful. Look for themes and conceptual and attitudinal patterns to emerge. Key words and phrases can trigger themes. Determine these themes by scanning the data, not by relying on your preconceived ideas of what you think the categories are. Narrow the themes down to something manageable. Look for those unique ideas that you had not considered; they might influence your thinking. Some ideas may fit into more than one theme. Create subgroups under each theme. Insights emerge unexpectedly.

Data we anticipate being very rich and illuminating may be less so than other sources of information and the importance of remaining open to our data collection methods is crucial. . . . It is important to avoid premature closure and pre-emptive judgments. (James, 1999, p. 88)

Try out different hunches about what the data mean. Look to see if there are any factors or variables that might cause you to distrust the data. Make an educated guess and then see if it is supported by the data. Don't stick rigidly to an assumption or hypothesis that was originally held.

7. Write continuously to document actions and ideas as they take place. Writing can reveal meaning and significance to you in the act of writing itself. As you proceed through the action research process, make notes. Jot down what you are seeing, what questions are emerging, and what you are learning. Keep notes on those new ideas that are unanticipated. These may be findings or surprises you had not planned. Rewrite the question several times, modifying or changing it when necessary to fit what's important from the data that have been collected. What is it that you really want to figure out? Sometimes, you will want to make the question more global, whereas sometimes, the question may become more tightly focused.

8. Create a visual representation for what you have collected. Look for patterns related to time and sequence as well as patterns related to differences in other factors. A grid, an idea map, a chart, or some visual metaphor—these are all possibilities to help make sense of the data and display a powerful presentation of your ideas. Map out your data; draw it all on one page. Sketch the metaphors that come to mind when thinking of the data and what it all means. Use colors and shapes to separate ideas. Think about creating visual images of what you are learning using diagrams, sketches of things, people, and happenings to show different ideas and groupings. (See Depka, 2006.)

9. Abstract and distill. State the core of your findings as if you had to summarize and encapsulate the essence of your study in an abstract of 50 words or less. What matters most in these data? Think about writing an abstract that would be part of a conference program. What story do you see emerging from the data?

10. Consult with and involve your students. Ask your students what they think about what you are observing and writing about. They may offer new ideas about their learning or validate what you are finding. Students may become coresearchers, but be careful of compromising confidentiality.

11. Take a break away from the study. Sometimes, it helps to take a break from the research process to clear your mind and give yourself a rest. Coming back to the process with a refreshed outlook will often lead to new understandings and perspectives.

12. Confer with colleagues—with your critical friends group. Share your findings with your research group, your critical friends. Discuss the research approach you used. Explain the data interpretations. Do they see the same things? Consider their different interpretations and use them to clarify, broaden, and otherwise validate the findings. Do new questions emerge from this discussion? State your theories. You build your ideas about teaching as you try out new strategies. Theories emerge from and are grounded in practice. Ask your research group to help you look at your data from multiple lenses and data sources, to help you interpret your findings, and to draw conclusions and implications for future teaching.

Drawing Conclusions: Finding Meaning

From the data analysis, one needs to develop the conclusions and implications of the research for teaching and learning. Data don't stand alone. It is the meanings we apply to the data that are critical. However, it is important not to make any inferences from the data that the data will not support or to generalize the findings of the research beyond the study's parameters as defined in the research question. Engage in dialogue with your critical friends to unearth the meanings and conclusions of your study and their implications for practice. What story or stories do the data tell? What meanings can be found as a result of the data analysis? What have you learned about your teaching practices? About student learning? What effect has the research had on you as an educator and person? What changes have you made in your teaching approaches? Does the data analysis confirm or disconfirm the effectiveness of the action or intervention you planned and implemented to improve student learning? Has your research question been answered, or have more questions emerged? What are the implications of your study for improving the teaching practices of colleagues? Were there unexpected findings? What new questions would you ask for future action research studies?

This phase of the action research process should bring the research together, providing an interpretation of the data, a summary of critical conclusions, and recommendations for further research. The conclusion section is important because it offers the last opportunity to communicate the significance and meaning of your research. The conclusions should be solidly anchored in the findings of the study. If there are significant differences between what the data say about the research question and what you expected, then these differences should be explored and viewed as rich opportunities for learning. Such differences can catalyze new perspectives and questions. In discussing the conclusions of your study, it is imperative that you delineate the limitations of your findings and of the research study. You do not want to inadvertently overgeneralize the findings or add an opinion that is not supported by the data.

Evaluating Your Action Research Study

As you proceed in completing your research study, it is important that you assess its development and outcomes. Waterman, Tillen, Dickson, and De Koning (2001) suggest helpful guidelines, which I have modified to include the present and past verb tenses in some instances to capture the fluidity and dynamics of your study in assessing it as you progress through various stages:

1. Is/was there a clear statement of the aims and objectives of each stage of the study?

2. Is/was the action research relevant to the participants in the study? Relevant to their issues, goals, and experiences?

3. Are/were the different phases of the study clearly outlined? Did recursion and iteration occur? For what reason?

4. Are/were the participants and the stakeholders and the process of their selection and involvement in the study clearly described?

5. Is/was the context of the research fully described?

6. Is/was the relationship between you and participants adequately considered?

7. Is/was there a clear discussion of the actions taken and how they may have been adjusted in response to local events, participants, and evolving data? Have you described how and why the action intervention was identified?

8. Are/were ethical issues encountered, and if so, how are/were they addressed?

9. Is/was the length and the timetable of the study realistic?

10. Are/were data collected in a way to address the research questions? What data are being/were collected and how are/were they collected?

11. What steps were taken to advance the rigor of the findings? To what degree was triangulation employed?

12. Are/were data analyses sufficiently rigorous? How valid and reliable are the data?

13. Is/was the study design flexible and responsive? To what extent was the study recursive and iterative in its process? Were any changes made reflecting recursion and iteration generated by changes in the data or interpretation of the data?

14. Are/were there clear statements of the findings and outcomes for each phase of the study?

15. Do/did you link the data and the findings to your own commentary and interpretation?

16. Is/was the connection to an existing body of knowledge made clear?

17. Are/were the findings transferable to other contexts and settings?

18. Are/were your biases, assumptions, and autobiographical stances clearly stated?

19. How has the research study affected your students? What impact did your action intervention have on student learning?

20. How has the research study affected you and your teaching?

❖ SUMMARY

In this chapter, I have offered a number of suggestions for conducting an action research study. Major points to remember include the following:

- Conducting action research is challenging because the researcher not only conducts research but simultaneously enacts change in implementing an intervention.
- Initially, a modest research study is preferable to a more ambitious undertaking.
- It is important to identify and engage colleagues as critical friends who will work with you throughout the action research process.
- Identifying and clearly stating the research question is one of the most critical steps in doing action research.
- A good research question engages your energy, passion, and commitment; is manageable and consonant with your work; benefits students; is authentic and owned by you the researcher(s); and is sufficiently open-ended to facilitate meaningful and deep exploration of teaching and learning.
- The research question should be carefully framed and include the action or intervention that will be implemented and the intended outcome of the study.
- A good literature review helps to define the social, historical, theoretical, educational, or cultural context of the research problem or question.
- The literature review is in a reciprocal relationship with the action research process and evolves, shifts, and changes over the life of the research.
- Sources for conducting a literature search include books, journals, Internet resources, government publications, research reports, theses, and dissertations.

- Collecting and analyzing data while you are implementing an intervention is one of the biggest challenges in doing action research.
- As you collect and analyze data, bear in mind that action research is a recursive and cyclical process of inquiry and that questions and data may change during the life of an action research study.
- Data don't stand alone. It is the meanings we apply to the data that are critical.

Glossary

Action research/teacher action research—A process of concurrently inquiring about problems and taking action to solve them. It is a sustained, intentional, recursive, and dynamic process of inquiry in which the teacher takes action—purposefully and ethically in a specific classroom context—to improve teaching and learning. Action research is change research, a nonlinear, recursive, cyclical process of study designed to achieve concrete change in a specific situation, context, or work setting, to improve teaching/learning.

Aggregate—A group of people who have certain traits or characteristics in common without necessarily having any direct social connection with one another. For example, "all female physicians" is an aggregate; so is "all European cities with populations over 20,000." Gross National Income is an aggregation of data about individual incomes.

Applied research—Research undertaken with the intention of applying the results to some specific problem, such as studying the effects of different methods of law enforcement on crime rates. One of the biggest differences between applied and basic research is that in applied work, the research questions are most often determined not by researchers, but by policymakers or others who want help. Types of applied research include evaluation research and action research.

Autoethnography—An analytical personal account about the self as part of a group or culture; an attempt to see the self as others might; an opportunity to explain differences from the inside and written for others as the major audience.

Biographical research—A narrative approach to research that is primarily qualitative and includes gathering/using data in the form of diaries, stories, autobiographies, and life histories.

Classroom/school studies—Teachers' explorations of practice-based issues using data based on observation, interview, and document collection involving individual or collaborative work.

Coded data—A way of recording material at data collection, either manually or on computer, for analysis. The data are put into groups or categories, such as age groups, and each category is given a code number. Data are usually coded for convenience, speed, and computer storage space and to permit statistical analysis.

Collaborative action research— Action research conducted by a team or teams of teacher-researchers. In teams, teachers form communities of reflective practitioners who together engage in cycles of research and action that lead to professional growth, improved teaching practice, and student learning.

Conceptual research—Theoretical/philosophical work or the analysis of ideas. The focus of conceptual research is essays that deal with teachers' interpretations of the assumptions and characteristics of classroom and school life and/or the research itself.

Construct—(a) Something that exists theoretically but is not directly observable. (b) A concept developed (constructed) for describing relations among phenomena or for other research purposes. (c) A theoretical definition in which concepts are defined in terms of other concepts. For example, intelligence cannot be directly observed or measured; it is a construct.

Constructivism—The belief that humans individually and collectively construct reality. Adherents of this perspective argue that social reality is constructed by those who participate in it. Aspects of the social environment do not have existence apart from the meanings that individuals construct for them. Constructivism emphasizes the need to put analyses in context, presenting the interpretations of many, sometimes competing groups interested in the outcomes of education.

Constructivist-interpretivist-qualitative paradigm—Analysis of curriculum and instructional programs that attempts to expose the values underlying these phenomena. There is an emphasis on the need to put analyses in context, presenting the interpretations of many, sometimes competing groups interested in the outcomes of education. Human beings are seen as the primary research instruments, rejecting the mathematical modeling of phenomena on which the quantitative paradigm depends.

Context—The circumstances in which a particular event happens. A combination of circumstances, variables, and conditions that affect an event or action at a given moment.

Control group—Members of a control group are used as a standard for comparison. For example, a particular study may divide participants into two groups: an experimental group and a control group. The experimental group is given the experimental intervention or program while the control group continues with a standard program or no intervention. At the end of the study, the results of the two groups are compared.

Controlled variable—See *Variable.*

Correlation—The extent to which two or more things are related ("co-related") to one another. This is usually expressed as a statistical correlation coefficient that documents the strength of the relationship between two variables. A **positive correlation** occurs when one variable increases at the same time as the other variable increases. A **negative correlation** occurs when one variable increases at the same time as the other variable decreases.

Cosmology—A branch of philosophy that deals with the nature of the universe and humanity's place in it. (See also *Metaphysics* and *Ontology*.)

Critical theory—A concern with questions of power, control, and epistemology as social constructions with benefits to some and not to others. Unlike traditional theory, which is oriented to understanding or explaining society or the world, critical theory is oriented to critiquing and changing society. Critical theory posits that the real world, although it exists, cannot be seen by anyone because of biases and values that they possess. Proponents of critical theory view themselves as forces of emancipation engaged with powers of oppression. The goal of inquiry is to empower those who are not in political power to see their oppression so they can transform the world.

Critical theory-postmodern-praxis paradigm—The values system that is used in scientific inquiry to reflect the political power of some groups over others. Proponents of this paradigm view inquiry as a political act, and they see themselves as forces of emancipation engaged in conflict with powers of oppression. Praxis is the art of acting on the conditions one faces in order to change them. Proponents seek to deconstruct the texts inherent in educational products, programs, and processes and reveal the contradictions and the exclusion of minority interests. Deconstruction is the process of revealing hidden meanings of texts. A dialogical approach to methodology is emphasized to eliminate false consciousness and facilitate transformation.

Data—Information collected by a researcher. Data is the plural term; datum the singular. Data are often thought of as statistical or quantitative, but they may take many other forms as well, for example, transcripts of interviews or videotapes of social interactions. Nonquantitative data such as transcripts or videotapes are often coded or translated into numbers to make them easier to analyze.

Database—A collection of data organized for rapid search and retrieval, usually by a computer; often a consolidation of many records previously stored separately.

Data set—A collection of related data items, such as answers given by respondents to all questions on a survey.

Deductive reasoning—Works from the general to the more specific. It is a method of inquiry in which a theory is verified or refuted by empirically testing hypotheses deduced from it. In deduction, inferences are drawn in which conclusions about particulars follow from general or universal premises.

Dependent variable—See *Variable.*

Eclectic-mixed methods-pragmatic paradigm—The most recent paradigm to emerge in the postmodernist era. The name refers to its openness in borrowing the methods of the other three paradigms to collect information and to solve complex problems. Within this paradigm, "mixed methods research is formally defined as the class of research where the researcher mixes or combines quantitative and qualitative research techniques, methods, approaches, concepts, or language into a single study" (Johnson & Onwuegbuzie, 2004, p. 17). In an age of methodological pluralism, the mixed methods approach is viewed as softening the competition between methodological paradigms. The mixed methods paradigm is deemed to be the paradigm of epistemological and methodological pragmatism most capable of handling the complexity of post-modern society.

Emancipatory research—Emancipatory research is conducted with people from marginalized groups or communities. It is led by a researcher (or research team) who is either an indigenous or external insider; it is interpreted within intellectual frameworks of that group; and it is conducted largely for the purpose of empowering members of that community and improving services for them. It also engages members of the community as co-constructors or validators of knowledge.

Emic—The interpretation of data that an "insider," "native," or "local person" brings to the table. Exploring the emic perspective offers the researcher an "insider's perspective" or explanation as to what is occurring in the observable society. (See also *etic*; these are two different perspectives and interpretations of information, and researchers must take both perspectives into account when analyzing human society.)

Empirical-positivist-quantitative paradigm—The most established of the paradigms, reflecting a belief in a mechanistic, determinist reality whereby parts can be separated from wholes, and cause-and-effect relationships among parts can be determined. Physical and social reality is independent of those who observe it. Observations of this reality, if unbiased, constitute scientific knowledge. The goals of inquiry are the definition, prediction, control, and explanation of physical phenomena as revealed through experience (induction) and experiments (deduction). There is a reliance on measuring variables and analyzing relationships among them with descriptive and inferential statistics. Adherents of this paradigm believe that if something exists, it can be measured.

Empirical research—Research that is based on observed and measured phenomena and that derives knowledge from actual experience rather than from theory or belief.

Epistemology—The study of the nature, origin, and limits of human knowledge; a philosophy of knowledge or of how we come to know. It is the study or theory of the nature and grounds of knowledge especially with reference to its limits and validity, the study of different ways of knowing. Epistemology is concerned with several questions: What is knowledge? What are the necessary and sufficient conditions of knowledge? What are its sources? What is its structure? What are its limits?

Ethnography—Originally understood as the descriptive anthropology of technologically primitive people; today, the ways in which people make sense of their social world. Ethnography is usually a long-term study of a group or culture that is based on immersion and participation in the group. It employs multiple methodologies (such as participant observation, interviews, and examination of artifacts and records) to arrive at a theoretically comprehensive understanding of a group or culture.

Ethnomethodology—The study of the ways in which people make sense of their "immortal ordinary society"; the methods that people use on a daily basis to accomplish their daily lives. The study of methods by which people construct reality and make sense of events in everyday life.

Etic—The interpretation of data that the "objective and external" researcher comes up with. The etic perspective is usually found in anthropological and analytical studies where there is a need to come up with a comparative or universal claim. (See also *emic*; these are two different perspectives and interpretations of information, and researchers must take both perspectives into account when analyzing human society.)

Experiment—A study undertaken in which the researcher has control over some of the conditions in which the study takes place and control over some aspects of the independent variables being studied. Random assignment of the subjects to control and experimental groups is usually thought of as a necessary criterion of a true experiment. For example, if you interviewed moviegoers as they exited a theater to see if what they saw influenced their attitudes, this would not be experimental research; you had no control over who the subjects were or what film they watched or the conditions under which they watched it. On the other hand, if you chose a room, a film, and subjects to assign randomly to control and experimental groups and interviewed these subjects about the effects of the film on their attitudes, that would be an experiment.

Experimental design—The art of planning and executing experiments.

The greatest strength of an experimental research design, due largely to random assignment, is its internal validity: One can be more certain than with any other design about attributing cause to the independent variables. The greatest weakness of experimental designs may be external validity: It may be hard to generalize results beyond the laboratory.

Experimental group—A group receiving some treatment in an experiment. Data collected about people in the experimental group are compared with data about people in a control group (who received no treatment) and/or another experimental group (who received a different treatment).

Experimental research—Activities in which (a) two (sometimes more) conditions are compared to assess the effects of a particular treatment (the independent variable) and (b) the independent variable (i.e., the treatment) is directly manipulated by the researcher. There are two types of experiments: In **true experiments,** the subjects are always randomly assigned, and the researchers control the administration of the treatments. In **quasi-experiments,** random assignment of subjects is not possible. Intact groups are compared. The researchers control the administration of the treatments.

External validity—See *Validity.*

Extraneous variable—See *Variable.*

Factor—(a) In analysis of variance, an independent variable, that is, a variable presumed to cause or influence another variable; (b) in factor analysis, a cluster of related variables that are distinguishable components of a larger set of variables; (c) a number by which another number is multiplied, as in the statement: real estate values increased by a factor of three, meaning they tripled.

Feminism—An intellectual commitment and a political movement that seeks justice for women and the end of sexism in all forms. Feminist inquiry provides a wide range of perspectives on social, cultural, and political phenomena. Important issues for feminist theory and inquiry include the body, class and work, disabilities, human rights, popular culture, the family, race and racism, the self, science, and sexuality.

First-person research—Research in which the individual focuses on becoming aware of the self and the individual's impact on the world while taking action. In first-person research, the teacher-researcher attends to such questions as Who am I? What is important and meaningful to me? What values, ideologies, worldviews, and assumptions do I bring to the process of inquiry? First-person approaches include autobiographical writing, journal writing, narratives, and reflection on audio and videotapes of one's behavior. (See also *Second-person research; Third-person research.*)

Focus groups—Open-ended, discursive groups, which are used to gain a deeper understanding of respondents' attitudes and opinions. Focus groups typically involve between 6 and 10 people, and their sessions last for 1 to 2 hours. A key feature is that participants are able to interact with, and react to, each other. To facilitate this group dynamic, it is important to ensure that participants do not know each other beforehand and that they are broadly compatible.

Generalizability—The extent to which you can come to conclusions about one thing (often a population) based on information about another (often a sample).

Independent variable—See *Variable.*

Inductive reasoning—The process of drawing generalized conclusions from particular instances; a process of moving from specific observations to broader generalizations and theories. It is the process by which the truth of a proposition is made more probable by the accumulation of confirming evidence, a common pattern in sociological and scientific research.

Inquiry as stance—An orientation to the construction of knowledge and its relationship to practice. With this stance, the work of teachers in generating local knowledge through inquiry communities is considered social and political, "making problematic the current arrangements of schooling, the ways knowledge is constructed, evaluated, and used, and teachers' individual and collective roles in bringing about change" (Cochran-Smith, 2002, p. 15). Inquiry as stance positions teachers to link their inquiry to larger questions about the ends of teacher learning in school reform and to larger social, political, and intellectual movements, emphasizing that teacher learning needs to be understood as a long-term collective project with a democratic agenda.

Internal validity—See *Validity.*

Interpretive research—Work based on the idea that investigations should be searches for meaning rather than experimental science in search of laws. The criteria or assumptions of this kind of research are: Attention is paid to interaction between people and environments; teaching and learning are continuously interactive; classroom contexts are nested within other contexts; and unobservable processes like thoughts and attitudes are important sources of data. This research is interested in causal relationships and addresses the immediate and local meanings of actions. In addition, it addresses the inferences made by the researcher. Finally, it is concerned with why things happen and not just with what occurs.

Journals—Teachers' written accounts of classroom life over time, including records of observations, analyses of experiences, and reflections and interpretations of practice.

Knowledge democracy—A school or educational organization characterized by collaborative, participatory, and democratic relationships between and among teachers, university faculty, students, and parents, who together build communities of inquiry that promote the democratization of the knowledge-building process. In a knowledge democracy, a transformational knowledge infrastructure characterized by systemic and relational trust evolves over time to support and facilitate the engagement of teachers, parents, and students in all aspects of the inquiry process. A culture of collaborative inquiry emerges and becomes embedded in the school.

Longitudinal research—Any method of data gathering (observation, survey, experiment, etc.) in which the process is repeated on several occasions over a period of time, as far as possible replicating the chosen methodology each time. It follows that a key aim of such research is to monitor changes over time.

Mean—The arithmetic average of a set of data in which the values of all observations are added together and divided by the number of observations.

Median—The outcome that divides an ordered distribution exactly into halves.

Meta-analysis—A collection of systematic techniques for resolving apparent contradictions in research findings. Meta-analysts translate results from different studies to a common metric and statistically explore relations between study characteristics and findings. Meta-analysis typically follows the same steps as primary research. The meta-analyst first defines the review's purpose. Organizing frameworks can be practical or theoretical questions of varying scope, but they must be clear enough to guide study selection and data collection. Second, sample selection consists of applying specified procedures for locating studies that meet specified criteria for inclusion. Typically, meta-analyses are comprehensive reviews of the full population of relevant studies. Third, data are collected from studies in two ways. Study features are coded according to the objectives of the review and as checks on threats to validity. Study outcomes are transformed to a common metric so that they can be compared. A typical metric in educational research is the effect size, the standardized difference between treatment and control group means. Finally, statistical procedures are used to investigate relations among study characteristics and findings.

Metaphysics—A branch of philosophy concerned with ideas and theories regarding what kinds of beings are real, the nature of those beings, and concepts and language used to think about these beings. Metaphysics refers to broad theories of reality and to broad issues regarding the nature of reality. Metaphysics includes ontology, cosmology, and sometimes epistemology. (See also *Cosmology* and *Ontology*.)

Mixed/multiple methods—Research that uses a variety of methods. This requires an openness in borrowing a variety of methods to collect data and solve problems. However, the methods chosen must fit appropriately with the research being conducted. Mixed methods researchers might employ surveys, videos, interviews, qualitative and quantitative data, process-product approaches, censuses, laboratory experiments, observation, description, case studies, interpretation, and any variety of combinations.

Mode—The most frequent score or number in a set of data or test scores.

Modernism—A school of thought that affirms the power of human beings to create and improve and reshape their environment, with the aid of scientific knowledge, technology, and practical experimentation. The movement emerged at the end of the 19th and beginning of the 20th century and argued that the new realities of the industrial and mechanized age were permanent and imminent and that people should adapt their worldview to accept that the new was equal to the good, the true, and the beautiful.

Multivariate analysis—Any of several methods for examining multiple variables at the same time. Usage varies: (a) Stricter usage reserves the term for designs with two or more independent variables and two or more dependent variables; (b) more loosely, multivariate analysis applies to designs with more than one independent variable or more than one dependent variable or both. Whichever usage is preferred, either allows researchers to examine the relation between two variables while simultaneously controlling for the influence of other variables.

Mutually exclusive—A term used to describe two events, conditions, or variables that cannot occur at the same time. For example, one cannot be both male and female, or both Protestant and Catholic. Thus, the categories male and female or Catholic and Protestant are said to be mutually exclusive.

Negative correlation—See *Correlation*.

Normative—Relating to norms or standards. Normative is used, in educational research, to refer to traditionally or commonly accepted criteria.

Observation—A method of gathering information by watching a situation. In **nonparticipant observation,** the researcher attempts to remove or detach him/herself as an actor from the research situation. In **participant observation,** the researcher is something of an insider, someone who is involved in the processes being observed.

Ontology—A branch of philosophy that deals with the nature of reality or with being. It raises questions about the nature of reality, and it refers to the claims or assumptions that a particular approach to social inquiry makes about the nature of social reality, that is, about what exists, what it looks like, what units make it up, how they interact with each other, and what counts as evidence. (See also *Cosmology* and *Metaphysics*.)

Open-ended questions—A style of questioning in which the answer is left entirely to the respondent, either by providing a blank space on the questionnaire for recording the reply or by phrasing an interview question in such a way as to elicit a longer answer. This approach is used when there is no way of knowing what answers the respondents are likely to give, or if you want quotable responses. Often, such questions are used in pilot studies to develop a pre-coded version for the main study.

Oral inquiries—Teachers' oral examinations of classroom/social issues, contexts, texts, and experiences including collaborative analyses and interpretations and explorations between cases and theories.

Paradigm—A "taken for granted" conceptual framework that offers a way of seeing, framing, and making sense of the world. Paradigms provide an overarching conceptual view as well as a social and cultural framework for doing research; they shape how we understand ourselves, determine what counts as valuable and legitimate scientific knowledge, define the experiences that can legitimately lead to knowledge, and establish the kinds of knowledge that are produced.

Participatory action research—A social participatory process that engages participants in the study of reality in order to change it. It assumes that ideology, epistemology, knowledge, and power are bound up together. It is a collective critical process in which participants deliberately contest and reconstitute unproductive, unjust, and alienating ways of interpreting and describing their ways of working and ways of relating with others. It seeks to emancipate people from the constraints of irrational, unproductive, unjust, and unsatisfying social structures that limit their self-development and self-determination.

Pilot study—A trial that is done both to examine the effectiveness of various aspects of the proposed research, such as procedures for data gathering, and to aid the completion of detailed project plans.

Population—A group of people that researchers want to describe or about which they want to generalize. To generalize about a population, one often studies a sample that is meant to be representative of the population. Also called *universe*.

Positive correlation—See *Correlation*.

Positivism—A doctrine in the philosophy of science, positivism is characterized mainly by an insistence that science can deal only with observable entities known directly to experience. The world is seen as a single reality existing independently of the observer, which can be known and understood only by an objective and uninvolved researcher in a situation in which all variables can be controlled and manipulated to determine causation. In positivism, the only authentic knowledge is scientific knowledge. The positivist aims to construct general laws, or theories, that express relationships between phenomena. Observation and experiment will then show whether the phenomena do or do not fit the theory; explanation of phenomena consists in showing that they are instances of the general laws or regularities.

Postmodernism—Most generally, abandonment of confidence in the achievement of objective human knowledge through reliance on reason in pursuit of foundationalism, essentialism, and realism. It refers to an intellectual state lacking a clear central hierarchy or organizing principle and embodies extreme complexity, contradiction, ambiguity, diversity, and interconnectedness. In philosophy, postmodernists typically express grave doubt about the possibility of universal objective truth, reject artificially sharp dichotomies, and delight in the inherent irony and particularity of language and life.

Postpositivism—Like positivism, a perspective that seeks universal laws and theories. Unlike positivism, however, postpositivism suggests that we can know these truths only imperfectly. Human knowledge is conjectural. To gather as much information as possible toward the goal of objectivity, multiple methods are recommended.

Poststructuralism—Like structuralism, a perspective that recognizes that individual meanings are subservient to their contexts. A word, for example, has meaning only relative to other words and to the structure of the language in general. This makes the structure or context the unit of study rather than the individual. Although poststructuralism retains this belief, it is critical of the structuralist view that these structures are fixed. Adherents of this view believe that structures and meanings are not universal. Moreover, they suggest that there is no way to objectively view the situation.

Praxis—The practical application of a branch of learning; the conversion of theory into action. In education research, praxis is used to denote research that connects the research process to action or research that sparks action and change.

Pre-coded questions—Questions that have a list of answers from which respondents choose. This method facilitates analysis and improves control of the interview process. In a self-completion questionnaire, the respondent chooses the option or options. In an interview, the options are either read out or shown to the respondent, who then chooses. In this type of question, care must be taken that the options are exclusive and exhaustive. The category "Other" is often added in case the list is not complete, but keep in mind that if there are possible answers that are not on your list, bias can ensue.

Qualitative research—A method that examines people's words or actions in narrative or descriptive ways more closely representing the experiences of the people involved. It focuses on understandings and meanings; and it takes seriously lay accounts and concepts. Qualitative research developed to account for the importance of context in education. Unlike quantitative research, which seeks to generalize about educational practices and their effects, qualitative research seeks to examine the particulars of a given setting. Qualitative research tends to be a residual category for almost any kind of nonquantitative research.

Quantitative research—Research or variables that can be handled numerically. It is usually contrasted with qualitative variables and research and is concerned with measurement. Quantitative research uses control groups and is typically not focused on describing the context, but rather measuring data within a context (like test scores).

Quasi-experimental research—A type of research design for conducting studies in field or real-life situations where the researcher may be able to manipulate some independent variables but cannot randomly assign subjects to control and experimental groups. The procedures of quasi-experimentation were developed mainly in the context of evaluation research projects. For example, you cannot cut off someone's unemployment benefits to see how well he or she could get along without them or to see whether an alternative job-training program would be more effective for some unemployed people. You could, however, try to find volunteers for the new program. You could compare the results for the volunteer group (experimental group) with those of people in the regular program (control group). The study is quasi-experimental because you were unable to assign subjects at random to treatment and control groups. (See also *Experimental research.*)

Questionnaire—A group of written questions to which subjects respond. Some restrict the use of the term questionnaire to written responses. In action research, the questions often change as the teacher-researcher proceeds recursively through the action research spiral of planning, acting, observing, and reflecting.

Recursion—A basic action research process, which implies that there are no fixed conclusions but rather continuing, infinite revision. Questions change and shift from the very beginning of an action research study through a cyclical process of data discussion and analysis. The approach develops and redevelops the research questions by submitting their parameters to a process of redefinition that takes into consideration whatever new data and contexts have accumulated. The data, the generalizations, and the research questions are resubmitted along with other new and emerging data to develop tentative findings and conclusions.

Reliability—The consistency or stability of a measure or test from one use to the next. When repeated measurements of the same thing give identical or very similar results, the measure is said to be reliable. In **quantitative research,** reliability is concerned with measurement error. A measure must have reliability if it is to have any validity; if the dependent variable contains nothing but measurement error, then the reliability coefficient will be zero. The reliability coefficient describes the degree to which scores on a measure represent something other than measurement error. In **qualitative research,** reliability is the extent to which what has been recorded is what actually occurred. It is enhanced by detailed field notes; researchers' accuracy; the review of field notes by participants; use of tape recorders, photographs, or videotapes; use of participant quotations and literal descriptions; and an active search for discrepant data.

Replicability/replication—The process of repeating a study undertaken by someone else, in the sense of using the same methodology. Commonly the location and research subjects will be different, although sometimes studies return to the same group of subjects after a period of time has passed, for example, in child development studies. A good research report always includes enough information on the methods used to enable someone else to carry out a replication.

Research design—The science and art of planning procedures for conducting studies so as to get the most valid findings; called *design* for short.

When designing a research study, researchers draw up a set of instructions for gathering evidence and for interpreting it.

Sample—A group of subjects selected from a larger group in the hope that studying this smaller group (the sample) will reveal important things about the larger group.

Sampling—The process by which the total number of possible respondents for a research project (the research population) is reduced to a number which is practically feasible and theoretically acceptable (the sample). In **nonrandom sampling,** the principle of randomness has not been maintained in the selection of a sample. Often, such work involves structured sampling, whereby the sample group is carefully matched to the overall population on key variables. Nonrandom sampling is often convenient or the only approach possible in the circumstances. In **random sampling,** the goal is to combine chance (that everyone in the frame has the same chance of being chosen) with balance (that the chosen sample will be an accurate microcosm of the research population as a whole).

Sampling frame—A report that includes all of those from the research population who genuinely can become respondents, if they are willing.

Scale—A group of related measures of a variable. The items in a scale are arranged in some order of intensity or importance. A scale differs from an index in that the items in an index need not be in a particular order, and each item usually has the same weight or importance.

Schoolwide action research—An action research approach that seeks to improve the school as a problem-solving entity, to improve equity for students, and to involve the entire school community in the process of inquiry, thereby creating a knowledge democracy. It is a process of conducting inquiry about the school to improve teaching and learning and to make the school a self-renewing organization permeated by inquiry.

Second-person research—Cooperative research in which individuals inquire face to face with others into issues of mutual concern, in small groups. In a typical cooperative inquiry group, 6 to 20 people work together as coresearchers and cosubjects, conducting research in cycles of action and reflection to address a problem of mutual concern. (See also *First-person research* and *Third-person research.*)

Self-study research—A form of action research or teacher research that focuses inwardly on teacher education and, in some instances, professional development in a comprehensive way of leaving no area of teacher education sacrosanct from inquiry.

Social justice—The belief that every individual and group is entitled to fair and equal rights and participation in social, educational, political, and economic opportunities. Adherents of this belief usually develop an agenda for increasing understanding of oppression and inequality and taking action to overcome them.

Standard variable—See *Variable.*

Survey—A research design in which a sample of subjects is drawn from a population and studied (usually interviewed) to make inferences about the population. This design is often contrasted with the true experiment, in which subjects are randomly assigned to conditions or treatments.

Teacher action research—See *Action research.*

Textual analysis—Analysis of secondary source data also used in qualitative research. It involves working on a text in depth, looking for keywords and concepts and making links between them. The term also extends to literature reviewing. Increasingly, much textual analysis is done using computer programs.

Third-person research—A research process that draws together the views of large groups of people and creates a wider community of inquiry involving people who cannot always be known to each other face to face. Small inquiry groups are networked into wider communities of organizational, regional, and national action research systems. An example is the National Writing Project, which emerged from the Bay Area Writing Project. (See also *First-person research* and *Second-person research.*)

Treatment—What researchers do to the subjects in the experimental group but not to those in the control group. A treatment is thus an independent variable.

True experiments—See *Experimental research.*

Validity—A term to describe a measurement instrument or test that measures what it is supposed to measure; the extent to which a measure is free of systematic error. For example, a bathroom scale provides a reliable measure of weight but cannot give a valid measure of height. **External validity** is the extent to which the findings of a study are relevant to subjects and settings beyond those in the study; it is another term for generalizability. **Internal validity** is the extent to which the results of a study (usually an experiment) can be attributed to the treatments rather than a flaw in the research design; in other words, the degree to which one can draw valid conclusions about the causal effects of one variable on another.

Variable—Any factor that may be relevant to a research study. In a survey, for example, you may choose to analyze data by the age and gender of respondents. *Age* and *gender* are variables. Researchers use **controlled variables** to allow the research to focus on specific variables without being distorted by the impact of the excluded variables. A common way to control a variable is to be selective; for example, gender is controlled by selecting as respondents only men or only women; age can be partially controlled by restricting a sample to one age range, rather than any age. In a research project that seeks to establish cause and effect between variables (most likely in an experimental or quasi-experimental project), the potential causal variable is known as the **independent variable,** and the variable(s) where effects are under scrutiny is the **dependent variable,** or is affected by the independent variable. The independent variable is the presumed cause, and it can be used to predict the values of another variable. Some authors use the term independent variable for experimental research only; for no experimental research, they use predictor variable. When an experiment is seeking to monitor the impact of one variable on another (like counseling on stress level), attention has to be paid to other variables that could have an impact (that is, other factors which could affect a person's stress level). These are called **extraneous variables**. In social science research, especially in survey analysis, a range of variables is usually considered **standard variables** or "key variables" in the sense that some analysis is undertaken in relation to each of them. The list will change according to the specific research project, but it may well include such items as age, gender, socioeconomic class, ethnicity, employment, family background, and housing.

Variance—A measure of the spread of scores in a distribution of scores, that is, a measure of dispersion. The larger the variance, the further the individual cases are from the mean. The smaller the variance, the closer the individual scores are to the mean.

Appendix A

Examples of Teacher Action Research Projects

Example 1: From Reading Recovery to Guided Reading

What happens to the reading levels of some of my second-grade students when I adapt the guided reading process to support the skills they developed in their first-grade Reading Recovery program?

Marie A. Lennon
Title I Reading Teacher
Boston Public Schools
Boston, Massachusetts

Abstract

Students who participate in a Reading Recovery Program in Grade 1 are identified as "at risk" students. My question seeks to understand what happens to the reading levels of these students as they enter Grade 2 when I adapt the guided reading process to support the skills they developed in their first-grade Reading Recovery program. Specifically, the adaptation consisted of introducing a think-aloud strategy to help three students develop their decoding strategies. The instructional technique of think-alouds is a research-based strategy that requires teachers to verbalize their cognitive processes as they interact with a text, making visible the active thinking process of an expert reader. Think-alouds "talk" about using alternative strategies to comprehend a text with the goal that this "self-talk" is eventually internalized by the student. The think-alouds in this study focused on five decoding strategies, with students self-assessing their usage during 10 intervention sessions over a 2-month period. Four diverse indicators were analyzed to measure pupil progress: reading level, strategy use, attitude, and engagement. Although each student exited on improved reading levels (one, two, and three levels, respectively) and recorded varying strategy usage and different attitudes about their improved ability to read, there was a marked consistency observed about the level of engagement. The think-aloud intervention jump-started each student to become an active reader when encountering a word that he or she could not read, requiring full engagement. Self-assessment of strategy use was an enjoyable activity and encouraged metacognitive development as students gained awareness of their own cognitive processes. While the research highlighted a connection between think-aloud strategy use and reading-level gains, it was difficult to account for the marked difference in home literacy environments and its impact on reading levels.

I am passionately interested in understanding how to help students with reading difficulties. Despite differences in educational needs and economic backgrounds, I believe that every child has the right and the ability to become literate. Becoming literate enables children to take advantage of educational opportunities, and this ultimately provides upward mobility. Growing up, I was a voracious reader and experienced the positive benefits this had on my success in school performance.

This semester, I observed three students in Grade 2 who completed the 20 weeks of a Reading Recovery (RR) program in Grade 1 at Cathedral Grammar School (CGS), an inner-city Catholic school in Boston. RR is an early intervention literacy program designed to close the gap between the lowest performing first-grade students and their average peers. It is estimated that one out of every five schools in the United States has a first-grade RR program. RR teachers deliver one-on-one literacy lessons with the goals of closing the gap for these at-risk students, reducing the need for longer term literacy support, and increasing educational opportunities for many of these students (Schwartz, 2005). But I wonder, what happens after this support is gone? Do the RR skills learned have sustainability? Although several longitudinal studies have found that former RR students have been successful in sustaining literacy progress with their peers (Cox & Hopkins, 2006), I am concerned if these students will, in fact, "make it" and continue their reading progress in Grade 2.

On the surface, these students demonstrated similar warning behaviors in the classroom. They rarely participated in choral reading, rarely volunteered to read a short sentence to the class, stumbled over short math word problems, and overall were timid and passive in the full classroom setting. Were they worried? Do they like to read but are embarrassed about their fluency? Did they lose skills over the summer? Do they read at home? Even in their small guided reading group, I observed them waiting for help if they did not know a word and listening passively to the other students as they made comments and connections to the text. Overall, I worried that they were losing confidence. My research question was directed to get at the heart of how to differentiate instruction to have a positive impact on their reading skills so that they did not lose ground but in fact made gains in their reading levels. Briefly, my proposed intervention introduced a teacher-directed think-aloud process during guided reading to assist the students in developing and internalizing decoding strategies.

I strongly desire to be a teacher who is supportive and encouraging to students struggling with the reading process. Each child is unique and needs to be "raised up" and to perceive that he or she possesses talents and gifts that we respect. Sometimes, that is all students need to spur them on. This question afforded me both the opportunity to strive to become this kind of teacher and to have a positive impact on pupil learning.

❖ RATIONALE

My research question is compelling to me as a future teacher and researcher because the guided reading process is such an important component of the reading program at CGS. In addition, Opitz and Ford (2001) state that guided reading (defined as planned, focused, and teacher-led instruction in a small-group setting with the goal of helping children construct meaning) is implemented by numerous classroom teachers all across the United States.

CGS is part of a Literacy Collaborative (Lesley University) and subscribes to leveled readers being used during the guided reading process three to four times per week. I was curious about how teachers at this school effectively bridge the gap between one-on-one RR instruction (Grade 1) and the small group setting (Grade 2). Did the second-grade classroom teacher employ different strategies during the guided reading process for RR students to ensure their long-term success in becoming independent readers? Sometimes, guided reading can take on a formulaic (almost passive) stance, in contrast to what I think these RR students need: active engagement in the process. I was concerned that following a strict guided reading format would not be enough of a scaffold for these students on their journey from reading recovery to independent reader. Looking deeply into this question could shed light on many facets of working with at-risk readers. Important to the field of research would be understanding RR students' learning during guided reading in some of the following areas:

- What specific decoding and comprehension strategies positively impact reading for meaning?
- Does the order in which the strategies are introduced impact comprehension, and if so, how?
- What specific type of teacher-directed questions activate thinking, increase students' interactions, and improve comprehension?
- What types of teacher modeling (e.g., think-alouds) increase decoding abilities and consequently comprehension?
- How/when do RR students become metacognitive about their reading?

Because so many U.S. resources have been dedicated to the early intervention RR program, a deeper understanding of how to continue the literacy learning of these at-risk students would be both beneficial to the student (pupil learning) and valuable for all teachers.

❖ CONTEXT

The setting in which I am teaching is in some respects very different from what I experienced as a child. CGS is an inner-city school; its student body is a diverse, multicultural mix of African Americans, Hispanics, and Asians, with most students coming from a low socioeconomic background. Fewer than half of the students are Catholic, and there is one white child in the entire student body of 200. (Aside: I grew up in a middle-class home and attended a Catholic grammar school in Boston in the 1970s, where most children were white and Catholic.) Although the student population is different from my childhood experience, there are aspects of this environment that remind me of my school days. Both schools value spiritual growth as well as academic growth, with an underlying sense of the importance of caring for one another—a strong scaffold for supporting social justice. The following mission statement of CGS reflects its sensitivity to the social context of education and its focus on promoting each child's social progress.

> Cathedral Grammar School educates and nurtures the whole child. As a multicultural Catholic school, we instill values to promote each child's spiritual and social progress.

As a white teacher in a nonwhite school, I currently feel deficient in understanding the cultural backgrounds of all 28 students in Grade 2. These children are special and have rich cultural heritages that I respect and desire to learn more about. There are many bilingual students in my class, and their languages range from Spanish to Igbo (Nigerian dialect) to French Creole. Being sensitive to cultural differences and differentiating instruction for English language learners (ELLs) is always at the forefront of my thinking when planning curriculum. On many occasions, I have consulted my notes from ED 346: Teaching Bilingual Students for sheltered instruction techniques. Representative of this highly diverse classroom are the three students I worked closely with this semester: Chism, Jasmine, and Ralph.

Chism

Chism is a quiet, intense child from a very strict Nigerian family. Chism tries very hard in all of her academic work, yet never makes a peep in class. She writes in her weekend journal that she loves school because it is "cool, fun, and great," but you would never know she feels this way. She cries silently at her desk when she cannot figure out a math problem or how to answer a question. She told me she "likes to read" and engages me whenever I stop by her desk. One on one, she smiles and talks nonstop. However, in a reading survey, she indicated that she feels sad when she reads aloud at home, and she believes both her family and teachers are unhappy with her reading abilities.

Chism's first-grade Terra Nova (a national standardized achievement test) scores at the end of Grade 1 placed her in the bottom third percentile in the nation for reading, vocabulary, and language. Chism made the most progress in the RR cohort, exiting as a Level G reader, which is the midway point in Grade 1.

Jasmine

Jasmine is an ELL whose mother speaks Spanish only but whose father is bilingual. Both kindergarten and first-grade teachers felt her oral language was delayed, and she isolated herself in the classroom. This year, she is more of a participant in the classroom and has forged several friendships with girls in the classroom. Both parents are involved in Jasmine's progress, and I was able to participate in Jasmine's core evaluation at a nearby public school in September. Jasmine presented with no learning disabilities. Given this, Jasmine's father feels responsible for her lack of literacy skills—blaming himself for not reading to her at home. He works at night and goes to school during the day. Jasmine is currently listening to books on tape at home (tape recorder and books provided by CGS). Jasmine's personality can be sullen, and she often complains about how her parents have no money.

In her reading survey, Jasmine described herself as someone who likes to read, and she believes that both her teachers and parents are happy with her reading abilities. She exited the RR program as a Level E reader, less than the midway point in Grade 1. Her Terra Nova scores from Grade 1 indicate a Grade 2 equivalent in both reading and language skills.

Ralph

Ralph is an ELL whose family speaks Spanish at home. Ralph has a happy personality and engaging smile; he desperately wants to please his teachers. He is an easy-going child who interacts well with all students and teachers. He is currently making very slow academic progress in the classroom in all subject areas. Ralph receives little homework support at home. Both parents work, and little time is available for literacy work. Although parent communication has been requested, the family has not contacted the school. Many times, Ralph is left at school without a ride home because it was unclear who had responsibility to pick him up.

In his self-assessment as a reader in September, Ralph indicated that he is happy about how well he can read. His Terra Nova scores at the end of Grade 1 indicate a kindergarten level equivalent in vocabulary. Ralph did make progress in RR last year, exiting on Level E, the same level as Jasmine. The annual RR report (June '06) indicated that Ralph's progress should be closely monitored in Grade 2.

Coming from a background where my parents made significant financial sacrifices to send me to Catholic schools and supported me in all aspects of school life (including homework), I struggle to understand the complexities of these students' home environments. Because home literacy is strongly correlated with children's literacy development (Dickinson & Tabors, 2002), I sometimes do not understand the choices some parents may make that impact their children; I wish things were different. These are biases grounded in my own experiences and culture, and I strive to be nonjudgmental. I realize that many parents of CGS students make choices for their children based on their economic situation, own educational upbringing, and cultural beliefs. For example, Ralph's parents do not appear available for homework assistance, read-alouds, and, in some cases, basic physical needs (he often comes to school without a coat). Jasmine's parents are ELLs with developing oral language skills themselves. Her father is learning how to speak and read English but not her mother. Finally, Chism has been forbidden to participate in class field trips (even if the cost is paid by the school), where she might have access to stimulating out-of-school experiences with adult-assisted exploration providing important world knowledge helpful in processing texts. Given my knowledge of the students' home life and my own interpretations, I did not let this negatively influence my interactions with the students in the classroom but instead used it as an opportunity to scaffold learning through my intervention.

❖ THE RESEARCH QUESTION
   CONNECTS TO BOSTON COLLEGE THEMES

This research project promoted social justice as it met the needs of diverse learners. I worked with students from a low socioeconomic background and three distinct cultures, all of whom had been identified as "at-risk" in the area of reading. The think-aloud intervention differentiated instruction during the guided reading process with the goal of expanding the students' decoding strategies and ultimately raising their reading levels through increased comprehension. With an improvement in reading level, they will be able to more fully participate in *all* classroom literacy activities and begin the path of becoming lifelong readers. Their improved ability to read will have positive benefits on their academic performance and ultimately in society where the ability to understand what they read has never been so pronounced as with the increased communication abilities of the Internet.

No progress would have been made in this action research project without the collaboration of my cooperating teacher, Primary Literacy

Coordinator, and RR teacher at CGS, Professor Gerald Pine, and the other student-teachers in my triad.

For example, the Primary Literacy Coordinator spent precious upfront planning time with me translating my proposed intervention from research to practical application. We created an observation checklist, a "think-aloud" script with tangible strategic tools for the students, a self-assessment activity for the students, and a method for collecting student data during the intervention. The RR teacher gave me a tutorial on the RR process and allowed me to observe her with this year's RR students so that I would more fully understand my students' background knowledge in this area. Dr. Pine was instrumental in refining my question until it reflected what I desired to research, and my classmates offered ideas and support in each phase. I am fortunate to be working with professionals who are both dedicated to children and willing to reflect on new practices.

By critically reflecting on how to adapt the guided reading process for my at-risk second-graders, I was able to bridge the gap between the research I gathered on RR, guided reading, and think-alouds with the reality of my second-grade classroom. This microcosm, albeit small, became an important site for teacher research. Because I was able to gain experience implementing the think-aloud process and observed how it could be beneficial, I plan on adding this strategy to my arsenal of tools when planning an effective reading curriculum.

Through the interaction of my three students, collaborating professionals, insights from my literature review, and the background knowledge gained from my coursework at Boston College (especially as it pertained to ELLs), I was able to construct new knowledge to have a positive impact on the decoding abilities of former RR students. Because I wish to continue working in an inner-city classroom helping at-risk readers in innovative ways, this project can serve as a building block for my future action research.

❖ LITERATURE REVIEW

The instructional technique of think-alouds is a research-based teaching strategy requiring the teacher to talk aloud to students as they interact with the task at hand, helping students "see" the process or strategy (Fuhler, Farris, & Nelson, 2006). When used in the reading process, the "talk" consists of statements describing what the teacher is thinking as she is reading, verbalizing her own cognitive processes (e.g., use of decoding and comprehension strategies) to make meaning from a text (Block & Israel, 2004). What makes think-alouds different from a teacher purely giving directions is that think-alouds "demonstrate how to select an appropriate comprehension process at a specific point in a particular text. They explain how expert readers elicit comprehension processes selectively and collectively" (Block, Rodgers, & Johnson, 2004, p. 22).

Without giving the think-aloud strategy a name, students have communicated a need for this kind of assistance. Block et al. (2004) references a study of 139 second- and third-graders who were asked what teachers could do to help them with the reading comprehension process. The student responses overwhelmingly cited the need for improved explanations and specifically a desire for the teacher to explain everything they did in their minds to comprehend better. Wilhelm (2001) delights in sharing one of his struggling reader's reactions after being exposed to this technique. "Why didn't you tell me this before? If I had known what to do, I would have done it! Is it supposed to be a big secret or something?" (p. 28).

The think-aloud technique is also two-sided. After the teacher explains his or her thinking, students are asked to verbalize their own thoughts and strategies as they read. Oster (2001) states that this metacognitive awareness is crucial to learning because readers must be able to self-assess their own comprehension and adjust strategies accordingly to become expert readers. This exchange also informs the teacher of the reader's strengths and weaknesses. Consequently, this real-time assessment informs subsequent instruction and potentially different think-alouds.

Walker (2005) focuses on why think-alouds are especially important to struggling readers (the focus of my research question). She makes the case that many struggling readers are passive; they sit back and rarely respond when questioned about what they are reading. Perhaps they do not know how to *think* about arriving at an answer. Struggling readers need more than just a model; they need a verbal demonstration of a concrete structure that they can consistently follow when challenged by a text. Many give up when they try one strategy and it does not work. The active thinking process of an expert reader needs to be visible to the struggling reader. Think-alouds "talk" about using alternative strategies with the goal being that this "self-talk" is eventually internalized by the student. Walker (2005) adds a crucial step to the think-aloud process that turns the passive reader into an active participant. This last step is for the students to self-evaluate themselves regarding strategy use with the help of the teacher. Walker found that self-evaluation improved strategy use, increased engagement, and promoted positive self-efficacy.

Think-aloud techniques can be used throughout different points of the reading comprehension spectrum (e.g., before, during, and after reading). Block and Israel (2004) developed 12 different types of think-alouds with instructional lessons. (Note: the think-aloud intervention used in this project focused on decoding, a universal need identified for the three second-grade students.) They described several decoding strategies under the title: "Determine Word Meanings Think-Alouds" (p. 161). Although each decoding strategy (e.g., context clues, sight words) is to be delivered separately when reading aloud a text, it is imperative to demonstrate how several of these decoding strategies might be needed to unlock the meaning of a new word.

Table A.1   The Essential Elements of Guided Reading: Teacher's Role

Per Fountas and Pinnell (1996, p. 7)	With the Think-Aloud Intervention
Teacher "listens in" during reading.	Teacher "listens in" during reading.
Observes reader's behavior for evidence of strategy use.	*Thinks aloud to demonstrate strategy use and selection.*
Confirms students' attempts and successes.	Confirms students' attempts and successes.
Interacts with students to assist with problem solving at difficulty.	Interacts with children to assist with problem solving *before and* at difficulty.
Makes notes about children's strategy use.	Makes notes about children's strategy use. *Students also self-assess by stamping personal strategy cards.*

NOTE: Italics = Change to guided reading process.

Finally, the impact on pupil learning as a result of delivering effective think-alouds has been positive. Oster (2001) references several studies that show higher comprehension scores for students who verbalize their thoughts while reading. Block et al. (2004) describes a recent study of 1,200 students from kindergarten through fifth grade in the southwestern United States who participated in multiple think-alouds and accompanying instructional activities. These students experienced increased scores on standardized tests in the areas of reading vocabulary, fluency, and comprehension.

❖ INTERVENTION

My intervention was to introduce a "think-aloud" process before, during, and after the guided reading process. CGS adheres to the guided reading process described by Fountas and Pinnell (1996) below. The italicized text in Table A.1 highlights the modifications I made to the teacher's role during the guided reading process.

I collaborated with the Primary Literacy Coordinator in developing a think-aloud intervention for this particular group of learners. She suggested that the language I use to "think aloud" should be consistent with the language that the students were exposed to during Reading Recovery. The Primary Literacy Coordinator offered that they were exposed to decoding strategies last year, but the think-aloud technique would be an excellent extension into making these strategies their own by requiring active participation and self-assessment.

Although I liked the self-evaluation sheets described by Walker (2005), I believed that my second-graders, particularly the two ELLs, would not be able to read and write them. As a substitute, I created five strategy cards after reviewing sample strategy card templates described by Hoyt (2000), which help students develop an awareness of the wide spectrum of strategies available to them to decode unknown words. During the guided reading session, these cards were available as visible reminders of ways for the students to decode a word. At the end of the session, I had each student stamp the strategy card(s) (a color-coded personal set was made for them) that they used during reading. Echevarria, Vogt, and Short (2004) emphasize the need to provide visual supplementary materials for ELLs who have difficulty processing a lot of auditory information. My ELLs benefited from these visual and kinesthetic supports. Finally, we discussed their strategy use together.

Based on the above, the detailed components of my think-aloud (task = decoding) was introduced as follows.

1. *Preview.* Before the oral read-aloud, I told the students that I will be explaining to them "what I do when I am reading and encounter a word I do not know."

2. *Thinking aloud.* I explained each strategy that I used to assist me in decoding a word while simultaneously pointing to a visible strategy card(s). I modeled statements about why one strategy worked and why another did not. I also pointed to my head and to the text explaining that I am always thinking when I am reading. This step was an iterative process and demonstrated how I am an active reader.

3. *Self-assessment.* At the end of the oral reading, I tallied which strategies helped me the most and marked them with a stamp on the card.

4. *Repeat.* I performed this same process with one of the students as another model to the group of three students.

5. *Internalize.* At the end of each session, we reviewed our strategy cards, stamped the ones used, and "thought aloud" about how we used them and why.

6. *Documentation.* At the end of the session, I completed my customized intervention checklist, especially noting strategy use.

Research Methodology

More than 10 data sources were collected to measure the students' progress in reading levels. These data sources ranged in a continuum from qualitative (e.g., anecdotal notes from classroom observations, student surveys) to quantitative (e.g., Terra Nova scores, number of decoding strategies used during self-assessment). Both types of data sources were collected and analyzed during all stages of the research process. Given this, my research methodology is technically defined by Johnson and Onwuegbuzie (2004) as a mixed-model methods research approach.

I believe that this combined approach provided greater reliability and validity to the results of my inquiry question than if a purely quantitative or qualitative approach had been chosen. For example, an analysis using only objective, quantitative data such as the national standardized Terra Nova reading and language scores, in conjunction with word error rates and book level, to measure pupil learning would have overlooked the richness provided by student attitudes toward reading and their home literacy environments. In a similar fashion, a strictly qualitative approach to measuring progress in reading level would have captured the students' increased engagement and confidence when interacting with new texts but would not have analyzed the quantitative frequency of strategy use during the think-aloud process supporting this behavior. In addition, because I was both the researcher and data collector of the qualitative research, my results could have been influenced by my personal biases. All sources were necessary for a holistic and expansive view of pupil progress.

Data Sources

The data sources I collected and analyzed to provide insights into my question were organized into the four categories described by Shea, Murray, and Harlin (2005): thinking evidence, work samples, in-the-classroom benchmarks, and standardized achievement tests.

Thinking Evidence

1. *Student surveys.* At the beginning and end of the semester, I surveyed the RR students to understand how they felt about reading in different venues and how they self-assessed their own reading ability. This survey provided two data points which highlighted changes in the students' attitudes toward reading.

2. *Transcripts of guided reading discussions (through field notes or tape recordings) and checklists prior to intervention.* I summarized the main points of the discussion that reflected the students' decoding abilities, comprehension, and level of engagement during the guided reading process *before* the intervention.

3. *Completion of a customized "intervention" checklist.* Areas I focused on included: frequency and type of decoding strategies used by the student, student's retelling abilities, and engagement. Ten intervention sessions were conducted yielding 29 checklists.

4. *Anecdotal notes on reading behaviors outside of the guided reading process.* I jotted down relevant student classroom behaviors that helped me determine if the skills and strategies the students were learning in the guided reading process were being transferred to other areas of the classroom.

5. *Independent reading selections.* Reviewing the students' independent book choices from their weekly school library visit gave me a window into their perceived reading level and interests.

6. *Parent interaction.* Due to limited access, data were collected on reading behaviors at home for only one of the students (Jasmine).

Work Samples

1. *Weekend journals.* Students are asked to write each Monday in their personal journals about what they did over the weekend. Cox and Hopkins (2006) note that "reading and writing are reciprocal and interrelated processes" (p. 260); thus, I reviewed eight journals per student looking for evidence in the following areas: Were decoding skills learned during the guided reading intervention process transferred to the writing process? At what stage is their writing?

In-the-Classroom Benchmarks

1. *Record of book reading progress.* This record is used by CGS to measure progress by book and grade level. I collected these for June 2006 (end of Grade 1), late September/early October 2006, and November 2006 (end of data collection period) for the three RR students.

2. *Running record summaries.* Information was gathered as available from the classroom teacher. This was used to assess students' fluency, expression, word error rates, and comprehension through retelling and other prompts.

3. *End-of-year RR assessment.* The RR teacher created an end-of-year summary report in Grade 1 for each student. The report referenced the results of Clay's Observational Assessment Summary given three times during the school year. I obtained this report to analyze the strengths and weakness of each RR student as he or she began second grade.

Norm-Referenced and Other Standardized Achievement Measures

I obtained the results of the Terra Nova test administered in May of 2006 for the RR students while they were in first grade.

Because a rich variety of data sources was collected, it was important for interpretation purposes to integrate the data in a thematic manner that documented pupil learning over the 3-month period. A summary student profile sheet was created that highlighted four diverse indicators of pupil progress.

1. *Reading level* (What is the student's reading level? Is it at the level of peers?). Data sources: End of year RR assessment, record of book reading progress, and Terra Nova standardized test results.

2. *Strategies used* (What strategies do the students use when reading?). Data sources: Think-aloud checklists, running record summaries, and anecdotal notes.

3. *Engagement* (Is the student engaged during guided reading? Did he or she make connections with the text and other students?). Data sources: Discussion checklists and anecdotal notes.

4. *Attitudes* (How does the student feel about reading? School in general?). Data sources: surveys, parent interaction, independent reading selections, writing journals, and anecdotal notes.

I believe that an analysis of these data sources will begin to answer the question of how adapting the guided reading process for former RR students impacts both pupil learning and pupil confidence.

❖   RESULTS

The results have been summarized by the indicators of pupil learning referenced above.

Reading Level

Chism experienced the most gain in reading level from her exit from RR until her most recent benchmark on November 15, 2006. She jumped five levels from G to L. In reviewing her running record generated prior to intervention, I noted she was benchmarked at "I" (two levels post-RR level). Her teacher indicated that she needed to attend to word structure including the

Figure A.1   Change in Reading Level

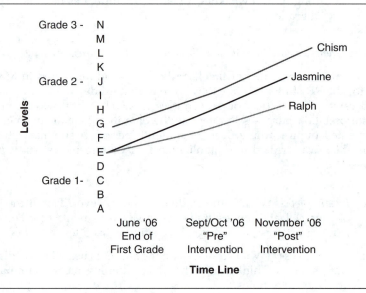

Table A.2   Chism's Reading Strategies

Strategy Number	Description	Self-Assessment = No. of Stamped Cards	Percentage
1	Look at the picture—picture cues	4	17
2	Think about the story—use your brain	2	8
3	Chunk the word—are there words I already know?	7	29
4	Use the beginning, middle, and ending sounds—what makes sense?	10	42
5	Read on to figure it out—reread	1	4
	Total	24	100

Table A.3   Jasmine's Reading Strategies

Strategy Number	Description	Self-Assessment = No. of Stamped Cards	Percentage
1	Look at the picture—picture cues	11	23
2	Think about the story—use your brain	8	17
3	Chunk the word—are there words I already know?	12	25
4	Use the beginning, middle, and ending sounds—what makes sense?	15	31
5	Read on to figure it out—reread	2	5
	Total	48	100

beginning, middle, and ending sounds of words. Postintervention work, Chism gained three more levels to L. This reading level puts her at the level of her peers and in fact, she is nearing the third-grade benchmark. This is outstanding, given her previous year's Terra Nova scores, which placed her in the bottom third percentile in reading.

Table A.4   Ralph's Reading Strategies

Strategy Number	Description	Self-Assessment = No. of Stamped Cards	Percentage
1	Look at the picture—picture cues	9	24
2	Think about the story—use your brain	2	5
3	Chunk the word—are there words I already know?	9	24
4	Use the beginning, middle, and ending sounds—what makes sense?	17	45
5	Read on to figure it out—reread	1	3
	Total	38	100

Jasmine exited first-grade reading on a Level E. Her most recent benchmark on November 20, 2006, placed her at Level I, one level below the start of the second-grade reading level (J). Immediately prior to the think-aloud intervention, Jasmine was reading at a G level, and her teacher noted that her fluency could be improved by a review of high-frequency words. Jasmine was able to gain two additional levels after the intervention work commenced.

Ralph made the least amount of progress from the original RR cohort. Like Jasmine, he exited first grade reading on Level E. In early October, his teacher performed a running record, and he was benchmarked at Level F. She indicated that he attended to the beginning sounds of words but did not follow through on middle and ending sounds. After the intervention work, Ralph gained one more level to Level G, the midway point of a typical first-grade reader. This level places him as an early reader (Fountas & Pinnell, 2000) and not at the level of his peers in second grade.

Strategies Used

Chism began the think-aloud process very tentatively. She is quiet and not a risk taker; it took multiple sessions before she was comfortable talking about her strategy use. Given her teacher's comments regarding word structure, I concentrated on thinking-aloud word structure strategies with her. Chism's self-assessment showed that more than 70% of the time (see Table A.2), she used "chunking" and "use the beginning, middle, and ending sounds" to decode a word. After our intentional conversations, she made excellent connections and progress and delighted in "chunking" words. I knew it was time for her to graduate from the guided reading group when she began thinking aloud for Ralph. When he stumbled over the word *couldn't*, she told him he already knew a word in that word (*could* is on their high-frequency word list), and he should try chunking it out. Chism had internalized the chunking strategy.

Jasmine used multiple strategies while reading for meaning. Her tendency was to start with picture support because she is very artistic and then quickly move to other strategies to corroborate the correct decoding of a word. Over time, she developed from a passive to an active reader. Her self-assessment cards had the most "stamps" and most variability compared to the other two students (see Table A.3).

Ralph's strategy use was the reverse. He often began with trying to sound out the word in question, and then when prompted, he would look for picture support. His top three strategies accounted for approximately 90% of his self-assessments (see Table A.4), and occasionally, he self-assessed fewer strategies than he actually used. Finally, these self-assessments did not always correspond with a correctly decoded word. Ralph stumbled over many sight or high-frequency words that are difficult to decode with these strategies.

Engagement

When I observed Chism in September during her guided reading group of six students, she was a passive group member. When she encountered a word she did not know, she stopped cold. Chism never engaged with the other students, and when asked a question, she answered politely. In contrast, as the think-aloud sessions progressed, she became increasingly engaged and often would read out of turn. Chism made comments throughout the sessions about the texts, sometimes interrupting others in her excitement.

Jasmine was also passive in the original guided reading group; also, she often lost her place and could not answer questions when asked. Given this, Jasmine surprised me by asking multiple questions during the intervention. She was the most curious about the strategy cards and asked for repeated clarification. She would state aloud that "I am always using my brain" when reading and appeared very pleased during the self-assessment process. When her teacher conducted a running record at the end of November (postintervention), she commented that Jasmine was self-correcting more frequently. She was finally engaged.

Ralph's level of engagement did not appear to change from pre- to post-intervention guided reading groups. He appeared consistently happy and eager to read. Although he often had difficulty decoding words, he never stopped trying.

Attitude

Chism demonstrated drastic changes in her attitudes toward reading and school. In September, she had indicated that both her family and teacher were indifferent and sad about her ability to read aloud. When resurveyed about her feelings toward reading in November, she stated that both her family and teacher are happy about her reading level. In fact, her survey had 100% happy faces, and she said "too many happy faces" with a big smile. Toward the end of the intervention, Chism also began raising her hand in class to answer questions during word study. She had never done this before. During choral reading, she now reads quietly with the class rather than staring at the pages.

In reviewing Chism's independent reading selections over a 3-month period, I noted that unlike her peers in this cohort, she consistently took out chapter books from the school library. Although she never actually finished one of these books, she did make progress in the number of pages read during independent reading time. She increased from four pages in September to multiple chapters read in mid-November. Chism's attitude is one of a proficient reader no longer requiring picture support to comprehend meaning.

Jasmine's attitudes about reading via the survey results had marginal changes. She steadfastly believed that both her family and teacher were happy when she read aloud. Jasmine's independent reading selections reflected her artistic tendencies. She selected books almost always based on their illustrations. Usually, they were too difficult for her to read, so consequently, she primarily used picture support to create meaning.

Ralph's reading surveys indicated a negative change in his feelings about his abilities from September to November. He drew a sad face to explain how he felt when he read aloud to his teacher in class and an indifferent face to show how he felt when he reads at home and how he believes his family feels when he reads aloud. As Chism's abilities grew rapidly in the group, she sometimes displayed negative body language (e.g., rolling her eyes) about Ralph's reading ability. To counteract this trend, the students (initiated by Jasmine) created a rule for the group, which stated that "no one could make fun of anybody when they were reading." Although this helped, I believe Ralph began to see himself as the poorest reader of the group when he compared himself to Jasmine and Chism.

Ralph's independent reading selections extended the reading we performed in the small group. For example, he chose a book we had read together, *A Kiss for Little Bear*, to reread and *Henry and Mudge in the Green Time* to continue reading the series we began during guided reading. These selections highlighted his "trying to improve" attitude, and re-reading texts also served as an excellent self-sustaining strategy for him.

❖ ANALYSIS

All of the students improved their reading levels after the think-aloud intervention. Chism, Jasmine, and Ralph gained 3, 2, and 1 level(s), respectively.

The student's frequency of decoding strategies did not correlate to these reading gains. For example, Chism's self-assessed strategies were the smallest in number at 24. This could be explained by the fact that she did not need to decode as many words as the other two students because she entered the group in October on a slightly higher level. Although the percentage of strategy use differed by student, the most frequent strategy used by all students was No. 4—"use the beginning, middle, and ending sounds—what makes sense?" This was a strategy they were all introduced to during RR; in second grade, they were continuing to practice it. The strategy least used was No. 5—"read on to figure it out—reread." Although I demonstrated strategy No. 5 with several think-alouds, the students did not like the idea of skipping and then coming back to a word. Although, in reality, they perform this strategy when they self-correct during oral reading, their explicit use of this strategy was not observed.

I found the most interesting relationship to be between changes in reading level and home language and literacy environments. The two ELLs, Ralph and Jasmine, did not gain as much in reading levels as the monolingual student, Chism. In addition to decoding, Jasmine and Ralph were also processing the differences between the English and Spanish sound systems during oral reading. Jasmine's parents were supporting her at home by listening to books on tape provided by CGS, and Chism was reading with an older sister, but Ralph had minimal home support. When I met his mother one time when he was "forgotten" after school, Ralph provided all the translations to his mother in Spanish and to me in English. His first-grade teacher said that no one reads to him at home, nor does he read by himself at home. Whereas the other two students were supplementing our work together with their reading at home, Ralph was not provided this opportunity for a number of reasons (e.g., parents' work schedules).

In Grade 2, having a large core of known words that are recognized automatically is imperative to move from an early reader to a transitional reader (Fountas & Pinnell, 2000). My cooperating teacher had generated lists of these high-frequency words to study at home and to be aware of when reading in school and at home. When Ralph was tested on these words, he could not read half of them. Given that these words often cannot be effectively decoded using a think-aloud strategy, it is perhaps not surprising that the intervention had limited measurable success for him.

Given the interrelated nature of the reading and writing processes, an analysis of the students' weekend journals was performed. Although the analysis highlighted that all three were phonetic spellers, the differences in writing supported each student's current reading abilities. Chism was more sophisticated in her use of punctuation and attempts at mastering the correct tense of verbs. Jasmine experimented with the spelling of words phonetically in the same way she was open to trying out different decoding strategies. Ralph's writing revealed his deficiency in the usage of high-frequency words and showed him repeating the same words over and over again to fill the page.

The data from my notes on students' think-aloud checklists supported a high engagement level for all students during the intervention. This may be attributable to the group size. In October, the three students were pulled out of the six-member guided reading group. They enjoyed the extra attention I gave them in the smaller group plus the personalized strategy cards, two factors that approximated their RR experience.

Although the think-alouds were primarily focused on decoding, we did not limit our guided discussions to this one task. I also "thought aloud" about the meaning of each story, and the children made predictions and inferences throughout reading as well. Their favorite text was *A Kiss for Little Bear* because that kiss ended up causing two skunks to get married. They thought this was hilarious and speculated that perhaps Little Bear knew this might happen all along, and that is why he sent a kiss "physically"—with the help of other animals—to his grandmother. An interesting inference indeed and an excellent example of their engagement.

Finally, changes in students' attitudes about reading were widely variable. While Chism became increasingly confident after each session, Ralph seemed to become aware of his limitations. Chism and Jasmine's confidence spilled over into the classroom, as observed in shared read-alouds and their increased participation in whole-class activities. Although Ralph remained happy in class, he made no progress in class participation as it related to reading activities.

❖ LIMITATIONS OF THE RESEARCH STUDY

Many variables could have impacted the validity and reliability of this research study. First and foremost, the number of students (small number of RR graduates) and the duration of the intervention (short period of time and number of sessions) could have placed limits on the results. Because the think-aloud intervention required multiple sessions before the students were comfortable with the process, a longer intervention period might have produced different results.

Second, while the research highlighted a possible connection between think-aloud strategy use and reading level gains, it is difficult to account for the marked differences in the students' home literacy environments and their impact on reading levels. Two of the three students appear to have sustained levels of independent reading at home, which could have accounted for their reading gains.

Third, another variable that was important was the impact that being an ELL had on overall literacy achievement and this study. Two of the three students in the study were Spanish ELLs. Would the results have been different if all or none were ELLs?

Fourth, this was the first time I had undertaken a think-aloud intervention; my ability to deliver effective instruction could have skewed results. As I gained experience and reflected over the 2 months dedicated to this study, my think-alouds became more concrete and opportunistic.

Finally, the research design was a major factor in this study. My initial selection of which decoding strategies to "think aloud" potentially impacted the usefulness of think-alouds to improve reading comprehension. Although I had more than 10 think-alouds from which to choose, I implemented only five.

❖ IMPLICATIONS FOR
TEACHING AND PUPIL LEARNING

Educators could benefit from the following findings of the impact a think-aloud strategy had on the reading levels of second-grade readers identified as "at risk." Although each student had varying success with different decoding strategies and exited on different reading levels (all improved), the intervention accomplished three things.

First, each student became active when encountering a word he or she did not know. Unlike their initial guided reading sessions, in these later sessions, none of the students was waiting for me before they started thinking. They may have needed encouragement to persevere in their thinking, but they did not require a jump-start.

The second thing it accomplished was the encouragement of the students' metacognitive development. Chism, Jasmine, and Ralph ended the guided reading sessions discussing their strategies (when and why they used them) and actually enjoyed self-assessing their abilities. They made connections to decoding words and active reading. An added benefit is that this awareness of their own cognitive processes is transferable to other academic areas such as writing.

Third, the engagement levels of the three students were positively impacted by modifying the guided reading curriculum. These students benefited from a smaller group size and more explicit teaching as they transitioned from one-on-one intervention work in first grade to small-group guided reading in second grade. (Note: I plan to share my results with the Primary Literacy team at CGS with the goal of brainstorming new grouping options in the second-grade guided-reading process for former RR students.)

One logical next step is to ask another question: Will the strategies introduced become internalized by the readers? A longitudinal study could be designed to follow these students at different points in the year and discuss what strategies (new or old) help them read for meaning. What think-aloud strategies would they want to tell next year's second-graders?

An additional question that interests me is "Do second-grade ELLs who are also RR graduates need specific support as they transition to guided reading?" Concentrating on Ralph's progress, it appeared that he needed more than a think-aloud strategy to bridge the guided reading process. Ideas have already started to formulate such as developing oral language through small-group shared readings, high-frequency word activities, and following up with Readers Theater to help build fluency.

I hope to discover through future research how adapting the guided reading process for struggling readers can have positive results on both pupil learning and pupil confidence.

❖ REFLECTION

My own learning as a teacher and a researcher grew exponentially throughout this process. I soon realized that I not only needed collaboration in the upfront planning but could also benefit from coaching in the execution of the intervention. After listening to a tape recording of the first intervention session, I realized that although the students were engaged, they could not handle an introduction to the five think-aloud strategies, actively use them, and then perform a self-assessment. In my zeal to help these students, I delivered too many concepts in one session and could hear the confusion. With the help of the Primary Literacy Coordinator, I was able to decouple tasks and reintroduce them slowly without lowering expectations. It is essential when conducting research not to force the time frames estimated in your project plan. One must plan for contingencies and the human factor.

The think-aloud intervention required a lot of teacher talk. Although I needed to be cognizant of my intervention and "think aloud" so that the students could "hear" and "see" how an expert reader reads, I did not want simply to talk at them. It was critical to strike a balance so that I could hear the students talk about their own thinking, too. Many conversations were started when I asked, "Tell me what you are thinking—I am really interested."

Most important, what I learned concretely as a teacher and researcher is that there is not one proven path to literacy development for children. What works for Chism may not work for Ralph. The selection of appropriate reading instruction needs to consider both the pedagogical knowledge of the complex dimensions of literacy and the knowledge of the diversity (e.g., cultural, learning style, etc.) of the children with whom you are working. This takes time, effort, and a continual reflection about one's practice.

In summary, I loved working with this group of students and sensing their excitement and pride when they were able to read and understand a new story. The think-aloud intervention provided me with experience implementing a research-based strategy to assist "at-risk" readers make meaning from text. My immediate plan is to research other think-aloud applications supporting the comprehension process. This action research project was an excellent way for me to begin my lifelong dream of helping struggling readers.

❖ REFERENCES

Block, C. C., & Israel, S. E. (2004). The ABCs of performing highly effective think-alouds. *The Reading Teacher, 58*(2), 154–167.

Block, C. C., Rodgers, L. L., & Johnson, R. B. (2004). *Comprehension process instruction: Creating reading success in grades K–3.* New York: Guilford Press.

Cox, B. E., & Hopkins, C. J. (2006). Building on theoretical principles gleaned from reading recovery to inform classroom practice. *Reading Research Quarterly, 41*(2), 254–265.

Dickinson, D. K., & Tabors, P. O. (2002, March). Fostering language and literacy in classrooms and homes. *Young Children,* pp. 10–18.

Echevarria, J., Vogt, M., & Short, D. J. (2004). *Making content comprehensible for English learners: The SIOP model.* Boston: Pearson Education.

Fountas, I. C., & Pinnell, G. S. (1996). *Guided reading: Good first teaching for all children.* Portsmouth, NH: Heinemann.

Fountas, I. C., & Pinnell, G. S. (2000). *Guided readers and writers, Grades 3–6: Teaching comprehension, genre, and content literacy.* Portsmouth, NH: Heinemann.

Fuhler, C. J., Farris, P. J., & Nelson, P. A. (2006). Building literacy skills across the curriculum: Forging connections with the past through artifacts. *The Reading Teacher, 59*(7), 646–660.

Hoyt, L. (2000). *Snapshots: Literacy minilessons up close.* Portsmouth, NH: Heinemann.

Johnson, R. B., & Onwuegbuzie, A. J. (2004). Mixed methods research: A research paradigm whose time has come. *Educational Researcher, 33*(7), 14–26.

Opitz, M. F., & Ford, M. P. (2001). *Reaching readers: Flexible and innovative strategies for guided reading.* Portsmouth, NH: Heinemann.

Oster, L. (2001). Using the think-aloud for reading instruction. *The Reading Teacher, 55*(1), 64–69.

Schwartz, R. M. (2005). Literacy learning of at-risk first-grade students in the reading recovery early intervention. *Journal of Educational Psychology, 97*(2), 257–267.

Shea, M., Murray, R., & Harlin, R. (2005). *Drowning in data? How to collect, organize, and document student performance.* Portsmouth, NH: Heinemann.

Walker, B. J. (2005). Thinking aloud: Struggling readers often require more than a model. *The Reading Teacher, 58*(7), 688–691.

Wilhelm, J. D. (2001, November). Think-alouds boost reading comprehension. *Scholastic Instructor,* pp. 26–28.

Example 2: Why Do I Have to Know This Stuff?

How Can I Make the Study of World
History Relevant to Ninth-Grade Students?

Maryann Byrne
History Teacher
Canton Public Schools
Canton, Massachusetts

Abstract

Responding to a persistent student question ("Why do I have to know this stuff?"), I examined strategies designed to make history more relevant to my ninth-grade World History students. To promote authentic methods of inquiry, I invited the students to collaborate with me as coresearchers on this project. Relying heavily on student input, the methods employed focused on constructing a working definition of what the relevance of studying history is for each individual in the class.

Together, we have explored ways to test and evaluate what beliefs and assumptions we bring to the history classroom. The result has been a dynamic and ongoing redefinition of how history is personally relevant to each of us, along with the understanding that this personal definition of the relevance of historical study can change over time.

"Why do I have to know this stuff?" Without realizing it, my research question was coming at me early and often as I began my teaching career in a ninth-grade World History classroom at Canton High School in September 2003. Readings from my Inquiry Seminar at Boston College implied that my research question would be a nagging idea or dilemma that pulled at me as I taught. This made sense to me, and I was expecting to hear a little voice gently leading me to my research question; instead, the voices that came at me loud and clear on an almost daily basis were those of my own students.

I responded to my students' question in a number of ways. Drawing on traditional history teacher responses, I told them that history can teach us how to be better citizens, how to appreciate diversity, how to develop critical thinking skills, how to construct an argument, and how to learn from the past. Drawing on my education courses and from the advice of other teachers, I worked on making my classes "engaging," "interesting," and "fun." These attributes made my classes more enjoyable, but still the question kept coming back.

"Why do *I* have to know this stuff?" Within a couple of weeks, I realized that it was easy for me to make history lessons entertaining, but if the information held no relevance for students' lives, they would not retain the crucial concepts I was trying to teach. I was telling the students why I— Maryann Byrne, new teacher—thought that they should know this stuff. I wasn't listening to the *I* of the question, the *I* that represented each student in class and how each individual student was asking for an explanation of why this stuff was important for him or her personally to know. Not important in the "need to know" sense of necessary for next week's test or future MCAS exams, but in the "need to know" sense of critical information or skills essential to their lives. In the end, my research question developed naturally out of my eventual connection with the individual *I* of each of my students.

My research question therefore is: How can I make the study of World History relevant to my ninth-grade students? I believe my research question has a number of implications for classroom practice. I have come to appreciate that to make history relevant for my students, I need first to determine what makes it relevant for me. To do this, I need to examine my own frame of reference, while keeping in mind that relevance for me may not constitute relevance for my students. Another implication of the research question is that, for history to have relevance for students, they would have to construct this understanding for themselves, using me and their classmates as guides and sounding boards. To accomplish this, students would need to have a voice in the choice of topics covered in class and in how the class was conducted in terms of procedures, activities, and level of discourse. My classroom climate would need to facilitate these types of interactions. Finally, I believe my research question opens up a timely debate in this era of standards-based education, accountability, and budget constraints. Why should we make students learn this stuff if we can't help them recognize for themselves that the habits of mind developed through the study of history are legitimate, practical, and crucial skills necessary to enhance and advance their lives?

❖ LITERATURE REVIEW

I may have conducted my literature review out of sequence, but the timing worked to my advantage in helping me to target the specific type of articles I needed. If I had undertaken my full practicum as a student teacher, I would have had more time to read up on current educational literature in my content area. Instead, I was hired as a contract teacher at Canton High School a few days before the start of classes, and all of my available reading time was devoted to sources that would help me create lesson plans for World History. As a result, I developed my inquiry question before I had a chance to carry out a literature review.

Even within the welcoming atmosphere at Canton High School, I was feeling overwhelmed. It was only after a few weeks that I was able to concentrate on articulating my inquiry question and begin to look for appropriate research literature. As I read, I felt that I had met a new group of collaborators who were as passionate about history as I was and who had experienced what I was experiencing in my classes. It quickly became apparent that I was not the only educator dealing with the question of how to make history relevant to students. I felt a sense of relief; if so many others in my field had dealt with the same dilemma, I must have hit on a legitimate research question. Even better, I found practical advice on how to make history relevant for my students interspersed with theories of history and practice.

Because my inquiry question developed prior to my literature review, I had already attempted strategies to promote relevancy for my students, including the use of controversy, narrative, role-plays, and simulations in an effort to engage student interest in and empathy with our flesh-and-blood predecessors. As a new teacher, it was encouraging to discover that techniques that I was already using in my classes were recommended by many of the authors I read (Akmal & Ayre-Svingen, 2002; Kennedy, 1998; Meyerson & Secules, 2001; Newmann & Wehlage, 1993; Rosenzwieg, 2003; Stanley, 2003).

In addition to discussing theories that informed my teaching, such as constructivism and the study of history as preparation for democratic citizenship (Akmal & Ayre-Svingen, 2002; Carrier, 2002; Foster & Padgett, 1999; Kornfeld & Goodman, 1998; Vanderstel, 2002), it was extremely useful to come across concrete, practical suggestions on how to incorporate these theories in my lessons, including advice on proper student preparation and step-by-step instructions on activities and assignments. Veteran teachers Bill Bigelow and Michele Forman (Rosenzweig, 2003) and Lee W. Formwalt (Formwalt, 2002) discussed how to make history relevant for students and how strategies such as narratives and simulations can play out successfully in classroom settings where students are properly prepared by informed teachers. The teachers also confirmed what I had discovered in class: that these techniques help bring history to life for students by allowing them to empathize and thus link their life experiences to the dynamic and continuing stories of fellow human beings, past and present. Bigelow and Forman also led me to understand that to make strategies authentic and successful in my classroom, I had to spend more time preparing students for these types of lessons.

One article directly confronted me with assumptions that I bring to the classroom, causing me to realize that to make history relevant to my students, I first must determine what makes history relevant for me. Meyerson and Secules (2001) state that "the first prerequisite to the creation of a meaningful and relevant social studies learning environment for students is to ensure that social studies learning is meaningful and relevant to its teachers" (p. 267). The authors go on to suggest that what constitutes relevancy for the teacher may not constitute relevancy for students and that the teacher's main task should be to establish a classroom environment that allows students to construct the meaning of history for themselves.

Although the authors sometimes had different perspectives, two main themes came through clearly in almost every article I read. First, there was overwhelming consensus on the value of constructivism—that for history to be real for students, they must construct this reality for themselves. Second, and closely related to the first, was the emphasis that to construct personal relevance, students must be active participants in authentic historical inquiry. In other words, they must "do" history, not just "receive" history from the teacher as passive receptacles. As Foster and Padgett (1999) state, for students:

> Involvement in historical study leads them to become "creators" of history and to discover the power, potential, and excitement that the study of the past can engender. For teachers and students alike, meaningful engagement in historical inquiry means that the history classroom need never again be a refuge for boredom, passivity, and irrelevance but a place of excitement, fascination, and discovery. (p. 364)

❖ WHO AM I AS A RESEARCHER?

I think of myself as a historian, which helps explain my frame of reference. From the outset, it is important to state that in my understanding of history, personal frames of reference change as they are impacted by factors both internal and external.

As a historian, I decided it would be best to investigate how the phrase *frame of reference* is defined. According to the Merriam-Webster Online Thesaurus (2002), a frame of reference is "the particular angle from which something is considered: see OUTLOOK." *Outlook* is defined several ways, all of which speak to my frame of reference as a new teacher.

Definition Number 1: "Chance of success or advancement, see *hope*." For me, teaching is the embodiment of hope, the hope that what my students learn in my classroom will truly improve their lives, make them more committed and active citizens, and encourage them to become lifelong learners. In addition, with the myriad differences of opinion over the direction and purpose of education, it has filled me with hope for the future to have met educators who may have different perspectives but are all committed to the success of their students.

Definition Number 2: "A high structure or place commanding a wide view, see *awareness*." Although it is an assumption, I believe that my life experience has already proven to be an asset to my students. I have been involved in a number of activities that constitute practical, applied social studies. I was active in trading stocks and also need to balance my family's checkbook, providing me with an awareness of macroeconomics and microeconomics and how one impacts the other. I have lived abroad and maintain contacts with friends in foreign countries. I am, therefore, familiar with how outsiders view America and Americans for good and ill, giving me a unique, firsthand perspective that many students and teachers do not possess. I have also lived in a number of places in the United States, including Atlanta, Boston, Cape Canaveral, and New York City, and have worked with people from a variety of backgrounds. As such, I believe I am able to expose my students to the range of diversity inherent in American society and how it has both helped and hindered us as a nation. I am a member of the Canton Historical Commission and am cognizant of local historical lore and developments that have enabled students to make connections between the subjects we are studying from the past and issues directly impacting their world today. In my first job out of college, I worked in the advertising section of a leading trade publication, from which I gained an appreciation of those phrases history teachers taught us: "The pen is mightier than the sword" and "A picture is worth a thousand words." Drawing on this experience, I teach my students to clearly and succinctly state their thesis or opinion, while simultaneously appreciating the power of images to influence what is seen as historical truth. I am a practicing Roman Catholic and feel that my religious beliefs help me aid students in understanding that all students are gifted, although not always with the same gifts. Finally, I am a mother, and believe this helps me to connect on a personal level with my students. It may sound trite, but the awareness that each student is someone's child is in the forefront of my mind as I teach. Drawing on this, I try to treat each student the way I would want my child to be treated and to follow the dictum to first do no harm.

Definition Number 3: "The act of predicting, see *foresight*." I believe that frames of reference are constantly shifting. My life experience is a good example of this. The way I view the world today is different from the way I saw it as a child, a teenager, a college student, a young professional, an American abroad, a newlywed, a mother, a graduate student, and now a teacher. Even the core beliefs that have remained present throughout these stages have been modified with each new experience. I believe that the stages of my life can serve as an exemplar for my students. My life experience is a good illustration of the difficulty of predicting where your future may lead, validating the importance of developing your individual gifts to be prepared for opportunities and roadblocks as they arise.

❖ SCHOOL CULTURE

Canton High School is a construction zone, both literally and figuratively. We are in the midst of an exciting, inspiring, and sometimes anxious time at Canton High School. Symbolized by the $38 million school renovation scheduled to be completed in 2005, innovative changes are being implemented in all areas, shored up by cultural footings that have proven successful in the past.

While this acceptance of change bodes well for positive learning experiences, collaboration, and collegial relationships, most members of the school community are also aware that cultural changes at the school cannot be accomplished as quickly as new classrooms are installed. Each member of the community is being forced through internal and external pressures to reflect critically on which facets of the Canton High School culture are worth overhauling and restoring and which may be remnants of cultural norms that should be scrapped.

The foundation of the school is embodied in its mission statement, which stresses the importance of helping each individual strive for excellence. This quest for quality in the midst of change is most visible in the person of the principal and in curriculum initiatives, the value placed on mentoring new teachers, time set aside to allow for collaboration among teachers in and across disciplines, and in open, far-ranging and collegial discussions about the direction of the school. The new principal, Edward Mulvey, exemplifies the notion of reaching for new heights by standing on the firm foundations of the past. Mr. Mulvey taught biology at the school for 30-plus years, was head of the teachers association, and has proven an approachable and supportive presence for teachers old and new. As the school community grapples with change, it is comforting to know that we are headed by a person who feels our pain and has the big picture of the school in sight—namely, how these innovations will result in improved instructional opportunities for students.

It is in the area of teaching and learning that I believe the scaffolding needs additional support. Some departments rely on curriculum guidelines that are a decade old. In a series of professional days this fall, teachers and administrators struggled to come up with curriculum that addresses standards-based instruction while allowing room for individual teaching and learning styles. It is very much a work in progress. Many of the older teachers are resistant to change, seeing standards-based education as just one of a number of educational fads that have come and gone over the years. The new teachers are recent graduates of education schools that dealt directly with this new reality, resulting in interesting and constructive dialogues between veteran and rookie teachers. Within this amorphous framework, exciting teaching is happening, supported by involved administrators and staff. Teachers comfortably drop in to observe their colleagues' classes, and a mentor program is in place to help new teachers navigate both the overt and less obvious cultural norms of the school.

The area of school culture that cries out for the services of an "interior designer" is demographics, which would be greatly improved with the inclusion of more color. A visitor to Canton High School is struck by the whiteness of both the students and the staff. I have not seen one minority staff member, from administrators to teachers to maintenance staff. This has been the case in Canton for years, and I'm not sure that the older members of the community truly appreciate what a disservice this is for students. We live in an increasingly complex world, both at home and abroad, and if one of the purposes of education is to prepare students to be successful in this world, we are letting them down by not providing exposure to teachers, administrators, and other authority figures who look different from them. The population of minority students is small, and the lack of diversity among staff, obvious to me as a middle-class white woman, must seem glaring and somewhat alienating to them.

Most students (in a school population of about 850) are white and middle to upper class. If asked to state a religious affiliation, the majority would say that they are either Christian (predominantly Roman Catholic) or Jewish. I have not met students from other faith backgrounds. In addition, although the school has hired ELL teachers, I do not have any students in my classes for whom English is not their first language. What heavy inclusion I do have is in the area of special needs, with nine students on Individualized Education Programs in my college-level class of 24 students. So far, this has worked out well, and these students—many of whom are experiencing full inclusion for the first time—have made the transition with few setbacks and are fitting in comfortably with their classmates.

For more than 100 years, Canton High School has been the center of the larger town community, playing an active role not only in the education of its citizens, but in other town proceedings including politics, memorials, and cultural events. One of the school's distinctions—currently causing some debate—is that it is the only high school campus in the country with a legally operating bar on its premises in the shape of the American Legion Hall. Older citizens defend this by pointing out that many of the town's veterans were classmates at the high school and have contributed time and money toward the school. Younger adult members of the community answer this by saying that, in this time of zero tolerance for substance abuse, having a bar on campus sends students the wrong message. This ongoing debate is one of the more obvious examples of values from the past clashing with values from the present.

Canton High School has in place the building blocks necessary to ensure a quality education for its students, and the school climate promotes collaborative innovations that benefit all members of the community. There is a feeling that we are all embarking on a new experiment and need to work together and get to know each other's areas of expertise to ensure that this experiment will have successful outcomes for our children, our school, our greater community, and ourselves. By appreciating the contributions from the past, and recognizing that some of the older building materials may not meet the standards laid out by more modern educational architects, we are on the way to constructing a house of learning in which we can all take pride.

❖ MY STUDENTS

I teach ninth-grade history to honors and college-level students. When I met them, some aspects of my students were immediately apparent. My students are mostly white; I have one African American and three Asian American students in my classes. My honors classes are more than three quarters female, whereas my college classes are more evenly balanced along gender lines.

Over the course of the semester, I have come to know my students on a deeper level. Many live in single-parent homes, mainly as the result of divorce. Most are very open about discussing issues of sexuality, substance abuse, and other topics that would not have been open for discussion when I was a freshman. Although in some ways I feel these students have lost some of the innocence or naïveté my generation had, one benefit is that young people are more accepting of differences than my classmates were, including such areas as ethnicity, sexual orientation, religious affiliation, and the inclusion of special education students in general education classes.

Over time, I have noticed a number of dichotomies between my honors and college-level students. With minimal support, my honors students can handle just about any assignment I give them. The college students need more scaffolding and support. I have had no classroom management issues with my honors students, but I am in a constant battle to keep my college students focused and on task. Compared to my college students, my honors students come from wealthier homes and have parents who take a more active interest in their child's education.

I have noticed that many of my college-level students have an inferiority complex, comparing themselves negatively with honors-level students. One thing I have observed and commented on to these students is that the honors class often tells me what they think I want to hear, whereas the college class is more willing to take risks and tell me how they truly are thinking and feeling about topics covered in class. As a result, in many ways, I am learning much more from my college-level students than I am from my honors students.

If I had a say in placement, students of all abilities would be placed in the same classroom. I have not observed this in my practicum placement, and I don't know the practical details of how this would be worked out. However, just as I suspect that students lose out due to the lack of ethnic diversity, I believe that they are also losing out by not experiencing more mixed ability levels in their classes.

❖ METHODOLOGY

Realizing that I needed their help to succeed, I decided early on to collaborate with my students as coresearchers. Their enthusiasm for this project has carried me through what has been a sometimes exhausting but always exciting process.

The idea of collaborating with my students was a natural development. I had taken an adolescent developmental psychology course at Boston College but had no firsthand knowledge of young adults between the ages of 13 and 15. I relied on my students to clue me in to their mind-set: what interests and concerns they might have, as well as what they think about school and history in particular. I tapped into their knowledge of the public school culture in Canton to become acclimated to my new environment. For the most part, the students in my classes knew each other and were aware of Canton Public School norms that could not be found in the faculty handbook. At the same time, we were all new to Canton High School and were able to empathize with each other over the myriad changes to our lives. I was anxious and excited about being a new teacher; they were anxious and excited about being freshmen.

This partnership deepened as time went on, especially as a number of inconsistencies confronted me. The history curriculum guidelines ask me to teach students to become critical thinkers: to construct reasoned arguments based on evidence, enter into debate, compare and contrast diverse perspectives, appreciate cause-and-effect relationships, and, most important, develop into active, democratic citizens; yet, most of the teachers I know do not allow students to exercise these same skills in the areas of curriculum choice or classroom decision making. Both Boston College and Canton High School promote collaboration with other teachers, professors, and administrators but do not address collaboration with the No. 1 constituency on whom teachers' actions have the greatest impact, the students. Over the course of the year, I have been evaluated by my Boston College supervisor and by Canton's history department chair, its director of curriculum, and my mentor-teacher; however, the people who could provide the most honest evaluation of my teaching performance had no input in this process. Who better to judge me than my students, with whom I am engaged in day-to-day interactions, both positive and negative? While I appreciate the constructive criticisms I have received from my evaluations and have acted on them to improve my instruction, I also want to know how my students value my teaching. Finally, we tell students we expect them to behave as respectful, responsible young adults ready to fully participate and express their opinions in class; we should then respect the knowledge, ideas, suggestions, and innovations that they bring to our classroom.

❖ DATA SOURCES

For my research, I concentrated on data sources that most directly addressed my inquiry question. These included:

1. *Surveys of history teachers at Canton High School.* The purpose of these was to determine whether other history teachers were getting the same question as I was ("Why do I have to know this stuff?") and how they responded. I also wanted to know what personal relevance they attached to the study of history and what their expectations were for their students.

2. *Interest Inventories and Multiple Intelligences Surveys conducted with students.* In the beginning, I relied on information from these sources to design lessons that directly addressed student interests and learning styles.

3. *Initial brainstorming session with students to define relevance.* To know where we were starting and where we wanted to go, I asked students to brainstorm and come to an agreement on how we would define relevance in reference to the study of history.

4. *Surveys of students.* In this instance, we were trying to focus on which classroom activities and interactions made history more relevant to students and which ones hindered this process.

5. *Class discussions on whether the historical events that we were studying have a direct impact on our lives today.* At the beginning of the year, many students had stated that history was irrelevant because it consisted of old facts about dead people who had no connection to their lives. Class discussions were initiated to see if students could come to their own understanding that history is not dead but is a dynamic, evolving story in which they play a part.

6. *History progress reports.* These were used to determine whether our understanding of the relevance of history was developing throughout the semester and what activities or interactions promoted this development.

7. *Historical significance paper.* Students were asked to write a short report on a historical event we had studied and state two reasons why the event was significant in history and two reasons why it was significant for them. They were also asked to pretend they were the teacher and to suggest a teaching method that would make the event interesting to ninth-grade students. My purpose was to have students make connections to their own lives, while also reflecting on what teaching methods had made history most relevant to them.

8. *Observational notes.* These notes were reviewed to determine if the process of collaborating with students promoted an understanding of historical relevance.

9. *Quotes activity.* The intent of this activity was to show students, especially those who felt no connection to the material we were studying, that people throughout history have struggled with the question of whether the study of history is relevant. Student groups were given quotes on the subject and agreed or disagreed with them in a class discussion.

10. *Recommendation letters from the students.* In keeping with the spirit of collaboration, and to emphasize that their voices were as important to me as were those of the Boston College and Canton High School authorities who had evaluated me, I asked the students to rate my performance as a teacher. These anonymous evaluations were based on the same categories that my Boston College supervisor rated me on: Plans Curriculum and Instruction; Plans Effective Instruction; Manages Classroom Climate

and Operations; Promotes Equity; and Meets Professional Standards. I also asked them to comment on whether they thought I was a good teacher. My purpose in designing this assignment was to discover whether the methods we had put in place had resulted in actual student learning outcomes.

❖ RESULTS

My results confirmed my initial assumption: For students to feel that the study of history is relevant to their lives, they must build this knowledge themselves by actively doing history and not receiving it. A teacher can guide a student in the construction of this knowledge, but in the end, the students must feel that they have ownership of the process or it will not be real to them. While I am pleased with the results of our research, I feel that there is much more that needs to be examined to determine if the results we experienced can be replicated in other class settings.

What is relevance? In our brainstorming activity, the students and I came up with the following meaning of relevance as applied to the study of history. For it to be relevant, it must be real, it must be beneficial and important to our lives, and we must feel some connection with the topics we are studying and the skills we are acquiring.

Did our results show that our classroom interactions had made history real to us? This appears to be proven from the data. Students commented on activities that made history come alive for them, particularly role-plays and simulations, class discussions focused on connections to current events and our lives today, the construction of narratives based on the historical figures we studied in class, interactive hands-on activities, the analysis of primary sources, and participating in games such as "Who Wants to be a Legionnaire?" and "Feudal Jeopardy." Students were also strongly in agreement on which classroom activities made history irrelevant to their lived experiences. Receiving the greatest mention in this regard were activities that relied on the textbook and lectures that did not include student interactions in some way.

Did our results show that our classroom interactions led us to appreciate whether the study of history was beneficial or important to our lives? Again, the data would appear to support this. Some representative comments from students include:

- To know yourself, you have to know your history. Who we are is history.
- If you only go by what you read in one source and don't do further research, you might not get the whole story.
- If we don't know our history, people can come in and write a history that suits them, which may be false or twisted.

- Learning about the past has helped me understand the present.
- I now see that studying the past can help you predict the future. My views on history changed as a result of class discussions and the war in Iraq. It will be important to predict what the aftermath of that war might be.
- We learn why we are here.
- History teaches us to make better decisions than people did many years ago.

Did our results show that our classroom interactions helped us forge personal connections to the topics we were studying? The data support this conclusion. Among the student comments are the following:

- I learned things about myself that I did not know.
- Her teaching has depended on what we think about history.
- Before I had you as a teacher, I never knew or had a good understanding of how the people who lived in the past felt.
- I learned about my own religion and others as well. This has changed the way I look at Muslims and other people.

Finally, did our results show that our classroom interactions helped students learn? The overwhelming response was yes.

- She gets the job done by teaching us the content, but sometimes, it happens in a different way. It's not busywork, it's just plain learning and teaching, which personally makes learning fun. Of course, that would be worthless if we don't learn anything, which is not the case.
- The classwork is done in a way that we learn in new ways. It's more hands-on. Not just lectures and reading the book. We get to do little skits and other things. I don't mind learning in that class. It is exciting and fun.
- Sometimes, the class had discussions that I don't think were planned, but I have noticed that if a teacher stands in front of a class and just tells the class the facts, that the students will get bored or distracted. Getting students involved makes the students pay attention and understand the topic more.
- The way she teaches with activities for some reason it makes me learn and have a better understanding on the subject.
- She has unique teaching methods that help us learn in an active way. I have learned a lot.
- I personally retain the information longer. It makes the information very clear.

❖ ANALYSIS AND INTERPRETATION

Looking back to the first days of the school year, I can see how the collaborative environment my students and I established has transformed our classroom. As mentioned earlier in this paper, this collaboration developed naturally out of an appreciation that we needed each other to succeed professionally and academically. What began in an atmosphere of some trepidation has become an honest, open space where the curriculum is actively explored on a daily basis.

At the start of the year, what did I see? Students who were bored, students who were hesitant to participate, students who were classroom management issues, students who were unsure of what was expected of them, students who missed handing in assignments, students who under-performed on assessments and evaluations, and a teacher anxious to prove that she could teach them.

What do I see now? I see high-energy, involved students who enjoy coming to class prepared to do history, not just receive it. In an atmosphere of honesty and trust, the students challenge each other and me, probing statements and assumptions that might go unquestioned in a different classroom environment. This newfound sense of empowerment has proved inspiring and infectious, starting out slowly and building as students have become more interested in participating and have seen the benefits both to their grades and to their enjoyment of the class. As Kornfeld and Goodman (1998) state,

> Knowledge generated by students and teachers as part of the formal curriculum, not in opposition to it, should be a fundamental feature of liberatory social studies classrooms. Students . . . should come to realize the power of their own interpretations of information and their own experience in the production of school knowledge. (p. 314)

By becoming active participants in their learning, my students have learned more. In living the history curriculum, they have made the study of history a part of their lives that I hope will continue beyond my classroom. Every day, we strive to learn history by doing history, putting into place authentic interactions that rely on the interpretation of evidence, appreciation of multiple perspectives, analysis of cause-and-effect relationships, and the ongoing examination of the assumptions and biases we all hold when we discuss issues of historical importance.

One unforeseen benefit of these classroom interactions is their positive effect on classroom management issues. In my college-level classroom, I have a number of students, nine of whom have been diagnosed with Attention Deficit Disorder, who were a constant challenge at the start of the school year. As roles were redefined and students were given more auton-omy and a greater voice in classroom procedures, these challenges have lessened considerably. My instinct tells me that they know I honestly respect their opinions and concerns and that they are reciprocating. We have established that our purpose in the classroom is to teach and learn from each other, and we enjoy tracking this process of discovery. It is easy for me to point out when behaviors are not facilitating this, and often that is the only action I have to take to maintain order. The alternative is return-ing to more traditional modes of teaching history—lecturing, using the textbook, with me "giving" history and students passively "receiving" it—and the students and I do not want this to happen.

While the experience has been an exhilarating one, there have been some disappointments. Despite my best efforts, there are still a few students who find history boring. While I will continue to explore ways to engage them, I also realize that some students will never have the passion for history that I have. For those few, I believe I have at least fostered an appreciation of why history is included in their curriculum and needs to be studied, although it may never be a study they enjoy.

I am even more concerned with the students who have not done well academically in my class. I have two students who failed the first semester, which truly upset me. Both students have a number of issues to deal with academically and in their personal lives, which puts schoolwork low on their order of priorities. Still, they have expressed that they enjoy my classes, and we have decided to try and work together to develop alternative ways for them to demonstrate what they know and can do.

Our classroom has become a site that embodies a number of the theories of why the study of history is relevant. Some students would agree with those who see the study of history as crucial in promoting democratic citizenship:

- Without history, a nation would have no purpose; it would be impossible for a nation to exist without it.
- History is important; you should know what happens where you live.
- To understand the way things are today, we need to know what went on years and years ago. Many things that went on during our history affect us today because they relate to events that occur these days.

Other students would support theorists who see the study of history as essential for promoting empathy and a sense of social justice:

- There has been so much conflict. When will we start taking care of each other?
- I actually paid attention. I had no idea women were treated so badly.

Finally, most of the students have come to realize that history is not a collection of old facts about people long gone, but an ongoing, unfinished story of the human condition in which we all play a role.

- I now see history is a cycle of recurring events, not just a bunch of facts.
- Sometimes we are in the same place as people from the past.
- Anything that happened in the past helps you move forward now.
- You learn stuff about your part in history.

❖ RECOMMENDATIONS FOR PRACTICE

You can never step into the same river twice.

—Heraclitus (cited in Mashalidis, 2003, p. 27)

This research project has been a wonderful experience. I hope my students will continue to "do" history in all areas of their lives for the best reasons: to become active, contributing members of our democratic society; to strive to promote social justice; and to become lifelong learners, examining their lives and the world around them.

In future classes, I will have new students with different interests, goals, and conceptions about history. Most will probably think history is a boring bunch of facts about dead people with no relevance to their lives. Drawing on what I have learned this semester, I will try to replicate the inquiry experience while at the same time realizing that the dynamics will inevitably change with the introduction of a new set of participants. Although success is not guaranteed, there are a number of factors that I as a teacher can put in place to facilitate the process. Acting on the definition we developed for relevance, I believe to make history real, I need to be real. To help students connect with history, I need to connect with my students. And finally, to make history beneficial, I need to be beneficial.

First, if you make it real, they will remember it. By real, I am referring not only to authentic methods of inquiry but also to the beliefs and attitudes the teacher brings to the classroom. It is not enough to model collaborative constructivist teaching methods. You need to believe in them, and your students must perceive that you value them in your instruction. To embrace this realism, I think it will be crucial to keep asking questions and to constantly reexamine my own beliefs and biases, as well as what works in my classes and what doesn't and why. This is an inquiry I will continue to pursue for the remainder of this school year, especially with the few students with whom I have not connected. For me, a future research project might focus on what elements in my classroom still serve as barriers to academic progress for these students. If students are not willing to enter into collaboration, what other methods can be used to connect with them and their experiences of history and school in general? How might other students help their classmates overcome these barriers to success?

Second, I will need to connect with and draw on my students' knowledge and skills to assess my own abilities and to access the information that they bring to class, adding value to my own and their classmates' education. Connecting students' interests, needs, and concerns with lives of the people we are studying made history relevant to my current students, and I hope it will do so for future classes. One method of connection that I incorporated this year was the use of controversy to engage and motivate students. This has worked well but can stir up strong emotions. A research project might examine how to effectively guide the use of controversy in history lessons so that emotions add to and do not detract from student learning.

Finally, for true teacher-student collaboration to take place, the students must feel that the classroom is a safe place for them to express their views and take risks without fear of failure or ridicule. I hope I can continue to establish a beneficial level of discourse and classroom structure, open to negotiation, that will allow all my students to feel empowered as active participants in their own education. I was pleasantly surprised at how this approach positively impacted classroom management issues and would like to look more deeply into how increased student autonomy influences student behaviors.

At the start of the year, "Why do I need to know this stuff?" seemed like a challenge. I now see it as an invitation to enter into authentic collaborations with my students, and I am looking forward to continuing to do so in the future.

❖ REFERENCES

Akmal, T. T., & Ayre-Svingen, B. (2002). Integrated biographical inquiry: A student-centered approach to learning. *The Social Studies, 93*(4), 272–277.

Carrier, R. C. (2002). The function of the historian in society. *The History Teacher, 35*(4), 519–526.

Formwalt, L. W. (2002). Seven rules for effective history teaching or bringing life to the history class. *Organization of American Historians Magazine of History, 17.* Retrieved November 15, 2003, from http://www.oah.org/pubs/magazine/ ww1/formwalt.html

Foster, S. J., & Padgett, C. S. (1999). Authentic historical inquiry in the social studies classroom. (Special Section: Dimensions of Middle School Social Studies). *The Clearing House, 72*(6), 357–364.

Kennedy, D. M. (1998). The art of the tale: Story-telling and history teaching. *The History Teacher, 31*(3), 319–330.

Kornfeld, J., & Goodman, J. (1998). Melting the glaze: Exploring student responses to liberatory social studies. *Theory into Practice, 37*(4), 306–314.

Mashalidis, S. (2003). Heraclitean thinking: Implications for philosophy of education. *Interchange, 34*(1), 23–33.

Merriam-Webster. (2002). *Merriam-Webster online thesaurus.* Retrieved November 11, 2003 from http://www.m-w.com/

Meyerson, P., & Secules, T. (2001). Inquiry circles can make social studies meaningful: Learning about the controversy in Kosovo. *The Social Studies, 92*(6), 267–272.

Newmann, F. M., & Wehlage, G. G. (1993, April). Five standards of authentic instruction. *Educational Leadership,* pp. 8–11.

Rosenzweig, R. (2003). Interviews with exemplary teachers: Bill Bigelow and Michele Forman. *The History Teacher, 36*(3), 397–406.

Stanley, G. (2003, Winter). Warts and all: Exposing history to high school students. *Educational Horizons,* pp. 86–91.

Vanderstel, D. G. (2002). "And I thought historians only taught": Doing history beyond the classroom. *Organization of American Historians*

Magazine of History, 16. Retrieved November 15, 2003, from http://www .oah.org/pubs/magazine/publichistory/vanderstel.html

Example 3: What Happens to Students' Writing When I Add a Self-Assessment Component to Each Writing Activity?

Jody McQuillan
Literacy Specialist and Modern Language Teacher
Noble and Greenough School
Dedham, Massachusetts

Abstract

Writing is a complex process that relies on students' abilities to orchestrate multiple components to arrive at a finished piece of writing. My research question focuses on the potential effects of self-assessment on students' writing. The intervention in this study involved adding a self-assessment piece to allow students to consider their own thinking processes while writing. I systematically incorporated a self-assessment component to writing activities, and I examined the effects of the self-assessments on students' learning about the writing process. Initially, students seemed unable to self-assess independently, as they consistently rated themselves very highly on the rubrics provided. After collaboratively assessing their writing pieces with their peers, they seemed to adopt a more critical stance toward assessing their own writing. This suggests that providing consistent rubrics, small-group discussions, and opportunities for constructive peer assessment of writing pieces can promote students' ability to assess the shortcomings of their own writing critically. While developing students' metacognitive skills about writing can improve future writing pieces, I also think that this reflective stance can be empowering for students, and it is critical for learning across the curriculum and in life.

Writing is a complex process that involves multiple steps—selecting topics, brainstorming ideas, organizing and sequencing these ideas, choosing effective words to convey messages, using appropriate mechanics, developing personal voice, and checking for conventions, as well as revising and editing skills. The writing process relies on a person's ability to orchestrate these varied components and to arrive at a finished piece of writing. Writing is thus a complex and often difficult process for many students.

There are many different types of writing assessments for educators to evaluate students' writing. My research question focuses on the potential effects of self-assessment. The question reads, "What happens when I add a self-assessment component to each writing activity?" As a teacher-researcher, I systematically added a self-assessment component to writing activities and examined the effects of these self-assessments on students' learning about the writing process. As Graves (1994) writes, "Teachers do have an important role in evaluation, but it consists primarily of helping children become part of the process" (p. 12). In other words, students' self-assessment of their writing pieces makes them more active learners, and it enhances their own learning. Black and his colleagues (2004) note that when students reflect about their learning and their thinking processes, they are "developing the capacity to work at a metacognitive level" (p. 14) and are becoming independent learners. I believe that developing students' metacognitive skills about writing could not only improve future writing pieces but also empower students' learning across the curriculum and even in life.

❖ RATIONALE

In my role as a literacy paraprofessional, I work with fourth- and fifth-grade students who are struggling with various elements of reading and writing. My job entails providing literacy support to these students both in the classroom and in pullout sessions with small groups of students. In the upper elementary grades, most students are no longer "learning to read" or learning to decode texts, but they are instead "reading to learn." That is, they are reading for information, and they are expanding their reading comprehension skills. Similarly, these students already have a basic understanding of writing, yet they need instruction on how to further develop their own writing pieces.

As a literacy teacher, I work with students on various writing activities, and I have observed many students who need support completing each step of the writing process. Specifically, some students need help using graphic organizers to help them brainstorm and organize their ideas during the prewriting phase. Some need guidance to use a thesaurus to find more effective words to incorporate into their writing pieces. Some students also need assistance with a checklist of the mechanics such as spelling, capitalization, and punctuation to set a purpose for the revising and editing phase of each writing activity. And still others need conversations and conferences to further develop and refine their ideas throughout each step of the writing process.

In my experiences, I have noticed that developing students' metacognitive skills is a beneficial use of instructional time. When students hone their own thinking processes, they can feel empowered. For example, a fifth-grade student and I were recently revisiting and rewriting an essay that he had previously turned in to his classroom teacher. The first draft was difficult to understand and to follow due to incomplete sentences, poor penmanship, and weak organization. When asked to read this paragraph to me, the student remarked that he couldn't read it and that it didn't make any sense. We then revisited the question, reexamined the graphic organizer used for the compare/contrast paragraph, and discussed topic sentences and concluding sentences. In rewriting the paragraph, the student easily generated ideas, and he quickly rewrote the paragraph. Afterward, we made a T-chart to compare how he worked on the paragraph the first time and the second time. He made specific comments about his different approaches, and together we talked about his needs as a writer.

Since our meeting, this student has more consistently found a quiet place to work at home, he has more carefully planned his writing pieces, and he has given more thought to each step of the writing process. Moreover, he has been able to articulate his needs as a writer for each assignment. That is not to suggest that a single conference resolved this student's needs as a writer but that developing his metacognitive skills benefits student learning.

Teaching students to think about their metacognitive strategies—that is, their own thinking processes—is critical to students' success in today's world, yet it is often overlooked and underestimated. If students can begin first to describe and then to analyze their thought processes while writing, teachers and students can work together to identify strengths and weaknesses in writing. They can, in turn, use this information to plan writing support and to strengthen students' writing. Encouraging students to think about their thinking processes during writing activities might help them develop as writers, and such thinking could strengthen future writing pieces. Moreover, these metacognitive skills and strategies might transfer to other areas of the curriculum as well as to real-life situations.

❖ LITERATURE REVIEW

Metacognition has often been defined as "the knowledge and control one has over his or her own thinking and learning activities" (Baker & Brown, 1984, cited by Kingery, 2000, p. 76).

Metacognition presents an important link between writing and self-assessment in that it promotes thinking about one's own thinking processes while writing. Reflection, as Tompkins (2005) writes, "requires children to pause and become aware of themselves as writers. Indeed, reflection is part of the writing process itself. Children write, pause, reflect, write some more, reflect, and so on" (p. 152). Tompkins (2005) continues to note that "this ability to reflect on one's own writing promotes organizational skills, self-reliance, independence, and creativity. Furthermore, self-evaluation is a natural part of writing" (p. 165).

While writing appears inextricably linked with self-assessment and metacognition, the research in this area is relatively recent. Beginning in the 1990s, researchers and educators focused on teaching students to self-assess while reading and writing since, as Rhodes and Shanklin (1993) claim, "Assessing metacognition allows us to discover students' perceptions of themselves as readers and writers, the reading and writing they do, and the strategies they employ to solve the problems they encounter in reading and writing" (p. 112). At this time, researchers and educators used questionnaires, interviews, group discussions, and conferences to teach students to self-assess during literacy activities (Rhodes & Shanklin, 1993, pp. 101–145). Various forms of self-assessment relied on open-ended questions to probe students' understanding of their thinking processes while reading and writing.

More recently, researchers and educators have focused on the importance of self-assessment during writing (Anderson, 2005; Routman, 2005;

Tompkins, 2004). With the current emphasis on writing as a constructive process, researchers and educators are teaching students to use checklists and process checklists to reveal the students' process of thinking while writing. As Tompkins (2004) writes, "Process assessment is designed to probe how children write, the decisions they make as they write, and the strategies they use rather than the quality of the finished product" (p. 150). In addition to checklists, researchers and educators are also relying on rubrics to help students learn to assess their own work and reflect on their thinking processes. Rubrics can be simple or complex in delineating the criteria against which a writing piece is to be judged. Yet, as Routman (2005) reminds researchers and educators alike, "In too many places students are being 'rubricized': every piece of writing is scored against a rubric, sometimes even in first grade. . . . It is not advisable to apply rubrics to all writing nor to score all writing" (p. 243).

Current research recognizes the need to develop students' ability to self-assess, and it promotes the importance of teaching students to reflect on their writing pieces. As Routman (2005) states,

> Self-evaluation is the missing piece in writing instruction. Ultimately, we want students to internalize the qualities of good writing and to have inner conversations about their writing—in other words, to have conferences with themselves in which they notice their strengths, critique their own writing, set reasonably high goals, know how and when to seek help, and work toward accomplishing their goals. The more work the child is able to do on his own, the more learning takes place. Teach writing with self-evaluation as an end goal for all students. (p. 253)

Educators now create child-friendly self-assessment tools that are grade-level and developmentally appropriate, and they solicit feedback about these assessments from students (Routman, 2005, p. 241). Further research into the link between writing, self-assessment, and metacognition will continue to clarify the benefits to student learning of developing students' reflective stance in writing activities, in other areas of the curriculum, and in real-life situations.

❖ THE RESEARCH QUESTION CONNECTS TO BOSTON COLLEGE THEMES

Teaching students to think about their metacognitive strategies, that is, their own thinking processes, is critical to students' success in today's world. The research question, "What happens when I add a self-assessment component to each writing piece?" provided an opportunity to link metacognitive skills with writing. If students can describe and analyze their thought processes while writing, students can, in turn, use this information to plan writing support and to strengthen future writing pieces.

This research question allowed me to grow as an educator and to construct my own knowledge about the writing process. Research on teaching writing offers prompts, graphic organizers, checklists for editing, and suggestions for classroom publishing. In looking at the research on teaching writing, I noticed that it sometimes includes a self-assessment piece and that this component often takes many different forms. I also noted that some of the literature on teaching writing adds a self-assessment to writing activities, yet, it seems an afterthought. I first examined several different forms of self-assessment to identify key elements involved in students' self-assessment of writing. I then created a self-assessment tool that promoted students reflecting about their writing. It seemed that this simple step of asking students to reflect on a more systematic basis could provide critical information about their metacognitive skills, and it could also enhance their future writing skills.

This research question also promoted social justice and accommodated diversity as I worked with students identified as "deficient" in the area of writing. I offered differentiated lessons and interventions to these students to strengthen their writing skills and to further their metacognitive skills while writing. If students can begin to reflect on the process of writing while they are writing, they can then more fully and more equitably participate in all academic classroom writing activities.

Collaboration among students, classroom teachers, and literacy specialists was also a critical part of this research question. In talking with the students, I explained that I wanted them to complete a self-assessment piece at the end of writing activities to determine if they were thinking about the writing process and if this thinking process might influence future writing assignments. I also explained my project to classroom teachers at one of our bi-weekly collaborative meetings. I asked for their help in collecting writing samples from the students, and I invited their observations of literacy students during writing activities in the classroom. In addition, the literacy specialists' expertise and teaching experience helped me identify examples of self-assessment across different grade levels. In all, this project was a collaborative project intended to benefit student learning by enhancing students' overall ability to reflect on and to learn from the writing process.

In all, this research question allowed me to explore a topic of interest to me on both a theoretical and practical level. After researching different forms of self-assessment, I integrated a self-assessment tool into the writing lessons, and I continually reflected on the process and the product. The processes of researching and reflection ultimately bridged the gap between theoretical research and classroom practice.

❖ TEACHING AND LEARNING CONTEXTS

This study took place in an elementary school in a suburb of a large New England city. The school currently enrolls 340 students in kindergarten through fifth grade, and there are often 10 to 12 students who enroll in the middle of the academic year. The elementary school is located in an upper middle-class town with a population of 17,000, and the inhabitants' primary language is predominantly English.

Various assessments were used to determine which students should receive literacy support and to identify the focus of the literacy services. Students were given the Qualitative Reading Inventory-3 (QRI-3) for reading comprehension, a word identification list, the *Words Their Way* spelling list, and a writing assessment. Students' scores from the most recent MCAS tests were also examined. The findings of these assessments, combined with classroom teachers' input, resulted in the selection of these four students to receive literacy support both in the classroom and in pullout sessions.

Stavros

Stavros is a fifth-grade boy whose primary language is English and who can speak a few words of Greek. He is an only child who excels at sports, and he actively participates in activities that are sports related, including recess activities and physical education. Stavros has been receiving literacy services since first grade, and he is currently on a 504 Education Plan to support processing information.

John

John is a fifth-grade boy whose primary language is English and who can speak a few words of Greek. He has an older brother, who is in eighth grade and currently receives SPED services, and a younger sister in first grade. John often has difficulty hearing in class. He continually states that he spends hours on the weekends playing video games. He has received literacy services since first grade. John has been recommended for testing several times, and his parents refused to sign the forms each time.

Sophie

Sophie is a fifth-grade girl whose primary language is English. Her parents both speak Italian fluently, and her grandmother speaks only Italian. Her grandmother cares for Sophie and her younger brother while her parents work. Sophie is a shy girl who seems to get along with everyone. Sophie has been receiving literacy services since fourth grade, when she received a "Needs Improvement" on a third-grade MCAS.

Alex

Alex is a fifth-grade girl whose primary language is English and who lives with her mother. Her parents are divorced, and her brother lives in a different state with her father. Alex's mother works full-time, and Alex attends an afterschool program at another elementary school in town. She often struggles to get along with other fifth-grade girls. She has been receiving literacy services since first grade.

Literacy services for these four students focus on writing development and reading comprehension strategies. As a literacy paraprofessional, I work with these four students in small groups two times a week. I am also involved in the literacy activities in their classrooms twice a week. In this way, I support them in literacy activities both in and out of the classroom.

❖ INTERVENTION

Writing is a complex process that involves orchestrating multiple interrelated skills to create a final product. It relies on a student's ability to select topics, brainstorm ideas, organize and sequence these ideas, choose effective words to convey messages, use appropriate mechanics, develop personal voice, check for conventions, and revise and edit the work. My intervention involved adding a self-assessment component to students' writing activities to see if it impacted their writing.

Over the course of 8 weeks and in the role of a literacy paraprofessional, I worked with small groups of students (two groups of two students) for 30 minutes twice a week on writing activities. Our lessons typically began with a mini-lesson about a specific component of writing, and the students then responded to a writing prompt. For example, one lesson focused on transition words, another highlighted writing about a "small moment" (Calkins, 1994), and yet another emphasized lively lead sentences. The focus of these mini-lessons was on individual student needs, and these needs were determined by examining prior writing samples and by conversations with their classroom teacher. To organize their writing pieces during the research study, as Buckner (2005) suggests, the students each kept a spiral notebook in which we recorded notes about each mini-lesson. These notes were in the back of the notebook so students could refer to them while completing later writing assignments. In the front of each notebook, students put in the writing prompt for which they could create a graphic organizer (a teaching strategy with which they are familiar) prior to writing, and they wrote responses to the prompts.

The intervention in this study involved adding a self-assessment to each writing activity. The self-assessment took two distinct forms, one that was open-ended and one that was more structured. Students had the self-assessment forms before they began writing. At the beginning of the study, students completed the first writing piece, and they then did the first self-assessment comprised of two open-ended questions. I introduced this project by explaining that we were working on strengthening their writing skills and that I wanted them to take a few minutes to think about how they did on the first writing piece. The questions read, "What do you think you did well in this piece?" and "What would you like to focus on in your next writing piece?" These two questions allowed the students to articulate which elements they used well in their writing and which elements they wanted to focus on in future writing assignments. These open-ended questions promoted students identifying the elements they deemed important in writing.

The second form of self-assessment was a rubric and thus a more structured form of self-assessment as it delineated different elements of writing and asked students to consider if they included specific elements in their writing. This form of self-assessment relied on a teacher generating the important elements in a writing activity and allowed the students to assess their use of specific elements or the lack thereof.

At the end of the study, students wrote a final piece and again completed a self-assessment similar to the first, that is, a self-assessment comprising two open-ended questions. I looked at whether students could identify and use various components of writing. I also looked at whether elements of the self-assessments promoted during this study could be linked to improvements in students' writing.

❖ RESEARCH METHODS

While this study technically employed a mixed-methods research approach, the methods were predominantly qualitative. Specifically, the qualitative research included analysis of graphic organizers as well as the associated writing samples, observations of students during writing activities, and conversations with students, classroom teachers, and literacy specialists about the students' performance. The quantitative research methods included the self-assessment rubrics, where students awarded themselves points.

These research methods allowed me to identify varied trends in the link between metacognition and writing and to describe progress in rich detail and thereby to document the changes that occurred during the course of the study. Moreover, the thick description generated by these qualitative data sources provided a rich context within which I could situate these developments in students' learning.

❖ DATA SOURCES

Various data sources were used to illuminate potential links between writing, self-assessment, and metacognition. I examined students' writing pieces from the prewriting phase to the finished works. Specifically, I began by looking at the use of graphic organizers that support brainstorming and organizing during the prewriting phase, then I continued to collect writing samples, and I ended each writing assignment with a self-assessment piece. After 8 weeks, I had six writing samples from each student as well as copies of the self-assessment rubric I developed for each lesson.

In addition to students' writing, data sources included ongoing informal assessments, observations, lesson plans, and conversations I had with students while they were writing. It was important to note students' questions and comments during these writing activities as well as during

Table A.5   Initial Self-Assessment

Name	What did I do well in this writing piece?	What will I focus on in my next writing piece?
Stavros	• Adjectives • Details • Clear sentences • Transition words	• Bette [sic] adjectives.
John	• I put capitals • I have no worn out words • I had good transision [sic] words	• Details • Adjetives [sic] • Better scentences [sic]
Sophie	• Capitals • Periods • Flow • Juicy words • No fluff words • Transation [sic] words	• Periods • Details • Flow • Transitionary [sic] words • Spelling • No fluff words/Juicy words
Alex	• Spelling • Transition words • Intresting [sic]	• How it goes together

Table A.6   Summary of Self-Assessment Scores

Name	Self-Assessment 1	Self-Assessment 2	Self-Assessment 3	Self-Assessment 4
Stavros	14	15	12.5	11
John	13	13	11.5	10
Sophie	13	14	10	11
Alex	15	14	12	8
Total	55	56	46	40
Total Possible Points	64	64	64	64

writing activities in their classrooms. Along the same lines, it was critical to take careful notes of student behaviors during writing activities. Data sources also included interviews and conversations with the focus students as well as with their classroom teachers.

In all, I interpreted the data by looking for emerging themes and patterns and by linking these themes to students' growth or lack thereof. Continually revisiting these data provided feedback about future teaching points and revealed emerging themes and patterns relevant to the potential link between writing, self-assessment, and metacognition.

❖ RESULTS

During the 8-week intervention, four 5th-grade students completed six writing pieces for the purpose of this study, and they performed six self-assessments of these writing activities. They completed the initial self-assessment that asked two open-ended questions about their strengths and weaknesses in writing, they finished two self-assessments after a writing activity, they filled out two self-assessments after a peer assessment and a small-group discussion, and they responded to two open-ended questions on the final self-assessment.

Students completed the initial self-assessment of a writing piece during the first week of the study. The initial self-assessment asked students to respond to two questions following a writing activity: "What did I do well in this writing piece?" and "What will I focus on in my next writing piece?" As a group, they named 16 features they felt they had done well, and they identified 12 features they wanted to focus on in future writing activities (see Table A.5).

Over the course of the next 5 weeks, students worked on four writing pieces, and they completed self-assessment rubrics for each piece. The students filled out the first two self-assessments following a writing activity, and each rubric had a total of 16 points. As Table A.6 shows, students gave themselves a combined score of 55 out of 64 possible points on Self-Assessment 1 and a score of 56 out of a possible 64 points on Self-Assessment 2. Table A.7 presents the scores in each category of the rubric, and it shows that they scored themselves as proficient writers in 31 of 32 categories. Only one student gave himself a two out of four points in one category.

Specifically, Table A.7 shows that the students rated themselves a 4 out of 4 in 15 of 32 categories on Self-Assessments 1 and 2. They also rated themselves a 3.5 out of 4 in 2 of 32 categories, a 3 out of 4 in 14 of 32 categories, and a 2 out of 4 in 1 of 32 categories.

The next two self-assessments, Self-Assessments 3 and 4, followed a writing activity and a peer assessment activity. During the peer assessment and ensuing small-group discussion, students used the same rubric to assess their peers' writing pieces, and they were required to give evidence to support their judgments. Then, students used the same rubric to perform a self-assessment of their own writing piece. Table A.6 shows that students gave themselves a combined score of 46 out of a possible 64 points on Self-Assessment 3 and a combined score of 40 out of a possible 64 points on Self-Assessment 4. Table A.6 also shows that the scores from the first two self-assessments completed individually differ from the last two self-assessments completed after a peer assessment and a small-group discussion. As Table A.8 shows, students did not give themselves a 4 out of 4 in any categories. The figures in Table A.9 show that they scored themselves a 3.5 out of 4 points on 5 of 32 categories, they rated themselves a 3 out of 4 points on 12 of 32 categories, they gave themselves a 2.5 out of 4 points on 9 of 32 categories, and they graded themselves a 2 or less on 6 of 32 categories.

The final self-assessment asked students to again answer the two open-ended questions from Self-Assessment 1. Students generated a total

Table A.7   Scores for Self-Assessment Rubrics 1 and 2

	Self-Assessment 1				Self-Assessment 2			
Name	"Slice of the Pie"	Word Choice	Grammar and Spelling	Caps and Punctuation	"Slice of the Pie"	Word Choice	Grammar and Spelling	Caps and Punctuation
Stavros	3	4	3	4	3.5	3.5	4	4
John	2	4	3	4	3	3	4	3
Sophie	3	4	3	3	4	3	3	4
Alex	4	3	4	4	4	4	3	3

Table A.8   Scores for Self-Assessment Rubrics 3 and 4

	Self-Assessment 3				Self-Assessment 4			
Name	Lively Leads	"Slice of the Pie"	Word Choice	Mechanics	Lively Leads	"Slice of the Pie"	Word Choice	Mechanics
Stavros	3.5	3	3	3	3	2.5	3	2.5
John	3	3.5	2	3	2.5	2	3	2.5
Sophie	3.5	3	2.5	1	2.5	3	3	2.5
Alex	3.5	3.5	3	2	2.5	2	2.5	1

of 11 features of writing they felt they did well in their final writing piece, and eight features they would focus on in future writing pieces. Table A.9 presents the students' various responses.

In all, there is a difference in the scores of the self-assessments completed individually and those completed after peer collaboration. As Table A.6 displays, the scores are higher on Self-Assessments 1 and 2 than on Self-Assessments 3 and 4. On Self-Assessments 1 and 2, which were completed individually, students awarded themselves an average of 55.5 points out of a possible 64. On Self-Assessments 3 and 4, the students scored themselves lower, and they gave themselves an average of 43 points out of a possible 64 points. The decrease in the self-assessment scores suggests that the students adopted a more critical stance in assessing their own writing after collaborating with their peers.

❖ DISCUSSION

This research project set out to explore and document the possible links between writing, self-assessment, and metacognition. Although the classroom teacher assured me that these students could use a rubric to self-assess their writing and although I thoroughly discussed each self-assessment rubric introduced during the study, students' inability to be objective about their performance was evident. As Table A.7 shows, students scored

Table A.9   Final Self-Assessment

Name	What did I do well in this writing piece?	What will I focus on in my next writing piece?
Stavros	• Word choice • Gramer [sic] • Voice • Hook the reader	• Hooking the reader
John	• Good lively leads • Good spellings • "Slice of pie" • Juicy words	• More description
Sophie	• Dicriptive [sic] • Orginizing [sic] my stories • "Slice of the pie"	• Periods • "Slice of the pie" • Juicy words • Orginizing [sic] • Dialogue
Alex	• Describing one piece of the pie	• Editing my writing

themselves as proficient writers in 31 of 32 categories on Self-Assessments 1 and 2, and only one student felt his writing was weak in one category. These scores suggest that the students have a positive self-image of themselves as writers, and this is a positive element for these students in terms of their receiving literacy support. Yet, these scores also suggest that the students were not objective about their writing performance.

After examining the results from Self-Assessments 1 and 2, I introduced a collaborative component into the assessment process with the intent of helping students begin to think more critically about their writing. Specifically, after each writing piece, students read each other's pieces, assessed them with the same rubric used for self-assessment, and provided textual evidence to support their judgments. Following the peer assessment and small-group discussion, students then completed a self-assessment of their writing pieces. Table A.6 documents a drop in scores, for example, from a total of 55 points out of 64 on Self-Assessment 1 and a 56 out of 64 on Self-Assessment 2 to a 46 out of 64 points on Self-Assessment 3 and a 40 out of 64 points on Self-Assessment 4. On average, while the students gave themselves 55.5 points out of a possible 64 points on Self-Assessments 1 and 2, they gave themselves 43 points out of a possible 64 on Self-Assessments 3 and 4. The scores on the last two self-assessments suggest that the students assessed themselves more critically as a result of peer collaboration.

When the students had completed the self-assessments both without collaboration and with peer collaboration, I asked them to reflect on the two different approaches to self-assessment. Their comments suggest that peer collaboration promotes a more critical stance and thus develops their abilities to self-assess their own writing. For example, John mentioned he preferred doing the collaborative peer assessment before performing the self-assessment. He wrote, "It helps me when we talk about it because before I just gave myself all 4s. It helped me because when I don't talk about it I just give myself all fours" (personal communication, April 12, 2006). Another student wrote that she preferred the collaborative peer assessment before the self-assessment because when she did the self-assessment without feedback from others, "I think it isn't that good because then you just want to give yourself good grades" (Sophie, personal communication, April 12, 2006). Stavros also preferred the collaborative assessment prior to the self-assessment because, as he wrote, "Its [sic] helping me in class and its [sic] beter [sic] when we talk about it because I know what to add next time. I thought this activety [sic] was OK because we got to discuss how you felt about your paragraph" (personal communication, April 12, 2006). These comments, combined with the lower scores on Self-Assessments 3 and 4 rubrics, further support the idea that the students gave more thought to the self-assessments after discussing their writing with their peers.

In concluding the research study, I asked the students what they had learned about themselves as writers, and their responses were insightful. Two students identified specific elements of writing they felt they did well. Stavros, for example, wrote that his writing can "hook the reader," and he has good word choice (personal communication, April 12, 2006). John focused on how he will strengthen his future pieces in writing: "I need better word choice [and] better description" (personal communication, April 12, 2006). Alex responded by writing, "I am a good writer. I need quiet. I need to think more about writing" (personal communication, April 12, 2006). And Sophie wrote that "I think more when I'm writing" (personal communication, April 12, 2006). These comments reveal that these students still have a positive image of themselves as good writers despite the drop in scores between Self-Assessments 1 and 2 and Self-Assessments 3 and 4. These comments also suggest that these students are beginning to think more about their thinking processes while writing, thereby signaling a link between writing, self-assessment, and metacognition.

In all, this research study set out to explore and document the possible links between writing, self-assessment, and metacognition. Initially, students seemed unable to self-assess independently, as they consistently rated themselves very highly on the rubrics provided. After collaboratively assessing their writing pieces with their peers, they developed a more critical stance toward assessing their own writing. This suggests that providing consistent rubrics, small-group discussions, and opportunities for constructive peer assessment of writing pieces can promote the students' ability to critically assess the shortcomings of their own writing. Specifically, the collaborative component resulted in the students beginning to adopt a more critical stance in their self-assessments. While the intervention does not point to a direct link between writing, self-assessment, and metacognition, I think the intervention was successful in revealing the benefits to students' developing writing skills.

❖ LIMITATIONS OF THE RESEARCH STUDY

There were several limitations that could have influenced the validity and the reliability of this study. First, the students needed to be able to articulate in writing or in an interview that they were thinking about their own thought processes. If they couldn't communicate these thoughts, it would have been difficult to determine what happened when I added a self-assessment component to each writing assignment. A second possible limitation was the small number of students involved in this research study. While the research highlighted a possible link between self-assessment and writing, it would be necessary to conduct a study looking at more students and a more diverse sample of students to document the potential effects on a larger scale. A third limitation was the students' level of literacy achievement in this research study. This study involved fifth-grade students who have been identified as needing literacy support and who are currently receiving literacy services. To further show the possible link between self-assessment and writing, it would be essential to work with a whole class of fifth-grade students to document a more random sampling of students' achievement and their development. Finally, another limitation to collecting writing samples was the number of MCAS exams scheduled for fifth-graders during the time of this study. Although it reduced the number of writing samples collected, the data about the possible link between writing, self-assessment, and metacognition still yielded interesting insights.

❖ IMPLICATIONS FOR TEACHING

Teaching writing is a challenge. This research study focused on the processes of writing, with hopes that I could document a link between self-assessment and writing skills. In theory, such a finding impacts many aspects of classroom teaching. For instance, educators need to be explicit about the learning goals they hold for students for every writing lesson so students are clear as to what they are trying to accomplish and how they are attempting to realize these goals. One way to make these learning goals explicit is for educators to develop rubrics that attend specifically to the goals and the means employed to realize them. While this entails carefully developing grade-appropriate rubrics for writing activities, Routman (2005) reminds teachers that while rubrics are helpful, they do not need to "rubricize" (p. 243) every piece of writing throughout the school year. During the research study, I solicited students' feedback about various rubrics, and I found that it was beneficial to students' learning to ask for their input about the rubrics. They offered insightful comments about rubrics that were too complex, too long, too wordy, or too confusing. It is important for educators to identify the goals of writing activities and to design rubrics that match these goals.

Linked with creating rubrics is showing students how to use rubrics to assess themselves. After learning goals are identified and a rubric is developed to match these goals, teachers need to set aside time so students have

opportunities to discuss the rubric before they write. It would also be beneficial to student learning to give students multiple opportunities to famil-
iarize themselves with the rubric and the assessment process. Teachers
need to have students write, give them opportunities to think about what
and how they have written, provide a rubric with which to assess their
writing, and then allow them to revise their work. Writing instruction cou-
pled with reflection can thus result in stronger writing skills.

Another implication of this research study involves the social dynamics of integrating a peer assessment component into the self-assessment
process. Educators need to offer mini-lessons to students on how to provide positive and constructive feedback to their peers and on how to give
textual evidence to support their judgments. This is a critical component
because it addresses the social dynamics within a classroom, and it creates
a "safe" environment within which students can collaborate. Peer assessment, as Alex noted, "is hard because sometimes it hurt my feelings if you
get bad grades" (personal communication, April 12, 2006). Yet she also suggested that it was a valuable experience, adding, "next time I will write
more carefully" (personal communication, April 12, 2006). Addressing the
social implications ultimately helps students learn to work together and to
help each other more effectively.

A final implication of this project is that students will gain greater
awareness of their own thinking processes and that this metacognition will
encourage them to think more while they are writing. When Alex commented, "next time I will write more carefully," she suggested she understood the potential positive impact of thinking about her thinking
processes while writing. In all, as Routman (2005) writes,

> Self-evaluation is the missing piece in writing instruction. Ultimately, we
> want students to internalize the qualities of good writing and to have
> inner conversations about their writing—in other words, to have con-
> ferences with themselves in which they notice their strengths, critique
> their own writing, set reasonably high goals, know how and when to
> seek help, and work toward accomplishing their goals. The more work
> the child is able to do on his own, the more learning takes place. Teach
> writing with self-evaluation as an end goal for all students. (p. 253)

Students' self-assessment of their own writing pieces makes them more
active learners, and it enhances their own learning. While developing
students' metacognitive skills about writing could improve future writing
pieces, I also think that these skills can be empowering for students, and they
are critical for learning across the curriculum and even in life.

❖ REFLECTION

At the beginning of 2006, educators and researchers across America are
participating in an ongoing debate about whether teachers should devote

more time to working with content material or with the processes necessary to understand content materials. Schools are being graded on the results of state standardized tests, recess is being shortened or eliminated to allow for more teaching time, and the school year is being lengthened in some towns to give teachers more time to work with students. There is an ongoing and widespread debate in America about teaching content over process in our schools.

Why can't we do both? In fact, we should do both. While many students can complete worksheets, and they can write five-paragraph essays without support, for other students, orchestrating the multiple strategies involved in the writing process is difficult. We, as educators, should teach developmentally appropriate, grade-level content material to our students, and at the same time, we should teach them multiple ways to organize and present their thoughts and responses in writing. We, as educators, should introduce our students to various writing strategies to strengthen writing skills and to develop an awareness of their metacognitive skills. This style of effective teaching would teach content and process to our young students. Moreover, as educators, we should help our students develop relevant skills to writing, and we should do this in an appropriate and supportive social context. In all, to be effective educators in the 21st century, it is critical that we work with our students to develop their metacognitive skills as they are writing and that we also guide them as they acquire the facility to use multiple strategies in the writing process. When we can teach our students the essential processes for organizing and presenting their thoughts in writing, they will be able to more fully and more effectively present their ideas in writing to others.

Writing is a demanding cognitive activity, and this research study examined the potential link between self-assessment and writing. The intervention in this study involved adding a self-assessment piece to allow students to think about their own processes of thinking while writing. It is my hope that students internalized the value of self-assessment and used this component to further enrich their writing skills. It is also my hope that students can ultimately transfer this reflective stance into other areas of the curriculum and into their lives.

❖ REFERENCES

Anderson, C. (2005). *Assessing writers.* Portsmouth, NH: Heinemann.

Black, P., Harrison, C., Lee, C., Marshall, B., & William, D. (2004). Working inside the black box: Assessment for learning in the classroom. *Phi Delta Kappan,* pp. 9–21.

Buckner, A. (2005). *Notebook know-how: Strategies for the writer's notebook.* Portland, ME: Stenhouse.

Calkins, L. (1994). *The art of teaching writing.* Portsmouth, NH: Heinemann.

Fountas, I., & Pinnell, G. (2001). *Guiding readers and writers Grades 3-6: Teaching comprehension, genre, and content literacy.* Portsmouth, NH: Heinemann.

Graves, D. (1994). *A fresh look at writing*. Portsmouth, NH: Heinemann.

Kingery, E. (2000). Teaching metacognitive strategies to enhance higher level thinking in adolescents. In P. Linder (Ed.), *Literacy at a new horizon*, 22 Yearbook of the College Reading Association (pp. 74–86). Commerce, TX: College Reading Association.

Rhodes, L., & Shanklin, N. (1993). *Windows into literacy: Assessing learners K–8*. Portsmouth, NH: Heinemann.

Rosaen, C. (1990). Improving Writing opportunities in elementary classrooms. *The Elementary School Journal, 90*(4), 418–434.

Routman, R. (2005). *Writing essentials: Raising expectations and results while simplifying teaching*. Portsmouth, NH: Heinemann.

Tompkins, G. (2004). *Teaching writing: Balancing process and product*. Upper Saddle River, NJ: Pearson Education.

Appendix B

Annotated Teacher Action Research Web Sites

These are Web sites that students in several sections of my graduate course, Inquiry Seminar, identified and collected as rich resources for learning about and conducting teacher action research.

Access Excellence: Let's Collaborate

http://www.accessexcellence.org/LC/

This site is useful for teachers who are new to action research. In addition to providing a brief overview of Teacher Action Research (TAR), it provides a guideline for selecting a research project and takes readers through the initial steps: (1) deciding on a focus, (2) developing a plan to gain insights, (3) analyzing data by looking at patterns or themes, and (4) reporting what one has learned. Also, the site emphasizes the importance of starting with a general idea. Finally, this site gives several examples of action research studies that have already been done by teachers.

Action Evaluation Research Institute

http://www.aepro.org

This Web site deals with action evaluation research, which is a method of evaluation that focuses on defining, monitoring, and assessing success. This evaluation approach has two key components: participation and reflexivity. Participation means that all stakeholders engage in the process from the beginning, articulating and negotiating their goals, values, and proposed action plans. Reflexivity means that all participants function as "reflective practitioners" together, reflecting and examining the interaction of goals, values, and activities. These reflections are done systematically and continuously during the project. A Web-based database and discussion forum, which is designed to sustain the reflective process, facilitate the process. However, regular ongoing and face-to-face dialogue and reflection are essential.

Action Research at Queen's University

http://educ.queensu.ca/~ar/

This Queen's University Web site is an internally based page that focuses mostly on the papers of graduate students and faculty. The sections that link to outside sources, such as American Educational Research Association (AERA) papers, are limited, with only one or two links per section. However, for the narrow scope of action research topics that are covered, the articles and cited sources are accurate and comprehensive.

ActionResearch.Net

http://www.bath.ac.uk/~edsajw/

This is a British Web site that gives some introductory information on action research. It defines action research as well as what it calls a living education theory approach to action research. It defines this as an approach to action research in which individuals produce accounts or explanations for their own learning. This Web site also includes a selection of theses for visitors to read, as well as multimedia presentations of action research findings and links to other action research sites. This Web site is aimed primarily at students at Bath University, but it might be an interesting site for

people doing research in the United States because it gives a European perspective.

Action Research Network

http://actionresearch.altec.org

This Web site is a helpful resource for teachers and those in the process of getting their degrees in education. It contains many features, including a brief outline and definition of education action research. The site is a useful tool for teachers to share their research and view the research of others. Teachers can log on to the site and use a template to enter and track their research. The site also provides a search engine which anyone visiting the site can use to find research by author's name, grade level, level of student achievement, method of intervention, school specifications, and research problem. It gives a clear sense of the current topics in action research.

Action Research Resources, Southern Cross University

http://www.scu.edu.au/schools/gcm/ar/arhome.html

This site, sponsored by Southern Cross University in Australia, is a heavily trafficked discussion site as well as a reference library. It includes an in-depth discussion of what action research is and why it is useful. It also includes a full list of action research articles and books, including those still in progress, as well as a library of theses and dissertations on the subject. There are also a significant number of discussion boards and mailing lists for those interested in discussing and debating action research with others in the community. Unique to this site is a 14-week correspondence course about action research, called Areol, which is offered over e-mail as a public service.

Center for Applied Linguistics (CAL) Digest

http://www.cal.org/resources/digest/0308donato.html

This site takes a scholarly approach to action research by basing its definition on those of several published action researchers. The site highlights the difference between a deductive approach, which focuses on implementation of an action plan, and an inductive approach, which focuses on planning for action. The site provides an example of action research in an experimental elementary school Spanish program, which highlights the features of action research.

Teacher Research at George Mason University

http://gse.gmu.edu/research/tr/

This site is extensive and informative; it gives readers a history of action research and explains the differences between this type of research and traditional educational research. The site explains the processes one must go through to conduct action research. It takes readers through the entire research process, beginning with formulating a question and ending with publication. The site also includes a list of links to other action research sites.

Educational Action Research Journal

http://www.tandf.co.uk/journals/titles/09650792.asp

This London-based Web site highlights an international journal that connects research to practice. One of its appeals is that it is concerned with "exploring the unity between education research and practice." Such studies are valuable because readers can gather ideas from different educational settings and experiences that can then be applied worldwide. The site provides examples of action research studies so viewers can see the latest topics of interest, different formats of how research is presented, and how research and practice are related. Viewers can scroll through the journals and read one-paragraph summaries of all the entries contained in the journal. Links to full articles are also provided if viewers want to read further. The journal is published four times a year.

Education as Inquiry

http://www.lupinworks.com/ar/index.html

This Web site has good reflective pieces by teachers who have done action research. These teachers found themselves frustrated by a situation in their classrooms and wanted to try to change the situation. Reflective pieces by teachers describe trying different strategies, reflecting, and collecting data on their positive and negative outcomes; this is a valuable form of action research.

Inquiry Units/iLabs

http://www.inquiry.uiuc.edu

This Web site, developed by the University of Illinois at Urbana-Champaign, centers on teacher inquiry and defines inquiry for researchers. The focus of the site is the 3,000-plus inquiry units that are available to researchers. These units involve research that has been previously done and are available for current teachers and students to use as background information or confirmation for their own research. The site also provides chat rooms and the ability to communicate with other member researchers. This interactive, shared capability is valuable for the teacher-researcher. In addition, the site provides assessment activities that can be used in the classroom as research is continuing. This is a particularly important capability, as it affords teacher-researchers the ability to test their theories and hypotheses in the classroom as research progresses to validate or refute the work.

Madison Metropolitan School District

http://www.madison.k12.wi.us /sod/car/carhomepage.html

This is an excellent Web site developed by the Madison Metropolitan School District in Wisconsin. The Madison District has been involved in action research since the early 1990s and therefore has a wealth of knowledge about the implementation and impact of actual research projects. The site includes basic ideas of how to approach a project and problems that may be encountered during a project. The best information on this site is contained in its wealth of documented projects. There are accounts of action research projects that can be searched through the criteria of grade level, data collection methods, and study descriptors. These abstracts provide a wealth of information about how to approach a

project. They can also stimulate ideas about what kinds of questions to propose for new projects.

Multicultural Pavilion

http://www.edchange.org/mul ticultural/tar.html

This Web site gives readers a brief overview and description of teacher action research, but more important, it looks at it through the scope of equity and multicultural education. The authors of this site believe that TAR is an effective tool for promoting equity within our schools. The authors feel that TAR works on an individual level as well as public, noting the transformative nature of TAR. In addition, this site provides an actual account of TAR at work and gives useful strategies for initiating action research in our schools.

The National Health Museum: Access Excellence

http://www.accessexcellence. org/LC/TL/AR/

This is an excellent starter site. It gives an overview of the teacher-as-researcher concept, tips on how to perform TAR correctly, examples of ongoing research, online resources for further information including a list of e-mail discussion groups teachers can join, access to a discussion board, and two indices that can be searched for further information.

Networks–Online Journal for Teacher Research

http://journals.library.wisc.edu/ index.php/networks

This is the Web site for *Networks*, the first online journal for teacher research. The site provides direct access to the current and previous issues of the journal, which contains original research projects conducted by classroom teachers, book reviews, works-in-progress, and discussions on current issues. It also provides a link to Research in News, a site that contains information regarding grants for conducting teacher action research for Canadian teachers. The site has a links section that provides links to Web sites related to various educational issues.

Project Site Support

http://www.sitesupport.org/actionresearch/

This site was developed by Johns Hopkins University and provides a brief summary of action research and its history. The site was created as a supplement to an education course. The summary of action research is clear and concise, and it provides helpful downloadable files that one may incorporate into an action research evaluation journal. The site is ideal for someone who wants to implement quickly some tools of action research.

Research for Action

http://www.researchforaction.org/

Research for Action is a non-profit, Philadelphia-based organization whose goal is to reform Philadelphia public schools. The Web site evaluates factors such as staff, parent, and student involvement in deciding what works best for different communities. A weakness of the site is that it does not specifically seek the opinion and experience of classroom teachers themselves.

Resource Papers in Action Research

http://www.scu.edu.au/schools/gcm/ar/arp/books.html

This Web site provides an updated list of recent books and articles on action research and related topics. It is especially helpful for planning the steps of action research. The authors update it frequently so that it provides some of the most current literature on action research that is available. Some of the books listed focus on methods used for action research, whereas others provide case examples that could prove helpful while brainstorming a topic for research.

Teaching Today

http://teachingtoday.glencoe.com/

Teaching Today is a subsidiary of the McGraw-Hill Publishing Company and is dedicated to providing secondary school teachers with practical classroom strategies. This site explains action research through the example of one teacher's experience with it. The site explains what action research is, why teachers should use it, and how one would conduct it in one's own classroom. Additional links are provided for further research on action research.

Teachers Network Leadership Institute

http://www.teachersnetwork.org/tnli/index.htm

The Institute's principles are based on "improving student achievement by bringing the teachers' voice to education policymaking," and by "teachers bringing their experience and expertise to current debates on education policy" through action research. On this site, there are a number of interesting and useful links, including: Where We Are, Our Growth and History, Impact of TNLI, Our Teacher

Research, Publications, and Readings and Resources. Another exceptional resource is a video on action research, which focuses on an example of how action research can be used to meet standards and improve class discussion. The professional development section is also particularly interesting, including completed research projects in both elementary and high school settings. There are also numerous other completed research projects on various topics, including: Curriculum Implementation, Classroom Management and School Culture, Assessment and Preparation for Assessment, Parent Involvement and Immigrant Engagement, and Policy and Practice. The site is fairly easy to navigate.

UCERC Collaborative Partners

http://ucerc.edu/teacherre search/teacherresearch.html

UCERC has composed a collection of journal articles that deal with the spectrum of issues surrounding teacher action research. The site is helpful for those doing scholarly work on the subject of TAR. The site is designed for easy navigation; article abstracts have links immediately below them. The full text of some articles is available from the Web site, while others must be ordered.

Appendix C

Curriculum and Instruction Web Sites

These curriculum and instruction Web sites were collected and annotated by students in my graduate course, Secondary Curriculum and Instruction. They identified Web sites that would assist them in their teaching internships and in addressing subject matter content in conducting teacher research studies.

The Academy of American Poets

http://www.poets.org

This site provides a complete anthology of English-language poets, with biographies, sample poems, and even readings of poems. The site also has lesson plans, forums for discussion, and a host of educationally oriented materials. News about poetry events and awards is updated frequently.

Artcyclopedia

http://www.artcyclopedia.com

This site is a helpful resource for history teachers. Teachers can obtain an electronic copy of a painting, photo, or other form of visual art relating to a time period or theme in history.

Best of History Web Sites

http://www.besthistorysites .net/LessonPlans.shtml

This site is useful for helping history teachers design interesting lesson plans for subjects students may consider mundane. There are links to more than 1,000 history content-related Web sites. Each link has a detailed annotation so one can easily identify if a link would be of interest. The side tool bar is organized into different areas of history, including Prehistory, Ancient/ Biblical, Medieval, U.S. History, Early Modern European, 20th Century, World War Two, and Art History. There are also links for general historical resources and maps.

Classroom Connect

http://corporate.classroom.com/

This Web site connects to hundreds of other sites on all different subjects. It also has options to get in touch with other teachers to discuss lesson plans and subject matter. This site can help a teacher research historical matters during the lesson planning process.

Daily Grind

http://ahighcall.blogspot.com/

The Daily Grind is a blog created by a teacher about his teaching experiences. It has sections for other teachers to comment on his experiences and his opinions on pedagogy. It also has links to other teachers' blogs. Having a blog relieves teachers' isolation and allows teachers to receive advice on teaching outside of their political and geographic location. The Web site is helpful for new teachers as well as experienced teachers.

Dave's ESL Café

http://www.eslcafe.com/

This page is sponsored by institutions that are engaged in improving teacher skills and granting TEFL (Teaching English as a Foreign Language) certificates. The Web site is well-organized and is intended for both students and teachers. The main page has three major links: Stuff for Teachers, Stuff for Students, and Stuff for Everyone. The Teachers link has information on job opportunities and general lesson plans appropriate for all student levels. The Students link has quizzes, grammar activities, and pronunciation activities.

Ed Helper

http://www.edhelper.com/

This site is helpful for both teachers and students and is focused primarily on English content. Teachers can find many lesson activities as well as worksheets. Students can use the page to practice their English. The site also offers support to students with other subjects, including math, science, geography, social studies, and health. Activities offered on the site are appropriate for any grade level. Teachers can also use the page to make word puzzles and graphs.

Education Development Center

http://main.edc.org/

For more than 40 years, EDC has built bridges among research, policy, and practice. It manages 335 projects in 50 countries, including projects on early child development, K–12 education, health promotion, workforce preparation, community development, learning technologies, and basic and adult education.

Education Index

http://www.educationindex.com/history/

This Web site is a compilation of historical resources on the Internet. It has links to Web sites that are applicable to any subject matter and is extremely comprehensive. The Web site is a good starting place to search for specialized knowledge and materials to add to lectures and presentations.

Education-World

http://www.education-world.com

This site has numerous lesson plan ideas from other teachers. Most of the lesson plans are geared for younger students, but with some work, they can be modified for secondary school students. While most of the lesson plan ideas are intended for history teachers, teachers of other subjects will still find the site helpful.

Educator Learning Center

http://www.educatorlearningcenter.com

This Web site includes tools and materials to better prepare students for the classroom. It also contains articles about everyday issues faced by teachers and lesson plans categorized by content area and age range.

Facing History

http://www.facinghistory.org/

This Web site is for the curriculum, "Facing History and Ourselves." The curriculum is designed to examine history and human behavior, using the Holocaust as the main focus. However, the curriculum also discusses oppression and genocide throughout history. The Web site provides access to numerous documents, lessons, and unit plans.

Fordham University Internet History Sourcebooks Project

http://www.fordham.edu/halsall/

This Web site designed by Fordham University provides educators with a collection of historical sourcebooks. The three main areas of history for which the site provides documents are ancient history, medieval history, and modern history. The site also provides some specific sourcebooks on African history, Asian history, global history, Indian history, Islamic history, Jewish history, and women's history. Theme sourcebooks of travelers' accounts and legal history are also available. The site's bibliography is extensive and serves as additional research materials for teachers. Despite being extensive and detailed, the site's sections are well-outlined and easy to navigate.

Google Earth

http://earth.google.com/

Google Earth is a free application that can be downloaded and then used in conjunction with an online community. Google Earth is a collection of satellite images, creating an atlas of the Earth that can be used in presentations. For example, history students can tour a series of Civil War battle sites or countries affected by the Napoleonic wars.

Historical Text Archive

http://www.historicaltextarchive.com

This Web site has numerous documents appropriate for a history class. The site also has links to other information, such as videos and books. Although the site is not intended specifically for teachers, they will undoubtedly find its resources helpful.

I Love Teaching

http://www.iloveteaching.com

This Web site is especially useful for student teachers and new teachers. Notable sections include the "Education Majors and Student Teachers" and the "Classroom

Management" sections. The "Getting a Teaching Job" section provides extensive lists of possible interview questions and what one should include in a portfolio. The site is not run by a major company, and it provides sound and reassuring advice.

Lesson Plans and Resources for Social Studies Teachers

http://www.csun.edu/~hcedu 013/index.html

This Web site is intended for social studies and history teachers. It contains links to lesson plans, unit plans, and thematic units.

Lewis and Clark

http://www.pbs.org/lewisand clark/

This is an interactive Web site about Lewis and Clark's exploration in search of the Northwest Passage. On each page, the reader is given a description of the trip at a certain geographical point and then asked to make a decision about the group's next move. This Web site would be useful at the end of a unit or lesson, after students have a strong understanding of the journey, because the interactive decisions students are required to make require thorough knowledge.

Library of Congress American Memory

http://www.memory.loc.gov

This is the Web site for the American Memory Project by the Library of Congress. It provides free access to historical images, maps, documents, and audio and video clips from American history. Most of the documents on the site are primary documents. The main page has

a list of topics to explore including African American history, presidents, immigration, and American expansion. The Web site provides pictures of actual sources, such as photographs of letters by former presidents.

National Council of Teachers of English

http://www.ncte.org

This is the homepage of the National Council of Teachers of English and is a resource specifically for English teachers. It offers numerous resources for teaching skills, assessment, working with English Language Learners, and conventions. A section entitled "Issues" discusses current issues such as No Child Left Behind. This Web site is a resource for teachers to examine what others think about education issues. Some aspects require a membership.

National Public Radio

http://www.npr.org/

This Web site is helpful for finding media that can be used as teaching tools. The site offers video tools for sale. Additionally, the Web site has audio interviews that teachers can download for free and incorporate into lesson plans.

onestopenglish

http://www.onestopenglish .com/

This site is especially useful for English teachers and ELL students. Its resources are appropriate for all grades and include sample lesson plans, activities, and worksheets. Teachers can register for free sources and receive materials directly to their e-mail account. Additional links give practical suggestions to teachers, such as how to teach with minimal sources. There are also links suggesting books teachers should incorporate into lessons and links students can access to practice their English. Adult language learners can also take exercises targeted for specific content areas, such as phrases and verbs.

Open Directory Project
http://dmoz.org

This Web site offers a large variety of Web resources for language arts classrooms, including lesson plans, reading tests, methods for music inclusion, and ELL activities and worksheets. There is a convenient search feature that allows for searching of a specific work or topic. Distinct links allow readers to be relocated to the specific lesson or resources for which they are looking.

PBS Teacher Source
http://www.pbs.org/teacher source/siteguide

This site has an array of resources by curricular subject, topic, and grade level. It offers in-depth online professional development through PBS TeacherLine. The site also includes details on PBS station outreach activities in the community as well as tips on how to effectively teach with technology. Interdisciplinary teaching suggestions are also posted on the site.

Purdue University
Online Writing Lab
http://www.owl.english.pur due.edu

This is a helpful site for teachers who are working with ELL students. The site includes online journals, online resources, and annotated bibliographies for ESL instructors. There are numerous handouts for ELL students, such as handouts explaining difficult English grammar concepts. Examples of handouts include "Adjective vs. Adverb" and "Verbals: Gerunds, Participles and Infinitives." One of the site's best features is an e-journal for ESL teachers entitled "Teaching English with Technology," which incorporates the Internet, computers, and various other technologies into academic agendas. Sample lesson plans, Web sites, and reviews are also included in the site.

ReadWriteThink
http://www.readwritethink.org

This site is a helpful resource when thinking of lesson ideas. The site includes a number of lesson plans for all ages, which can be easily modified to suit individual classrooms. A helpful feature of the site is a thorough student materials index. The lesson plans offered on the site are notably innovative.

Shakespeare's Globe Theatre
http://www.shakespeares-globe.org/

This Web site is invaluable when teaching Shakespeare. In addition to lots of educational materials and opportunities for conversing with actors or others in the Royal Shakespeare Company, this Web site provides excellent visual resources for understanding the Globe Theatre. This site has virtual 3-D tours as well as conventional photographs. It is an excellent visual archive.

Special Needs Ontario Window

http://snow.utoronto.ca/best/accomodate/

This site focuses on strategies to assist students with special needs. It includes strategies for helping students with language problems, students with learning disabilities, students who are slow learners, and students who are gifted. Behaviors are listed for each category of student along with classroom strategies aimed at accommodating special needs. Specific areas, including mathematics, test-taking, and social skills, are included in each category.

Teachers.Net

http://www.teachers.net

This very comprehensive Web site contains more than 3,500 lesson plans. The site also has a classified section, where one can look throughout the country for teaching positions. Users can post teaching materials for sale, scan tutor ads, and read evaluations about where to buy good inexpensive software for classrooms. In addition, the site has chat rooms and forums broken down by subject area, grade level, and interest group. While much of the site is geared for younger grades, it does have a number of links for secondary grade teachers.

Teachers.com

http://www.teachers.org (The URL "www.teachers.org" is correct for Teachers.com. The URL "www.teachers.com" leads to an insurance site.)

This Web site is an excellent Web site for those who are concerned with student equity. This Web site is very comprehensive, giving many full-length articles in the "Equity Index," such as identifying seven principles for instructional design in which all students thrive and achieve excellence. There are various examples of alternative assessments, all with rubrics. In addition, there is a link to QuizStar, a free site in which teachers can manage the quizzes from all of their classes in one contained place.

Teaching Methods
Web Resources

http://www.mhhe.com/socscience/education/methods/resources.html

This site is pertinent to all content area teachers. It offers a plethora of resources for content area teaching as well as strategies for covering curriculum guidelines. The homepage is dedicated to developing teaching methods and offers a link for subject area-specific Web sources. The site is especially helpful for first-year teachers who need to develop teaching style, curriculum, classroom management, lesson planning, and assessment.

Teaching Today

http://teachingtoday.glencoe.com/

This Web site is a pedagogy-based site, focusing on teaching using a standards-based approach. It offers strategies and lessons that will help teachers meet standards. The Web site offers a subset of topics in the left margin in which one can search by topic, find other Web resources, and look up teaching tips. It offers teaching tips for each week, including tips on cultural diversity.

U.S. Department of Labor, Bureau of Statistics

http://stats.bls.gov

This Web site details the conditions, training, qualifications, and additional resources needed to work as a teacher in different levels. This Web site is helpful in outlining for prospective teachers what they may expect from their future profession.

Voices of the Shuttle

http://www.vos.ucsb.edu

Launched in 1994 by the University of California, Santa Barbara, as a collection of static Web pages, VoS has now been rebuilt as a database that serves humanities content dynamically on the Web. Unlike major university databases, which require subscriptions, VoS allows teachers or students to search its contents for free. Students might be intimidated by the intellectual rigor of the site, but for more advanced research projects, it is excellent, and teachers can use it for their own professional development in humanities-related content areas.

WhippleHill

http://www.whipplehill.com

Whipplehill is a Web development company that provides software customized to meet the marketing and administrative needs of independent schools. It can provide scheduling, grade book, and homework site software as well as host Web pages for teachers. The company also handles Registrars. The cost may be prohibitive for many schools.

Wikipedia

http://en.wikipedia.org/wiki/Main_Page

Wikipedia is an online encyclopedia that provides many entries that exceed traditional encyclopedias in depth and thoughtfulness as well as many that are just a few sentences. Articles may contain extensive media on subjects, including pictures, music, video, and animations. All media used in the articles are free for reproduction. Articles also contain links to other nonprofit Wikipedia foundation projects, including the Wiktionary (dictionary and thesaurus), Wikisource (a free online library), Wikibooks (textbooks and manuals), and Wikiquotes (collection of quotations). The collection of resources is helpful in assembling engaging PowerPoint presentations for students. Be aware in using this resource that it is not entirely trustworthy: Anyone may add, delete, or change an entry; entries are not peer reviewed; and there is only the most cursory oversight of entries.

2Learn

http://www.2learn.ca

This Web site is the winner of the 2004 NSDC Award for Exemplary Use of Technology for Staff Development. It is an excellent asset for teachers who are technologically impaired. This site includes a glossary of technical education jargon to help users find meaning in current buzzwords such as "authentic learning" and "empowering students." There is a helpful section on multimedia teacher tools which explains how to incorporate new technologies to better classrooms. The site is also helpful for Language Arts classrooms because it includes sections on the writing process, different types of compositions, and skill builders for students.

References

Abramson, P. R. (1992). *A case for case studies*. Newbury Park, CA: Sage.

Adelman, C. (1993). Kurt Lewin and the origins of action research. *Educational Action Research, 1*(1), 7–24.

Adelman, C., Kemmis, S., & Jenkins, D. (1980). Rethinking case study: Notes from the second Cambridge conference. In H. Simon (Ed.), *Towards a science of the singular* (pp. 45–61). Norwich, UK: University of East Anglia, Centre for Applied Research in Education.

Airasian, P. W., Gullickson, A. R., Hahn, L., & Farland, D. (1995). *Teacher self-evaluation: The literature in perspective*. Kalamazoo: Western Michigan University, Center for Research on Educational Accountability and Teacher Evaluation.

Altrichter, H. (1993). The concept of quality in action research: Giving practitioners a voice in educational research. In M. Schratz (Ed.), *Qualitative voices in educational research* (pp. 40–55). London: Falmer Press.

Anderson, C. S. (1982). The search for school climate. *Review of Educational Research, 32*(3), 368–420.

Anderson, E. S., Jackson, A., Wailoo, M. P., & Peterson, S. A. (2003). Successful parent researchers in child care project. *Journal of Reproductive and Infant Psychology, 21*(2), 125–128.

Anderson, G. L., Herr, K., & Nihlen, A. S. (2007). *Studying your own school: An educator's guide to practitioner action research*. Thousand Oaks, CA: Corwin Press.

Anderson, R. C. (1993). *Voices of change: A report of the clinical schools project*. (ERIC Document ED 353252)

Angus, B. B. (2003, March 1–7). Discovering action research: The evolution of my research question. *Networks: An On-Line Journal for Teacher Research, 6*(1). Retrieved July 4, 2008, from http://jour nals.library.wisc.edu/index.php/ networks/article/view/97/98

Armstrong, F., & Moore, M. (Eds.). (2004). *Action research for inclusive education: Changing places, changing practices, changing minds*. London: Routledge Falmer.

Atkin, J. M. (1989). Can educational research keep pace with educational reform? *Phi Delta Kappan, 71*(3), 200–205.

Atweh, B., Kemmis, S., & Weeks, P. (Eds.). (1998). *Action research in practice: Partnerships for social justice in education*. London: Routledge.

Avery, C. (1990). Learning to research/researching to learn. In M. Olson (Ed.), *Opening the door to classroom research*. Newark, DE: International Reading Association.

Ayers, W. (2001). *To teach: The journey of a teacher*. New York: Teachers College Press.

Back, L. (2001, April 24). A write off. *Guardian Education*, pp. 30–33.

Bailey, K. J., & Rios, H. (2005). Bully prevention. *Networks: An Online Journal for Teacher Research, 8*(1), 1–7.

Bambino, D. (2002).Critical friends. *Educational Leadership, 59*(6), 25–27.

Bangs, J. (1998). "Yes, but. . . ." *Improving Schools, 1*(1), 20–21.

Barlow, D. H., Hayes, S. C., & Nelson, R. O. (1984). *The scientist practitioner: Research and accountability in clinical and educational settings*. New York: Pergamon.

Barnard, N. (1999, September 17). Teacher panel to block irrelevant research. *Times Educational Supplement*, p. 14.

Barrett, F. J., & Fry, R. E. (2005). *Appreciative inquiry: A positive approach to building cooperative capacity*. Chagrin Falls, OH: Taos Institute.

Barritt, L., Beekman, T., Bleeker, H., & Mulderij, K. (1985). *Researching educational practice*. Grand Forks: University of North Dakota, North Dakota Study Group on Evaluation.

Barth, R. (2001). *Learning by heart*. San Francisco: Jossey-Bass.

Bassey, M. (1999). *Case study research in educational settings*. Philadelphia: Open University Press.

Battaglia, C. (1995). Confused on a higher level about more important things. In S. E. Nofke & R. B. Stevenson (Eds.), *Educational action research: Becoming practically critical*. New York: Teachers College Press.

Battaglia, C. F. (1996). Active voice. *Teaching and Change, 4*(1), 90–92.

Beattie, M. (1995). *Constructing professional knowledge in teaching: A narrative of change and development*. New York: Teachers College Press.

Bednarz, S. W. (2002). Using action research to implement the National Geographic standards: Teachers as researchers. *Journal of Geography, 101,* 103–111.

Belenky, M. F., Clinchy, B. M., Goldberger, N. R., & Tarule, J. M. (1986). *Women's ways of knowing: The development of self, voice, and mind*. New York: Basic Books.

Benne, K. D., Bradford, L., Gibb, J. R., & Lippitt, R. C. (Eds.). (1975). *The laboratory method and application*. Palo Alto, CA: Stanford University Press.

Berliner, D. C. (2002). Educational research: The hardest science of all. *Educational Research, 31*(8), 18–20.

Berry, B., Boles, K., Edens, K., Nissenholtz, A., & Tractman, R. (1996). *Inquiry and professional development schools: A working paper prepared for NCREST*. New York: Teachers College Press.

Biel, A., Eek, D., Garling, T., & Gustafson, M. (Eds.). (2008). *New issues and paradigms on social dilemmas*. New York: Springer.

Biesta, G. (2007). Bridging the gap between educational research and educational practice: The need for critical distance. *Educational Research and Evaluation, 13*(3), 295–301.

Black, S. (2006, July). Students as researchers. *American School Board Journal, 193*(7).

Bluedorn, A. D., Kaufman, C. J., & Lane, P. M. (1992). How many things do you like to do at once? An introduction to mono-chronic and polychronic time. *The Academy of Management Executive, 6*(4), 17–26.

Boardman, A. G., Arguelles, M. E., Vaughn, S., Hughes, M. T., & Klinger, J. (2005). Special education teachers' views of research-based practices. *The Journal of Special Education, 39*(3), 168–180.

Bochner, A. (1981). Forming warm ideas. In C. Wilder-Mott & J. Weakland (Eds.), *Rigor and imagination: Essays from the legacy of Gregory Bateson.* New York: Praeger.

Bogdan, R., & Biklen, S. (1982). *Qualitative research for education: An introduction to theory and methods.* Boston: Allyn & Bacon.

Bohm, D. (1996). *On dialogue.* London: Routledge.

Bok, D. (1987, May-June). The challenge to schools of education. *Harvard Magazine,* pp. 47–49, 79–80.

Boler, M. (1999). *Feeling power: Emotions and education.* New York: Routledge.

Bolgar, H. (1965). The case study method. In B. Wolman (Ed.), *Handbook of clinical psychology.* New York: McGraw-Hill.

Bolton, G. (2006). Narrative writing: Reflective enquiry into professional practice. *Educational Action Research, 14*(2), 203–218.

Book, C. L. (1996). Professional development schools. In J. Sikula, T. J. Buttery, & E. Guyton (Eds.), *Handbook of research on teacher education* (2nd ed., pp. 194–210). New York: Macmillan.

Brewer, J. D., & Hunter, A. (2005). *Foundations of multimethod research: Synthesizing styles.* Thousand Oaks, CA: Sage.

Briod, M. (1982). *School, society, and teacher work time.* Unpublished paper, Oakland University, School of Education and Human Services, Rochester, MI.

Britzman, D. (2003). *Practice makes practice: A critical study of learning to teach* (Rev. ed.). Albany: SUNY Press.

Broekkamp, H., & van Hout-Wolters, B. (2007). The gap between educational research and practice: A literature review, symposium, and questionnaire. *Educational Research and Evaluation, 13*(3), 203–220.

Brookfield, S. (1988). *Training educators of adults.* New York: Routledge.

Brookfield, S. (1995). *Becoming a critically reflective teacher.* San Francisco: Jossey-Bass.

Brookmyer, J. (2007). Findings from a survey of the CRESS Teacher Research Program. In *Windows on our classroom* (Vol. 12, pp. 123–133). Davis: University of California, Davis, School of Education, CRESS Center.

Brough, J. A., & Irvin, J. L. (2001). Parental involvement supports academic improvement among middle schoolers. *Middle School Journal, 32,* 52–61.

Brown, L., Henry, C., Henry, J., & McTaggart, R. (1982). Action research-notes on the National Seminar. In J. Elliott & D. Whitehead (Eds.), *Action research for professional development and the improvement of schooling.* Cambridge, UK: Institute of Education.

Brown, T., & Jones, L. (2001). *Action research and post-modernism: Congruence and critique.*

Philadelphia: Open University Press.

Bryden-Miller, M., Maguire, P., & McIntyre, A. (Eds.). (2004). *Traveling companions: Feminism, teaching, and action research.* Westport, CT: Praeger.

Bryk, A. S., & Schneider, B. (2002). *Trust in schools: A core resource for improvement.* New York: Russell Sage Foundation.

Buchmann, M. (1983). *Argument and conversation as discourse models of knowledge use.* East Lansing, MI: The Institute for Research on Teaching. (ERIC Document Reproduction Service No. ED 242493)

Buckingham, B. R. (1926). *Research for teachers.* New York: Silver, Burdett.

Buckingham, B. R. (1939). The value of research to the classroom teacher. In AERA and the Department of Classroom Teachers National Education Association, *The implications of research for the classroom teacher* (pp. 24–37). Washington, DC: National Education Association.

Calhoun, E. (1993). Action research: Three approaches. *Educational Leadership, 51*(2), 62–65.

Calhoun, E. F. (1994). *How to use action research in the self-renewing school.* Alexandria, VA: Association for Supervision and Curriculum Development.

Calhoun, E. F. (2002). Action research for school improvement. *Educational Leadership, 59,* 6.

Cambone, J. (1995). Time for teachers in school restructuring. *Teachers College Record, 96*(3), 512–543.

Cammarota, J., & Fine, M. (2008). *Revolutionizing education: Youth participatory action research in motion.* New York: Routledge.

Campbell, A., & Groundwater-Smith, S. (Eds.). (2007). *An ethical approach to practitioner research: Dealing with issues and dilemmas in action research.* New York: Routledge, Taylor, & Francis.

Campbell, D. T., & Stanley, J. C. (1963). *Experimental and quasi-experimental designs for research.* Chicago: Rand McNally.

Campbell, K. H. (2004). *Beginning teachers as researchers: Developing knowledge for teaching through classroom inquiry.* Unpublished doctoral dissertation, Portland State University, Portland, OR.

Capobianco, B. M., & Feldman, A. (2006). Promoting quality for teacher action research: Lessons learned from science teachers' action research. *Educational Action Research, 14*(4), 497–512.

Caracelli, V. J., & Greene, J. C. (Eds.). (1997). *Advances in mixed method evaluation: The challenges and benefits of integrating diverse paradigms* (New Directions for Program Evaluation, No. 74). San Francisco, CA: Jossey-Bass.

Carini, P. F. (1975). *Observation and description: An alternative methodology for the investigation of human phenomena.* Grand Forks: University of North Dakota Press.

Carini, P. F. (1986). *Prospect's documentary process.* Bennington, VT: Prospect School Center.

Carini, P. F. (2000). Prospect's descriptive processes. In M. Himley & P. Carini (Eds.), *From another angle: Children's strengths and school standards* (pp. 8–22). New York: Teachers College Press.

Carnegie Forum on Education and the Economy. (1986). *A nation prepared: Teachers for the 21st century.* New York: Author.

Caro-Bruce, C. (2000). *Action research facilitator's handbook.* Oxford,

OH: National Staff Development Council.

Caro-Bruce, C., Flessner, R., Klehr, M., & Zeichner, K. (Eds.). (2007). *Creating equitable classrooms through action research.* Thousand Oaks, CA: Corwin Press.

Carpenter, W. A. (2000). Ten years of silver bullets: Dissenting thoughts on educational reform. *Phi Delta Kappan, 82*(5), 383–389.

Carr, W. (1987). What is an educational practice? *Journal of Philosophy of Education, 21*(2), 163–175.

Carr, W., & Kemmis, S. (1986). *Becoming critical: Education knowledge and action research.* Philadelphia: Falmer Press.

Carson, T. R., & Sumara, D. (Eds.). (1997). *Action research as a living practice.* New York: Peter Lang.

Catelli, L. A., Padovano, K., & Costello, J. (2000). Action research in the context of a school-university partnership: Its value, problems, issues, and benefits. *Educational Action Research, 8*(2), 225–242.

Cazden, C. B., & Mehan, H. (1989). Principles from sociology and anthropology: Context, code, classroom, and culture. In M. C. Reynolds (Ed.), *Knowledge base for the beginning teacher* (pp. 47–55). New York: Pergamon Press.

Chandler, D., & Torbert, B. (2003). Transforming inquiry and action: Interweaving 27 flavors of action research. *Action Research, 1*(2), 133–152.

Chatterji, M. (2004). Evidence on "what works": An argument for extended-term mixed-method (ETMM) evaluation design. *Educational Researcher, 33*(9), 3–13.

Chittendon, E., Charney, G., & Kanevsky, R. (1978). Collaborative research: Implications for in-service development. In R. Edelfelt & E. Smith (Eds.), *Breakaway to multidimensional approaches* (pp. 49–59). Washington, DC: Association of Teacher Educators.

Clandinin, D. J., & Connelly, F. M. (1992). Teacher as curriculum maker. In P. W. Jackson (Ed.), *Handbook of research on curriculum* (pp. 363–401). New York: Macmillan.

Clandinin, D. J., Huber, J., Huber, M., Murphy, M. S., Orr, A. M., Pearce, M., & Steeves, P. (2006). *Composing diverse identities: Narrative inquiries into the interwoven life of children and teachers.* New York: Routledge.

Clarke, H., Egan, B., Fletcher, L., & Ryan, C. (2006). Creating case studies of practice through Appreciative Inquiry. *Educational Action Research, 14*(3), 407–422.

Clauset, K. H., Lick, D. W., & Murphy, C. U. (2008). *Schoolwide action research for professional learning communities.* Thousand Oaks, CA: Corwin Press.

Clay, W. C. (1998). *The evolution of an instructional coordinator's role: Action research for school improvement.* Doctoral dissertation, University of Missouri–St. Louis.

Clifford, G. J., & Guthrie, J. W. (1988). *Ed school: A brief for professional education.* Chicago: University of Chicago Press.

Cochran-Smith, M. (2002). Inquiry and outcomes: Learning to teach in the age of accountability. *Teacher Education and Practice, 15*(4), 12–34.

Cochran-Smith, M., & Lytle, S. L. (Eds.). (1993). *Inside/outside: Teacher research and knowledge.* New York: Teachers College Press.

Cochran-Smith, M., & Lytle, S. L. (1998). Teacher research: The question that persists. *International Journal of Leadership in Education, 1,* 19–36.

Cochran-Smith, M., & Lytle, S. L. (1999). Relationships of knowledge and practice: Teacher learning in communities. *Review of Research, 24,* 249–305.

Cole, A. L., & Knowles, J. G. (1996a). *The politics of epistemology and the self study of teacher education practices.* Paper presented at the International Conference: Self-Study in Teacher Education: Empowering Our Future. East Sussex, England.

Cole, A. L., & Knowles, J. G. (1996b). Reform and being "true to oneself": Pedagogy, professional practice, and the promotional process. *Teacher Education Quarterly, 23*(3), 109–126.

Collier, J. (1945). United States Indian Administration as a laboratory of ethnic relations. *Social Research, 12*(3), 265–303.

Collier, J. (1963). *From every zenith.* Denver, CO: Alan Swallow.

Committee on Research in Education and National Research Council. (2005). *Advancing scientific research in education* (L. Towne, L. L. Wise, & T. M. Winters, Eds.). Washington, DC: National Academies Press.

Connelly, F. M., & Clandinin, D. J. (1996). Teachers' professional knowledge landscapes: Teacher stories-Stories of teachers-School stories-Stories of school. *Educational Researcher, 19*(5), 2–14.

Connelly, F. M., & Clandinin, D. J. (2000). *Narrative inquiry: Experience and story in qualitative research.* San Francisco: Jossey-Bass.

Connelly, F. M., Clandinin, D. J., & He, M. F. (1997). Teachers' personal practical knowledge on the professional knowledge landscape. *Teaching and Teacher Education, 13*(7), 665–674.

Cook, T. (1998). The importance of mess in action research. *Educational Action Research, 6*(1), 93–108.

Cooper, M. (2008). *Reflection: Getting learning out of serving.* Miami: The Volunteer Action Center at Florida International University. Retrieved June 26, 2008, from http://www.fiu.edu/~time4chg/Library/reflect.html

Cooperrider, D. L., Sorenson, P. F., Whitney, D., & Yaeger, T. F. (2000). *Appreciative inquiry: Rethinking human organization toward a positive theory of change.* Champaign, IL: Stipes.

Cooperrider, D. L., & Srivastva, S. (1987). Appreciative inquiry in organizational life. In W. Pasmore & R. Woodman (Eds.), *Research in organization change and development* (pp. 129–169). Greenwich, CT: JAI Press.

Cooperrider, D. L., & Whitney, D. (1999). *Appreciative inquiry: Collaborating for change.* San Francisco, CA: Berrett-Koehler Communications.

Cooperrider, D. L., & Whitney, D. (2005). *Appreciative inquiry: A positive revolution in change.* San Francisco, CA: Berrett-Koehler.

Cooperrider, D. L., Whitney, D., & Stavros, J. M. (Eds.). (2003). *Appreciative inquiry handbook: The first in a series of AI workbooks for leaders of change.* Bedford Heights, OH: Lakeshore Communications.

Corbett, H. D., Dawson, J. A., & Firestone, W. A. (1984). *School context and school change.*

New York: Teachers College Press.

Corey, S. (1953). *Action research to improve school practices.* New York: Teachers College Press.

Covey, S. R. (1989). *The 7 habits of highly effective people: Powerful lessons in personal change.* New York: Simon & Schuster.

Crepps, S. (1999). Reading, writing, and mathematics in a fifth grade class. In *Windows on our classrooms.* Davis: University of California, Davis, School of Education, CRESS Center.

Creswell, J. W. (2003). *Research design: Qualitative, quantitative, and mixed approaches.* Thousand Oaks, CA: Sage.

Creswell, J. W., & Plano-Clark, V. L. (2007). *Designing and conducting mixed methods research.* Thousand Oaks, CA: Sage.

Cunningham, S. J., & Jones, M. (2005). *Autoethnography: A tool for practice and education* (ACM International Conference Proceeding Series, Vol. 94 archive). New York: ACM Press.

Cushman, K. (1998). How friends can be critical as schools make essential changes. *Horace, 14*(5).

Czamiawska, B. (2004). *Narratives in social science research.* Thousand Oaks, CA: Sage.

Dabish, D. (2001). From desks to a quest: Understanding the process of teacher research. *Networks: An Online Journal for Teacher Research, 4*(2). Retrieved June 11, 2008, from http://journals.library.wisc.edu/index.php/networks/article/view/37/42

Dadds, M. (1995). *Passionate enquiry and school development.* London: Falmer Press.

Damasio, A. (1994). *Descartes' error: Emotion, reason, and the human brain.* New York: G. P. Putnam's Sons.

Dana, N. F., & Yendol-Hoppey, D. (2008). *The reflective educator's guide to classroom research.* Thousand Oaks, CA: Corwin Press.

Daniels, L. Y. (1998). *Student teachers' use of action research in the classroom (behavior management).* Doctoral dissertation, University of Virginia.

Dantonio, M. (2001). *Collegial coaching: Inquiry into the teaching self* (2nd ed.). Bloomington, IN: Phi Delta Kappa.

Datta, L. (1990). *Case study evaluations* (Transfer paper 10.1.9). Washington, DC: U.S. General Accounting Office.

Davey, L. (1991). *The application of case study evaluations.* Washington, DC: U.S. Department of Education. (ERIC Clearinghouse on Tests, Measurement, and Evaluation, ED 338706)

Davis, S. H. (2007). Bridging the gap between research and practice: What's good, what's bad, and how can one be sure? *Phi Delta Kappan, 88*(8), 569–579.

Day, C. (1993). Reflection: A necessary but not sufficient condition for professional development. *British Educational Research Journal, 19*(1), 83–93.

Deal, T. E., & Peterson, K. D. (1998). *Shaping school culture: The heart of leadership.* San Francisco: Jossey-Bass.

De Marrais, K. B. (1998). *Inside stories: Qualitative research reflections.* Mahwah, NJ: Lawrence Erlbaum.

Denzin, N. (1984). *The research act.* Englewood Cliffs, NJ: Prentice Hall.

Denzin, N. K. (1989). *Interpretive interactionism.* Newbury Park, CA: Sage.

Denzin, N. K. (1997). *Interpretive ethnography: Ethnographic practices for the 21st century.* London: Sage.

Denzin, N., & Lincoln, Y. (1994). Entering the field of qualitative research. In N. Denzin & Y. Lincoln (Eds.), *Handbook of qualitative research* (pp. 1–18). Thousand Oaks, CA: Sage.

Depka, E. (2006). *The data guidebook for teachers and leaders.* Thousand Oaks, CA: Corwin Press.

de Sousa, R. (2003). Emotion. *Stanford encyclopedia of philosophy.* Retrieved from http://plato.stanford.edu/entries/emotion/

Dewey, J. (1929). *The sources of a science of education.* New York: Liverright.

Dewey, J. (1933). *How we think.* Boston: Houghton Mifflin Co.

Dinkelman, T. (2003). Self-study in teacher education: A means and ends tool for promoting reflective teaching. *Journal of Teacher Education, 54*(1), 3–16.

Donawa, W. D. (1998, May). *Friendship: An epistemological frame for narrative inquiry.* Paper presented at the Connections Conference sponsored by the University of Victoria, British Columbia, Faculty of Education.

Doyle, W. (1986). Classroom organization and management. In M. C. Wittrock (Ed.), *Handbook of research on teaching* (3rd ed., pp. 392–431). New York: Macmillan.

Durkheim, E. (1965). *The elementary forms of religious life.* New York: Free Press.

Durrant, J., & Holden, G. (2006). *Teachers leading change: Doing research for school improvement.* London: Paul Chapman.

Ebbutt, D. (2002). The development of a research culture in secondary schools. *Educational Action Research, 10*(1), 123–139.

Ebbutt, D., Robson, R., & Worrall, N. (2000). Educational research partnership: Differences and tensions between the professional cultures of practitioners in schools and researchers in higher education. *Teacher Development, 4*(3), 319–337.

Egan-Robertson, A., & Bloome, D. (Eds.). (1998). *Students as researchers of culture and language in their own communities.* Creskill, NJ: Hampton Press.

Eisenhart, M., & Howe, K. (1992). Validity in qualitative research. In M. LeCompte, W. Milroy, & J. Preissle (Eds.), *The handbook of qualitative research in education* (pp. 643–680). San Diego, CA: Academic Press.

Eisner, E. W. (1975). Curriculum development in Stanford's Kettering project: Recollections and ruminations. In J. Schaffarzich & D. H. Hampson (Eds.), *Strategies for curriculum development.* Berkeley, CA: McCutchan.

Eisner, E. (1985). *The educational imagination: On the design and evaluation of school programs.* New York: Macmillan.

Elliott, J. (1977). Developing hypotheses about classrooms from teachers' practical constructs: An account of the work of the Ford Teaching Project. *Interchange, 7*(2).

Elliott, J. (1991). *Action research for educational change.* Philadelphia: Open University Press/Milton Keynes.

Elliott, J. (2005). *Using narrative in social research: Qualitative and quantitative approaches.* Thousand Oaks, CA: Sage.

Elliott, J. (2006). *Reflecting where the action is: The selected works of John Elliott.* New York: Routledge.

Elliott, J., & Adelman, C. (1975). *Classroom action research*. Cambridge, UK: Cambridge Institute of Education, Ford Teaching Project.

Ellis, C., & Bochner, A. P. (2000). Autoethnography, personal narrative, reflexivity: Researcher as subject. In N. Denzin & Y. Lincoln (Eds.), *The handbook of qualitative research* (2nd ed., pp. 733–768). Thousand Oaks, CA: Sage.

Emery, F. E., & Trist, E. L. (1973). Re-evaluating the role of science. In F. E. Emery & E. L. Trist (Eds.), *Toward a social ecology*. New York: Plenum Press.

Ericson, F. (1986). Qualitative methods in research on teaching. In M. C. Wittrock (Ed.), *Handbook of research on teaching* (3rd ed., pp. 119–161). New York: Macmillan.

Ericson, F., & Gutierrez, K. (2002). Culture, rigor, and science in educational research. *Educational Researcher, 31*(8), 21–24.

Fals Borda, O. (2001). Participatory action research in social theory: Origins and challenges. In P. Reason & H. Bradbury (Eds.), *Handbook of action research: Participatory inquiry and practice* (pp. 27–37). Thousand Oaks, CA: Sage.

Feldman, A. (1993). *Conversation as methodology in collaborative action research*. Unpublished paper, University of Massachusetts, Amherst.

Feldman, A. (2002). Existential approaches to *action* research. *Educational Action Research, 10*(20), 233–251.

Feldman, A. (2003). Validity and quality in self-study. *Educational Researcher, 32*(3), 26–28.

Feldman, A. (2007). Validity and quality in *action* research. *Educational Action Research, 15*(1), 21–32.

Fendler, L. (2003). Teacher reflection in a hall of mirrors: Historical influences and political reverberations. *Educational Researcher, 32*(3), 16–25.

Fenstermacher, G. D. (1987). On understanding the connections between classroom research and teacher change. *Theory into Practice, 26*(1), 3–7.

Fielding, M., & Bragg, S. (2003). *Students as researcher: Making a difference*. Cambridge: Pearson.

Fieleke, M. (2002). *How teachers talk about teaching: A phenomenological, phenomenographical, narrative, and heuristic study*. Unpublished doctoral dissertation, Boston College.

Firestone, W., & Louis, K. S. (1999). Schools as cultures. In J. Murphy & K. S. Louis (Eds.), *Handbook of research on educational administration* (2nd ed.). San Francisco: Jossey-Bass.

Fischer, D., Mercado, M., Morgan, V., Robb, L., Sheehan-Carr, J., & Torres, M. N. (2000). The curtain rises: Teachers unveil their processes of transformation in doing classroom inquiry. *Networks: An On-Line Journal for Teacher Research, 3*(1), 1–15.

Fishman, S. M., & McCarthy, L. (2000). *Unplayed tapes: A personal history of collaborative teacher research*. New York: Teachers College Press.

Fox, S. A. (1971). A *practical image of the practical*. Paper presented to the AERA Annual Meeting.

Frank, C. (1999). *Ethnographic eyes: A teacher's guide to classroom observation*. Thousand Oaks, CA: Corwin Press.

Freeman, D. (1998). *Doing teacher research: From inquiry to understanding.* New York: Heinle & Heinle.

Freire, P. (1970). *Pedagogy of the oppressed.* New York: Seabury Press.

Freire, P. (1973). *Education for critical consciousness.* New York: Seabury Press.

Frost, D., Durrant, J., Head, M., & Holden, G. (2000). *Teacher-led school improvement.* London: Routledge-Farmer.

Fry, R. (Ed.). (2002). *Appreciative inquiry and organizational transformation: Reports from the field.* Westport, CT: Quorum Books.

Fullan, M. (1993). Why teachers must become change agents. *Educational Leadership, 50,* 6.

Fullan, M. (1998). Leadership for the 21st century: Breaking the bonds of dependency. *Educational Leadership, 55*(7), 6–10.

Fullan, M., & Hargreaves, A. (1996). *What's worth fighting for in your school?* New York: Teachers College Press.

Gajewski, J. (1978). Wisdom of the practitioner. In *Communication Quarterly.* East Lansing, MI: Institute for Research on Teaching.

Gallagher, J. J. (2002). What next for OERI? *Education Week, 21,* 28, 52.

Gant, J., South, O., & Hansen, J. (1977). *Temporary systems.* Tallahassee, FL: Authors.

Gardner, H. (2002). The quality and qualities of educational research. *Education Week, 22*(1), 72.

Garmston, R., & Wellman, B. (1998, April). Teacher talk that makes a difference. *Educational Leadership,* pp. 30–34.

Gary, T. (2007). *Education and theory: Strangers in paradigms.* Maidenhead, Berkshire, England: Open University Press.

Gay, L. R., & Airasian, P. W. (2000). *Educational research: Competencies for analysis.* Upper Saddle River, NJ: Merrill.

Geertz, C. (1973). *The interpretation of cultures.* New York: Basic Books.

Geertz, C. (1983). *Local knowledge: Further essays in interpretive anthropology.* New York: Basic Books.

Gersti-Pepin, C. (2002). Magnet schools: A retrospective case study of segregation. *The High School Journal, 85*(3), 47–52.

Gibbons, L. C. (1997). *An action research study of middle grade students' perspectives about sustained silent reading.* Doctoral dissertation, University of Alabama.

Gibbs, J. C. (1979). The meaning of ecologically oriented inquiry in contemporary psychology. *American Psychologist, 34,* 127–144.

Gibson, R. (1985). Critical times for action research. *Cambridge Journal of Education, 15*(1), 59–64.

Giroux, H. A. (1989). *Schooling for democracy: Critical pedagogy in the modern age.* London: Routledge.

Giroux, H. A. (1997). *Pedagogy and the politics of hope: Theory, culture, and schooling: A critical reader.* Boulder, CO: Westview Press.

Glewwe, P., Kremer, M., Moulin, S., & Zitzewitz, E. (2004). Retrospective vs. prospective analyses of school inputs: The case of flip charts in Kenya. *Journal of Development Economics, 74*(1), 251–268.

Goldstone, M. J., & Shroyer, M. G. (2000). Teachers as researchers: Promoting effective science and mathematics teaching. *Teaching and Change, 7,* 327–346.

Goldwasser, M. (2004). *A guide for facilitating action research for* youth. Philadelphia, PA: Research for Action.

Good, C. V., Barr, A. S., & Scates, D. E. (1936). *The methodology of educational research.* New York: Appleton-Century.

Goodlad, J. I. (1977). What goes on in our schools? *Educational Researcher, 6*(3), 3–6.

Goodlad, J. (1994). The National Network for Educational Renewal. *Phi Delta Kappan, 75*(8), 632–638.

Goodlad, J. I., Klein, F., & Associates. (1970). *Behind the classroom door.* Worthington, OH: Jones.

Goodman, R. A., & Goodman, L. P. (1976). Some management issues in temporary systems: A study of professional development and manpower, the theater case. *Administrative Science Quarterly, 21*(3), 494–501.

Goodson, I. F. (1993). The devil's bargain: Educational research and the teacher. *Educational Policy Archives, 1*(3), 1–7.

Goodwin, D. R., Jr. (1999). *A qualitative study of the personal and professional growth of teachers involved in collaborative educational action research projects.* Doctoral dissertation, University of Illinois at Urbana.

Gore, J. M., & Zeichner, K. M. (1995). Connecting action research to genuine teacher development. In J. Smyth (Ed.), *Critical discourses on teacher development.* London: Cassell.

Goswami, D., & Stillman, P. R. (1987). *Reclaiming the classroom: Teacher research as an agency for change.* Portsmouth, NH: Heinemann.

Graham, P. A. (1978, February/March). Let's get together on educational research. *Today's Education,* pp. 57–63.

Grant, C. A., & Zeichner, K. M. (1984). On becoming a reflective teacher. In C. A. Grant (Ed.), *Preparing for reflective teaching* (pp. 54–68). Boston: Allyn & Bacon.

Green, T. D., Brown, A., & Robinson, L. (2008). *Making the most of the web in your classroom.* Thousand Oaks, CA: Corwin Press.

Greene, J. C., Caracelli, V. J., & Graham, W. F. (1989). Toward a conceptual framework for mixed evaluation designs. *Educational Evaluation and Policy Analysis, 11*(3), 255–274.

Griffin, G. A., Lieberman, A., & Jacullo-Noto, J. (1983). *Interactive research and development on schooling: Executive summary of the final report.* Austin: University of Texas, Research and Development Center for Teacher Education.

Griffiths, M. (1994). Autobiography, feminism, and the practice of action research. *Educational Action Research, 2*(1), 72.

Grimmett, P. P., & Erickson, G. L. (Eds.). (1988). *Reflection in teacher education.* New York: Teachers College Press.

Gross, R. R. (2002). Research-driven school improvement. *Principal Leadership, 2,* 35–40.

Grumet, M. (1988). *Bitter milk: Women and teaching.* Amherst: University of Massachusetts Press.

Grundy, S. (1994). Action research at the school level: Possibilities and problems. *Educational Action Research, 2*(1), 23–38.

Guba, E. (Ed.). (1990). *The paradigm dialogue.* Newbury Park, CA: Sage.

Guba, E. G., & Lincoln, Y. S. (1981). *Effective evaluation: Improving the usefulness of evaluation results through responsive and naturalistic approaches.* San Francisco: Jossey-Bass.

Habermas, J. (1971). *Knowledge and human interests.* Boston: Beacon Press.

Hall, B. (2001). I wish this were a poem of practices of participatory research. In P. Reason & H. Bradbury (Eds.), *Handbook of action research: Participative inquiry and practice* (pp. 171–178). London: Sage.

Hall, E. T. (1959). *The silent language.* Garden City, NY: Doubleday.

Hall, E. T., & Hall, M. R. (1987). *Hidden differences: Doing business with the Japanese.* Garden City, NY: Doubleday.

Hall, R.V., Cristler, C., Cranston, S. S., & Tucker, B. (1970). Teachers and parents as researchers using multiple baseline designs. *Journal of Applied Behavioral Analysis, 3*(4), 247–255.

Halsall, R. (Ed.). (1998). *Teacher research and school improvement.* Philadelphia: Open University Press.

Hamilton, M. L. (Ed.). (1998). *Reconceptualizing teaching practice: Self study in teacher education.* London: Falmer Press.

Hancock, D. R., & Algozzine, B. (2006). *Doing case study research: A practical guide for beginning researchers.* New York: Teachers College Press.

Handscomb, G., & MacBeath, J. (2003). *The research-engaged school.* Essex Forum for Learning, Research, and Inquiry (FLARE), Essex County Council, England.

Hansen, J. (1997). Researchers in our own classrooms: What propels teacher researchers? In D. Leu, C. Kinzer, & K. Hinchman (Eds.), *Literacies for the 21st century: Research and practice* (pp. 1–14). Chicago: National Reading Conference.

Hargreaves, A. (1994). *Changing teachers, changing times: Teachers' work and culture in the postmodern age.* New York: Teachers College Press.

Hargreaves, A. (1996). Revisiting voice. *Educational Researcher, 25*(1), 12–19.

Hargreaves, D. H. (1999). The knowledge-creating school. *British Journal of Educational Studies, 47*(2), 122–144.

Hargreaves, D. H. (2001). A capital theory of school effectiveness and improvement. *British Educational Research Journal, 27*(4), 487–503.

Harris, N. (1992). A philosophical basis for an Afrocentric orientation. *The Western Journal of Black Studies, 16*(3), 154–159.

Hart, A. W., Sorensen, N. B., & Naylor, K. (1992). Learning to lead: Reflective practice in preservice education. In F. Wendel (Ed.), *Leadership in the profession* (pp. 7–24). University Park, PA: University Council for Educational Administration.

Hart, C. (1998). *Doing a literature review: Releasing the social science imagination.* London: Sage.

Hawkins, D. (1974). *The informed vision: Essays on learning and human nature.* New York: Agathorn Press.

Heibert, J., Gallimore, R., & Stigler, J. W. (2002). A knowledge base for the teaching profession: What would it look like and how can we get one? *Educational Researcher, 31*(5), 3–15.

Heikkinen, L. T., Huttunen, R., & Syrjala, L. (2007). Action research as narrative: Five principles for validation. *Educational Action Research, 15*(1), 5–19.

Heikkinen, L. T., Kakkori, K., & Huttunen, R. (2001). This is my truth, tell me yours: Some aspects of action research quality in light of truth theories. *Educational Action Research, 9*(1), 22.

Hendricks, C. C. (2006). *Improving schools through action research: A comprehensive guide for educators.* Boston, MA: Allyn & Bacon.

Henry, R. (2003). *Leadership at every level: Appreciative inquiry in education.* Seattle, WA: New Horizons for Learning.

Henson, K. T. (1996). Teachers as researchers. In J. Sikula (Ed.), *The handbook of research on teacher education.* New York: Macmillan.

Henze, R., & Hauser, M. (1999). Exploring culture: A dialogue among teachers and anthropologists (Educational Practice Report 4, *Personalizing Culture Through Anthropological and Educational Perspectives*). Santa Cruz, CA: Center for Research on Education, Diversity, and Excellence.

Heron, J. (1996). *Co-operative inquiry: Research into the human condition.* London: Sage.

Heron, J., & Reason, P. (1997). A participatory inquiry paradigm. *Qualitative Inquiry, 3*(3), 274–294.

Hicks, E. (1999). *Ninety-five languages and several forms of intelligence.* New York: Peter Lang.

Himley, M., & Carini, P. F. (Eds.). (2000). *From another angle: Children's strengths and school standards.* New York: Teachers College Press.

Hingley, V. (2008). Action research diagrams. Retrieved August 24, 2008, from the Hospitality, Leisure, Sport and Tourism Network Web site: http://www.heacademy.ac.uk/hlst/resources/detail/resources/heinfe/Action_Research_Diagrams

Hitchcock, G., & Hughes, D. (1995). *Research and the teacher: A qualitative introduction to school-based research* (2nd ed.). New York: Routledge.

Hodgkinson, H. L. (1957). Action research—a critique. *Journal of Educational Sociology, 31,* 137–153.

Hollingsworth, S., & Cody, A. (1994). *Teacher research and urban literacy education: Lessons in a feminist key.* New York: Teachers College Press.

Holly, M. L., Arhar, J., & Kasten, W. (2005). *Action research for teachers: Traveling the yellow brick road.* Upper Saddle River, NJ: Pearson/Prentice Hall.

Holmes Group. (1986). *Tomorrow's teachers: A report of the Holmes Group.* East Lansing, MI: Author.

Holmes Group. (1990). *Tomorrow's schools: Principles for the design of professional development schools.* East Lansing, MI: Author.

Holmes Group. (1995). *Tomorrow's schools of education.* East Lansing, MI: Author.

hooks, b. (1994). *Teaching to transgress: Education as the practice of freedom.* New York: Routledge.

Howard, G. S. (1988). Science, values, and teleological explanations of human action. *Counseling and Values, 32*(2), 93–103.

Howe, K. (1988). Against the quantitative-qualitative incompatibility thesis or dogmas die hard. *Educational Researcher, 17*(8), 10–16.

Hubbard, R. S., & Power, B. M. (1993). Finding and framing a research question. In L. Patterson, C. M. Santa, K. G. Short, & K. Smith (Eds.), *Teachers are researchers: Reflection and action* (pp. 19–25). Newark, DE: International Reading Association.

Huberman, M. (1995). Networks that alter teaching: Conceptualizations, exchanges, and experiments. *Teachers and Teaching: Theory and Practice, 1*(2), 193–211.

Huling, L. L. (1982). *The effects on teachers of participation in an interactive research and development project.* Unpublished dissertation, Texas Tech University.

Hustler, D., Cassidy, A., & Cuff, E. C. (Eds.). (1986). *Action research in classrooms and schools.* London: Allen & Unwin.

Ianni, F. (1978). *Documentation as a process* (Teacher Corps National Conference Report). Washington, DC: U.S. Office of Education.

Jackson, P. W. (1968). *Life in classrooms.* New York: Holt, Rinehart and Winston.

Jacob, E. (1995). Reflective practice and anthropology in culturally diverse classrooms. *Elementary School Journal, 95*(5), 451–463.

Jacob, E., Johnson, B. K., Finley, J., Gurski, J. C., & Lavine, R. S. (1996, March). One student at a time: The cultural inquiry process. *Middle School Journal,* pp. 29–35.

Jalongo, M. R., & Isenberg, J. P. (1993). Teachers' stories: Reflections on teaching, caring, and learning. *Childhood Education, 69*(5), 260–261.

Jalongo, M. R., & Isenberg, J. P. (1995). *Teachers' stories: From personal narrative to professional insight.* San Francisco: Jossey-Bass.

James, P. (1999). Rewriting narratives of self: Reflections from an action research study. *Educational Action Research, 7*(1), 85–102.

Jamieson, C. (2000). Learning together: Transformative action research. *The Ontario Action Researcher, 3*(3), 1–6.

Janis, I. L., & Mann, L. (1977). *Decision making: A psychological analysis of conflict, choice, and commitment.* New York: Free Press.

Jeffrey, S. G. (1996). The transformative nature of action research. *Teaching and Change, 4*(1), 96–97.

Jeffs, T., Morrison, W. F., Messenheimer, T., Rizza, M. G., & Banister, S. (2003). A retrospective analysis of technological advances in special education. *Computers in the Schools, 20*(1/2), 129–152.

Jensen, J. L., & Rodgers, R. (2001). Cumulating the intellectual gold of case study research. *Public Administration Review, 61*(2), 236–246.

Jensen, P. J., & Kolb, D. A. (2002). Streams of meaning making in conversation. In A. C. Baker, P. J. Jensen, & D. A. Kolb (Eds.), *Conversational learning: An experiential approach to knowledge creation.* Westport, CT: Quorum Books.

Johnson, A. P. (2008). *A short guide to action research* (3rd ed.). Boston: Pearson/Allyn & Bacon.

Johnson, M., Munoz, V., & Street, E. (2003). *Building parents as researchers.* Washington, DC: Education Resources Information Service. (ERIC Document Reproduction Service No. ED 478210, pp. 1–12).

Johnson, R. B., & Onwuegbuzie, A. J. (2004). Mixed methods research: A research paradigm whose time has come. *Educational Researcher, 33*(7), 14–26.

Kanevsky, R. (1993). Descriptive review of a child: A way of knowing about teaching and learning. In M. Cochran-Smith & S. Lytle (Eds.), *Inside/outside: Teacher research and knowledge* (pp. 150–162). New York: Teachers College Press.

Kaplan, A. (1964). *The conduct of inquiry.* Scranton, PA: Chandler.

Kellett, M. (2005a). *Children as active researchers: A new research paradigm for the 21st century?* Paper written for the Economic

& Social Research Council National Centre for Research Methods.

Kellett, M. (2005b). *How to develop children as researchers: Step by step guidance to teaching the research process.* London: Sage.

Kember, D. (2000). *Action learning and action research: Improving the quality of teaching and learning.* London: Kogan Page.

Kemmis, S. (1988). Action research in retrospect and prospect. In S. Kemmis & R. McTaggart (Eds.), *The action research reader* (3rd ed., pp. 27–39). Geelong, Victoria: Deakin University Press.

Kemmis, S., & DiChiro, G. (1987). Emerging and evolving issues of action research praxis: An Australian perspective. *Peabody Journal of Education, 64*(3), 101–130.

Kemmis, S., & McTaggart, R. (1988). *The action research planner* (3rd ed.). Victoria, Australia: Deakin University.

Kemmis, S., & Wilkinson, M. (1998). Participatory action research and the study of practice. In B. Atweh, S. Kemmis, & P. Weeks (Eds.), *Action research in practice: Partnerships for social justice in education* (pp. 21–36). London: Routledge.

Kennedy, M. M. (1997). The connection between research and practice. *Educational Researcher, 26*(7), 4–12.

Kenway, C. A. (1997). *Conflict resolution for peaceful schools: The implementation of a conflict manager program as collaborative action research.* Doctoral dissertation, University of Alberta, Canada.

Killion, J., & Todnem, G. (1991). A process of personal theory building. *Educational Leadership, 48*(6), 14–17.

Kincheloe, J. L. (1991). *Teachers as researchers: Qualitative inquiry as a path to empowerment.* London: Falmer Press.

Kirsch, G. (1999). *Ethical dilemmas in feminist research.* Albany: State University of New York Press.

Kirst, M. (1982). How to improve schools without spending more money. *Phi Delta Kappan, 64*(1), 6–8.

Knowles, J. G., & Cole, A. L. (Eds.). (1996). Beginning professors and teacher education reform [Special issue]. *Teacher Education Quarterly, 23*(3).

Koch, S. (1959). Some trends in study I. In S. Koch (Ed.), *Psychology: A study of a science* (Vol. 3). New York: McGraw-Hill.

Kochendorfer, L. (1994). *Becoming a reflective teacher.* Washington, DC: National Education Association.

Kochendorfer, L. (1997). Types of classroom teacher research. *Teaching and Change, 4*(2), 157–173.

Kohli, W. (2000). Teaching in the danger zone: Democracy and difference. In D. Hursh & E. Ross (Eds.), *Democratic social education: Social studies for social change.* New York: Falmer Press.

Korthagen, F. A. J. (2007). The gap between research and practice revisited. *Educational Research and Evaluation, 13*(3), 303–310.

Krathwohl, D. R. (1998). *Methods of educational and social science research.* New York: Addison Wesley Longman.

Kuhlthau, C. C. (1993). *Seeking meaning: A process approach to library and information services.* Norwood, NJ: Ablex.

Kuhn, T. (1962). *The structure of scientific revolutions.* Chicago: University of Chicago Press.

Kyle, D. W., & Hovda, R. A. (Eds.). (1987a). The potential and practice of "action research" (Part I). *Peabody Journal of Education, 64*(2).

Kyle, D. W., & Hovda, R. A. (Eds.). (1987b). The potential and practice of "action research" (Part II). *Peabody Journal of Education, 64*(3).

Ladkin, D. (2004). The phenomenological roots of action research. *Action Research, 3*(1), 109–127.

Lagemann, E. C. (2000). *An elusive science: The troubling history of education research.* Chicago: University of Chicago Press.

Lather, P. (1986). Issues of validity in openly ideological research: Between a rock and a soft place. *Interchange, 17*(4), 63–84.

Lather, P. (1991). *Getting smart: Feminist research and pedagogy within the postmodern.* New York: Routledge.

Law, J. (2004). *After method: Mess in social science research.* London/ New York: Routledge.

Leitch, R., & Day, C. (2000). Action research and reflective practice: Towards a holistic view. *Educational Action Research, 8*(1), 179–193.

Leonard, R. L. (1997). *A case study of the action research process in a school for at-risk students.* Doctoral dissertation, Virginia Polytechnic and State University.

Levine, M. (1992). *Professional practice schools: Linking teacher education and school reform.* New York: Teachers College Press.

Lewin, K. (1945). The research center for group dynamics at Massachusetts Institute of Technology. *Sociometry, 2,* 126–136.

Lewin, K. (1946). Action research and minority problems. *Journal of Social Issues, 2,* 34–46.

Lick, D. W. (2000). Whole-faculty study groups: Facilitating mentoring for school wide change. *Theory into Practice, 39*(1), 43–49.

Lick, D. W., & Murphy, C. U. (Eds.). (2006). *The whole-faculty study groups fieldbook: Lessons learned and best practices from classrooms, districts, and schools.* Thousand Oaks, CA: Corwin Press.

Lincoln, Y. (1995). Emerging criteria for quality in qualitative and interpretive research. *Qualitative Inquiry, 1*(3), 275–289.

Lincoln, Y., & Guba, E. (1985). *Naturalistic inquiry.* Beverly Hills, CA: Sage.

Lincoln, Y. S., & Guba, E. G. (2000). Paradigmatic controversies, contradictions, and emerging confluences. In N. K. Denzin & Y. S. Lincoln (Eds.), *Handbook of qualitative research* (2nd ed., pp. 163–188). Thousand Oaks, CA: Sage.

Little, J. W. (1982). Norms of collegiality and experimentation: Workplace conditions of school success. *American Educational Research Journal, 19*(3), 325–340.

Little, J. W. (1999). Colleagues of choice, colleagues of circumstance: A response to M. Fielding. *The Australian Educational Researcher, 26*(2), 35–43.

Livingston, C., Castle, S., & Nations, J. (1989). Testing and curriculum reform: One school's experience. *Educational Leadership, 45*(7), 23–26.

Lomax, P. (1994). Standards, criteria, and the problematics of action research within an award bearing course. *Educational Action Research, 2*(1), 113–126.

Longstreet, W. S. (1982, Winter). Action research: A paradigm. *Educational Forum,* pp. 135–158.

Longstreet, W. S. (1985). *On generalizability, recursion, and the action research paradigm* (Meadow brook Conference on Action Research). Rochester, MI: Oakland University.

Lord, B. (1994). Teachers' professional development: Critical colleagueship and the role of professional communities. In N. Cobb (Ed.), *The future of education: Perspectives on national standards in education* (pp. 175–204). New York: College Examination Entrance Board.

Lortie, D. C. (1975). *School teacher: A sociological study.* Chicago: University of Chicago Press.

Loucks-Horsley, S., Hewson, P. W., Love, N., & Stiles, K. E. (1998). *Designing professional development for teachers of science and mathematics.* Thousand Oaks, CA: Corwin Press.

Louden, W. (1991). *Understanding teaching: Continuity and change in teachers' knowledge.* New York: Teachers College Press.

Loughran, J., Hamilton, M. L., LaBoskey, V., & Russell, T. (Eds.). (2004). *International handbook of self-study of teaching and teacher education practices.* Dordrecht, The Netherlands: Kluwer.

Loughran, J., & Russell, T. (Eds.). (2002). *Improving teacher education practices through self study.* New York: Routledge Falmer.

Love, N. (2001). *Using data/getting results: A practical guide to school improvement in mathematics and science.* Norwood, MA: Christopher Gordon.

Luhmann, N. (1979). *Trust and power.* New York: John Wiley.

Lykes, B. (1997). Activist participatory research among the Maya of Guatemala: Constructing meaning from situated knowledge. *Journal of Social Issues, 53*(4), 725–746.

Lynn, M., & Smith-Maddox, R. (2007). Preservice teacher inquiry: Creating a space to dialogue about becoming a social justice educator. *Teaching and Teacher Education, 23*(1), 94–105.

Macbeath, J., Demetriou, H., Ruddick, J., & Myers, K. (2003). *Consulting pupils: A toolkit for teachers.* Cambridge, UK: Pearson.

MacDonald, D. C. (1997). *Action research: A catalyst for school improvement.* Doctoral dissertation, Memorial University of Newfoundland, Canada.

MacLean, M. S., & Mohr, M. M. (1999). *Teacher-researchers at work.* Berkeley, CA: National Writing Project.

MacLeod, R. B. (1964). Phenomenology: A challenge to experimental psychology. In T. W. Wann (Ed.), *Behaviorism and phenomenology: Contrasting bases for modern psychology.* Chicago: University of Chicago Press.

Magolda, M. B. (1995). The integration of relational and impersonal knowing in young adults' epistemological development. *Journal of College Student Development, 36,* 203–216.

Maguire, P. (1987). *Doing participatory research: A feminist approach.* Amherst: University of Massachusetts Press.

Maguire, P. (2001). Uneven ground: Feminisms and action research. In P. Reason & H. Bradbury (Eds.), *Handbook of action research* (pp. 59–69). Thousand Oaks, CA: Sage.

Maguire, P. (2002). Reflections on cooperative inquiry in this historic moment. *Systemic Practice and Action Research, 15*(3), 263–270.

Marion, R. D. (1998). *When teachers examine their practice: Action research as a vehicle for teacher learning in one urban school district.* Doctoral dissertation, University of Wisconsin–Madison.

Marrow, A. J. (1977). *The practical theorist: The life and work of Kurt Lewin.* New York: Basic Books.

Marshak, D. (1997). *Action research on block scheduling.* Larchmont: Eye on Education.

Massanari, K. (1978). Demonstration of delivery systems for inservice education. In R. A. Edelfelt (Ed.), *Inservice education: Demonstrating local programs.* Bellingham: Western Washington University Press.

McDonald, B., & Walker, R. (1975). Case study and the social philosophy of educational research. *Cambridge Journal of Education, 5,* 1.

McIntyre, A. (2007). *Participatory action research.* Thousand Oaks, CA: Sage.

McIntyre, D. (2005). Bridging the gap between research and practice. *Cambridge Journal of Education, 35*(3), 357–382.

McKenna, B. (1978). School-based interactive research and development on teaching: A promise for a more effective teaching profession. In *Interactive Research and Development on Teaching Newsletter.* San Francisco: Far West Regional Laboratory.

McLaren, P. (1997). *Revolutionary multiculturalism: Pedagogies of dissent for the new millennium.* Boulder, CO: Westview Press.

McLaren, P. (1998). *Life in schools: An introduction to critical pedagogy in the foundations of education* (3rd ed.). New York: Longman.

McLaren, P., & Lankshear, C. (Eds.). (1994). *Politics of liberation: Paths from Freire.* London: Routledge.

McLaughlin, C. (2003). The feeling of finding out: The role of emotions in research. *Educational Action Research, 11*(1), 65–76.

McLaughlin, M. W., & Yee, S. M. (1988). School as a place to have a career. In A. Lieberman (Ed.), *Building a professional culture in schools.* New York: Teachers College Press.

McNiff, J., Lomax, P., & Whitehead, J. (2006). *All you need to know about action research.* Thousand Oaks, CA: Sage.

McPherson, M., & Nunes, M. B. (2004). *Developing innovation in online learning: An action research framework.* London: Routledge Falmer.

McTaggart, R. (1991). *Action research: A short modern history.* Geelong, Victoria, Australia: Deakin University Press.

Mellor, N. (2001). Messy method: The unfolding story. *Educational Action Research, 9*(2), 465–484.

Menley, A., & Young, D. J. (2005). *Autoethnographies: The anthropology of academic practices.* New York: Broadview Press.

Mergendoller, J. R. (1979, April). *Collaborative research on teaching.* Paper presented at the Conference on Alternative Research Models, St. Louis University, St. Louis, MO.

Merriam, S. B. (1998). *Qualitative research and case study applications in education.* San Francisco, CA: Jossey-Bass.

Mertens, S. K., & Yarger, S. J. (1979). *Documenting success: A guidebook for teacher centers.* Albany, NY: State Education Department.

Messick, S. (1993). *Foundations of validity: Meaning and consequences in psychological assessment.* Princeton, NJ: Educational Testing Service.

Mettetal, G., & Cowen, P. (2000). Assessing learning through classroom research: The supporting teachers as researcher project. *Classroom Leadership Online, 3*(8). Retrieved July 2, 2008, from http://www.ascd.org/readingroom/classlead/0005/1may00.html

Meyers, E. (2003). Whither teachers? Trying to be heard. *Education Week, 32*(28), 32–33.

Michigan Partnership for New Education. (1992). *Professional development schools: A discussion paper.* East Lansing: Michigan State University.

Miles, M. (1964). On temporary systems. In M. B. Miles (Ed.), *Innovation in education.* New York: Teachers College Press.

Miller, D., Snell, C., & Snell, R. (1987). *Grass roots staff development: A strategy.* Mt. Clemens, MI: Macomb Intermediate School District.

Miller, D. W. (1999, August 6). The black hole of educational research. *The Chronicle of Higher Education,* pp. 17–18.

Miller, M. B., Maguire, P., & McIntyre, A. (2004). *Traveling companions: Feminism, teaching, and action research.* New York: Praeger.

Mishler, E. G. (1979). Meaning in context: Is there any other kind? *Harvard Educational Review, 49*(1), 1–19.

Mishler, E. G. (1990). Validation in inquiry-guided research: The role of exemplars in narrative studies. *Harvard Educational Review, 60*(4), 415–442.

Mitchell, C., O'Reilly-Scanlon, K., & Weber, S. (2006). *Just who do we think we are?: Methodologies for autobiography and self study in education.* New York: Routledge.

Mohr, M. (1985). *The teacher researcher: How to study writing in the classroom.* Urbana, IL: ERIC Clearinghouse on Reading and Communication Skills and the National Council of Teachers of English.

Mohr, M. (1987). Teacher researchers and the study of the writing process. In D. Goswami & P. R.

Stillman (Eds.), *Reclaiming the classroom: Teacher research as an agency for change* (pp. 94–106). Portsmouth, NH: Boyton/ Cook-Heinemann.

Moore, J. (2002). Teacher research: Learning to listen. *Networks: An Online Journal for Teacher Research, 5*(3). Retrieved June 11, 2008, from http://journals .library.wisc.edu/index.php/ networks/article/view/136/135

Moore, R. A. (1996). *Reflective action research through classroom inquiry: Seven workplace teachers examine their teaching beliefs.* Doctoral dissertation, University of Missouri–Columbia.

Morley, E., & Silver, A. (1977). A film director's approach to managing creativity. *Harvard Business Review, 55*(2), 59–70.

Motlong, M. K. (2000). My reflective journey in action research. *The Ontario Action Researcher, 3*(2), 1–7. Retrieved June 10, 2008, from http://www.nipissingu. ca/oar/archive-Vol3No2-V322 E.htm

Murphy, C. U., & Lick, D. W. (2005). *Whole-faculty study groups: Creating professional learning communities that target student learning* (3rd ed.). Thousand Oaks, CA: Corwin Press.

Murray, D. (1996). *Crafting a life in story, essay, and poem.* Portsmouth, NH: Boynton/Cook.

Murray, D. (2002). *Writing to learn* (7th ed.). New York: Harcourt College.

Murray, D. (2004). *The craft of revision* (5th ed.). Boston, MA: Thomson/Wadsworth.

Mutua, K., & Swadener, B. B. (Eds.). (2004*). Decolonizing research in cross cultural contexts: Critical personal narratives.* Albany: SUNY Press.

Naples, N. A. (2003). *Feminism and method: Ethnography, discourse analysis, and activist research.* New York: Routledge.

National Academy of Sciences. (2003). *Strategic education research partnership.* Washington, DC: The National Academies Press.

National Research Council, Center for Education, Division of Behavioral and Social Sciences and Education. (2004). *Advancing scientific research in education* (L. Townes, L. L. Wise, & T. M. Winters, Eds.). Washington, DC: National Academies Press.

Nelson, K. J. (2008). *Teaching in the digital age* (2nd ed.). Thousand Oaks, CA: Corwin Press.

Newmann, F., & Associates. (1996). *Authentic achievement: Restructuring schools for intellectual quality.* San Francisco: Jossey-Bass.

No Child Left Behind Act of 2001. Pub. L. No. 107-110, 115 Stat. 1425 (2002).

Nuthall, G. (2004). Relating classroom teaching to student learning: A critical analysis of why research has failed to bridge the theory/practice gap. *Harvard Educational Review, 74*(3), 273–306.

Ogusthorpe, R. T. (1999). *The role of collaborative reflection in developing a culture of inquiry in a school-university partnership.* Paper presented at the annual meeting of the American Educational Research Association, Montreal, Canada.

O'Hanlon, C. (1996). *Professional development through action research.* London: Falmer Press.

Oja, S. N., & Pine, G. J. (1983). *Final report: A two-year study of teacher stages of development in relation to collaborative action research in schools.* Durham, NH: UNH Collaborative Research Project

Office (ERIC Document Reproductive Service No. ED 248227).

Oja, S., & Pine, G. J. (1987). Collaborative action research: Teacher stages of development and school contexts. *Peabody Journal of Education, 65*(2), 96–115.

Oja, S., & Smulyan, L. (1989). *Collaborative action research: A developmental approach.* Philadelphia: Falmer Press.

Olson, L. (1988). Children flourish here. *Education Week, 2*(18), 18–19.

Olson, M. W. (1990). The teacher as researcher: A historical perspective. In M. W. Olson (Ed.), *Opening the door to classroom research.* Newark, DE: International Reading Association.

Onwuegbuzie, A. J. (2002). Positivists, post-positivists, post structuralists, and post modernists: Why can't we all get along? Towards a framework for unifying research paradigms. *Education, 122*(3), 518–530.

Onwuegbuzie, A. J., & Dickinson, W. B. (2006). *Action research: An update.* Unpublished manuscript, University of South Florida.

Onwuegbuzie, A., & Leech, N. (2005). A typology of errors and myths perpetuated in educational research textbooks. *Current Issues in Education, 8*(7). Retrieved June 26, 2008, from http://cie.ed.asu.edu/volume8/number7/index.html

Osterman, K. F., & Kottkamp, R. B. (2004). *Reflective practice for educators* (2nd ed.). Thousand Oaks, CA: Corwin Press.

Oyler, C. (2006). *Learning to teach inclusively: Student teachers' classroom inquiries.* Mahwah, NJ: Lawrence Erlbaum.

Palmer, P. (1983). *To know as we are known: The spirituality of education.* San Francisco: Harper & Row.

Palmer, P. (1998). *The courage to teach: Exploring the inner landscape of a teacher's life*. San Francisco: Jossey-Bass.

Pardini, P. (1999). Making time for adult learning. *Journal of Staff Development, 20*(2).

Parker, S. (1997). *Reflective teaching in the postmodern world*. Philadelphia: Open University Press.

Parsons, B. (2007). *Building a culture of inquiry through communities of learning, inquiry, and practice (CLIPS)*. Paper presented at conference of the League for Innovation in Community Colleges, New Orleans, LA.

Pasko, M. (2004). Curriculum connection: Linking literature and math. *Networks: An Online Journal for Teacher Research, 7*(2). Retrieved June 11, 2008, from http://journals.library.wisc.edu/index.php/networks/article/view/117/118

Patterson, J. L., Purkey, S. C., & Parker, J. V. (1986). *Productive school systems for a nonrational world*. Alexandria, VA: Association for Supervision and Curriculum Development.

Peshkin, A. (1988). In search of subjectivity. *Educational Researcher, 17*(7), 17–21.

Peterson, K. D. (1999). Time use flow from school culture: River of values and traditions can nurture or poison staff development hours. *Journal of Staff Development, 20*(2), 16–19.

Phillips, D. K., & Carr, K. C. (2006). *Becoming a teacher through action research*. New York: Routledge.

Pinar, W. F. (2004). *What is curriculum theory?* Mahwah, NJ: Lawrence Erlbaum.

Pinar, W. F., & Grumet, M. R. (1976). *Toward a poor curriculum*. Dubuque, IA: Kendall/Hunt.

Pine, G. J. (1979). Teacher adaptation of research findings through in-service education. In *Adapting educational research: Staff development approaches*. Washington, DC: U.S. Office of Education.

Pine, G. J (1980a). Collaborative action research: the integration of research and service. In *Research adaptation and change* (pp. 31–53). Washington, DC: U.S. Department of Education.

Pine, G. J. (1980b). *Deans as teachers in the field*. Portsmouth, NH: New England Teacher Corps.

Plano-Clark, V. L., & Creswell, J. W. (2007). *The mixed methods reader*. Thousand Oaks, CA: Sage.

Polanyi, M. (1962). *Personal knowledge*. Chicago: University of Chicago Press.

Power, B. M. (1996). *Taking note: Improving your observational notetaking*. York, ME: Stenhouse.

Prejean, A. I. (1996). *A study of the effects of action research on elementary teachers' belief systems*. Doctoral dissertation, University of Central Florida.

Purves, A. C. (1975). The thought fox and curriculum building. In J. Schaffarzich & D. H. Hampson (Eds.), *Strategies for curriculum development*. Berkeley, CA: McCutchan.

Radford, M. (2007). Action research and the challenge of complexity. *Cambridge Journal of Education, 37*(2), 263–278.

Raymond, L. (2001). Student involvement in school improvement: From data source to significant voice. *Forum, 43*(2), 58–61.

Reagan, T. G., Case, C. W., & Brubacher, J. W. (2000). *Becoming a reflective educator: How to build a culture of inquiry in the schools*. Thousand Oaks, CA: Corwin Press.

Rearick, M., & Feldman, A. (1999). Orientations, product, reflections: A framework for understanding action research. *Teaching and Teacher Education, 15,* 333–350.

Reason, P. (2001). Learning and change through action research. In J. Henry (Ed.), *Creative management.* London: Sage.

Reason, P. (2003). *Choice and quality in action research practice.* Bath, England: University of Bath, School of Management Working Paper Series.

Reason, P. (2006). Choice and quality in action research. *Journal of Management Inquiry, 15*(2), 187–203.

Reason, P., & Bradbury, H. (2001). Inquiry and participation in search of a world worthy of human aspiration. In P. Reason & H. Bradbury (Eds.), *Handbook of action research: Participatory inquiry and practice* (pp. 1–14). London: Sage.

Reason, P., & Heron, J. (1986). Research with people. *Person Centered Review, 1*(4), 456–476.

Reason, P., & Heron, J. (1995). Cooperative inquiry. In R. Harre, J. Smith, & L. Van Langenhove (Eds.), *Rethinking in psychology.* London: Sage.

Reason, P., & McArdle, K. (2004). Brief notes on the theory and practice of action research. In S. Becker & A. Bryman (Eds.), *Understanding research, social policy, and practice.* Bristol, UK: Polity Press. Retrieved August 31, 2008, from http://people.bath.ac.uk/mnspwr/Papers/BriefNotesAR.htm

Reason, P., & Torbert, W. R. (2001). Toward a transformational science: A further look at the scientific merits of action research. *Concepts and Transformations, 6*(1), 1–37.

Reed, J. (2006). *Appreciative inquiry: Research for change.* Thousand Oaks, CA: Sage.

Reed-Danahay, D. E. (Ed.). (1997). *Auto/ethnography: Rewriting the self and the social.* Oxford, UK: Berg.

Reeves, T. (1996). *A hopefully humble paradigm review.* Retrieved May 7, 2008, from University of Georgia, Instructional Technology Forum Web site: http://it.coe.uga.edu/itforum/

Regan, E. M. (1971). The development and dissemination of a curriculum program package. *Curriculum Theory Network, 7,* 63–71.

Reynolds-Johnson, Y. O. (1997). *A case study of a primary school using the action research process to study parental involvement practices.* Doctoral dissertation, Virginia Polytechnical Institute.

Richardson, L. (1994). Writing: A method of inquiry. In N. K. Denzin & Y. Lincoln (Eds.), *Handbook of qualitative research* (pp. 516–529). Thousand Oaks, CA: Sage.

Richardson, W. (2006). *Blogs, wikis, podcasts, and other powerful web tools for classrooms.* Thousand Oaks, CA: Corwin Press.

Riessman, C. K. (2008). *Narrative methods for the human sciences.* Thousand Oaks, CA: Sage.

Rinaldi, C. (2003). The teacher as researcher. *Innovations in Early Education: The International Reggio Exchange, 10*(2), 2.

Robinson, S., & Darling-Hammond, L. (1994). Change for collaboration and collaboration for change: Transforming teaching through school-university partnerships. In L. Darling-Hammond (Ed.), *Professional development schools: Schools for developing a profession.* New York: Teachers College Press.

Rodgers, C. (2002). Defining reflection: Another look at John Dewey and reflective thinking. *Teachers College Record, 10*(4), 842–866.

Roman, L. (1989). *Double exposure: The politics of feminist research.* Paper presented at the Qualitative Research in Education Conference, Athens, GA.

Rosaen, C. L. (1995). Collaboration in a professional culture: Renegotiating barriers to improve practice. *Advances in Teaching, 5,* 355–385.

Ross, L., & Cronbach, L. J. (1976). Review of the *Handbook of evaluation research. Educational Researcher, 5*(10), 9–19.

Rowe, A. (2006). The effect of involvement in participatory research on parent researchers in Sure Start program. *Health and Social Care in the Community, 14*(6), 465–473.

Rubin, B. C., & Jones, M. (2007). Student action research: Reaping the benefits for students and school leaders. *NASSP Bulletin, 92*(4), 363–378.

Rudduck, J., & Flutter, J. (2004). *How to improve your school: Giving pupils a voice.* London: Continuum Press.

Russell, T., & Korthagen, F. (Eds.). (1995). *Teachers who teach teachers: Reflections on teacher education.* London: Falmer Press.

Sabelli, N., & Dede, C. (2001). *Integrating educational research and practice: Reconceptualizing the goals and process of research to improve educational practice.* Retrieved July 18, 2002, from http://www.virtual.gmu.edu/SS_research/cdpapers/integrating.htm

Sachs, J. (1999). Using teacher research as a basis for professional renewal. *Journal of Inservice Education, 25*(1), 39–53.

Sagor, R. (1997). Collaborative action research for educational change. In A. Hargreaves (Ed.), *ASCD Yearbook: Rethinking educational change with heart and mind.* Alexandria, VA: Association for Supervision and Curriculum Development.

Sagor, R., & Curley, J. (1991). *Can collaborative action research improve schooleffectiveness?* Paper presented at the annual meeting of the American Educational Research Association, Chicago.

Samaras, A. P. (2002). *Self-study for teacher educators: Crafting a pedagogy for educational change.* New York: Peter Lang.

Sanford, N. (1965). Will psychologists study human problems? *American Psychologist, 20,* 192–202.

Sanford, N. (1970). Whatever happened to action research? *Journal of Social Issues, 26*(4), 3–23.

Sarason, S. B. (1982). *The culture of the school and the problem of change* (2nd ed.). Boston: Allyn & Bacon.

Sarason, S. B. (1996). *Revisiting the culture of school and the problems of change.* New York: Teachers College Press.

Schaefer, P. M. (1989). Becoming researchers: Teaching mathematics to gray area students. In C. Livingston & S. Castle (Eds.), *Teachers and research in action* (pp. 35–40). Washington, DC: National Education Association.

Schaefer, R. I. (1967). *The school as a center of inquiry.* New York: Harper & Row.

Schein, E. H. (1992). *Organizational culture and leadership* (2nd ed.). San Francisco: Jossey-Bass.

Schön, D. A. (1983). *The reflective practitioner.* New York: Basic Books.

Schön, D. A. (1987). *Educating the reflective practitioner.* San Francisco: Jossey-Bass.

Schön, D. A. (1995). The new scholarship requires a new epistemology. *Change, 27*(6), 29–34.

Schubert, W. H. (1980, January). Recalibrating educational research: Toward a focus on practice. *Educational Research, 9,* 17–24.

Schwab, J. J. (1969). The practical: A language for curriculum. *School Review, 78,* 1–24.

Schwab, J. J. (1970). *The practical: A language for curriculum?* Washington, DC: National Education Association.

Schwab, J. J. (1975). Foreword. In W. A. Reid & D. F. Walker (Eds.), *Case studies in curriculum change.* London: Routledge & Kegan Paul.

Schwandt, T. A. (1994) Constructivist, interpretist approaches to human inquiry. In N. Denzin & Y. Lincoln (Eds.), *Handbook of qualitative research* (pp. 118–137). Thousand Oaks, CA: Sage.

Sechrest, L., & Sidana, S. (1995). Quantitative and qualitative methods: Is there an alternative? *Evaluation and Program Planning, 18,* 77–87.

Seidl, B. L., & Friend, G. (2002). The unification of church and state: Working with communities to prepare teachers for diversity. *Journal of Teacher Education, 53*(2), 142–152.

Senese, J. C. (2002). Energize with action research. *Journal of Staff Development, 23,* 39–41.

Sessums, C. (2005). *Collaboration and teacher reflection.* Weblog of Christopher Sessums, http:// edu spaces.net/csessums/weblog/

Shager, E. (2007). *Been there, done that: Student inquiry about high school dropouts.* In C. Caro-Bruce, R. Flessner, R. Klehr, & K. Zeichner (Eds.), *Creating equitable classrooms through action research.* Thousand Oaks, CA: Corwin Press.

Sharp, C. L. (1996). *The implementation of an elementary school's mentoring program: An action research study.* Doctoral dissertation, Wilmington College, Delaware.

Shea, M., Murray, R., & Harlin, R. (2005). *Drowning in data? How to collect, organize, and document student performance.* Thousand Oaks, CA: Corwin Press.

Sherman, F. T., & Torbert, W. (Eds.). (2000). *Transforming social inquiry, transforming social action: New paradigms for crossing the theory/practice divide in universities and communities.* Boston: Kluwer Academic.

Shih-hsein Yang, Y. (2005). EFL teacher learners' collaborative reflection through web-blogging. *US-China Education Review, 2*(9), 14–17.

Shor, I. (1992). *Empowering education: Critical thinking for social change.* Chicago: University of Chicago Press.

Shulman, L. (1986). Paradigms and research programs in the study of teaching: A contemporary perspective. In W. C. Wittrock (Ed.), *Handbook of research on teaching* (pp. 3–36). New York: Macmillan.

Shulman, L. (1987). Knowledge and teaching: Foundations of the new reform. *Harvard Educational Review, 57*(1), 1–32.

Skelton, C., & Francis, B. (Eds.). (2005). *Feminist critique of education: Fifteen years of gender and education.* New York: Routledge.

Smith, L. T. (1999). *Decolonizing methodologies: Research and indigenous people.* New York: Zed Books.

Snipes J., Doolittle, F., & Herlihy, C. (2002). *Case studies of how urban school systems improve student achievement.* New York: Manpower Demonstration Research Corporation.

Solomon, R. C., & Flores, F. (2001). *Building trust in business, politics, relationships, and life.* New York: Oxford University Press.

Spradley, J. (1979). *The ethnographic interview.* New York: Holt, Rinehart, & Winston.

Stainback S., & Stainback, W. (1988). *Understanding and conducting qualitative research.* Reston, VA: Council for Exceptional Children.

Stake, R. E. (1995). *The art of case study research.* Thousand Oaks, CA: Sage.

Stanfield, J. H. (1993). Methodological reflections: An introduction. In J. H. Stanfield & R. Dennis (Eds.), *Race and ethnicity in research methods* (pp. 3–15). Thousand Oaks, CA: Sage.

Stanley, L., & Wise, S. (1993). *Breaking out again: Feminist ontology and epistemology.* New York: Routledge.

Stavros, J. M., & Torres, C. B. (2005). *Dynamic relationships: Unleashing the power of appreciative inquiry in daily living.* Chagrin Falls, OH: Taos Institute.

Steinberg, S. R., & Kincheloe, J. L. (1998). *Students as researchers: Creating classrooms that matter.* London: Routledge, Taylor & Francis.

Stenhouse, L. (1975). *An introduction to curriculum research and development.* London: Heinemann Educational Books.

Stenhouse, L. (1983). *Authority, education, and emancipation.* London: Heinemann Educational Books.

Stevenson, R. B. (1987). Staff development for effective secondary schools: A synthesis of research. *Teaching and Teacher Education, 3,* 233–248.

Stevenson, R. (1991). Action research as professional development: A US case study of inquiry-oriented in-service education. *Journal of Education for Teaching, 17*(3), 277–292.

Stevenson, R. (1996, March). *What counts as "good" action research?* Paper presented at the Ethnography in Educational Research Forum, Philadelphia.

St. Pierre, E. A. (2002). "Science" rejects postmodernism. *Educational Researcher, 31*(8), 25–27.

Stringer, E. T. (2007). *Action research* (3rd ed.). Thousand Oaks, CA: Sage.

Suarez, E. V. (1997). *Staff collaboration in the school restructuring process: An action research study.* Doctoral dissertation, Temple University.

Susman, G. I., & Evered, R. D. (1978). An assessment of the scientific merits of action research. *Administrative Science Quarterly, 23,* 582–603.

Taggart, G. L., & Wilson, A. P. (2005). *Promoting reflective thinking in teachers.* Thousand Oaks, CA: Corwin Press.

Tarnas, R. (1991). *The passion of the Western mind.* New York: Ballantine Books.

Tashakkori, A., & Teddlie, C. (Eds.). (2003). *Handbook of mixed methods in social and behavioral sciences.* Thousand Oaks, CA: Sage.

Teddlie, C., & Tashakkori, A. (2008). *Foundations of mixed-methods research: Integrating qualitative and quantitative techniques into social and behavioral sciences.* Thousand Oaks, CA: Sage.

Thatchenkery, T. (2005). *Appreciative sharing of knowledge: Leveraging knowledge management for strategic change.* Chagrin Falls, OH: Taos Institute.

Thompson, J. (2000). *Emancipatory learning* (NIACE Briefing Sheet 11). Leicester, UK: National Institute of Adult Continuing Education.

Thomson, P., & Gunter, H. (2007). The methodology of students-as-researchers: Valuing and using experience and expertise to develop methods. *Discourse: Studies in the Cultural Politics of Education, 28*(3), 327–342.

Tickunoff, W. J., Ward, B. A., & Griffin, G. A. (1979). *Interactive research and development on teaching study: Final report.* San Francisco, CA: Far West Regional Laboratory.

Torbert, W. (2004). *Action inquiry: The secret of timely and transformative leadership.* San Francisco: Berrett-Koehler.

Torre, M. E., & Fine, M., with Alexander, N., Billups, A. B., Blanding, Y., Genao, E., Marboe, E., Salah, T., & Urdang, K. (2008). Participatory action research in the contact zone. In J. Cammarota & M. Fine (Eds.), *Revolutionizing education. Youth participatory action research in motion.* New York: Routledge, Taylor & Francis Group.

Traugh, C. (2000). Whole school inquiry: Values and practice. In M. Himley & P. Carini (Eds.), *From another angle: Children's strengths and school standards* (pp. 182–198). New York: Teachers Collage Press.

Tschannen-Moran, M., & Hoy, W. K. (1998). Trust in schools: A conceptual and empirical analysis. *Journal of Educational Administration, 36*(3/4), 334–352.

Tschannen-Moran, M., & Hoy, W. K. (2000). A multidisciplinary analysis of the nature, meaning, and measurement of trust. *Review of Educational Research, 70*(4), 547–593.

Tschannen-Moran, M., & Hoy, W. K. (2001). Collaboration and the need for trust. *Journal of Educational Administration, 39*(4), 308–331.

Valli, L. (1997). Listening to other voices: A description of teacher reflection in the United States. *Peabody Journal of Education, 72*(1), 67–88.

Van Buskirk, W. (2002). Appreciating appreciative inquiry in the urban Catholic school. In R. Fry, F. Barrett, J. Seiling, & D. Whitney (Eds.), *Appreciative inquiry and organizational transformation: Reports from the field* (pp. 67–98). Westport, CT: Quorum Books.

Van Dunk, E., & Dickman, E. (2003). *School choice and the question of accountability.* New Haven, CT: Yale University Press.

van Manen, M. (1977). Linking ways of knowing with ways of being practical. *Curriculum Inquiry, 6*(3), 205–208.

van Manen, M. (1991a). Reflectivity and the pedagogical moment: The normativity of pedagogical thinking and acting. *Journal of Curriculm Studies, 23*(6), 507–536.

van Manen, M. (1991b). *The tact of teaching: The meaning of pedagogical thoughtfulness.* Albany: SUNY Press.

van Manen, M. (1997). *Researching lived experience: Human science for action sensitive pedagogy* (2nd ed.). London, ON: Althouse Press.

van Manen, M. (Ed.). (2002). *Writing in the dark: Phenomenological studies in interpretive inquiry* (2nd ed.). London, ON: Althouse Press.

Van Tiem, D., & Rosenzweig, J. (2006). *Appreciative inquiry.* Alexandria, VA: ASTD Press.

Viadero, D. (2003). Scholars aim to connect studies to schools' needs. Research into practice-part one. *Education Week, 22*(27), 1.

Walker, D. F. (1975). Curriculum development in an art project. In W. A. Reid & F. Walker (Eds.), *Case studies in curriculum change.* London: Routledge & Kegan Paul.

Waples, D., & Tyler, R. W. (1930). *Research methods and teachers' problems.* New York: Macmillan.

Waterman, H., Tillen, D., Dickson, R., & De Koning, K. (2001). Action research: A systematic review and guidance for assessment. *Health Technology Assessment, 5*(23), 1–166.

Watkins, J. M. (2001). Review of *From another angle: Children's strengths and school standards. Anthropology and Education Quarterly, 32*(1). Retrieved July 5, 2008, from http://aaanet .org/ sections/cae/aeq/br/himley .htm

Watkins, J. M., & Mohr, B. J. (2001). *Appreciative inquiry: Change at the speed of imagination.* San Francisco, CA: Jossey-Bass/Pfeiffer.

White, P. (1998). Understanding prolepsis through teacher research. *Networks: An On-line Journal for Teacher Research, 1*(1). Retrieved September 2, 2008, from http:// journals.library.wisc.edu/index. php/networks/index

Whitehead, J. (1989). Creating a living educational theory from questions of the kind, "How Do I Improve My Practice?" *Cambridge Journal of Education, 19*(1), 41–52.

Whitehead, J., & McNiff, J. (2006). *Action research: Living theory.* Thousand Oaks, CA: Sage.

Whitney, D., Trostem-Bloom, A., Cherney, J., & Fry, R. (2005). *Appreciative team building.* Taos, NM: iUniverse.

Wiggan, G. (2007). Race, school achievement, and educational equality: Toward a student inquiry perspective. *Review of Educational Research, 77*(3), 310–333.

Willig, C. (2001). *Introducing qualitative research in psychology: Adventures in theory and method.* Buckingham, UK: Open University Press.

Wilson, S. (2007). "*What about Rose?*": Using teacher research to reverse school failure. New York: Teachers College Press.

Winter, G. (2000). A comparative discussion of the notion of "validity" in qualitative and quantitative research. *The Qualitative Report, 4*(3/4). Retrieved from http:// www.nova.edu/sss/QR/QR4-3/winter.html

Winter, R. (1989). *Learning from experience: Principles and practice in action research.* Philadelphia: Falmer Press.

Winter, R. (1996). Some principles and procedures for the conduct of action research. In O. Zuber-Skerritt (Ed.), *New directions of action research.* London: Falmer Press.

Wise, R. I. (1977). *A case for the value of retrospective accounts of curriculum development.* Paper presented at AERA Annual Meeting, New York.

Wolf, F. M. (1986). *Meta-analysis: Quantitative methods for research synthesis.* Beverly Hills, CA: Sage.

Yankelovich, D. (1981). *New rules: Searching for self-fulfillment in a world turned upside down.* New York: Random House.

Yin, R. K. (2008). *Case study research: Design and methods* (4th ed.). Thousand Oaks, CA: Sage.

York-Barr, J., Sommers, W. A., Ghere, G., & Monte, J. (2006). *Reflective practice to improve schools: An action guide for educators* (2nd ed.). Thousand Oaks, CA: Corwin Press.

Zehm, S. J., & Kottler, J. A. (1993). *On being a teacher: The human dimension*. Newbury Park, CA: Corwin Press.

Zeichner, K. M. (1996). Teachers as reflective practitioners and the democratization of school reform. In K. Zeichner, S. Melnick, & M. M. Gomez (Eds.), *Currents of reform in preservice teacher education* (pp. 1–8). New York: Teachers College Press.

Zeichner, K. M. (2003). Teacher research as professional development for P–12 educators in the U.S.A. *Educational Action Research, 11*(2), 301–323.

Zeichner, K. M. (2007). Accumulating self knowledge across self-studies in teacher education. *Journal of Teacher Education, 58*(1), 36–46.

Zeichner, K. M., & Liston, D. P. (1996). *Reflective teaching: An introduction*. Mahwah, NJ: Lawrence Erlbaum.

Zeni, J. (Ed.). (2001). *Ethical issues in practitioner research*. New York: Teachers College Press.

Zerubavel, E. (1981). *Hidden rhythms: Schedules and calendars in social life*. Chicago: University of Chicago Press.

Index

Cook, T., 236
Cooper, M., 182
Cooperrider, D. L., 218–219, 220
Corbett, H. D., 19
Corey, S., 40–41, 42, 68, 74, 84, 90, 110, 112
Costello, J., 60
Covey, S. R., 63
Cowen, P., 116
Cox, B. E., 289
Cranston, S. S., 154
Crepps, S., 34
Creswell, J. W., 65
Crewe Primary School (Virginia), 115
Cristler, C., 154
"Critical friends" colleagues, 235–236
Critical reflection, 181
Critical theory-postmodern-praxis paradigm, 65
Critical thinking, 191
Critical-incident case studies, 217–218
Cronbach, L. J., 98
Cross Cultural Roundtable, 150
Cuff, E. C., 108
Cultural inquiry process (CIP)
  assumptions of, 225
  description of, 224–225
  implementation steps of, 225–228
Culture. *See* School culture
Cumulative case studies, 218
Cunningham, S. J., 202
Curley, J., 56
Curriculum development
  case studies on, 222–223
  as educational research focus, 222
  Web sites on instruction and, 338–345
  See also Instruction
Cushman, K., 235
Cynewski, L., 125
Czamiawska, B., 197

Dabish, D., 247–248
Dadds, M., 76, 84, 85, 87
Daily Grind Web site, 339
Damasio, A., 76
Dana, N. F., 57, 113, 238
Daniels, L. Y., 33
Darling-Hammond, L., 160

Data analysis
  drawing conclusions/finding meaning from, 259–260
  Reading Recovery to Guided Reading project, 294–296
  rules of thumb for, 254–255, 257–259
  Why Do I Have to Know This Stuff? project, 310–312
Data collection
  case studies, 216–217
  issues addressed by plan for, 251
Data sources
  examples of classroom/school, 253t–254t
  identifying, 251–254t
  Reading Recovery to Guided Reading project, 288–290
  three categories of, 252
  triangulation of, 66–67, 82, 83, 87–88, 255, 256t
  What Happens to Students' Writing? project, 322–323t
  Why Do I Have to Know This Stuff? project, 307–309
  See also Methodology
Datta, L., 217
Dave's ESL Café Web site, 339
Davey, L., 217
Davis, S. H., 6, 8
Dawson, J. A., 19
Day, C., 144, 185
Deal, T. E., 22
Dede, C., 4
De Koning, K., 260
Deliberative reflection, 181
de Marrais, K. B., 202
Democratic validity, 85–86
Denzin, N. K., 64, 82, 202, 216
Depka, E., 258
Descartes' Error (Damasio), 76
Descriptive review
  characteristics of, 228–229
  examples of observations made during, 229–231
  procedures for conducting, 231–233
Descriptive Review of the Child, 229–231
de Sousa, R., 76
Development of study, 66

About the Author

Gerald J. Pine is professor emeritus of education in the Lynch School of Education at Boston College. He has served as dean of the Boston College School of Education; dean of the School of Education and Human Services at Oakland University, Rochester, Michigan; and chair of the Education Department at the University of New Hampshire. While at the University of New Hampshire, he served as director of a Teacher Corps Project that focused on teacher adaptation of research findings through professional development and teacher action research. Following this project, he was the codirector and co-principal investigator of a National Institute of Education study on teacher development, action research, and educational change. He is the author or coauthor of 11 books and more than 120 articles and book chapters dealing with teacher action research, learner-centered teaching, educational collaboration, and counseling. He served 6 years as the editor of the journal *Counseling and Values* and 6 years as an associate editor of the *Journal of Teacher Education*. He has received major grants from the Kellogg Foundation, National Institute of Education, U.S. Office of Education, and the UAW-Chrysler Foundation. From 1990 to 1994, while serving as dean of education and human services at Oakland University, he was also staff associate for the Michigan Partnership for New Education at Michigan State University, where he worked as part of a team to establish and coordinate a statewide network of professional development schools. His current research efforts focus on professional development schools, learner-centered teaching, educational change, and collaborative action research.

In 1996, he received the Arthur D. Wilde Award from the Boston University Education Alumni Board for his significant contributions to education, and he was the corecipient of the American Association for Counselor Education and Supervision Publication Award for his contributions to the professional literature of counselor education and supervision.